THE STATE OF LEBANON

Stanford Studies in Middle Eastern and Islamic Societies and Cultures

THE STATE OF LEBANON

Popular Politics and Institution Building in the Wake of Independence

Ziad Abu-Rish

STANFORD UNIVERSITY PRESS
Stanford, California

Stanford University Press
Stanford, California

Library of Congress Cataloging-in-Publication Data

Names: Abu-Rish, Ziad author
Title: The state of Lebanon : popular politics and institution building in the wake of independence / Ziad M. Abu-Rish.
Other titles: Stanford studies in Middle Eastern and Islamic societies and cultures
Description: Stanford, California : Stanford University Press, 2026. | Series: Stanford studies in Middle Eastern and Islamic societies and cultures | Includes index.
Identifiers: LCCN 2025028718 (print) | LCCN 2025028719 (ebook) | ISBN 9781503645295 cloth | ISBN 9781503645820 paperback | ISBN 9781503645837 ebook
Subjects: LCSH: Political participation—Lebanon—History—20th century | Institution building—Lebanon—History—20th century | Lebanon—Politics and government—1946-1975
Classification: LCC DS87 .A5996 2026 (print) | LCC DS87 (ebook) | DDC 956.9204—dc23/eng/20251118
LC record available at https://lccn.loc.gov/2025028718
LC ebook record available at https://lccn.loc.gov/2025028719

Cover design: Susan Zucker
Cover art: Jana Traboulsi
Typeset by Newgen in 10.5/14.4 Brill

The authorized representative in the EU for product safety and compliance is: Mare Nostrum Group B.V. | Mauritskade 21D | 1091 GC Amsterdam | The Netherlands | Email address: gpsr@mare-nostrum.co.uk | KVK chamber of commerce number: 96249943

Contents

Acknowledgements

I owe a tremendous amount of gratitude to the many people that have supported me in the journey of researching and writing this book. These pages cannot adequately express my appreciation.

I received financial support from several institutions: UCLA's Department of History, International Institute, Graduate Division, and Alumni Association; Ohio University's Department of History and Office of the Vice President for Research and Creative Activity; Georgetown University's Center for Contemporary Arab Studies and its ADF Fellowship in Druze and Arab Studies; and Bard College's Human Rights Project and Faculty Research and Travel Fund.

At Stanford University Press, Kate Wahl showed genuine interest and gave sound advice across a number of years. I am grateful for the productive comments and encouragement of four anonymous readers of the manuscript. I also thank Thane Hale for his efforts in the production process. Haitham Haddad helped me think through cover concepts and Jana Traboulsi was kind enough to permit me to use one of her powerful illustrations.

At the University of California, Los Angeles, I had the honor of working with a group of outstanding scholars that provided the building block of this project. I am deeply indebted to James L. Gelvin, whose mentorship, teaching, and scholarship continue to shape me. I was lucky to benefit from the early engagement with this project by several faculty members whose theoretical and methodological precision remain models for me to aspire to.

In Lebanon, my work would not have been possible without the countless conversations with, thoughts of, and introductions by Andrew Arsan, Sami Atallah, Nadine Bekdache, Joelle Boutros, May Haider, Mona Harb, Ilham Khuri-Makdisi, Muzna al-Masri, Maya Mikdashi, Jamil Mouawad, Helena Nassif, Hicham Safieddine, Abir Saksouk, Nisreen Salti, Rosemary Sayigh, Petra Serhal, Hana Sleiman, and Fawwaz Traboulsi. I am especially indebted to Bassel Kassem, whose unending identification of private archives and sharing of collected materials transformed my understanding of Lebanon's archival terrain. Institutional affiliations granted to me by the Center for Arab and Middle Eastern Studies, the Center for Behavioral Studies, and the Issam Faris Institute for Public Policy and International Affairs, all at the American University of Beirut; the Lebanese Center for Policy Studies; and The Policy Initiative afforded me campus access, office space, research credentials, and opportunities to present and improve my analysis.

I am grateful to Brooke Atherton, Ghanem Bibi, Ahmad Dallal, Rayan El-Amine, William El Khoury, Dalal El Madade, Maha Issa, Maroun Karam, Aline Khoury, Pierre Khoury, Najibeh Rachid, and Abdul Rahman Zahzah. Their kindness, hospitality, and genuine engagement throughout more than a decade of research trips to Lebanon helped anchor me. Home-cooked meals, evening conversations, and day trips were a wonderful occasion to take breaks; connect with a broader set of interests, passions, and concerns; and affirm that Lebanon has always been a lived place, one to which historical research and writing must be responsible and accountable.

I joined the History Department at Ohio University in 2014, and remain grateful for the intellectual community and personal friendships forged with Mariana Dantas, Alec Holcombe, Steve Howard, Katherine Jellison, Loren Lybarger, Kevin Mattson, Jaclyn L. Maxwell, Joe McLaughlin, and Nukhet Sandal. I am particularly indebted to Assan Sarr, Miriam Shadis, Kevin Uhalde, and Julie White for their comradery.

I joined the faculty at Bard College in 2020, and I continue to appreciate the gifts of the experience. The friendships, collaborations, and accomplishments of so many inspire me. There are more individuals than I can practically mention, but a short list must include Thomas Keenan, Peter L'Official, Gideon Lester, Gregory B. Moynahan, Michelle Murray, and Danielle Riou.

For feedback on various stages of this work and support in conducting research, I am thankful to Betty Anderson, Beth Baron, Joel Beinin, John Chalcraft, Ziad Dallal, Lara Deeb, Carol Hakim, Waleed Hazbun, Michael Gasper, Laleh Khalili, Akram Khater, Owain Lawson, Sean Lee, Zeina Maasri, Ussama Makdisi, Nada Moumtaz, Tsolin Nalbantian, William Parry, Jeremy Randall, Awatef Sheikh, Abdel Razzaq Takriti, Sana Tanoury-Karam, Éric Verdeil, and Murat Yıldız. Reem Bailony and Graham Auman Pitts shared much of their insights and primary sources with me. Rony Abi Aad, Abboud Abou Jaoude, and Kaoukab Chebaro opened up whole new archival terrains for me. Kevin Martin moved this work forward with his editing. I am forever indebted to Aslı Ü. Bâli, Rosie Bsheer, Nadya Sbaiti, and Sherene Seikaly, who have accompanied this project from its inception and have supported it in countless ways.

Since 2004 I have held various editorial and other positions at the Arab Studies Institute, primarily through its *Arab Studies Journal* and *Jadaliyya*. This network of researchers, writers, editors, and friends has immeasurably impacted my thinking about elite coalitions, popular mobilizations, state formation, and the care, rigor, and responsibility about writing on and with the Middle East. Maya Mikdashi and Hesham Sallam each inspired new ways of thinking through the complexities of historical legacies and contemporary politics. Sinan Antoun suggested the title of the book, *The State of Lebanon*. Owain Lawson is an indispensable collaborator in researching Lebanon, one I continue to learn a great deal from. He also shouldered the entirety of our coeditorship of *Arab Studies Journal* as I completed this book. Nadya Sbaiti was the first person to encourage me to take up this project, and she guided and facilitated my initial fieldwork in Lebanon. Our collaboration on the Lebanon Dissertation Summer Institute has only deepened my learning from her theoretical and empirical brilliance as a historian of Lebanon. Rosie Bsheer has shared in the highs and lows of my academic life in general and this project in particular. Her wisdom, generosity, and intellectual prowess are inspirational. I consider myself a student of Sherene Seikaly, and am privileged to call her my friend, mentor, role model, and editor.

I am grateful for the unconditional love of Noura Erakat, Bassam Haddad, Elie Haddad, Carole Namez, Khalid Namez, and the late Asma Haddad. I owe a particular debt to Bassam for first inspiring me to learn about state formation and for all his efforts at introducing me to Beirut. Erin Blakeny and Teresa Kinkade are ever present whenever I reflect on my personal and professional trajectory because of their unflinching support.

My late father, Munif Abu-Rish, did not live to see this project published. His passion for reading, writing, and telling stories inspired me in unexpected ways. His reputation for remembering the details imbues the following pages. My brother Walid has taught me much about standing tall in the face of life no matter the blows. He is an exemplar of believing in oneself and realizing one's goals. Words will never capture the gratitude I have for Wagih and Eileen Abu-Rish. They have been role models in so many ways. Without them, none of this would be possible.

My chance meeting with Tania El Khoury in the midst of my research is one of the more consequential events of my life. She opened up new vistas of Lebanon, research methodologies, public engagement, and myself. She reminds me to be in the present and with those closest to me. She also read several chapters, helped translate many French documents, and took on the lion's share of childcare during my writing phase. Leyl Abu Rish fills me with joy and inspires me to laugh, dance, and live in the moment. My hope is that one day this book will help her understand a part of me, and in so doing learn more about one of the places she calls home. I am so fortunate to have her in my life.

Note on Transliteration and Translation

This manuscript follows a simplified version of the transliteration system of the *International Journal of Middle East Studies*, with modifications intended to keep the narrative accessible to all readers. I do not use diacritics or long vowel markers, with the exception of the glottal stop hamza (') and the pharyngeal fricative ayn ('). All translations are mine unless otherwise noted.

THE STATE OF LEBANON

Introduction

BEYOND EXCEPTIONALISM

IN DECEMBER 1951, RESIDENTS OF BEIRUT LAUNCHED A SEVEN-MONTH campaign boycotting the payment of their electricity bills. The initiative began as an ad hoc and diffuse attempt by certain residential, commercial, and industrial subscribers to resist the exorbitant electric utility rates and fees of the Beirut Electricity Company (EDB, Sharikat Kahruba' Bayrut). These sporadic efforts subsequently evolved into an organized campaign spearheaded by a joint committee led by the Kata'ib Party (Hizb al-Kata'ib) and the National Organization (al-Hay'a al-Wataniyya), and involved the participation of over 50 percent of Beirut's electricity subscribers. At the heart of this campaign were questions related to the affordability and quality of Beirut's electricity utility service, as well as its ownership structure. Equally important were the demands on the state (*al-dawla*) to adjudicate these questions and fulfill its presumed role in promoting development and securing sovereignty.

The 1951–52 campaign featured a three-way struggle between Beirut residents, the electricity company, and incumbent politicians and bureaucrats. This seven-month period is replete with official and back-channel negotiations, ad hoc commissions of inquiry, parliamentary debates, protests, and the issuing of pamphlets by all stakeholders. The contours of these debates and struggles were at times specific to the issue of electricity. At other times they intersected with and were framed within a broader debate about development, foreign capital, and sovereignty. The campaign around the pricing, quality of service, and ownership structure of the EDB also provided bureaucrats and business groups opportunities to promote their long-standing ideas, plans, and interests in electricity and development. Partisans and critics of the EDB variously drew on foreign expertise and solicited foreign consultants. At the same time, local experts used the opportunity to demonstrate their knowledge and relevance. While the French government sought to support the EDB as a Paris-based joint-stock company whose concession dated back to the late Ottoman period, the US and British governments were concerned with the potential implications for economic nationalism while also cautiously optimistic about exploring ways to advance their influence and that of their own companies working in the electricity field.

The organized boycott campaign against the EDB ended in July 1952 with the government intervening to reduce the price of electricity. Yet electricity remained a central issue around which popular groups, business interests, and state officials mobilized. Residents in cities and towns outside of Beirut mounted similar campaigns, either concurrent with or subsequent to the campaign against the EDB. As the government expanded its role in the electricity sector of Beirut, culminating in the nationalizing of the EDB's offices and installations in 1953–54, the locus of demands (and criticism) narrowed to focus on government officials and ministerial bureaucrats. By 1955, the functioning of electricity in the country was a litmus test for development and sovereignty. Parliamentary and party opposition groups drew on the issue to challenge the president or cabinet. Incumbent politicians and long-time bureaucrats prioritized it as a means of bolstering their legitimacy (and in some cases their financial interests).

The 1951–52 electricity boycott campaign and its reverberations are but one manifestation of mobilizations that characterized the early postindependence period in Lebanon. Therein, incumbent politicians, career civil servants, businesspersons, political entrepreneurs, activists, and residents routinely debated the "proper" relationship between the state, the citizen, and the postcolonial. Which state institutions and functions were necessary to consolidate independence? What was the place of different classes, sexes, or regions in the political economy of Lebanon? How best to shed the legacies of French colonial rule and fulfill the promise of development? For most Lebanese, these questions were at the heart of imagining their country's future.

Resolving these questions was more than an intellectual exercise. It was a crucial component of the discussions and struggles that constituted politics after independence. The primary locus of elite and popular mobilizations shifted from the struggle for decolonization to the battle over state formation. These mobilizations played out in parliamentary debates and party meetings, through newspapers and leaflets, and—frequently—in street protests. This shift from decolonization to state formation would have consequences for every aspect of daily life and the broader political, social, and cultural landscapes.

These struggles and their consequences reflect the different and overlapping registers of this book's title, *The State of Lebanon*. In one register, this book attends to social life and the political during the 1943–55 period. Patterns of elite competition and popular mobilization during these years share some continuity with previous or subsequent years. They nevertheless also featured patterns unique to the imaginative possibilities, strategic opportunities, and institutional flux of what I define as the early postindependence era (1943–55). The period begins with formal political independence in 1943 and lasts through 1955, after which shifts in the organization of social conflict transformed the positionality, interests, and strategies of a range of bureaucrats, politicians, parties, and other organizations into the often-narrated dynamics in scholarship on postcolonial Lebanon. Elites and popular groups mobilized around a broad array of issues during this period. Some focused on electoral politics and the specific policies governing voting, candidacy, and serving in office. Others emphasized economic policies related to trade, manufacturing, and agriculture. Still others highlighted taxation and social safety nets. Some also sought to remake the privileges of religious institutions in adjudicating matters of personal status. Despite the different—and for many, numerous—issues that motivated them, these groups shared an understanding that the transition to independence and the construction of a postwar regional system and global order opened up new possibilities for the production of political power, economic life, and social hegemony in Lebanon. They all called for the primacy of state institutions and the need to reorganize these bodies. Thus, the second register of this book's title addresses the ways in which the idiom of state building and the materiality of specific state institutional arrangements were central to both elite and popular mobilizations.

Most of the struggles alluded to above do not appear in academic histories of Lebanon. There are several reasons for this absence. The first is to be found in the history and historiography of Lebanon. The second reason is three tropes that continue to dominate the historiography of Lebanon: sectarianism, nationalism, and the merchant republic. Finally, there are the broader assumptions and frameworks of comparative work on the Middle East in particular and the Global South in general.

THE HISTORY AND HISTORIOGRAPHY OF POSTINDEPENDENCE LEBANON

The bulk of the scholarship on the history of the territories that constitute present-day Lebanon has focused on the late Ottoman period (1839–1918), the French colonial period (1918–43), or the period of the civil war (1975–90).[1] By contrast, scholars have paid little attention to the postindependence period of 1943–75. One reason for this gap in the scholarship is the alleged dearth of local archival sources. This has been explained through various combinations of a number of factors. One is the devastating effects of the fifteen-year civil war (1975–90), which included the looting and destruction of archival collections. Another factor is the heterogenous archival practices of Lebanese state institutions. A third factor is the degree to which access to extant archival collections can be determined by sectarian identity or personal contacts.

A more important factor in explaining this specific gap in the scholarship of modern Lebanon concerns the ways in which scholars have conceptualized the three decades after Lebanese independence vis-à-vis the *longue durée* of history. When juxtaposed to the spectacular violence of the mid-nineteenth century and that of the 1975–90 civil war, the absence of prolonged, organized violence during—and the concomitant relative political stability of—the period between 1943 and 1975 has prompted some scholars to characterize the period as the exception to the norm of violence in the modern history of Lebanon.[2] This might help explain why much of the scholarship that does exist on this period pivots around the three-month rebellion or civil war of 1958, its terminology depending on analytic preference and political worldview.[3]

However, despite the alleged archival absences and the emphasis on spectacular events, a subset of scholars has provided intriguing portrayals of postindependence Lebanon as a dynamic site of cultural production and of significant social transformations that included labor organizing, political party formation, and other forms of institution building.[4] Yet the critical picture of political, economic, social, and cultural life that we have skews toward the late 1950s and subsequent years. As such, much of what we know about the early postindependence period (1943–55) continues to be shaped by a body of scholarship that—despite various disciplinary, theoretical, and methodological orientations—reifies the same old story of politics in Lebanon.

SECTARIANISM, NATIONALISMS, AND THE MERCHANT REPUBLIC

Recent scholarship on Lebanon has complicated if not overturned long-held understandings about politics in the territories that constitute present-day Lebanon. Ussama Makdisi and Max Weiss demonstrate the contingent nature and geo-temporal specificities of the production of sectarianism as a modern political discourse and practice.[5] Ilham Khuri-Makdisi, Elizabeth Thompson, Malek Abisaab, and Betty Anderson highlight how mobilizations by middle-class intellectuals, workers, women, and students were constitutive of particular periods and spaces of Lebanon.[6] At the same time, Akram Khater, Andrew Arsan, and Stacy Fahrenthold explore how outward and return migration helped establish the political economy of ideas and power relations that constituted the territories of Lebanon during the late Ottoman and French colonial periods.[7] Others like Maya Mikdashi and Hicham Safieddine have insisted on the role of state institutions in the production of power, whether in the form of categories of citizenship or banker privilege.[8]

Yet as historical inquiry focuses on the early postindependence years (1943–55), there is a dearth of narratives based in this period. When such narratives do form, most are hampered by one of two methodological faults. Some scholars consider the period from 1943 to 1975 a single unit and reduce it to a simple teleology leading directly to the civil war.[9] Others identify 1958 as a pivot during the period of independence.[10] However, viewing 1958 or 1975 as a decisive turning point reifies the mythologizing of personalities and coalitions whose fates pivoted around either of those dates. It renders 1943–58 or 1943–75 as ostensibly cohesive (linear) periods making invisible critical turning points, shorter-lived dynamics, and foreclosed possibilities. Both periodization schemes transform our understanding of the interregnum into a "prequel," rendering all events prior to the period's end date as explanatory and reflective of its outcome. In parallel, individuals, groups, events, and dynamics with no significant role during the end-point event of 1958 or 1975 are almost completely ignored.

A related methodological fault is to focus on a single event or personality of the postindependence period while nonetheless reading the sources and narrating developments with an implicit or explicit foreshadowing of the post-1958 status quo or the 1975–90 civil war. In such readings, the assumption that politics and social life in Lebanon are "always the same" continues to constrain our thinking. Accompanying this assumption is an intensified scholarly investment in the predictability of elite behavior, popular mobilizations, and the universe of interests and possibilities of both. Hicham Safieddine's work on the shifting relationship of the banking sector to the prospects and then realities of a central bank is a recent and important corrective to this general trend of homogenizing not just groups within Lebanese history but the history of Lebanon itself.[11] He explores the consolidation of bankers' power and its imbrication in state institutional arrangements while destabilizing stock characters, static interests, and stale strategies.

Yet scholars continue to insist that elites, popular groups, and the state are fundamentally unchanging and thus easily understood. Most existing research on the early postindependence period is characterized by adherence to one of three schools of analysis about the politics of the period. Scholars have in turn used the sect, rival nationalist groups, and the mercantile-financial elite to flatten politics in Lebanon in familiar ways.

The first school takes the sect as its central unit of analysis, whereby the history of Lebanon is the history of different sects (i.e., Druze, Greek Orthodox, Maronite, Shi'i, and Sunni) struggling with one another for political power, economic resources, and foreign support.[12] These scholars consider the sectarian identities of individuals and movements as so primary and fixed that the sect is narrated as the fundamental agent of historical change. They suggest a binary relationship between sectarian identity and the nation-state in which Lebanese citizens privilege the former; or the latter does not really exist at all. The problem with making the sect the central unit of analysis is that it is based on an essentialist conception of identity and a static conception of political community. More recently, scholars have challenged us to interrogate the shifting terrain of sectarian markers and the ways in which the meaning of those markers was constantly changing in relation to a range of processes.[13]

A second dominant framework of analysis assumes that the primary cleavage animating the early postindependence history of Lebanon is a struggle between the forces of Lebanese nationalism and those of Arab nationalism.[14] Each of these nationalist orientations is assumed to be a function of a particular sectarian identity. In this rendering, a Lebanese Christian is said to more likely be oriented toward a more exclusive conception of the Lebanese nation, one that is set apart from the broader Arabo-Islamic history and more closely aligned with the West. The counterpart to this is that a Lebanese Muslim is more likely to be oriented toward a more expansive conception of the Lebanese nation, one that is part of the region's history and thus more closely aligned with an Arab nationalist foreign policy orientation. The competition between Lebanese nationalists and Arab nationalists, this narrative contends, is implicated in all aspects of Lebanese politics including conflicts over foreign relations, internal politics, and economic policies.

Assumptions about nationalism that divide the population of Lebanon into Arab nationalists and Lebanese nationalists are—like those that privilege the sect—rooted in essentialist and teleological conceptions of identity. Over the past two decades, a number of scholars have highlighted complex processes that caused the majority of the post-Ottoman successor states' populations to internalize specific national identities that conformed to their respective territorial boundaries. They also highlight how these processes were uneven across time and space as well as the contingent conditions under which this internalization potentially gives way to new or other nationalist projects. We thus have a better understanding of how specific individuals transitioned from one form of nationalist attachment to another in response to changing circumstances. At the same time, other scholars have taken critical stock of the alleged binary between a specific state nationalism (e.g., Lebanese or Iraqi) and Arab nationalism. In particular moments, these were symbiotic—rather than alternative—forms of nationalist identification.[15] Furthermore, assertions of Arab identity or calls for Arab unity meant different things at different times and in different contexts.

The third school of analysis variously centers the consolidation of a "merchant republic," whereby the political economy of postindependence Lebanon coalesced around a laissez-faire and service-based model.[16] For scholars adopting this approach, the history of postindependence Lebanon is one of a mercantile-financial elite that consolidated its preferred political economy, and one that features internal competition between its composite networks of familial and sectarian relations. Some scholars consider the merchant republic an almost natural corollary to politics in Lebanon, either due to its alleged complementarity with political sectarianism or its assumed privileged status as the default economic vision overriding all other potential constructions of the economy. These scholars also suggest a binary relationship between the merchant republic and the centrality of state institutions in which the former precludes the latter.

The merchant republic framework and the parallel assumption of the laissez-faire state inform most histories of postindependence Lebanon. Yet even some of the most critical works operating under this assumption confront common pitfalls in the historiography of Lebanon. The focus on macroeconomic and sectoral trends has taken for granted several areas of inquiry. One example is the mercantile-financial elite. On the one hand, it is presented as a preexisting group whose formation and historical evolution are not worthy of mention. On the other hand, we are provided with little to no account of its collective struggles with other social classes or groupings.[17]

The adoption of these three frameworks—sectarianism, nationalism, and the merchant republic—reflects more fundamental assumptions about the history of Lebanon and the broader Middle East, and their continued usage by scholars has hindered our understanding of the early postindependence period. In particular, much of the scholarship on postcolonial Lebanon views it as the example par excellence of the deficiencies and exceptionalisms that undergird much knowledge production on the region. In such scholarship the "strength" of sectarianism, the "lack" of national identity, and the "weakness" or "failure" of the state stand as metonyms for politics. We should not underestimate the civil war's power to engender such representations; for in many ways, that conflict demarcates what we can know about Lebanon before, during, and after it.

This book tells a different story. It analyzes the politics of the early postindependence period on their own terms. It also takes seriously how individuals and groups identified themselves, articulated their interests, and innovated strategies, all actions taken under specific conditions and with imaginative possibilities unincumbered by the specter of civil war, armed rebellion, or foreign intervention. Instead, they envisioned a future defined by decolonization, sovereignty, and development in ways that preceded the domestic transformations of 1956–58 and the transnational dynamics of the Bandung Conference of 1955 and the articulation of Third Worldism. While there were multiple and competing visions of such a future, they all featured the assumption of state building.

RETHINKING THE STATE OF LEBANON

This book is both a social and an institutional history of how people pursued their visions of the postcolonial in the years between 1943 and 1955. It demonstrates that state institutions were important sites for the projection of power and of collective action in the wake of independence. It further argues that state building and popular mobilizations were co-constitutive in Lebanon during the 1943–55 period. This was a time of exceptional elite and popular mobilization over the creation and control of state institutions. In the territories that comprise Lebanon, late Ottoman and French colonial rule left significant legacies. Also important were new global norms that emerged during the post–World War II era and the parallel imperial machinations of the United States. Most crucial were the elite and popular mobilizations that built on, appropriated, challenged, or rejected these legacies and norms as they sought to remake institutional arrangements in the wake of independence.

This book maps several of these efforts and the hitherto overlooked worldviews and strategies that Lebanese politicians and activists developed while it also traces the trajectories of specific state institutions generated by these actors' struggles. This book accomplishes that by emphasizing state institutions as an object of analysis. These institutions were objects of mobilization and brokers of political, economic, and social privilege. Exploring their trajectories sheds new light on the fortunes and limits imposed on postcolonial state building in Lebanon and beyond.

The literature on state building in the Middle East is copious yet scattered, and thus not sufficiently cohesive to identify many shared propositions. Three dynamics contribute to this character of the literature. First, scholarship on state building has come from a variety of disciplines, including anthropology, economics, history, political science, and sociology.[18] The diversity of research methodologies, theoretical frameworks, and research questions has in turn developed several isolated thematic research agendas. Second, the literature on state building ranges from studies focusing on the state as an object of analysis to others that focus on alternative social formations (e.g., civilizations, interest groups, or classes).[19] While scholars with the former focus view the state in its totality, scholars with the latter focus tend to study a collection of individuals performing a specific function or a specific institution within the state.[20] Finally, developments in the social sciences have shifted the types of questions posed and models used.[21] For example, while "the Alawi community" and "the military in politics" were once foci of attention, institutional capacities and discursive frameworks currently attract the bulk of attention.[22] One product of this eclectic range of research agendas is the near absence of dialogue between scholars across disciplines, time periods, or countries.

Most scholarship on state building can nevertheless be grouped into one of three categories based on what order of phenomena they address. One set of scholars recognizes the modern state as a unique form of social organization defined by new constellations of political rationalities and power relations. For these scholars, the modern state is a compulsory model for organizing political communities in the modern era and involves techniques of governance that permit the state to intervene into subjects' daily lives in unprecedented ways. These scholars diverge, however, over precise definitions of the political rationalities, power relations, and techniques of governance that constitute the modern state. The theoretical observations of Max Weber and Michel Foucault have played an influential role in this regard.[23] For Weber, the extension of bureaucratic organization and procedures throughout society becomes a crucial and specifically "modern" way to legitimize domination and rule.[24] Accordingly, the routine operation of bureaucracy creates and maintains political authority, the socioeconomic order, and social hierarchies. For Foucault, the modern state is defined by "governmentality," a system of correlation between three mechanisms of power: sovereignty over territory, discipline over bodies, and security of the population.[25] Accordingly, the social order is one in which each individual is disciplined and policed (i.e., individuation) while the totality of individuals is abstracted as a population and managed through biopolitics (i.e., totalization).

In applying such theories of the modern state to the Middle East, this first set of scholars—who recognize the modern state as a unique form of social organization—have variously sought to understand the emergence of the modern state as an evolving mode of sociopolitical organization in the Middle East. Their research demonstrates how, throughout the long nineteenth century, the Khedival, Ottoman, and Persian states introduced instruments of modern governance, thereby transforming their political systems into modern states and introducing the requisite institutions (e.g., the modern military, mass education, and the census) and corollary social formations (e.g., market economies and a wage-earning class).[26] Their studies are attentive to the impulses, contingencies, difficulties, and resistance such projects encountered.

A second set of scholars researching state building is interested in the territorial delineation of contemporary states and the making of their borders. It is in this context that many scholars have analyzed the post–World War I dismemberment of the Ottoman Empire and the border drawing integral to the creation of its successor states: Iraq, Lebanon, Palestine, Syria, Transjordan, and Turkey.[27] They have also highlighted numerous alternative geographic imaginaries concerning each of these states. Over time, and in many cases not until the 1930s, the boundaries between states started to resemble the outline of the region's present-day map. These scholars demonstrate how this was the result of a slow process of "resolving competing claims to territory" of local groups, rulers of the new states, and colonial powers. This resolution was always reached via the application of power, frequently in the form of war. Comparable exertions of applications of violence were required to maintain these borders.

The nature of a specific state's regime constitutes the mainstay of a third set of scholarly works. The term *regime* broadly refers to the particular organization of mass politics in a given state, formed through rules, norms, and practices that structure formal political participation and economic privilege.[28] Some scholars also deploy the term more narrowly to refer to "ruling coalitions: the principal power holders who exercise definitive policy making authority" in a state.[29] These researchers are particularly interested in the emergence, consolidation, and sometimes collapse of specific systems of rule in a given country or as a regional model for specific eras. Scholars analyzing such dynamics have usually examined several facets, including the historical mechanisms that led to the emergence of such a regime;[30] the effects of such a regime on the domain of political activity;[31] the developmental consequences of this model;[32] and prospects for economic and political reforms within the context of a changing international system.[33]

This book draws inspiration and builds on all three categories of scholarship on state building outlined above. It eschews two tendencies among a subset of scholars. The first is to confuse the modern state, as unique form of sociopolitical organization, with the demarcation of a given state's territorial boundaries and/or the consolidation and unraveling of particular regimes therein. As one example, let us consider the post–World War I settlement that ushered in a new political order in large parts of the Middle East. The creation of new national borders defining the successor states of Iraq, Jordan, Lebanon, Palestine, Syria, and Turkey, as well as the consolidation of new regimes within them, characterized this new order. Yet it would be profoundly ahistorical to argue that the modern state as a form of sociopolitical organization had no existence prior to the onset of postwar British and French colonial rule. The post–World War I division of the Ottoman Empire into successor states radically redefined the borders, symbols, and "histories" of various populations but not their categories of thought or social practice. In fact, it built on the late Ottoman precedent of introducing techniques of governance and the political sociabilities of the modern state to the local population.[34]

This book points to the enormous "success" of the internalization by residents of the territories that constitute Lebanon of the modern state as conveyor of political sociability as well as the recognized boundaries of the regional state system. It nevertheless details the institutional arrangements that shaped political incumbency, economic privilege, and social inclusion within this system. More specifically, it argues that the particular contours of those institutional arrangements were predicated less on a preexisting kind of knowledge about how to rule than on an organic, tentative, and ad hoc process managed from above, but also shaped and defined from below. Put differently, during the early independence period of Lebanon, the country's presidents, cabinets, and parliaments created new institutional arrangements to address problems stemming from popular mobilizations. Furthermore, these mobilizations made demands concerning institutional arrangements on those in power that were both normative and strategic in nature. Sometimes they succeeded in imposing their visions upon the state. It is therefore analytically impossible to write a history of state institutions that is not simultaneously a history of popular mobilizations.

PLAN OF THE BOOK

The previous distinction between the modern state as a unique form of sociopolitical organization, the demarcation of a given state's territorial boundaries, and the consolidation of particular regimes therein provides the scaffolding for chapter 1. It takes a new look at Ottoman (1839–1918) and French (1918–43) practices of governing the territories that constitute present-day Lebanon. The chapter frames these practices as underpinning the co-constitutive processes of state, market, and class formation. The late Ottoman period featured the initial introduction of governing techniques associated with the modern state into the territories of present-day Lebanon as it did to other parts of the empire during the same period. French invasion and occupation intensified the deployment of those techniques while territorializing them around the new national and imperial borders of the post-Ottoman successor state of Lebanon and the broader French Mandate in Lebanon and Syria. Concomitant with this period was the establishment of particular institutional arrangements—some of which were built on Ottoman precedents—that organized formal politics, economic development, and social relations. This chapter introduces several of these arrangements and the social actors who mobilized around them, setting the stage for the struggles and institutional transformations that would shape the early postindependence period.

The transition to independence opened up a host of new questions and strategic possibilities concerning the future of political incumbency, economic privilege, and social standing. Chapter 2 explores the macro-institutional contours of postcolonial state building in Lebanon, with a particular emphasis on the bureaucratic expansion underpinning this process between 1943 and 1955. While this period featured the construction of an open laissez-faire service-based model for economic development, the chapter demonstrates how critical the role of state institutions was to the realization of that model and a range of other arrangements shaping political, economic, social, and cultural life. The current and future natures of state institutional arrangements were nevertheless a contentious topic. This chapter therefore also attends to the ways in which global dynamics and regional trends combined with elite and popular mobilizations to (re) shape state institutions.

Chapter 3 explores the military and education (both public and private) as key domains in which the interplay between global and regional dynamics, elite jockeying, and popular mobilization gave specific shape to state institutional arrangements. It engages particularly with calls for the evacuation of all foreign troops; for the creation of sovereign, national armed forces; and for the reforming and expansion of public education. In contrast to the usual scholarly concern with intra-elite factionalism and foreign intervention, the chapter traces how these calls and the resultant transformations of the military and education worked to help produce the Lebanese state and national identity. The point is not to minimize competing visions, preferences, and interests in the shaping of the military and education. Rather, it is to explore the widespread agreement around the very idea of Lebanese society and state institutions as the foundation of sovereignty.

Chapter 4 turns to how, both as part of the transition to independence and subsequent to it, labor became increasingly important as an economic resource, a social experience, and a political force. Throughout the French colonial period, the mobilization of workers was intertwined with ideas about sovereignty and the nature of state institutional arrangements. But it was only after 1943 that the Lebanese state adopted a comprehensive labor law. Yet rather than view the passage of that law as the culmination, successful or not, of labor mobilizations, I propose viewing it as a turning point in the normalization—for both workers and managers—of state intervention into labor. The chapter examines labor mobilizations around the 1946 labor law as well as subsequent calls for its implementation or expansion. This dynamic was intimately linked to the changing nature of state institutional arrangements regulating labor, both its exploitation by employers and mobilizations by workers.

If the bureaucracy, national military, public schools, and labor were all flash points for elite and popular mobilizations, their trajectories are unpredictable. Chapter 5 looks at how women's organizations and a key subset of women activists worked to secure women's suffrage. Women had demanded the right to vote in Lebanon since the state's establishment in 1920. Yet they only secured that right in 1953. The chapter explores the broader shifts that enabled a renewed mobilization for women's suffrage as well as the strategic and organizational innovations of that mobilization.

Chapter 6 returns to the topic with which I began this Introduction, the controversies over the affordability, quality, and sourcing of electricity in Beirut. It also explores the murky origins yet clear trajectory of a campaign against the primarily French-owned concessionaire, the Beirut Electricity Company, which resulted in the government mandating a price reduction. I argue that the campaign featured multiple—and at times competing—objectives that were nevertheless viewed and presented through the idioms of sovereignty and state building. Public utilities in general, and electricity in particular, represented a critical site for the coming together of various struggles that centered state institutional arrangements in general and active government intervention in particular. It is in this context that a campaign that officially called for greater transparency and lowering of prices laid the groundwork for the nationalization of the Beirut Electricity Company and the inauguration of a public electricity sector.

This book's conclusion explores some of the implications of the histories explored and arguments advanced in this book. I am interested in how a focused study on the 1943–55 period might prompt us to rethink the role of the state in Lebanon, including the historiographic and analytic implications for later periods. Yet I am equally if not more interested in how the research for, organization of, and analysis in this book might push us to question long-held assumptions about those living in Lebanon and their capacity to dream, envision, strategize, innovate, and realize.

A NOTE ON METHODOLOGY

This book is not a history of Lebanon or the Lebanese state as a "coherent sociohistorical or conceptual subject."[35] Each chapter explores specific aspects of early postindependence Lebanon's varied struggles over state institutional arrangements. These struggles were not part of some scripted logic of political rule, sectarianism, or class conflict. They were usually attempts to address—in real time—urgent issues viewed as obstacles to the realization of both national independence and particular views of development. It was only in the waging of a particular struggle or the implementation of a specific campaign that a given "problem" became legible in broader national and comparative terms.

This methodological point is related to state institutional arrangements on which I choose to focus. There are manifold spheres and issues in which state institutions are implicated. There is an equally ubiquitous array of elite and popular mobilizations that a book like this could explore. But there are several reasons this book features the specific domains of mobilizations and concomitant institutional arrangements that it does. First, in surveying several newspapers from the 1943–55 period, one is struck by the ubiquity of the military, education, labor, women, and electricity as privileged topics of coverage and recurring subjects of controversy. Second, there is the question of sources. One could interpret all matters as being related to state building and the co-constitutive nature of popular mobilizations and institutional arrangements. However, the reality of primary sources is such that there are clusters of sources around particular institutional arrangements and particular moments of popular mobilization. Some of these sources were extant in state and private archives. In other cases, these sources had previously been collected by activists or researchers.

I have made use of sources drawn from archives, as well as library stacks and special collections scattered across three continents. I use many sources not previously exploited by scholars of Lebanon. My research coincided with the recent availability of new documents and collections across the archives, bookshops, and antique dealers of Beirut. I owe a particular debt to the MA theses collection at the American University of Beirut. Those written between the 1940s and the 1970s reflect both a bygone orientation to taking seriously state institutions in Lebanon and the ability to access government officials and archives in the country. I have also reexamined sources previously utilized by other scholars. My research differs from most of the scholarship on Lebanon in several ways.

First, the state institutions covered in this book helped form "the deep structural basis" for reproducing a political regime within which sectarian politics were critical.[36] Yet at the same time, the institutions under study are largely "one step removed from [those] sectarian politics."[37] Unlike many of the period's other domains in which the sectarian composition of bureaucrats or the sectarian implications of policies were readily identified or debated in the sources (e.g., the parliament, the personal status courts, and sectarian employment quotas), the historical record of the struggles covered in the following chapters makes scant mention of such concerns. I suggest two reasons for this absence. The first is the rather simple fact that not everything was reducible, or relevant, to issues of sect and sectarianism. The second reason is a more complicated and thus understudied reality: the very concept of sectarianism is unstable as an idiom for claim making or a basis of mobilization.

Another way in which my research diverges from narratives about the transition to independence and differs from much recent scholarship on Lebanon is the near complete absence from my analysis of what has come to be known as the National Pact (*al-mithaq al-watani*). Most scholars of Lebanon (if not Lebanese people themselves) consider the 1943 National Pact as the cornerstone of Lebanon's postcolonial political system.[38] The primary narrative about the pact is that it was an unwritten agreement between Riyad al-Sulh, as representative of the Sunni community and the Arab nationalists of Lebanon, and Bishara al-Khuri, as representative of the Maronite community and the country's Lebanese nationalists.[39] For everyone, the key element of the pact related to the country's foreign relations: Lebanon would be independent and oriented toward the Arab world in its foreign affairs. A second element of the pact is the 6:5 Christian to Muslim ratio of seats in parliament and the understanding that sects would be equitably represented in government positions, particularly the bureaucracy and high offices like cabinet positions. The Maronite, Sunni, and Shi'a communities' exclusive claim on the three highest offices—president, prime minister, and speaker of parliament, respectively—is considered by many to be a third element of the pact. These three elements elevate the National Pact to the status of Lebanon's central institutional arrangement.

How is it then that this book does not explore in depth—let alone discuss—the National Pact? There is a simple yet primary reason for this: the National Pact makes little to no appearance in the extant primary sources from the period under study. The National Pact as a sociohistorical or conceptual subject is not present in the newspaper articles, political pamphlets, public speeches, and other sources of the period. In fact, during the 1943–55 period the very term "national pact" is variously used by several political parties to describe their own internal organization or those with other parties. In all of these cases, these national pacts are never presented as an alternative to or different order of phenomenon from the alleged status of the 1943 National Pact.

It is important to clarify what are the stakes of such assertions. There is little doubt that the National Pact as a sociohistorical and conceptual subject occupies an important place in the elite jockeying, popular mobilizations, and scholarly writings of Lebanon during and after the 1960s. But that is precisely the point. The overwhelming majority of references to the National Pact cite the memoirs of Bishara al-Khuri—published at the turn of the 1960s.[40] Previous substantive discussions of the 1943 National Pact date to the 1958 rebellion.[41] The National Pact as a sociohistorical or conceptual topic is thus better understood as a product of a later (and significantly different) set of struggles to reshape the political system or to maintain the status quo. The struggles directly linked to 1958 and its aftermath appear to be the context for the idea of a 1943 National Pact as a precisely defined bargain underpinning the entire political system and assuming a privileged position in the national political imagination.[42] Beyond serving as an explanation for the absence of the National Pact—the presumed fundamental institutional arrangement of politics in Lebanon—as a matter of analysis in this book, the preceding discussion serves to highlight what is perhaps the fundamental methodological underpinning of this book. To understand the state of Lebanon in 1943–55, we cannot read history backward from current understandings or even past understandings that are subsequent to the period. We must read history forward, beginning with the events through which the subjects of our analysis emerge and through the terms by which they defined themselves. Only then can we learn about politics and social life in Lebanon in ways that transcend the limitations of the same old story.

One
THE FORMATION OF LEBANON

THE FORMATION OF LEBANON AS A MODERN STATE IS MOST PRODUCtively understood through a historical comparative perspective that deexceptionalizes the Lebanese state and Lebanese national identity. Scholars have often narrated its history as a battle between the forces of Lebanese nationalism and those of Arab nationalism. Accordingly, this fundamental cleavage animated the populations and territories constituting present-day Lebanon since at least the nineteenth century. This narrative certainly reflects the language of some local debates during World War I (1914–18) and the French colonial period (1918–43) between those favoring the postwar establishment and maintenance of a Lebanese state and those favoring the inclusion of potential territories and populations in a broader national state (i.e., Ottoman, Arab, or Syrian). Such a narrative nevertheless elides the contingent nature of those positions and the fact that by the eve of independence in 1943 there was a broad-based commitment to Lebanon as the national framework for sovereign state building, economic development, national identity formation, and mass politics. This is not to give credence to the Lebanese national narrative that renders the institutions of semiautonomous rule in Ottoman Mount Lebanon as commensurate with an independent state.[1] Such narratives frame the Shihabi emirate (1697–1841) and the *mutasarrifiyya* (a subprovince directly subordinate to the imperial capital) of Mount Lebanon (1861–1915) as earlier incarnations of the Lebanese state and harbingers of Lebanese national identity. The emirate was part and parcel of early modern Ottoman administrative structures and political culture, while the *mutasarrifiyya* is best understood as the product of empire-wide debates about decentralization (not independence), the introduction of modern governance (at the imperial, provincial, and municipal levels), and the broader context of colonial competition and intervention.[2]

The project of creating a Lebanese state was in fact a product of the later years of World War I and its aftermath. The success of establishing and maintaining Lebanon as a territorial state was more a function of Ottoman legacies of modern statecraft and the post–World War I regional and international order than it was of any alleged nationalist antecedents. Like their regional counterparts, postwar state builders in Lebanon owed an unacknowledged debt to the late nineteenth- and early twentieth-century expansion of the Ottoman state, for they could not have succeeded in their endeavors in the absence of that legacy.[3] Furthermore, most of the project of Lebanese state building's early detractors ultimately became its supporters. This signifies a shift in the terrain of struggle away from questions about the territorial division of the post-Ottoman Levant toward issues of controlling the state apparatus and otherwise shaping its production of political power, economic privilege, and social experience.

One central aim of this chapter is defamiliarizing the prevalent story of Lebanese state formation. This approach rejects both the nationalist view of the Republic of Lebanon as the inevitable culmination of previous autonomous institution building in Mount Lebanon as well as the idea of Lebanon as the ex nihilo construction accomplished by the French and their Maronite clients. This chapter instead attends to how modern formations of governance manifested through specific institutional arrangements that engendered particular political dynamics, many of which were subsequently expanded, deepened, and encaged within the territorial borders of the state in question. These arrangements were neither uncontested nor ineffective. Thus a second aim of this chapter is to introduce the institutional arrangements, social groups, political coalitions, and individual personalities that constitute the starting point of this book's exploration of the trajectory of state formation and popular politics in postcolonial Lebanon.

LATE OTTOMAN LEGACIES

Lebanon was established in 1920 as one of several successor states of the Ottoman Empire. The current territory of the Republic of Lebanon is an amalgamation of the Ottoman *mutasarrifiyya* of Mount Lebanon and parts of the *vilayet* (province) of Beirut and the *sanjaks* (ordinary subprovinces) of Damascus, Hama, and Hawran. Prior to World War I, these territories—like those that would constitute Iraq, Palestine, Transjordan, and Syria—were administratively, politically, economically, and culturally part of the late Ottoman Empire.[4] To insist on the significance of Ottoman legacies is not to deny the agency of local inhabitants and their counterparts in the diaspora, who critiqued Ottoman policies or advocated a particular post-Ottoman future. Rather, it is to argue that both the experience and collapse of the Ottoman system were the conditions of possibility for a sustained and broad-based national imagining of an independent state of Lebanon.

During the Ottoman Empire's final century of existence, modern forms of statecraft, economy, and sociability began to emerge in its territories.[5] The period also featured the integration of these areas and their populations into the modern world system.[6] Two overarching processes undergirded this integration. The first was the introduction of techniques of modern governance and the unprecedented degree to which they permitted state intervention into subjects' daily lives.[7] The second was the shift from subsistence to market production.[8] Both processes were uneven across time and space, resulting in heterogeneous patterns of cultural identification, political affiliation, land ownership, capital accumulation, and labor, gender, and sectarian relations. An overall effect of the transformation of Ottoman rule and the shift to market production was the redefinition of social categories: tax farming and the slave trade were abolished, new urban businesses began to appear, rural landowning and wage-earning (rural and urban) classes began to form, normative gender roles shifted, and the relationship of Ottoman subjects to one another and to the sultan increasingly came to be defined through a negotiated—however unequally—set of rights and responsibilities.

One key element of pre–World War I transformations was that peasants—the overwhelming majority of the local population—along with rural and urban landed elites increasingly turned to production for the world capitalist market. The rise and fall of the silk economy in Mount Lebanon is the most studied aspect of this transformation.[9] French and local economic interests spurred a dramatic expansion in sericulture between the 1840s and 1880s. Previously, silk production had not been a significant part of the region's economy.[10] However, the entry of Chinese and Japanese silk into the world market, coupled with the global recession of 1873–96, caused the local silk economy to decline from the early 1870s. Consequently, large numbers of landowners and peasants turned to new crops. Tobacco was particularly popular.[11] Such developments dovetailed with those affecting less-studied regions and communities that did not take up sericulture in the first place, but rather anchored their shift to market production in the cultivation of grains and tobacco.[12]

A second key development of the pre–World War I period was the establishment of institutions and practices of modern governance. This marked an unprecedented level of state intervention into everyday life and the standardization of both. This process was uneven yet cumulative, occurring over four consecutive phases of modern institution building in the Levant: the Egyptian occupation (1831–40), the Ottoman Tanzimat (1839–78), the reign of Sultan Abdulhamid II (1876–1909), and the second Ottoman constitutional era (1908–14). The Ottomans introduced a new system of provincial administration.[13] They also inaugurated municipal governance and restructured rural governance.[14] These reforms created a bureaucratic hierarchy within every province, featuring the *vilayet* (province), *sanjak* (subprovince), *qada* (district), *kariye* (village) or *nahiyya* (commune) in rural areas, and *mahalla* (neighborhood) in the cities. This hierarchy featured the heads of each administrative division, who were accompanied by other appointed or elected officials and councilors. The inclusion of provincial representatives on the Ottoman Council of State (Şura-yı Devlet) served both to coordinate and control the work of the new provincial councils and to allow for provincial input into the empire's legislative process.[15] Through these and other modern administrative structures, the Ottomans conducted the census, registered land ownership, imposed direct taxation, and established urban and rural policing.[16] They also created a modern military, public civil and military education systems, and unprecedented regulations affecting public health and public life.[17] The empire intended for these institutions and practices to centralize and expand state authority through forms of disciplinary and biopolitical power.[18] Such developments, their attendant hierarchies, and the relations they engendered shaped subsequent approaches to and dynamics of state formation.

The influx of European investment capital in the form of loans, concessions, and monopolies facilitated, and was shaped by, the emergence of market relations and modern statecraft.[19] The development of tramways, roads, railways, ports, telegraphs, and urban amenities like water, lighting, and electricity systems was tied to the region's emerging commodity markets and their connection to the global economy.[20] Yet they were profit-generating enterprises in their own right.[21] They also offered important technologies of power to both Ottoman bureaucrats, who sought to facilitate more effective communication and transportation, and European agents, who sought new forms of influence in the region. Such infrastructure therefore further linked the history of these territories to a broader pattern of European investment and political interference in the region.

A fourth key element in the pre–World War I transformations was the changing nature and significance of various urban centers. The rise of Beirut as a major port city (and, in 1888, a provincial capital) and of Zahleh as a commercial center was linked to modern statecraft, emerging commodity markets, and infrastructural investments during the late Ottoman period.[22] Previously, Beirut was of little relevance to the local or regional political economy. Only in the 1830s and 1840s did Beirut begin its transformation into a major port city. The region's increasing integration into the world economy was one factor.[23] Also important were the lobbying efforts of local politicians, merchants, and landowners and the intervention of European governments to give Beirut precedence over Acre, which was already an established port.[24] Similarly, the late eighteen and nineteenth centuries featured administrators, merchants, and landlords repositioning Zahleh as a major node for controlling regional production and sale of grains and cattle. They did so within the multiple contexts of the local dominance of Bashir Shihab II (r. 1789–1840), the Egyptian occupation (1831–40), the Crimean War (1853–56), and the intensification of sericulture in Mount Lebanon (1860–73).[25] These developments also negatively affected more traditional urban centers, trading towns, and ports. For example, the attendant increase in maritime trade, the construction of new road and rail networks, and changing administrative frameworks rendered interior towns like Bint Jbayl and Tibnin as well as coastal cities like Tripoli and Sidon less consequential than they had been prior to the late nineteenth century.[26] These shifts in the balance of power between urban centers was accompanied by an overall restructuring of urban space through the introduction of modern urban planning, street lighting, and tramway infrastructures; parks, squares, other public leisure zones; and other products of development.[27] Both dynamics contributed to an increase in the overall and relative size of the region's urban population.[28]

The fifth key element of the pre–World War I transformations was mass emigration from Mount Lebanon and nearby areas to (primarily) the Americas. This process, which began in the 1880s and accelerated between 1890 and 1915, occurred largely in response to the global depression and the decline of the silk economy.[29] New transportation and communication infrastructures greatly facilitated migration, as well as flows of information and capital between local communities and the diaspora. A significant number of these émigrés returned.[30] This return migration transformed home villages and towns, as returnees brought back capital, purchased land, built houses, educated their children, and embodied new gender norms and relations.[31] Diasporic networks also informed local developments through remittances (transfers of capital) and political mobilizations.[32] Consequently, the emergence of a middle class in the territories that would become Lebanon followed a slightly different trajectory than other parts of the Middle East.[33]

A final key element of this period was the emergence of mass politics, whereby the middle class, urban workers, and peasants increasingly established a more salient presence and discursive legitimacy in the formal domains of politics than had previously been the case.[34] The transformation of economic, administrative, infrastructural, and demographic conditions reshaped daily life and made possible a contingent restructuring of social categories.[35] This restructuring process affected the boundaries, identities, and composition of elite and popular segments of the population. Combined with the increasing turn to wage labor, rural-urban migration, and urban restructuring, this process changed the nature of family bonds, loosened neighborhood-based loyalties, and undermined traditional forms of social protection. These shifts made relationships of power along horizontal, associational, sectarian, and national lines more practicable. The repeated political mobilizations mounted by members of these new social categories helped develop internal bonds of solidarity. This in turn precipitated new concepts for identifying these bonds and new strategies for maintaining them.

It was in this context that new types of organization like the association (*al-jam'iyya*) emerged in Beirut, other cities, major towns, and select villages, as it did across the Ottoman Empire.[36] Use of the term *jam'iyya* reveals little about the institution's recognition by the state, its legal personhood, or its internal structure.[37] Most associations were based in horizontally defined constituencies who participated—even if in limited ways—in the selection of their officers. Regular meetings served as a central ritual of these groups. Many of them established, or emerged from networks that produced, periodicals of one kind or another.

Early manifestations of mass politics displayed a diverse array of interests, objectives, constituencies, and activities.[38] Some wealthy individuals professionalized and institutionalized benevolence through establishing charitable associations to address what their members deemed the root causes of poverty.[39] Many upper- and middle-class men also sought new forms of knowledge, or the status that came with demonstrating such knowledge, by forming literary and scientific societies.[40] Reflecting new ideas about bodies, health, exercise, and modernity, several sports enthusiasts created athletic clubs offering gymnastics and competition in team sports.[41] Significant numbers of notables, businessmen, and male intellectuals established political parties (both secret and public) to influence—if not seize control of—municipal, provincial, or imperial decision-making bodies.[42] Freemasonry offered a particular outlet for political and social organization, as well as a potential vehicle for political influence, as its lodge members embraced its associated philosophy and networking opportunities.[43] Workers also founded "associations" in the form of strike committees and mutual-aid networks.[44] Largely excluded from most of these formations, elite women created their own organizations to cultivate similar interests or those that they viewed as specific to their gender.[45]

By World War I, such associations were visible in public spaces and across the broader public sphere. The interregnum after the 1908 Ottoman

Revolution featured the intensification of the emergence of mass politics as political parties, professional associations, labor organizations, and other formal and semiformal groups multiplied, reflecting the diversity of interest representation and ideological formations.[46] Three sets of state policies facilitated this intensification. The discursive transformation of Ottoman subjects into Ottoman citizens was one.[47] Electoral cycles at the parliamentary, provincial, and municipal levels were another set of policies.[48] The party branch structure of the Committee of Union and Progress—beginning in 1908—and that of a range of formally recognized parties opposing it—during the 1910–12 period—further intensified the spread of mass politics. As associations and other less formal groupings increasingly demonstrated novel and effective ways to mobilize material resources, people, and political loyalty, laws were passed to monitor and constrain them. The Law of Associations and the Law of Public Gatherings are two notable examples.[49] These measures introduced new forms of state surveillance and required association officials to submit documentation detailing their organization's goals, structure, membership, activities, and funding. Simultaneously, old and new elites whose access to the state's coercive capacities was more limited developed informal means of disciplining subaltern groups like workers and peasants.

As previously noted, World War I was an important juncture in the trajectory of state, market, and class formation. Famine, disease, and conscription produced demographic, socioeconomic, and political crises. Equally important was the governorship of Ahmet Cemal Pasha (1872–1922) over the Levant (1915–18). It featured an intense campaign of policing loyalties, repressing opposition, and the arrest and deportation or execution of numerous persons deemed to be a security threat. This was the background context for the joint public executions in Beirut and Damascus of dozens of local notables the Ottoman authorities accused of Arab separatism. Also during World War I, the Entente powers—particularly the British and French—imposed a crippling blockade on the Eastern Mediterranean, resulting in food shortages and price hikes that culminated in famine.[50] Ottoman fiscal policies and grain requisitions aggravated this crisis, and Ottoman wartime conscription exacerbated the loss of life. In addition, local urban and rural as well as foreign elites compounded the blockade through hoarding of and speculation in wheat and other staples, thereby accumulating vast wealth.[51] They also used wartime exigencies to consolidate their control of land, removing competing claims to usufruct rights, shares of revenues, or shares of ownership.[52] Wartime also hastened the decline of the silk economy, especially as the Ottoman military requisitioned mulberry and other trees for timber. In contrast, the wartime blockade created a boom in demand for tobacco, which expanded and intensified its cultivation.[53] Estimates vary, but most historians agree that Mount Lebanon was hit hardest by the famine, with approximately 50 percent of its residents perishing.[54] Surrounding areas, including Beirut, fared only slightly better.

Famine and the broader set of wartime dynamics helped create the conditions enabling the establishment of a Lebanese state. Food shortages, other crises, and the Ottoman authorities' inability to effectively address them significantly undermined the Ottoman order in Mount Lebanon and its surroundings. This in turn created opportunities and incentives to organize and campaign for alternative and competing political projects.[55] The French Empire, the Hashemite-led Arab revolt, separatist movements in Mount Lebanon, and other forces appropriated wartime death, impoverishment, and repression to advance the tropes of "Turkish occupation" that featured the intentional starvation of the local population.[56] These tropes would continue to serve as key elements in the national myth of the Lebanese nation-state throughout the French colonial period and well into the postcolonial era.[57] Furthermore, wartime food shortages in Mount Lebanon were a decisive factor in motivating and justifying the inclusion of adjacent grain-producing regions (e.g., the Biqa' Valley) into the postwar state project of Lebanon.[58]

At the end of World War I, British, French, and Hashemite military forces occupied the Levantine regions of the Ottoman Empire. The particular balance of power, division of territory, and differential roles between Britain, France, and the Hashemites manifested in the establishment of the Occupied Enemy Territory Administration.[59] All three parties had very little interest in surrendering their new territories. Meanwhile, pursuing the "Open Door Policy" articulated at the turn of the century, the US government sought to end the prewar system of imperial trading preferences and secure access for US businesses. While the Entente powers made multiple promises of self-determination or statehood, none were honored. The Paris Peace

Conference (1919–20), London Conference (1920), and San Remo Conference (1920) sanctioned British occupation of what would become Iraq, Palestine, and Transjordan, as well as the French occupation of territories that today constitute Lebanon and Syria. The colonial Mandate system of the League of Nations (est. 1922) legitimated these maneuvers.[60]

The creation of Lebanon as a national state in its present territorial configuration, however, was not inevitable from the perspective of the French colonial authorities or the local population. Both the particular contours of the political geography of Greater Lebanon (as opposed to Mount Lebanon) and the permanent commitment to it as an independent territorial state were the results of various factors. These included diverse local and diasporic mobilizations and lobbying efforts, the strategic considerations of French—and various local—actors, and frequently changing French military capacities.[61] Competing movements across the Levant mobilized to define the nature of the post-Ottoman framework.[62] Such mobilizations took place on the ground by means of armed revolt, petition campaigns, and various forms of protest. Mobilizations also manifested in different arenas, including the King-Crane Commission (1919),[63] the Paris Peace Conference (1919–20) and its follow-up meetings (1920–23), and the League of Nations (1920–46).[64] These movements' relative success in realizing their particular visions was contingent upon a range of factors. These included the level to which such movements institutionalized themselves, the financial and other resources at their disposal, and the degree to which foreign powers supported them. The future relationships of Mount Lebanon to its adjacent areas, a Damascus-based state, and France was an open question for approximately two years after the end of World War I. The interregnum featured a fluidity of opinions, where some of the inhabitants committed to a single vision; others vacillated between independence, federation, and integration; and many (if not most) hedged their bets either due to genuine uncertainty or for fear of compromising their future interests with those who championed the prevailing status.

The Commander of the French Army of the Levant and High Commissioner of France to the Levant Henri Gouraud (1867–1946) declared the State of Greater Lebanon (Dawlat Lubnan al-Kabir) on September 1, 1920.[65] He accomplished this by amalgamating the coastal cities of Beirut, Tripoli, Sidon,

Tyre, and their surrounding areas, the 'Akkar plain, Jabal 'Amil, and Biqa' Valley, and Mount Lebanon.[66] Such a political project was neither a reflection of a preexisting national identity nor the restoration of some suppressed or otherwise aborted independent entity. Four dynamics highlight its novelty. While local and diasporic actors made various arguments for the enlargement of the administrative territory of Mount Lebanon prior to World War I, they were all partial in their claims to the coastal cities, the Biqa' Valley, or some other adjoining region—never advancing more than one claim at a time.[67] Simultaneously, autonomy within the framework of the Ottoman Empire (as opposed to national independence) always defined these proposals.[68] It was only in the last years of the war that any protagonists articulated a full-fledged call for the establishment of an independent state based on Mount Lebanon (including its amalgamation with multiple surrounding regions).[69] Finally, in 1920 there was no unanimous support for such a project, including among the inhabitants of Mount Lebanon in general or the members of its Administrative Council in particular.[70] The League of Nations officially confirmed the French Mandate over Lebanon and Syria in August 1922.[71]

The establishment of Lebanon was not a reflection of a predetermined French policy, even if ultimately part of a broader dynamic whereby colonial powers sought to divide, combine, and administer territories as they saw fit.[72] The status of a Lebanese entity in relation to both Damascus and France was subject to conflicting and competing views within the French Empire and across its top echelons in Paris and in Beirut.[73] The ultimate outcome was neither planned nor inevitable. A host of historical, strategic, personal, and contingent factors produced such an outcome—two consequences of which animate the remainder of this chapter. First, the territorial delineation and international recognition of Greater Lebanon could have been no more than a diplomatic representation with little basis in the everyday lived experience of the local inhabitants. Top-down and bottom-up processes of institution building both consecrated and reified the declaration of a state of Lebanon. Second, the power of armed resistance, political organizing, and lobbying of would-be Lebanese nationals (both locally and in the diaspora) paled in comparison to the military violence of French imperialism. Nevertheless, such mobilizations shaped the contours of the new state in critical ways.

COLONIAL STATE FORMATION

The colonial period featured the accelerating shift to market production, the institutionalization of modern techniques of governance, and a host of transformations associated with these processes. This acceleration was fundamentally marked by the territorial encaging of spaces, people, resources, and their relations within an increasingly geographically delimited modern state structure.[74] French colonial rule in the Levant revolved around the immediate concern of security, which relied on disciplinary, biopolitical, and (at times) necropolitical power.[75] Yet such rule ultimately produced Lebanon as "a bounded territorial space" over which "sovereignty could be asserted and economic development conducted." The French Mandate affected such transformations through three pillars of its rule: the army, the bureaucracy, and mediating elites.[76]

French-commanded military forces played a central role in defeating Ottoman soldiers and securing French control over territory. They also served as the primary pillar of French rule in the face of recurring, localized armed revolts, while also suppressing nonviolent protests and movements.[77] These forces collectively formed the Army of the Levant, which comprised infantry, cavalry, and artillery units variously drawn from the Foreign Legion, French colonial troops, and other regiments of the French Army recruited in North Africa.[78] The French also organized locally recruited forces, eventually transforming them into the Special Troops of the Levant (al-Quwwat al-Khassa fi al-Sharq in Arabic; Les Troupes spéciales du Levant in French).[79] Some of the local recruits had served in one or both of two other forces, the Ottoman Imperial Army and Amir Faysal bin Husayn's Arab Army. The Special Troops in both Lebanon and Syria shared a single budget, organizational structure, officer corps, and military academy. The French nevertheless established several units that were specifically Lebanese.[80] The creation, recruitment, and repeated reorganization of such formations were ultimately responses to contingent developments, most notably the 1925–27 Syrian revolt, mass protests against the 1936 Franco-Lebanese treaty negotiations, the Great Revolt in Palestine (1936–39), and the 1943 reinstatement of the constitution.

The French also reorganized and expanded the remnants of the Ottoman gendarmerie and police and unified their respective command and control structures across the Lebanese territories.[81] The gendarmerie formed a single regiment, composed of one company serving as a paramilitary police force, primarily in rural areas, in each governorate.[82] The French introduced a new division of labor and specialization into the police system, dividing it into a judicial police who conducted investigations, suppressed gambling and drugs, and maintained criminal records, and an administrative police, who operated prisons, policed traffic, and supervised provincial matters.[83]

The French further established their own "general security" police force, organizing its personnel around five primary issues: border control (including visas and residence permits), censorship (films and publications), human trafficking (both women and children), narcotics, and Communist activities. Several officers of this general security force supervised the Lebanese police and gendarmerie. The proportion of locally recruited security personnel (whether in the Special Troops, the gendarmerie, or the police) increased throughout the colonial period. French personnel nonetheless dominated the top echelons of the officer corps.

The civilian bureaucracy was another key pillar of French colonial rule in Lebanon. Though it initially grew out of the expediencies of military occupation and war relief, the French shaped the colonial bureaucracy into a centralized and efficient administration.[84] At the top of the Mandate system was the French High Commission, which represented the French Empire in Lebanon (and Syria) and ruled over the French Mandate states. The High Commission governed through a network of French military and civilian administrative units, each headed by a French "advisor" and all reporting to a coordinating body known as the Office of the Secretary General.[85] These administrative units included the armed forces, intelligence services, and the police; bureaus of finance, economics, public works, hygiene, and public education; and other units dealing with customs, quarantines, antiquities, the mail, and telegraphs. The French created different types of colonial administrative units based on their assessment of the degree of administration required. In contrast to the narrowly focused bureaus mentioned above, the French also created general inspectorates for customs as well as the post and telegraph, and an office for patents protection. The High Commission grouped those French administrative units working exclusively in Lebanon under the rubric of the Directorate of Lebanon.[86]

An important component of the bureaucracy was the set of local/national administrative units specific to each state.[87] These units formed the institutional nucleus of what would later be reorganized into state ministries and thus the public institutions that constituted the core of the colonial and postcolonial Lebanese bureaucracy. This set of local administrative units (one for each of the states created within the French Mandate) was distinct from yet subservient to the High Commission bureaucracy. The Lebanese units did not always mirror those within the High Commission's Office of the Secretary General. The Lebanese units were nevertheless attached to at least one of the French units of the Secretary General, in addition to reporting directly to other French administrative units within the Directorate of Lebanon.[88] The Lebanese bureaucracy managed many of the localized functions like census taking, assessing and collecting taxes, and organizing national and municipal elections. Another of the Lebanese bureaucracies' significant tasks was the reproduction of French colonial policies as Lebanese-issued policies and the issuing of government contracts—however, coerced by the High Commission.

The third and final pillar of French rule was a diverse set of mediating elites. They buttressed French power while also seeking to make it serve their own interests. These elites included French missionaries, foreign concessionary companies, and local notables, businessmen, landlords, tribal shaykhs, village heads, and religious leaders.[89] Operating under considerable financial and staffing constraints due to the destruction wrought on France during World War I, the High Commission turned to these elites in various ways to fulfill administrative and military functions. Yet the commission tightly orchestrated such control, whether directly through the French colonial bureaucracy or through the Lebanese bureaucracy. The colonial state consolidated these alliances through the distribution of resources.[90]

For example, the High Commission invited French missionaries and local religious institutions to establish the bedrock of the post–World War I education and health systems.[91] French missionaries solicited funds from their global network of dioceses and parishes, and the High Commission provided subsidies to them and to local religious institutions. As a result, the education and health sectors expanded dramatically during the 1920s and 1930s, with privately funded entities spending the most funds, building and maintaining the most infrastructure, and serving the most students and patients. Three instances capture the codependence this collaboration created. Responding to French Foreign Ministry elements calling for a greater emphasis on public education, High Commissioner Gouraud pointed out that it would be far more costly than relying on subsidized private schools.[92] Furthermore, private schools in Lebanon repeatedly claimed during the 1930s that they would be forced to close should subsidies be significantly reduced or eliminated. Finally, two orders of French nuns (the Sisters of Charity and the Sisters of St. Joseph) ran so many clinics and hospitals that they were officially designated as part of the High Commission's health inspectorate.[93]

In another example, the High Commission built local alliances through granting control of former Ottoman imperial lands, providing credit and access to equipment, and backing certain local personalities and groups—including actively supporting or providing legal cover to acts of violence against their rivals and popular unrest. The northern region of 'Akkar featured significant anti-French sentiment and limited French military presence. The collaboration between a French captain (known locally as "Mieg") and Abbud Bey Abd al-Razzaq al-Muhammad (1880–1958) helped secure the region.[94] Based in Berqayl, 'Akkar, al-Muhammad was a local bey who mobilized the men he controlled to disrupt local protests, mobilize votes, and provide legitimacy to the French colonial project. In exchange, Mieg facilitated al-Muhammad's expanding land ownership through the French-introduced land registration process as well as the leasing and/or sale of state lands. Mieg also facilitated privileged access to French colonial and Lebanese national state-sponsored economic and social programs as well as legal indulgences for al-Muhammad and his followers' criminal conduct.

Through these three pillars of French colonial rule—the army, the bureaucracy, and mediating elites—French policies contributed to the formation of a distinctly Lebanese social hierarchy. On the one hand, the High Commission's reliance on missionary and local religious institutions, combined with its uneven financial support for them, effectively rendered access to education and health unequal between Christians and Muslims as well as between the wealthy and the poor. On the other hand, French policies reorganized and nourished the familial, regional, and sectarian composition of local political and economic elites.[95] Some families—like the al-As'ads of Jabal 'Amil, the Bayhums of Beirut, and the Jumblatts of the Shuf, Mount Lebanon—retained their late Ottoman political and economic status in the new state.[96] Others, like the Harfushes of the Biqa', experienced a precipitous decline.[97]

At the same time, war and colonialism created opportunities for some to consolidate significant new financial and political resources. Alfred Sursuq (1870–1924) and Selim 'Ali Salam (1869–1938) made immense profits from wartime speculation on wheat and other grains while also consolidating significant urban and rural property holdings.[98] It was during the French colonial period that al-Muhammad of Berqayl (discussed above) transformed himself and his family into the leading Sunni notables of 'Akkar, expanding his land holdings and displacing rivals to whom he had been subordinated during the late Ottoman period.[99] One significance of this newly established status was al-Muhammad representing Akkar in every parliament elected during French colonial rule.[100] Mandate-era political offices, whether appointed or elected, served as a critical node in elite formation and reproduction. Between 1922 and 1943, representatives of 103 families held all parliamentary seats, while cabinets featured members of 45 of those families.[101]

A 1926 constitutional proclamation consecrated the new state, changed its name to the Republic of Lebanon (al-Jumhuriyya al-Lubnaniyya), and further institutionalized many of the practices introduced since 1920.[102] Buttressed by military force, French colonial authorities built on this constitutional framework to channel elite and popular mobilizations into formal institutions and to further instantiate the idea of Lebanon as an organizing principle of political sociability.[103] The constitutional provisions were not drawn on a tabula rasa, even if the document marked a new stage in the processes of institution building and political socialization in Lebanon. The constitution drew from and expanded upon late Ottoman and early French colonial precedents. One example of this concerns the set of representative bodies and electoral systems: the Ottoman parliament (1876–78 and 1908–20), the Administrative Council of Mount Lebanon (1861–1915), the Provincial Council of Beirut (1888–1920), the Municipal Council of Beirut (1860–present), the Administrative Council of Greater Lebanon (1920–22), and the Representative Council of Greater Lebanon (1922–26). The constitution established a parliamentary government that was elected via universal suffrage, abolishing the Ottoman property requirements and lowering the voting age from twenty-five to twenty-one. It retained the Ottoman precedent of delegating to parliament the design and supervision of elections. Parliament thus passed an electoral law that set the number of representatives; designated the boundaries, sizes, and seats of electoral districts; outlined procedures for the preparation of voter registers and their amendment; established voting procedures; delineated requirements for candidacy; created rules and duties for electoral management and monitoring; and enumerated penal clauses that established penalties for violations.[104] A cornerstone of all Mandate-period electoral laws was their specification of candidates and voters as men. The constitution created the office of the president of the republic and specified his election by the parliament; it also created the office of the prime minister and specified his appointment by the president. While the constitutional system was subject to some modifications by the eve of independence,[105] the above-described dynamics continued to impinge on the nature of both institution building and political mobilization throughout the late colonial and early independence periods.

The political regime of the Republic of Lebanon was not juridically limited to the 1926 constitution. The system was in fact an amalgam of legal categories, institutions, and practices that drew on late Ottoman, French colonial, Mandate, and local/national governments' sources of authority. Neither an unaltered remnant nor a newly invented regime, this amalgam was facilitated by selectively incorporating, creating, and reorganizing institutional arrangements. This amalgamation was fundamental to the reorienting of everyday practices within the framework of the new state.[106] Through such institutional arrangements, the colonial state produced the very territory, population, and identity it claimed to have been established to reflect.

The Republic of Lebanon reconfigured relationships between the individual and the collective, the local and the foreign, the public and the private, and the people and the state. The constitution defined Lebanon as a mandated territory and recognized the French High Commission as the ultimate authority. It denied the Lebanese state true sovereignty, empowering the High Commission to conclude treaties, abolish laws, dissolve parliament, and even suspend the constitution.[107] The High Commission twice suspended the constitution: May 9, 1932, through January 4, 1937, and then again September 21, 1939, through March 18, 1943. Such powers helped to secure French control over representative institutions and were a more effective means of managing electoral governance than those the High Commission initially constructed between 1920 and 1925.

The institutional practices of the new state produced and instantiated the new category of "Lebanese citizen."[108] Sectarian, gender, and class differences were central to the construction and experience of this new category. The constitution laid the foundation for incorporating and expanding the principle of political sectarianism. It deferred the adjudication of matters of personal status (i.e., marriage, divorce, inheritance, and child custody) to officially recognized sects (Article 9). It also stipulated temporary confessional-based representation at the cabinet and civil service levels (Article 95).[109] A key modality of state power pivoted around the articulation of sectarian and sexual differences through legal, bureaucratic, and discursive processes.[110]

In addition to the constitution, other bureaucratic arrangements—most notably the 1932 census and 1936 personal status law—restructured sectarian and gender relations.[111] They empowered religious institutions, expanded the number of officially recognized sects and shaped their leadership, established new personal status courts, and otherwise consolidated sectarian boundaries, practices, and identifications.[112] The personal status system served as an important mechanism of gender differentiation—both between women and men within a given sect and between women across sects. The Mandate Charter provided another mechanism by prohibiting discrimination based on race, religion, or language, but not on sex.[113] While the High Commission and local elites technically expanded suffrage to women through a constitutional provision, the electoral laws repeatedly confined it to male citizens. Furthermore, the nationality law prohibited children from inheriting Lebanese citizenship from their mothers. This gendering of citizenship encouraged the formation of diverse and internally contentious women's movements.[114]

The French alliance with Lebanese urban and rural elites, the new land tenure regime based on a cadastral survey (1926), a land registry (1926), and a land code (1930) all enshrined class differences in the new politico-legal system.[115] Furthermore, certain corporate interests were legally recognized while others were denied. For example, the High Commission maintained

Ottoman laws or passed new laws recognizing foreign and local business interests individually and collectively. These included laws regulating chambers of commerce (1910), patents (1924), foreign corporations (1926), contracts (1932), and commercial transactions (1942).[116] However, the absence of a labor code meant that workers' interests were governed by the Ottoman Law of Associations.[117] A 1934 law built on this Ottoman precedent by requiring workplace associations to include workers, employees, managers, and owners in a single organization.[118] As a result, labor was a legally invisible collective interest, even as the ranks of wage earners in general and urban workers in particular increased significantly. The simultaneous invisibility and expansion of the working class contributed to the mobilization of a labor movement coalescing around the issue of securing a comprehensive labor code. As was the case with the women's movements, differences within the labor movement resulted in compromises, negotiations, and alliances with the state bureaucracy, politicians, and other movements (e.g., women's organizations, tenants' associations, and parliamentary blocs).

The Lebanese state bureaucracy expanded continuously throughout the colonial period. This trend further integrated the daily lives of the local population within the bureaucratic routines of what came to be recognized as the Lebanese state. Shortly after the promulgation of the 1926 constitution, the Lebanese government issued Decree no. 5 of May 31, 1926, which established the various ministries of the republic and defined their functions.[119] These ministries included justice, internal affairs, finance, public works, education, health, and agriculture. The decree also assigned all Lebanese administrative units created prior to the constitution to one of these newly created ministries. French advisors and bureaus continued to function in parallel, often times monitoring and intervening in the workings of Lebanese state institutions. Mandate-era laws on municipal (1922), village (1928), and provincial (1930) administration built on late Ottoman precedents and supplemented the expanding ministerial bureaucracy.[120]

COLONIAL ECONOMY

Two principles undergirded French economic policy in Lebanon (and Syria) during the colonial period. The first principle was self-sufficiency: locally generated revenue was to cover state expenditures. Except for continuing military subsidies, the Mandate paid for itself, even during the depression of the 1930s and World War II.[121] The second principle was economic stabilization. From early on, the French Mandate sought to soften the economic impact of colonialism while responding to the fiscal, monetary, and economic instability of the immediate postwar period.[122] The High Commission regularly intervened to affect the supply and pricing of certain goods and services. However, self-sufficiency and the economic imperatives of the imperial metropole took precedence over stabilization.

These policy principles resulted in specific institutional arrangements. First, the French unified the monetary and customs systems of Lebanon and Syria. Beginning in 1920, the High Commission introduced the Syrian-Lebanese lira and implemented various policies to establish it as the sole currency accepted in the execution of local French and Lebanese government expenditures and payment for taxes, custom, and monetary debt.[123] This policy came in the aftermath of the introduction of several "new" currencies during World War I and the Occupied Enemy Territory Administration.[124] The High Commission's decision to render the Syrian-Lebanese lira sole legal tender while pegging it to the French franc both centralized and enhanced French fiscal capacity in the Mandate. This policy enabled the French government to pay its army and other expenditures in a local currency representing the French franc, thus strengthening the monetary position of the High Commission. The policy eliminated the necessity of purchasing Egyptian paper notes or Turkish gold money for local expenditures, both of which were financed through internal government loans in France and had contributed to inflationary pressures and the depreciation of the French franc relative to the British pound and the US dollar. The Egyptian currency the High Commission received in exchange for Syrian-Lebanese currency helped to increase French foreign exchange reserves (vis-à-vis the international market) given that the Egyptian currency was pegged to the British pound sterling. Despite a diverse array of local opposition, the High Commission was able to institutionalize this new currency regime between 1925 and 1929.[125] The use of nonmarket measures like outlawing the use of other currencies facilitated this process. The increase in the value of the French franc in late 1926 further buttressed the currency's institutionalization. More importantly, the Lebanese state (along with the Syrian states) officially sanctioned the new legal currency in 1924 and by 1928 required all public accounting and pricing to be in the new lira, highlighting the important role local bureaucracies were already playing in this period.[126] In addition to monetary union, the High Commission established a customs union throughout its territories in the Levant.[127] A single customs regime thus grouped the Republic of Lebanon and the different Syrian states (the latter only unified into a single Syrian state in 1936). Goods entering the French Mandate in the Levant were subject to the same tariff legislation irrespective of their point of entry. No customs barriers existed between the various states in the Levant under French Mandate.

The monetary and customs union did not mean that all economic policies and practices operated across all states. Both the High Commission and the local bureaucracy organized the majority of economic activities within the framework of individual states. These included the standardization and collection of direct taxes; the registration of commercial and industrial enterprises, business chambers, and various associations; the securing of credit; and the disbursement of rations.[128] Furthermore, beginning in 1937 the sole currency of legal tender in Lebanon were Syrian-Lebanese lira paper notes with a Lebanon-specific insignia—fully equal to and exchangeable with their Syrian counterpart.[129]

Second, monopolies and concessions established centralized control over key aspects of the economy.[130] The High Commission defined various functions, services, and commodities as contributing to the public good, thereby justifying their monopolization. It contracted out the provisioning and management of most of these services and commodities to private persons and companies in accordance with a 1924 law of concessions.[131] In some cases the High Commission affirmed late Ottoman arrangements while in others it facilitated the penetration of new (primarily) French capital.[132] One important example of this practice concerns the Compagnie du Port, des Quais et des Entrepôts de Beyrouth. The High Commission maintained the 1887 Ottoman-era concessionary agreement for the management of the Beirut port, readapting the agreement (in 1925) relative to the Lebanese law of concessions, and facilitating an additional agreement (in 1937) to extend the harbor.[133] The tobacco sector featured another key example. Initially, the High Commission honored the Ottoman-era monopoly and concessionary rights of the Régie Co-Intéressée de Tabac de l'Empire until they expired in 1929.[134] The High Commission reestablished a state monopoly over the production, processing, and sale of tobacco and granted a 1935 concession to the newly created private joint-stock company Régie Co-Intéressée Libano-Syrienne des Tabacs et Tombacs.[135] An additional example is Banque de Syrie et du Liban (BSL).[136] The High Commission (in 1919) and later the local governments (in 1924) contracted the BSL to serve as the bank of issue for the Syrian-Lebanese lira.[137] The High Commission also reconfigured, expanded, or introduced new concessions for various urban utilities. These included electricity (e.g., Société d'Électricité du Liban Nord), water (e.g., Société des Eaux de Beyrouth), and railways (Société du Chemin de fer de Damas-Hamah et Prolongements).[138] The use of monopolies and concessions for what were effectively developmental purposes had two key effects. First, currency issue, urban utility services, and major crop cultivation were subject to the logics of private profit maximization. A further effect of this system was the empowerment of government officials (through state institutions) to privilege certain groups over others by cultivating relationships with both foreign and local capitalists.

A third outcome of French colonial economic policies was the government's unusual budgetary structure.[139] The colonial state was funded by three operating budgets, the High Commission, the Common Interests, and the Republic of Lebanon, which reflected the tripartite (French, Mandate, and Lebanese) bureaucratic organization of colonial Lebanon. Its fiscal priorities were self-sufficiency and co-optation. These budgets were technically independent of one another. However, the High Commission supervised and enabled the coordination of all three budgets and the strategic transfer of funds between them.

The High Commission directly funded its own bureaucracy as well as the units of the French Army of the Levant, excepting the locally recruited Special Troops. In addition, there are indications of direct contributions to missionary or local organizations whose activities were focused on education and health.[140] Consequently, even those ostensibly private endeavors in the field of social welfare were implicated in the broader budgetary dynamics of the Mandate. It appears that revenues from the treasury of the French government covered most of the expenses of the High Commission.[141]

After the High Commission budget came that of Common Interests. The High Commission established the Revenue and Expenditure Management Account of Common Interest Services (henceforth Common Interests) as a distinct institution in 1928 to centralize management of previously autonomous administrative units whose services spanned the entirety of the French Mandate in the Levant.[142] The Common Interests included those departments, bureaus, and other administrative units that managed customs, monopolies, concessions, economic services, quarantines, and a host of other activities.[143] The Common Interests budget drew the overwhelming share of its revenue from trade tariffs.[144] What little income certain economic services, concessions, and monopolies generated for the Common Interests budget generally did not exceed 7 percent and in very rare instances peaked at 15 percent.[145] On the expenditure side, the Common Interests budget covered the salaries and costs of all administrative units listed above. In addition, this budget paid for the Special Troops of the Levant and (until 1933) the servicing of Lebanon's share of the Ottoman public debt.[146] The Common Interests budget almost always had a surplus. The High Commission annually distributed a portion of this surplus among the local bureaucracies of each of the states that made up the French Mandate. Whatever amount was left from the surplus was either carried over to the next fiscal year or transferred to a reserve account within the Common Interests budget.

The third and final budget was that of the Republic of Lebanon. Revenue transfers from the Common Interests budget provided significant funds for this state budget.[147] Direct and indirect taxes also comprised important sources of revenue, while public enterprises and public domain land did so to a much smaller extent.[148] These taxes facilitated the process of territorial encaging as they formed an important pillar in the unification and standardization of bureaucratic practices across the populations and territories of Lebanon.[149] On the expenditure side, the state budget covered localized activities and their associated institutions, primarily those of security, administration, economic development, and social welfare.[150]

This tripartite division of fiscal budgets (French, Mandate, and Lebanese) would prove to be important in the postcolonial period. Its institutional legacies shaped how state elites consolidated these budgets into one state budget. On the one hand, postcolonial governments in Lebanon and

Syria struggled over their relative administrative control and revenue shares of the Common Interest budget. On the other hand, the elimination of the High Commission's subsidies to select educational and health care organizations altered the balance of power within the field of postcolonial social welfare provisioning and produced new demands on the Lebanese state.

ELITE AND POPULAR MOBILIZATIONS

The colonial political regime generated both the reproduction of and shifts in local hierarchies of power. During the 1930s, incumbent politicians and their elite allies coalesced around two parliamentary camps. Bishara al-Khuri (1890–1964) and Émile Eddé (1883–1949) respectively led what by the eve of independence came to be known as the Constitutional Bloc (al-Kutla al-Dusturiyya) and the National Bloc (al-Kutla al-Wataniyya). Both men launched their political careers during the Mandate, building on family legacies of service in late-Ottoman administrative bureaucracies and the capital accumulation this service enabled. Their rivalry originated in the first half of the 1930s as they competed for the presidency.[151] It crystalized around calls for the restoration of the constitution the first time the French suspended it (1932–37) and subsequently framed much of the elite-level political competition.

Many Lebanese outside these two centers of formal parliamentary power turned to other organizational forms to articulate their visions, mobilize constituencies, and build alliances. These dynamics originated during the late Ottoman period and World War I, intensifying during the subsequent decades. The French colonial period thus featured a growing number of formal and informal associational groups, whose projects increasingly shaped the political landscape of Lebanon's major urban centers and informed national politics more generally. These groups did so through public meetings, circulating petitions, mounting demonstrations or strikes, and other forms of mobilization. Along with forming organizations, establishing publications, installing plaques and statues, and sponsoring lectures, commemorations, performances, and festivals, such mobilizations shaped public discourses and produced potent cultural symbols.

The expansion of public space was a critical factor in facilitating this intensification of associational life during French occupation. The proliferation of hotels and cafés made them important sites for socialization: public ceremonies were held in the former and public meetings in the latter.[152] The introduction of new technologies (e.g., radios and telephones) and the rapid spread of older ones (e.g., print material and the telegraph) allowed for information to be shared faster and over greater distances.[153] New road networks combined with the spread of privately owned automobiles (a significant number of which were for hire as taxis or rentals) rendered travel between cities and into the countryside increasingly accessible.[154] Combined with the expanded systems of public and private education, such public spaces created physical environments and discursive realms that united otherwise anonymous individuals in sociability and collective action.

Numerous individuals representing a range of social backgrounds and ideological orientations turned to the political party as a specific organizational form. Between 1924 and 1925, Yusuf Ibrahim Yazbak (1901–82), Fu'ad al-Shimali (1894–1939), and Artin Madoyan (1904–90) founded the Communist Party of Syria and Lebanon (al-Hizb al-Shuyu'i fi Suriyya wa-Lubnan).[155] In 1932, Antun Sa'ada (1904–49) established the Syrian Nationalist Party (al-Hizb al-Suri al-Qawmi).[156] Pierre al-Jumayyil (1905–84) founded the Lebanese Phalange (al-Kata'ib al-Lubnaniyya) in 1936.[157] Muhyi al-Din al-Nsuli (1896–1961) formed the Rescuers (al-Najjada) in 1937.[158] Three other parties combined to play a dominant—though not exclusive—role within Lebanon's Armenian communities: the Huntchak Social Democrat Party (al-Hizb al-Hunshaq al-Dimuqrati al-Ijtima'i); the Dashnak Armenian Revolutionary Federation (al-Ittihad al-Thawri al-Armani al-Tashnaq); and the Ramgavar Democratic Liberal Party (Hizb al-Ramghavar).[159]

These organizations differed in their ideological and strategic positioning vis-à-vis French colonial authorities, incumbent politicians, other organizations, and a host of political and social issues. They also fluctuated in terms of their official status, how openly they operated, and what organizational forms they took. They nevertheless formed the primary party-like organizations that politicized and mobilized many sectors of the urban population around the trajectory of state formation and economic development.[160] Lesser-known parties that sometimes operated clandestinely, like 'Ali Nasir al-Din's (1888–1974) Lebanon chapter of the League of Nationalist Action ('Usbat al-'Amal al-Qawmi, est. c. 1933–36) and Constantine Zurayq's

(1909–2002) Arab Nationalist Party (al-Hizb al-Qawmi al-'Arabi, est. 1935), also played an important role.[161]

During the colonial period a host of other types of organizations and movements emerged to challenge existing hierarchies and pursue their own political visions. For example, 'Adila Bayhum (1900–75), Julia Dimashqiyya (1884–1954), Ibtihaj Qaddura (1893–1967), 'Anbara Salam (1897–1986), Salma Sayigh (1889–1953), and others established numerous women's organizations, playing leading roles in the development of a self-conscious women's movement during the French Mandate.[162] At the same time, workers employed by printing presses, railways, tramways, ports, and the tobacco monopoly, and those in construction, carpentry, and automobile driving took the lead in forming labor syndicates, organizing strikes, or both.[163] Other types of professionals also created associations to unify their growing ranks and lobby the government. Journalists and private school teachers, for example, organized some of the most systematic and consistent mobilizations.[164] Leftists like Ra'if Khoury (1913–76) and 'Umar Fakhuri (1895–1946) founded the League Against Nazism and Fascism ('Usbat Mukafahat al-Naziyya wa-l-Fashistiyya) in 1935.[165] They supported the internationalist struggle against fascism (whether as part of the Spanish Civil War or elsewhere) and confronted fascist propaganda and networks in Lebanon and elsewhere in the Arab world.[166] More ad hoc and contingent coalitions also formed. In 1922 and 1931, Beirut residents created committees to organize boycott campaigns against the Beirut tramway and electricity company, demanding lower prices and better service while challenging the company's ownership structure.[167]

Diasporic individuals and networks also informed state, market, and class formation during the Mandate. For example, the diaspora constituted an important recruiting and funding base for the French-sponsored Légion d'Orient that fought alongside the Entente powers against the Ottoman army and formed one of the early nuclei of what would become the Special Troops.[168] Diasporic networks also mobilized in times of crisis to lobby global powers, the Lebanese government, their own governments, and the League of Nations. This was particularly the case during negotiations over the postwar settlement (1918–23) and the Syrian Revolt (1925–27).[169] Such engagement with on-the-ground developments was motivated by the diversity of political visions present among diaspora activists, as well as uneven access to financial resources and political influence. This was indeed the case in creating and/or supporting various political parties, women's organizations, and other associational groups in Lebanon.[170]

Elite and popular groups increasingly challenged, shaped, and integrated into the system. Lebanon's political regime facilitated this process by channeling struggles away from insurgency and revolt and into the new bureaucracy. In the 1920s, military repression and state patronage were the pillars of colonial rule.[171] In the 1930s, however, popular movements demanding political and social rights challenged these pillars in an unprecedentedly consistent manner.[172] At the same time, the size and scope of the French colonial and local state bureaucracies significantly expanded.

THE MAKING OF POLITICAL INDEPENDENCE

World War II underpinned the transition from colonial rule to independence in Lebanon and formed a key conjuncture in state, market, and class formation. The High Commission suspended the constitution in September 1939 and, after the fall of France in June 1940, pledged its loyalty to the Vichy regime. The Allied invasion of Lebanon and Syria in June–July 1941 overthrew the Vichy colonial government and facilitated the emergence of new alliances and institutional arrangements that reconstituted the local, regional, and global balance of power.[173] The Free French Forces assumed administrative responsibility for the French Mandate in Lebanon and Syria. Seeking to rally the local population around their invasion of and subsequent rule over the Levant, the Free French Forces officially promised to end the Mandate while the British guaranteed that promise.[174] It was in this context that the Free French replaced the title of high commissioner with delegate-general.[175] In parallel, the British followed their introduction of military troops and installations with the establishment of a Levant branch of their liaison mission to the Free French,[176] and eventually established a diplomatic mission to Lebanon and Syria.[177] The preponderance of British personnel, French recognition of overall British military authority, and the pro-Vichy sympathies of many French colonial officials ultimately undermined French power in both countries.

Concomitant to these strategic changes were transformations in the Lebanese, regional, and global political economy during World War II. The period featured an unprecedented degree of state intervention in socioeconomic life. Key depression-era and wartime developments transformed relations between the High Commission, local elites, and popular groups to produce a colonial welfare state.[178] The Lebanese bureaucracy now administered a wide range of social welfare programs and policies, including minimum wage, family allowances, cost-of-living increases, rudimentary labor protections for women and children, bread subsidies, and price controls on fuel and rent. In addition, public spending on health care and education increased as a proportion of the state budget, while an expanded public works program created new employment opportunities. These new legal protections, state-provided services, and their attendant financial commitments established welfare as a right of citizenship and more directly and securely bound the local population to state institutions.[179] Furthermore, the Anglo-American Middle East Supply Centre's (MESC) wartime control of the movement of goods and capital impacted state institutional capacities in different ways across the Middle East.[180] In Lebanon, like many other arenas of its operation, MESC imposed strict controls on imports and exports while facilitating the expansion of import-substitution industrialization and food production.[181] New colonial welfare policies and wartime state management of trade, production, and consumption fundamentally transformed state regulatory capacities while significantly broadening administrative norms and repertoires.[182]

A significant number of Lebanese businessmen made fortunes during World War II. Increased demand, speculation, and smuggling activities all contributed to this development. Allied troop deployments and limitations on imports increased domestic consumption severalfold. Between 1941 and 1945, total Allied expenditures in Lebanon and Syria equaled eight hundred million liras.[183] Between May 1942 and May 1943, military expenditures equaled more than three times the total combined expenditures of the Lebanese and Syrian budgets, and about a third of the combined national incomes of the mandated states.[184] Local businessmen captured a large proportion of this influx of capital. For example, one year into the Allied occupation, seven Lebanese individuals secured forty-two million liras in war-related profits—equal to approximately half of total demand deposits in Lebanon that same year.[185] Speculation in commodities, land, buildings, and gold, parallel market operations, and trafficking in import licenses were critical means of accumulating wealth. Lira-denominated demand deposits doubled from 1939 to 1945.[186] Wartime purchases of precious metals, foreign currencies, stocks, and property further attest to the large profits made from trade, manufacturing, agriculture, and corruption. These purchases also reflect a diversified strategy to hedge against inflation and reduce risk.[187] Between 1941 and 1945, Lebanese and Syrians bought more than eight hundred million liras in sterling and gold on the open market.[188] During that same period, Lebanese alone purchased over six hundred million liras worth of foreign currency.[189] Furthermore, the Beirut Stock Exchange (est. 1920) featured more than a fourfold increase in equity prices between 1939 and 1945 at the same time that annual transactions in commercial real estate were two to three times their prewar levels.[190]

These strategic, material, and normative transformations fundamentally altered the relationship of individuals—of both the elite and popular classes—to the Lebanese state. One aspect of these transformations was the further instantiation of Lebanon as a nation-state in people's everyday practices. A related aspect was how various individuals, networks, and social groups increasingly understood that exercising control over state institutions was critical to the future of their material well-being and to their political aspirations. At the same time, the British and US governments invested in the Lebanese political economy, each with their own preferences and stakes in relationships between politicians, businessmen, and bureaucrats. This new balance of power and resultant local political alliances facilitated the transition from Mandate rule to independent state. The imperative of maintaining stability in the face of growing anticolonial mobilization that risked disrupting the Allied war effort undergirded this convergence.

Resistance to French colonial rule was a constant feature of the Mandate period. Yet during World War II a select number of politicians, religious leaders, business groups, political parties, labor syndicates, and women's organizations formed a broad anticolonial coalition. This collaboration represented multiple centers of power within both elite and popular groups and sought to secure exclusive local control over state institutions. This effort originated in the 1930s when the ubiquity of political-economic reformism increasingly gave way to a generalized rejection of French rule.[191] Partly in response to promises of independence made by the Free French and the British, starting in 1941 an increasing number of Lebanese abandoned the accommodationist discourse of national politics and swelled the ranks of those calling for full independence. Eventually, popular mobilizations, elite jockeying, and British and US interventions in support of independence—all in the context of wartime exigencies—combined to produce political independence for Lebanon in 1943, the incremental transfer of the Common Interests to local administration in 1944–45, and the evacuation of all foreign troops in 1946. Control of state institutions and popular mobilizations around the issue were at the heart of this prolonged transition as well as the spark that initiated it.

Lebanese politicians engaged one another as well as the High Commission and British military and diplomatic missions in a series of debates and struggles over the restoration of constitutional life and the rules governing parliamentary elections.[192] They ultimately agreed upon a new formula that would shape the next four decades of parliamentary formation: a wholly elected chamber of deputies with a Christian-Muslim seat ratio of six-to-five.[193] Al-Khuri's Constitutional Bloc won a critical combination of seats in the parliamentary elections of August–September 1943.[194] By September 1943 the bloc had built a coalition strong enough to elect al-Khuri to the presidency and to form a cabinet under the premiership of Riyad al-Sulh (1894–1951).[195]

The Constitutional Bloc had increasingly taken up a pro-independence position. This was a belated political orientation on the part of al-Khuri and his associates, and was a function of their increasing alienation from the High Commission, strategic opportunities created by British and US wartime support, and the bloc's expanding alliances with popular sectors of society.[196] The event that prompted the bloc's public and definitive call for independence was the High Commission's denial of the new cabinet's request for increased control of and access to the revenues of the Common Interests.[197] On November 8, 1943, the six-member cabinet secured parliamentary passage of constitutional amendments eliminating all references to the High Commission, Mandate, and League of Nations, describing Lebanon instead as a sovereign state, and removing French as an official language on a par with Arabic.[198] It was a unilateral declaration of independence that rejected the legitimacy of French political authority.

French reaction was swift. By the end of November 10, the High Commission repealed the constitutional amendments, dissolved parliament, and suspended the constitution pending new elections.[199] It appointed Eddé president and prime minister, tasking him to form of a new cabinet.[200] At around dawn the next day, the High Commission arrested al-Khuri, al-Sulh, and cabinet ministers Kamil Sham'un (1900–87), Salim Takla (1895–1945), and 'Adil 'Usayran (1905–98). Anticipating popular outcry, the French also declared a curfew in Beirut, dispatched military patrols throughout major urban centers, suspended telephone service, and imposed strict censorship on newspapers. Lebanese woke up on Thursday, November 11, to a radio address by French Delegate-General Jean Hellou (r. June–November 1943), pamphlets of which were airdropped by French military aircrafts throughout subsequent days.[201] He made no mention of the constitutional amendments or the arrests, but instead explained recent developments in terms of "needing to put a stop to the reckless behavior that only sought to deprive Lebanon from France's historical assistance and subject the country to a genuine dictatorship."[202] On the same day, Eddé issued a statement acknowledging his appointment and calling on the Lebanese people to trust him and remain calm.[203] He also announced the implementation of measures to maintain general security and punish those who threatened it.

Speaker of the Parliament Sabri Hamada (1902–76) attempted to convene the legislature several times despite French determination to prevent such meetings. Seven parliamentarians met at ten in the morning on November 11.[204] They addressed a memo to the British, US, Russian, Egyptian, and Iraqi governments denouncing the arrests while insisting on the legitimacy of the constitution and the parliament.[205] A larger group of twenty-eight parliamentarians convened at four in the afternoon that same day.[206] They included those from the morning session as well as the two cabinet members who remained at liberty: Habib Abi Shahla (1902–57) and Majid Arslan (1908–83). The parliamentarians unanimously passed a motion of confidence in support of the Sulh cabinet. They also insisted on the validity of the constitution, denounced the arrests, rejected the High Commission's appointment of a new government, and asserted the parliament's status as the legitimate representative of the nation. Sensing the need to maintain a working body to represent the Khuri regime, the cabinet, Abi Shahla, and Arslan temporarily assumed the powers of the presidency, premiership, and various ministries, respectively.[207] Such measures did little to fundamentally alter the status quo. Expanding their repression, the High Commission sealed the parliament building to prevent further meetings. The next day (Friday, November 12), thirty-three parliamentarians met at the home of Sa'ib Salam (1905–2000).[208] They declared the Eddé government illegitimate and its laws, decrees, and decisions invalid. They passed a confidence motion in support of the temporarily reconfigured Abi Shahla-Arslan cabinet and empowered it to take any and all measures to restore constitutional life and release those arrested.

Abi Shahla and Arslan fled Beirut southward to Bashamun in Mount Lebanon. From there, they issued communiqués as a rebel government and organized a militia to fend off French attempts to arrest them.[209] Securing the allegiance and collaboration of Lebanese politicians and bureaucrats was a key focus of the struggle between the Bashamun government and that of Eddé and the High Commission. The stakes were both symbolic and material. Unable to find parliamentarians to form a cabinet, Eddé on November 13 constituted a governing council (*majlis hukumi*) to assist him as head of state.[210] The French publicized this development via radio broadcast. The Bashamun government in turn called on all Lebanese state employees to disobey the Eddé government, and to stop work until the legitimate cabinet is restored to power.[211] They also issued directives to the Ministry of Finance and the Banque de Syrie et du Liban banning the transfer of funds to the Eddé government under penalty of prosecution.[212] During the subsequent days, word spread of at least four directors—whom Eddé announced as part of his council—declining to participate.[213] At a later point, the Bashamun government issued a decree stripping specific bureaucrats of their positions, labeling them traitors, and reserving the right to prosecute them.[214] While not all bureaucrats sided with the rebel government or were brave enough to break ranks with Eddé and the High Commission, a critical mass of them did.

Popular mobilizations buttressed the efforts of politicians and bureaucrats, transforming the power struggle with the High Commission into an anticolonial uprising.[215] These campaigns disrupted French strategies and pressured Hamada, Abi Shahla, and Arslan to take more radical measures. The aggressive posture and effective role played by popular groups, including their empowerment of various constituencies, alarmed both the Allied powers and the local political establishment. In the lead-up to and shortly after the constitutional amendments of November 8, 1943, the Sulh cabinet committed itself—through communications with British and US officials—to keep matters "on the constitutional plane," containing potential demonstrations and ensuring that shops were open. From November 11 onward, the Bashamun government and most parliamentarians maintained that commitment but repeatedly, although confidentially, expressed frustration at being outflanked by popular mobilizations.[216]

Popular groups played a key role in spreading word of the arrests and mobilizing the broader population around three central demands: the release of al-Khuri and other detained officials, reinstatement of the constitution, and recognition of the Khuri-Sulh government. In support of these demands, Beiruti newspapers and shopkeepers staged a general strike starting November 11. Several labor syndicates soon joined. Political parties coordinated (and sometimes enforced) these efforts while organizing marches, issuing communiqués, and distributing flyers providing the public with updates and instructions.[217] The Kata'ib and Najjada were at the forefront of these efforts in Beirut. These parties formed a joint command and issued a series of communiqués titled *In the Service of Lebanon* (*Fi Khidmat Lubnan*).[218] They also facilitated the distribution of rations in various Beirut neighborhoods. The Communist Party also mobilized, primarily through its affiliated labor syndicates in Beirut and a coordinating committee with other parties in Tripoli.[219] Lesser-known, and often short-lived, groups also mobilized. For example, in Beirut, a group identifying itself as the Lebanese Patriotic Youth (al-Shabab al-Watani al-Lubnani) plastered the walls with flyers and graffiti.[220] In other cities, unsigned flyers and pamphlets addressed Lebanese citizens and celebrated the general strike as the nation's most powerful weapon and most concrete symbol.[221]

Various notables, politicians, political parties, and labor unions established the National Congress (al-Mu'tamar al-Watani) on November 12, 1943.[222] The initial gathering featured approximately 1,500 people who subsequently formed an executive committee.[223] Acting as a national front in support of the Bashamun government, the National Congress brought together otherwise politically disparate individuals and constituencies who nevertheless shared in that moment a rejection of French colonial rule.[224] It issued regular communiqués, sent delegations to meet with religious leaders and foreign diplomats, and organized a series of public meetings that frequently transformed into rallies and demonstrations. The congress also raised money to fund the Bashamun government, support striking shopkeepers, and print flyers and leaflets.[225] Some sources claim the National Congress adopted the underground newspaper titled *??* [*sic*] as its mouthpiece.[226] The publication initially emerged in response to French press censorship banning local newspapers from covering the parliament's amendment of the constitution.[227]

High school and university students formed another important component of the November 1943 uprising. Political parties, local notables, and unsigned flyers called on students to strike.[228] Yet students also took the initiative and organized their own activities. Those of the American University of Beirut (AUB) are best documented. A broad coalition of approximately two thousand students petitioned AUB President Bayard Dodge (r. 1923–48), requesting he transmit their protest to "the proper authorities."[229] Others helped collect supplies and funds in support of the Bashamun government.[230] Students also participated in or organized their own demonstrations at great risk to themselves. In one such instance, students from AUB, Université Saint-Joseph, College of Benevolent Intentions (Kulliyyat al-Maqasid al-Khayriyya), Collège de la Sagesse (Kulliyyat al-Hikma), and Collège du Sacré-Cœur (Kulliyyat al-Frayr) teamed up to send a delegation to the British chancery in Beirut while holding a demonstration outside.[231] This was one of many deliberate attempts during the November 1943 uprising to display cross-confessional alliances (if not community). Thirty French troops arrived and immediately fired shots in the air and on the ground to disperse the crowd, injuring at least nineteen students. French colonial troops regularly fired live ammunition to disperse student protesters, wounding and/or issuing arrest warrants for many of those who participated.[232]

Eventually, schools and universities joined the general strike. This was in part a function of the closure of streets and the suspension of tramway services, rendering the commute to schools difficult and making administrators reluctant to permit student gatherings.[233] Yet the closures were also a response to student activists who pushed to extend the strike to their school buildings and university campuses. AUB officials were not necessarily in support of such student activism. In fact, Dodge used US military police to seal the university grounds, thereby effectively confining approximately eight hundred boarding students to campus.[234] He then pursued a policy of "keeping the students happy" by screening films and staging sporting events. Amid these developments, Dodge also appointed AUB's first Student Council, an apparent attempt to co-opt students involved in the uprising.[235] The council members defiantly continued their activism, prompting Dodge to disband the inaugural council and organize elections to select its successor.[236]

Women also played a central role in the uprising.[237] Many of them participated in the general strike, in demonstrations, and in marches. On Friday, November 12, a women's march from Ras al-Naba' to Martyrs' Square was staged. Many of those participating were elite women who, given the absence of telephone service, sent their domestic workers to relay plans for the march.[238] Some two hundred women joined the march, many as members of organized contingents, and others joined as individuals. The crowd proceeded down Ma'rad Street, passing Bab Idris before stopping at the British, US, Iraqi, and Egyptian diplomatic missions to meet with official representatives. The march ended at Bishara al-Khuri's home, where his wife Laure Chiha al-Khuri (b. 1900) received a large contingent of marchers, many of whom were wives, sisters, and daughters of Lebanese politicians.

Building on the march's success, Najla Sa'b (1908–71), Jamal Karam Harfush (1914–2000), and Eva Badr Malik (1914–88) took the lead in establishing the Lebanese Women's Strike Committee (Lajnat al-Idrab al-Nisa'iyya al-Lubnaniyya). Committee members met daily and organized interested women into specialized committees: general strike coordination, food provisioning, fundraising, countering French propaganda, and liaising with the Bashamun government.[239] The committee issued a daily bulletin entitled *The Woman's Voice* (*Sawt al-Mar'a*).[240] They lobbied British and US diplomats, and sent delegations to persuade Maronite, Greek Orthodox, Armenian, and Sunni religious leaders to support the Khuri-Sulh government. Women organized at least four major marches in Beirut, each one featuring one hundred to five hundred participants, that sometimes successfully evaded French military patrols and broke through checkpoints.[241]

Such popular mobilizations were critical to resolving the standoff between the Khuri government and the High Commission in favor of the former and its call for independence. The French utilized all available means to suppress the uprising, deploying their armed forces to barricade public squares, block streets, and close off entire neighborhoods. They arrested, injured, and killed Lebanese who defied them. Working through their most trusted local allies, the French also attempted to break the strike and sow sectarian strife.[242] Yet by Thursday, November 18, shopkeepers, students, and lawyers had joined the general strike, buttressed by a group of workers.[243] The unrest also spread beyond major cities, as locally organized militias began to attack French installations.[244] The lobbying efforts of women's organizations and political parties compelled local religious leaders to support independence and the restoration of the Khuri-Sulh regime. The Syrian government made similar demands, while Syrian citizens took to the streets to express their solidarity.[245] In addition, Lebanese politicians, women, and party activists organized telegram campaigns requesting the support of the Egyptian and Iraqi governments, demands amplified by demonstrations and other expressions of popular opinion in the two countries.[246]

Ultimately, British and US intervention proved decisive. Both governments privately expressed their objections to the French, offered moderate public support for the principle of Lebanese independence, and continued to receive delegations of Lebanese citizens throughout the uprising. Perhaps more significantly, the US State Department instructed its legation in Beirut to refrain from official relations with the Eddé regime,[247] and the British Ninth Army deployed approximately ten thousand troops to Lebanon.[248] The primary concern of both governments in the lead-up to the constitutional amendments and throughout the uprising was a breakdown of public order that would materially or ideologically impair the Allied war effort.[249] The uprising diverted British military resources, disrupted work at the Beirut naval port, risked sparking unrest in other Middle Eastern states, provided fodder for German propaganda, and undermined British and US standing as democratic alternatives to the Axis powers. These concerns animated repeated British deliberations on the potential necessity of imposing martial law in Lebanon.[250] Whereas their initial assessments reflected a reluctance to do this in support of the French, on November 20 the British government issued an ultimatum to the French to release and reinstate the Khuri-Sulh regime by 10 a.m. on November 22 or face British-imposed martial law.[251] This shift in British position from expressing misgivings about French policy to threatening the imposition of martial law in Lebanon reflected the power of popular mobilizations in the country.[252] The British also feared the further radicalization of popular groups, resulting in the complete marginalization of Lebanon's traditional political elites, assessments with which the US legation in Beirut concurred.[253] Throughout this time, Lebanese émigrés to the United States and Latin America also lobbied the White House in the name of freedom and liberty.[254] In sum, there was simply no turning back the clock on Lebanese sovereignty.

On November 21, the French announced they were reinstating al-Khuri as president and releasing Sulh, Sham'un, Takla, and 'Usayran—yet for the moment, they balked at restoring the cabinet and parliament, reinstating the constitution, and recognizing Lebanese independence. British extension of their deadline by forty-eight hours gave the French respite to do so.[255] Despite initial celebrations, popular mobilizations continued.[256] On Monday, November 22, 1943, the French released all government officials. The following day, as Abi Shahla and Arslan returned from Bashamun to Beirut, the French announced the revocation of most measures taken since the parliament amended the constitution.[257] Throughout November 22–23, tens of thousands of Lebanese celebrated in the streets, many raising the newly designed Lebanese flag.[258] Groups that participated in the uprising thanked "the people" for their efforts and called upon them to end the general strike.[259]

CONCLUSION

The November 1943 uprising inaugurated Lebanon's transition to independence. The focus of formal politics and popular mobilizations would henceforth shift to securing national control of all state institutions and a concomitant struggle to reconfigure them in line with competing Lebanese visions of the postcolonial future. As the next chapters highlight, this uprising for independence spurred the creation of new groups and the swelling of the ranks of several existing organizations. Such an expansion in popular mobilization was not simply a correlate to a generic transition to independence. Rather, it was a function of the heightened expectations that the new imaginative possibility and unfolding reality of jettisoning French colonial control made possible. The participation of popular groups in the struggle for independence both made its outcome possible and served as a new legitimating force for the Lebanese state. This mass participation in politics also marked the consecration of a new era in which these groups would demand both inclusion in existing state projects and the initiation of entirely new state projects.

Without doubt, the November 1943 uprising also created additional significant legacies for the postindependence period. Foremost is the elaboration of the founding myths of Lebanon as a nation-state bounded by a natural territory and embodied in a community. The 1943 achievement of Lebanese political independence provided the nationalist mythology with the ideal outcome of a linear historical narrative whose previous junctures were the Ma'nid emirate of Fakhr al-Din II (r. 1595–1635), the *mutasarrifiyya* of Mount Lebanon (1860–1915), the famine of the Great War (1915–18), and the establishment of Greater Lebanon (1920). A second legacy of the 1943 uprising was the expansion of Lebanon's pantheon of national heroes. Lebanese of all political orientations could associate al-Khuri, al-Sulh, and/or any of their compatriots with Emir Fakhr al-Din II, the 1858–61 Kisirwan peasant revolt leader Tanyus Shahin (1815–95), and the seventeen men executed by the Ottomans in May–June 1916. Both these legacies of founding mythology and national heroes underpinned the production of a plethora of historical writings and cultural artifacts in the postindependence period. First, their material embodiments helped shape the built environment of Lebanon. Significant examples include Riyad al-Sulh Square (Sahat Riyad al-Sulh) in Beirut and the House of Independence (Bayt al-Istiqlal) in Bashamun. In addition, Lebanese songwriters and authors have incorporated elements of the 1943 uprising in their artistic expressions. Mansur Rahbani's *The Story of Independence* (*Hikayat al-Istiqlal*) is the most notable example.[260] Such manifestations are accompanied by the most obvious one: the Lebanese Ministry of Education's mandatory history curriculum. Therein, the transition to independence marks the final moment in the country's political history to which Lebanese students are exposed.

The November 1943 uprising inaugurated the transition to independence in Lebanon. The following chapters explore the possibilities, debates, and struggles to shape the meaning and substance of that transition. State institutions as objects of elite and popular mobilizations were critical to these dynamics. Various contests over the meaning of independence and the bureaucratic expansion accompanying them demonstrate the relationship between state formation and popular mobilization. The following pages tell the stories of these top-down and bottom-up mobilizations and their interactions with the forces that would determine the present and future of Lebanon.

Two

BUREAUCRATIC EXPANSION

THE NOVEMBER 1943 UPRISING INITIATED LEBANON'S TRANSITION from French Mandate to independent state. The more notable turning points in this process were the transfer of the Common Interests and the Special Troops of the Levant to local control and the evacuation of all foreign military personnel. Yet visions of independence, sovereignty, and a postcolonial Lebanon also included the perceived necessity of taking control of—and transforming—state institutions. For diverse reasons and with oft-differing aims, bureaucrats, elites, and popular groups publicly advocated "state building" (bina' al-dawla). They identified both the need and the opportunity to restructure political, economic, and social relations in Lebanon, while sharing a belief that state institutions were central to such processes. That a broad-based coalition of Lebanese did so was not merely a function of shared nationalist assumptions. It reflected the deepening of statist norms locally, regionally, and globally. Material interests were also a factor. Elected officials wanted to consolidate their incumbency and profit from their offices, while various social groups attempted to realize their particular visions of a postcolonial political economy.

The starting point for most visions of postcolonial state building was autonomy from overt foreign control. Almost immediately after acquiring political independence, the Lebanese government began purging state institutions of personnel suspected of supporting the French during the November 1943 uprising, expelling a number of officials from throughout the bureaucracy.[1] Furthermore, the parliament passed a law stripping former president Émile Eddé (r. 1936–41 and November 11–22, 1943) of his parliamentary seat.[2] The government also abolished the mixed courts that provided French and other foreign nationals with extraterritorial rights.[3] All future legal proceedings in the country would occur within a wholly Lebanese judicial system.[4] Reflecting continuities with the colonial period, the Lebanese judicial system consisted of three parts: the ordinary courts (dealing with civil, commercial, and criminal cases), the administrative courts (assessing the legality of state regulations and the conduct of state institutions), and religious courts (addressing personal status matters). That system, however, was itself subject to several waves of complaint, protest, and reform throughout 1946–55.[5]

Such measures may in retrospect appear to be logical corollaries to decolonization. They nevertheless entailed significant debate and disagreements among politicians, bureaucrats, and the public.[6] As this and subsequent chapters demonstrate, how Lebanese officials pursued the logic of state building and national sovereignty was subject to fluctuations in personnel, ideologies, revenues, international pressures, and popular mobilizations. The outcome had varying consequences for the organization of state institutions and the concomitant dynamics of political incumbency and economic privilege. Nevertheless, the cumulative effects of these efforts were bureaucratic expansion and the valorization of the state.

State building and state institutions' centrality to restructuring political, economic, and social relations in Lebanon became defining elements of discourses of legitimacy deployed by incumbent politicians, career civil servants, opposition leaders and activists, ordinary citizens, and other residents of Lebanon. Individuals from across the geographic, political, socioeconomic, and sectarian spectrums articulated these views in a diverse combination of pamphlets, articles, books, speeches, lectures, petitions, and protest banners and chants.[7] State officials at the national, regional, and municipal levels invested significant energy and resources in presenting the accomplishments of public institutions through similar media.[8]

Such broad support for the state as a mechanism for political, economic, and social engineering among such a diverse set of actors does not mean that they spoke with a single voice on issues of state building. They were especially divided over the nature of political sectarianism, the parliamentary electoral system, and the respective roles of the public and private sectors in economic development. Nor should historians interpret these actors' conduct as anything other than pursuing what they deemed necessary to advance their own visions for Lebanon's postcolonial reality. Yet between November 1943 and December 1955, debates and struggles conducted in the context of two presidents, four parliaments, twenty-two cabinets, and countless acts of protest significantly expanded, strengthened, and centralized state institutions in Lebanon. Two key developments demonstrate this process: the repeated reorganization of government ministries and the continuous growth of the state budget.

The number of government ministries almost doubled during this period. While retaining the seven ministries created as part of the colonial state, the government established new ministries of post and telegraph (1943), defense (1945), foreign affairs (1945), national economy (1946), information (1949), social affairs (1951), and planning (1954). It also regularly restructured lines of authority, classifications of administrative units, and divisions of labor between and within individual ministries, standardizing their administrative structure. The major subdivision of every ministry was the directorate general (*al-mudiriyya al-'amma*), which was subdivided into directorates (s. *mudiriyya*), which were in turn subdivided into services (s. *maslaha*) or departments (s. *da'ira*), and finally into sections (s. *qism*). Accordingly, variations across ministries were henceforth largely limited to the number of subdivisions. Such expansion, reorganization, and standardization reflected three intertwined processes. The first was the incorporation into the Lebanese state of institutions and functions previously administered by the French High Commission. The second process was the deepening and broadening of bureaucratic reach into previously existing realms of state intervention. A third process was the creation of new bureaucratic realms. Unsurprisingly, these developments were accompanied by an increase in the state budget. Both annual estimates of the ordinary state budget and the actual expenditures increased fourfold between 1944 and 1955.[9] Access to revenues hitherto controlled by the French High Commission as well as new revenue streams and collection capacities facilitated this increased spending.[10]

As budgets grew, so did salaries and capital expenditures. Government spending on the basic salary and wages (excluding cost of living, family, and other allowances) of the permanent civil service nearly quadrupled, reflecting increases in both salary scales and the total number of persons employed.[11] In fact, the number of public sector employees more than doubled between 1943 and 1955.[12] Such increases reflected the expansion of existing administrative units and the creation of new ones. During that same period, the total number of directors general, directors, and service or department chiefs (i.e., the top-three positions below that of minister) also more than doubled.[13] Increases in public sector employment were not even across the bureaucracy and instead reflected how the shifting and competing priorities of state officials and public mobilizations rendered contingent the nature of bureaucratic expansion. For example, the four ministries that experienced the greatest expansion in the number of permanent employees (in both absolute and relative terms) were those of education, post and telegraph, public works, and finance.[14]

Expenditures on development projects expanded comparably between 1945 and 1954, with government capital investments increasing from 15 percent to 25 percent of ordinary expenditures.[15] In addition, to finance multiyear development projects, the government established a Development Works Fund (al-Sanduq al-Mustaqil li-l-Ashghal al-Insha'iyya) in 1944, whose funding was independent of the ordinary budget and based on project-specific allocations.[16] These investments manifested as major infrastructural projects—including the Beirut airport, an expanded national road network, and various potable water and irrigation schemes—as well as more mundane activities like the construction and renovation of government buildings and monuments.

In addition to the overall increase in the ordinary budget and Development Works Fund, bureaucratic expansion also featured the creation and growth of a number of financially independent budgets for newly established state agencies or private agencies recently incorporated into the state bureaucracy. These include the Directorate General of Telephone (al-Mudirriyya al-'Amma li-l-Hatif, est. 1947), the Beirut Water Service (Maslahat Miyah Bayrut, est. 1951), the Electricity and Common Transport Service (Maslahat al-Kahruba' wa-l-Naql al-Mushtarak, est. 1954), and the Litani

National Authority (al-Maslaha al-Wataniyya li-Nahr al-Litani, est. 1954).[17] This growth in the number of budgets and in the volume of their receipts and expenditures featured increasingly contentious debates about the nature of these new agencies. As a result, the government established new public accounting laws and practices that necessitated the disaggregation of the state budget into current expenditures (nondefense), capital expenditures (nondefense), and defense-related expenditures.[18]

BUILDING THE STATE

State institutional transformation was not merely quantitative in nature. It represented a qualitative shift in the scope, reach, capacity, and efficiency of the state bureaucracy. Between 1943 and 1955, Lebanese bureaucrats established direct links with significantly larger segments of the population. These links manifested in the proliferation of courts, post and telegraph offices, public schools, land and water surveyors, security service personnel, and facilities of the Lebanese armed forces. The reach of state institutions extended across geographic regions and economic sectors as well as intruding deeper into the lives of the country's citizens and noncitizen residents. This reach was symbolic, encompassing visual and other representations of Lebanon in the form of flags, other insignia, maps, statistics, a national radio broadcast, and government buildings. It was also material, in routine bureaucratic encounters related to crossing the border; registering births and deaths; securing identity cards, drivers licenses, or passports; applying for permits of various kinds; looking up the government-mandated price of a commodity or service; and lodging complaints. It was primarily through such experiences that individuals learned about "the state" (al-dawla).[19] The expanding network of institutional arrangements and the political practices they made possible constituted the material basis of the "structural effect" that individuals in Lebanon abstracted and subjectively experienced as "the Lebanese state" (al-dawla al-lubnaniyya).[20]

Several factors facilitated the postindependence expansion, strengthening, and centralization of Lebanese state institutions between 1943 and 1955. One factor was state officials' efforts to consolidate presidential, cabinet, and ministerial authority. Establishing national sovereignty, centralizing political authority over public institutions, and asserting ministerial autonomy required the creation of new bureaucratic arrangements to replace those of the French High Commission. At the same time, incumbent politicians sought to utilize public institutions to buttress their personal power by selectively responding to the needs and aspirations of Lebanese citizens. These goals were not accomplished immediately or in a linear fashion. Rather, state officials' success in these endeavors ebbed and flowed over time and involved formal and informal processes of negotiation with colleagues, with popular groups, and with foreign governments in the context of a shifting regional and global environment.

Another factor that supported the postindependence expansion of state institutions was the development-friendly environment created by the postwar international system. The International Bank for Reconstruction and Development (est. 1944), the International Monetary Fund (est. 1945), the Food and Agriculture Organization (est. 1945), the UN Educational, Scientific, and Cultural Organization (est. 1946), and the International Labor Organization (est. 1919) generally championed the role of governments in development, financial management, education, and labor. These multilateral institutions stopped short of advocating the full repertoire of state intervention embraced by Soviet socialism and (later) Third Worldism. They nevertheless provided models and incentives for newly independent states to adopt institutional reform that would facilitate more effective planning, administration, and social control.[21] Lebanon's membership in these organizations and participation in their programs served the goals of successive governments in at least three ways: It demonstrated the national independence and sovereignty of the Lebanese state, facilitated building alliances with blocs of states, and provided access to technical and financial resources not otherwise available. The 1943–55 period featured Lebanon's adherence to a variety of multilateral conventions and organizations, including participation in a range of programs and hosting many international meetings. Politicians, bureaucrats, and activists also selectively appropriated the discourses and logics of these multilateral institutions to buttress their own demands vis-à-vis state building.[22]

US imperialism was a third factor that facilitated the expansion of state institutions in postindependence Lebanon. In the aftermath of World War II, the United States sought to expand its military, political, and economic interests in Lebanon (as it did the rest of the Middle East), thereby bolstering the position of its local, regional, and global allies while subverting local leftist movements and Soviet influence.[23] In this way, US policy toward Lebanon promoted the creation of new state institutions and the expansion of existing state capacities to more effectively shape political, economic, and social life.[24] The United States did so through a multifaceted approach, drawing on the social sciences and on ideologies prevalent in US policy circles. Much of this was evident in the US Point Four Program in Lebanon, which between 1952 and 1955 allocated more than $13.5 million in development grants and more than $850,000 in scholarships for students to attend the American University of Beirut.[25] Whether through Point Four, the US diplomatic mission to Lebanon, or US influence in multilateral institutions, the United States encouraged and supplied expertise for state-sponsored planning. It also funded and otherwise facilitated technical training in public administration as well as more specific realms of bureaucratic management.[26] US policy also helped design and realize large-scale infrastructural projects.[27] Furthermore, the United States supported state-sponsored social policies that putatively empowered the middle class and ameliorated the plight of the urban and rural working classes.[28] At the same time, US policy bolstered the capacity of specific state institutions to surveil, police, and disrupt political projects and popular movements deemed threatening.[29] While British and French imperialism also facilitated the expansion of state institutions in postindependence Lebanon, they nevertheless could not compete with the breadth of issues, volume of funding, and political dominance of the United States.

The final, and perhaps most important, factor that supported postindependence expansion of state institutions was elite and popular mobilizations. The previous chapter demonstrated how the late Ottoman (1831–1918) and French colonial (1918–43) periods featured the introduction and expansion of mass politics. Yet the 1943–55 period was characterized by significant restructuring of the political field and the intensification of elite and popular mobilizations. Lebanese elected officials and government bureaucrats were liberated from certain decision-making constraints inherent to direct French colonial rule. The population experienced a concomitant expansion of imaginative possibilities, combined with new understandings of independence, sovereignty, development, and the proper role of state institutions in realizing them. Successive economic fluctuations associated with wartime inflation, postwar contraction, the partition and ethnic cleansing of Palestine (1948), the dissolution of the economic union with Syria (1950), and the Korean War (1950–53) drove many Lebanese to demand that the state expand its role in managing trade, prices, wages, and various social safety nets. At the same time, political crises, corruption scandals, and various elite and popular grievances generated continuous debate and demands for institutional arrangements capable of upholding notions of sovereignty, accountability, representation, and civil liberties. Parliamentary elections in 1943, 1947, 1951, and 1953 served as important events in the politicization and mobilization of the public at the same time they further centered the affairs of the state.[30]

During this period, incumbent politicians and their allies coalesced around multiple parliamentary camps, formed primarily in response to the presidencies of Bishara al-Khuri (r. 1943–52) and Kamil Sham'un (r. 1952–58). In the aftermath of the 1943 uprising, the late colonial diarchy of the Constitutional and National Blocs gave way to new, contingent, yet significant poles. The Constitutional Bloc emerged from the 1943 elections and uprising as the dominant parliamentary bloc with active support from the United Kingdom and United States. Alternatively, the National Bloc was politically compromised by Émile Eddé's collusion with the French and strategically weakened by his expulsion from parliament. With each round of legislative elections, new configurations of parliamentary blocs formed to reflect shifting relationships between presidents, prime ministers, cabinet members, and fellow MPs. Starting in 1946, al-Khuri and his Constitutional Bloc began to face an expanded and increasingly well-organized opposition among elite politicians. It took form as the Reform Bloc (Kutlat al-Islah, est. 1946), the National Liberation Bloc (Kutlat al-Taharrur al-Watani, est. 1947), and the Patriotic Socialist Front (PSF, al-Jabha al-Ishtirakiyya al-Wataniyya, est. 1951). This opposition ultimately helped force al-Khuri's resignation in September 1952. His successor Kamil Sham'un inherited the support of the US and British governments. Yet he too faced his own formal parliamentary opposition, the first iteration of which was the Popular Socialist Front (al-Jabha al-Ishtirakiyya al-Sha'biyya, est. 1953).

These parliamentary opposition blocs couched their criticisms of elected officials in terms of the organization, role, and performance of state institutions. While corruption scandals were a key feature of the rhetoric and list of grievances lodged against al-Khuri and his supporters, the electoral platforms and political programs of his critics in parliament featured a significant set of policies aimed to reshape political, economic, and social life through the creation of new state institutional arrangements. For example, the Reform Bloc called for administrative, budgetary, judicial, and electoral reforms.[31] It also demanded that the government study and ameliorate the rising cost of living and unemployment rate, provide guidance to revive various economic sectors, and better attend to the policy of rationing. In addition, the program of the National Liberation Bloc included mandatory voting in parliamentary elections, new regulations and administrative structures for budgetary oversight, state investment in concessionary companies so as to have a voice in their policies, and a social security system.[32] Furthermore, the PSF called for increased government attention to unemployment, the transformation of major foreign corporations into employee-run cooperatives, and the provision of free elementary and secondary education to all, health insurance for all citizens, and housing allowances for state employees.[33] Similarly, the Popular Socialist Front program also included calls for the end of political sectarianism, the protection of civil liberties and the prosecution of state officials who violate them, government planning for economic development, and a variety of social welfare provisions.[34] These varied platforms reflected diverse coalition constituents and levels of commitment to specific elements. Yet they also spoke to the ubiquity of normative and idiomatic assumptions about the centrality of state institutions as a panacea for political, economic, and social ills.[35]

The postindependence period featured the numerical and geographic expansion of different types of popular organizations and movements. They variously served as important nodes for debates about and mobilizations around the proper role of the state and the necessary attendant institutional arrangements. Several Mandate-era groups like the Women's Federation of Lebanon (al-Ittihad al-Nisa'i fi Lubnan, est. 1924), the Teacher's Syndicate (Naqabat al-Mu'allimin, est. 1938), the Railway Workers Syndicate (Naqabat 'Ummal Sikkat al-Hadid, est. 1908), and the United Islamic Youth

Association (Jam'iyyat Ittihad al-Shabiba al-Islamiyya, est. 1929) continued to thrive. They were joined by other organizations created in response to both the general context of independence and specific contingencies.[36] Several members of the Lebanese Women's Strike Committee (Lajnat al-Idrab al-Nisa'iyya al-Lubnaniyya), which was formed during the November 1943 uprising, sought to institutionalize their relationships. Thus they established the Union of Lebanese Women (Jami'at Nisa' Lubnan) in 1943. The union was one of numerous women's groups that continued to demand equal political rights and increased state commitments to education and health care. Workers in an increasing number of economic sectors formed syndicates and/or organized strikes. They sought the passage and enforcement of a comprehensive labor legislation that would establish new minimum wages, various benefits, better working conditions, job security, and the right to organize. Many of these syndicates in turn coalesced around a number of labor federations formed in the wake of independence: the Federation of Workers and Employee's Syndicates (Ittihad Naqabat al-'Ummal wa-l-Mustakhdamin, est. 1945), the League of Workers and Employees' Syndicates (Jami'at Naqabat al-'Ummal wa-l-Mustakhdamin, est. 1946), and the United Syndicates of Workers and Employees (al-Naqabat al-Muttahida li-l-Mustakhdamin wa-l-'Ummal, est. 1952). Athletic clubs also continued to proliferate, either as wholly new institutions or as expansions of existing clubs. In 1945, al-Nadi al-Riyadi (est. 1934) expanded its Rawshe-based club to include several new sports.[37] By 1947, the club had moved to the Sanayi' neighborhood of Beirut, appointing Sa'ib Salam (1905–2000) its first honorary president and inaugurating its first basketball court.[38] In 1954, the club relocated to its current location in the al-Manara neighborhood. The mobilization of sports clubs and their supporters prompted the passage of new regulations governing the establishment of such clubs as well as state-sponsored national federations like the Lebanese Football Federation (al-Ittihad al-Lubnani li-Kurat al-Qadam, est. 1944).[39] Sports clubs also regularly lobbied the government for financial, infrastructural, and other support for the local development of sport and for participation in international competitions like the Mediterranean Games and the Olympics.[40] Many Lebanese and non-Lebanese residents used these diverse organizational forms and arenas to articulate their visions, mobilize constituencies, and build alliances.

One of the most notable popular movements established during this period was the Committee for the Defense of Tenants (Lajnat al-Difa' 'an al-Musta'jirin). This organization, which emerged in 1944 from a series of public meetings, soon demanded state intervention into the rental market, primarily to lower rents and prevent evictions in the context of urban population growth, wartime real estate speculation, and the general shortage of affordable housing.[41] Landlords also mobilized, first opposing the premise of rent control, and then seeking to influence its substance in their own interests. Despite such resistance, in early 1944 the coalition of urban residential, commercial, and industrial tenants—consisting of workers, employees, engineers, doctors, lawyers, artisans, merchants, and shop and factory owners—succeeded in renewing a much-expanded version of Lebanon's first (1942) rent control law (*qanun al-ijarat*).[42] Prior to that date, most rental agreements were subject to the terms contained in a specific contract, many of which were for one-year leases. The 1944 law automatically extended all rental agreements expiring during 1944 to December 31, 1944. The law concurrently banned any rent increases for agreements signed after July 1941 and limited the rent increases of agreements reached before that date. In addition, the law allowed tenants to sublet a portion of their rented property without notice or compensation to the landlord. Furthermore, the law forbade landlords from collecting more than three months' rent in advance.[43] It also stipulated that no evictions could occur without a court order, and limited lawful evictions to three scenarios: failure to make due payment for three months, damage to the rental property, or a landlord's need of the property due to the loss of current housing. The committee successfully pressured the government to extend this law without any substantive modifications in 1945, 1946, and 1947, effectively securing a multiyear rent freeze for increasing numbers of tenants.[44]

The Committee for the Defense of Tenants appears to have formally established itself by that name by 1949.[45] The timing reflects the intensification of struggles over rent control, which tenants conducted with varying degrees of success. The committee successfully pressured the government to extend until the end of a given year any contracts that would expire that year. It failed, however, to secure what it regularly demanded: a significant reduction in rents. Nevertheless, the committee succeeded in lowering some rents in 1948, freezing most rents to their previous year's amounts in 1949, 1950, 1952, 1953, and 1955, and limiting—to a considerable extent—rental increases in 1948, 1951, and 1954.[46] The government increasingly expanded the grounds for eviction through the 1948–55 laws (as compared to those of 1944–47).[47] In 1954 it reduced the grace period for overdue payments from three months to one month, thereby making earlier evictions possible, and required tenants who sublet a portion of their rental space to compensate their landlords accordingly. The persistence of rent control as an issue and the fluctuations in its substantive nature reflected the ebbs and flows of the contest between tenant and landlord mobilizations. Despite these shifts, the law and its various iterations established and maintained state institutions' integral role in arbitrating the rental market, offering specific protections to tenants, and serving as the focus of mobilizations by landlords and tenants alike.

The 1943–55 period also featured incredible transformation and experimentation with the form of the political party. World War II and the transition to independence prompted the effective closure or abandonment of several Mandate-era political parties, among them the Republican Independence Party (Hizb al-Istiqlal al-Jumhuri) and the Arab Nationalist Party (al-Hizb al-Qawmi al-'Arabi).[48] Yet the period also featured the creation of new parties that would influence postindependence popular mobilizations for decades to come. In 1944, Kadhim al-Sulh (1904–76) and other former members of the then-defunct Arab Nationalist Party established the National Appeal Party (Hizb al-Nida' al-Qawmi),[49] while in 1950, Muhammad Khalid formed the National Organization (al-Hay'a al-Wataniyya).[50] Lesser-known and more short-lived parties, like Rashid Baydun's (1889–1971) Vanguard Organization (Munazzamat al-Tala'i') and Nasim Majdalani's (1912–91) Ghassassina Organization (Munazzamat al-Ghasassina), also played an important role in popular mobilizations.[51] These parties variously championed and mobilized around key administrative, political, economic, and social policies, including reforming the electoral law, designing new educational curricula, inaugurating infrastructural projects, supporting workers or unions on strike, and nationalizing the Beirut Electricity Company. In some instances, these parties coordinated their efforts, forming ad hoc coalitions around specific objectives for various lengths of time.[52] In other instances, they bitterly disagreed over specific policy recommendations and competed with one another for members and control of urban space.[53]

Preexisting groups and parties also reorganized themselves in relation to the shifting terrain of Lebanese, regional, and international politics. For example, the 1946–49 program of repatriating diasporic Armenians to the Armenian Soviet Socialist Republic restructured the balance of power between the Armenian political parties in Lebanon.[54] More than a third of the approximately one hundred thousand Armenians who repatriated came from Beirut or traveled through it en route.[55] Such demographic shifts drastically reduced the social base of the leftist Huntchak Social Democrat Party (al-Hizb al-Hunshaq al-Dimuqrati al-Ijtima'i) and the centrist Democratic Liberal Party (Hizb al-Ramghavar). Conversely, it facilitated the Dashnak Armenian Revolutionary Federation's (al-Ittihad al-Thawri al-Armani al-Tashnaq) consolidation of its power in the Armenian community and its representation in the parliament.[56]

The postindependence context posed different challenges and opportunities for the Communist Party of Syria and Lebanon, the Kata'ib, and the Syrian Nationalist Party. In 1944, the Communist Party formally separated into the Communist Party of Lebanon (al-Hizb al-Shuyu'i fi Lubnan) and its Syrian counterpart.[57] While state repression severely limited its ability to operate openly between 1949 and 1952, it played a critical and continuous role in mobilizing individuals around issues of state building, economic development, and social justice, primarily through its support of the labor, women's, and student movements.[58] At the same time, the Kata'ib transformed from a paramilitary youth movement to a political party, broadening its social base and inaugurating its first-ever comprehensive program for administrative, political, economic, and social reform.[59] Its success in doing so contrasted sharply with the fate of the Rescuers (al-Najjada). The latter remained a paramilitary youth movement until its dissolution in 1949. Starting in 1951, Adnan al-Hakim (1914–90) reconstituted the Rescuers as a political party.[60] Yet the group never regained the central place in popular mobilizations that it had enjoyed during the late Mandate period. In 1944 the Syrian Nationalist Party secured government authorization to operate legally under the name of the Nationalist Party (al-Hizb al-Qawmi).[61] Founder Antun Sa'ada amended the name in 1947 to the Social Nationalist Party (SNP, al-Hizb al-Qawmi al-Ijtima'). Despite its oscillating relationship to the Lebanese government, including its failed 1949 revolt and the subsequent execution of its founder, the SNP continued to play an important role in domestic politics through 1955.[62]

The Zionist expulsion of over 700,000 Palestinians during the 1948 Nakba intersected with the expansion of popular organizations and movements in Lebanon. By 1955, the temporary emergency facing the more than 100,000 Palestinian refugees in Lebanon (in addition to those in the West Bank, Gaza Strip, Jordan, Syria, and elsewhere) had given way to a condition of permanent precarity as the new Israeli state denied them the ability to return and confiscated their properties.[63] In parallel, Palestinians consolidated themselves as a critical part of popular mobilizations in Lebanon. Some joined (and took up leadership roles) in existing organizations, including political parties such as the Lebanese Communist Party, SNP, and the Arab Socialist Ba'th Party (al-Hizb al-Ba'th al-'Arabi al-Ishtiraki, est. 1947–52), as well as student groups like al-'Urwa al-Wuthqa (The Indissoluble Bond, 1918–55), the American University of Beirut Student Council (1943–44 and 1949–54), and the national coalition known as the Student Committee (Lajnat al-Tullab, c. 1949–53). Others formed new organizations, such as the short-lived Jaffa and District Inhabitants Council (est. 1949) and the much longer-lasting Palestinian Arab Women's League in Lebanon (al-Ittihad al-Nisa'i al-'Arabi al-Filastini fi Lubnan, est. 1950).[64] Still other Palestinians mobilized through pre-existing Palestinian organizations such as The Youth (al-Futtuwwa, est. 1936).[65] As early as 1949, some Palestinians formed clandestine paramilitary or commando units with the aim of carrying out armed resistance operations against Israeli rule. Through these various forms of mobilization, Palestinians in Lebanon challenged their exile, their living conditions, and the broader constellation of political forces shaping their lives, whether they were in the rural south, the urban neighborhoods of Beirut and other cities and towns, or the growing network of refugee camps.

Recognizing the ubiquity of popular mobilizations and the strategic potential they offered, several elite politicians turned to political parties as a mechanism to establish or institutionalize a popular base beyond a single electoral cycle. In 1946, former president Émile Eddé attempted to resuscitate his political career by amalgamating the remnants of his old parliamentary bloc into the National Bloc Party (Hizb al-Kutla al-Wataniyya).[66] While Eddé's reputation never recovered from his collaboration with the French during the 1943 uprising, the party became a key vehicle for his two sons, Raymond (1913–2000) and Pierre (1921–77), to launch their own political careers. Raymond took over the party leadership after his father's 1949 death, an event that helped pave the way for the party's rebranding and ascendence with the expanding opposition to the Khuri regime. In this vein, the National Bloc Party sought relations with popular groups through supporting specific polices like women's suffrage. In alliance with President Sham'un, the party helped shore up support for policies that consolidated bankers' power in Lebanon's economy.[67] Another example is Philippe Takla's (1915–2006) 1955 creation of the Constitutional Union Party (Hizb al-Ittihad al-Dusturi), an entity conceived as the vehicle for his return—along with other remnants of al-Khuri's Constitutional Bloc (discredited and effectively disbanded due to al-Khuri's downfall in 1952)—to electoral politics.[68]

Kamal Jumblatt's (1917–78) founding of the Progressive Socialist Party (PSP, Hizb al-Taqaddumi al-Ishtiraki) in 1949 both represented the trend of elite politicians forming political parties while also serving as an exceptional case of success. Few such attempts genuinely succeeded, and most eventually ended in the party's closure. For example, little trace of newspaper editor Iliyas Harfush and former minister George Philippe Tabet's Lebanese Christian Socialist Party (al-Hizb al-Ishtiraki al-Masihi al-Lubnani, est. 1946) remains beyond the flyer announcing its creation and a CIA report on its final meeting.[69] In 1952, former parliamentary deputies Kadhim al-Khalil (1901–90), Gabriel al-Murr (b. 1895), and Joseph Skaff (1922–91) founded the short-lived Lebanese People's Party (Hizb al-Sha'b al-Lubnani), envisioning it as a mechanism to build a new political base after their loss in parliamentary elections.[70] Although, as noted above, many of these parties closed down, others merged with larger, more successful parties. In 1950, the Ghasassina merged into the PSP while the Republican Union Party (Hizb al-Ittihad al-Jumhuri, est. 1948) merged with the National Bloc Party.[71] These examples signify elite politicians' newfound understanding of how to create a broad social base and harness the power of popular mobilization through the apparatus of a political party. They also highlight the contingent nature of success in such endeavors.

Politicians and parliamentary blocs that declined—or tried and failed—to create their own political parties increasingly collaborated and coordinated with popular groups, including other political parties, labor unions, women's organizations, and student groups. The National Liberation Bloc, for example, sought to work in collaboration with several political parties, leading to the creation of the Committee of Allied Parties (Lajnat al-Ahzab al-Mu'talifa, est. 1949). This collaboration began with a joint meeting between the bloc and representatives of the Kata'ib Party, the Ghasassina Organization, the National Appeal Party, the Republication Unity Party, and the PSP.[72] The committee helped deepen the popular base supporting the bloc's rejection of the legitimacy of the parliament elected in 1947.[73]

The case of the previously mentioned PSF is particularly telling because the coalition took shape and developed in a climate of intense popular mobilizations like the strikes, marches, protests, petitions, flyers, pamphlets, and booklets that seemed ubiquitous throughout much of 1951–52. The PSF included parliamentary representatives of the PSP, the National Bloc Party, and the SNP while meeting regularly with the Kata'ib, National Congress, National Appeal Party, and the National Organization. These last four parties created the Popular Front (al-Jabha al-Sha'biyya) in July 1952 to coordinate their own efforts, which they in turn coordinated with the PSF.[74] It is difficult to imagine the success (or even the possibility) of the two-day general strike held on September 15–16, 1952, that forced al-Khuri's resignation in the absence of effective leadership.[75] In fact, the final day of the strike and the following day featured intense disagreements between these two poles of the opposition to al-Khuri, who could not agree whether to continue the strike in order to ensure the fulfillment of demanded policy changes.[76] Although Jumblatt and other members of the PSF advocated continuing the strike, the Popular Front's desire to end it settled the matter.

This experience was a key learning moment for Jumblatt. He subsequently supplemented his work creating and maintaining a parliamentary opposition to the new presidency of Sham'un with coalition-building efforts among various popular groups. These efforts began with a series of meetings in 1953 that brought Jumblatt's PSP together with the Women's Federation of Lebanon, the Islamic Youth Association, the National Appeal Party, the National Organization, the Partisans of Peace, and the Syrian Social Nationalist

Party.[77] By 1955 this coalition had formalized itself as the National Conference of Parties and Organizations (al-Mu'tamar al-Watani li-l-Ahzab wa-l-Hay'at), which issued a platform of administrative, political, economic, and social demands, and episodically mobilized to respond to regional developments.[78]

THE COMMON INTERESTS

In the wake of the November 1943 uprising, the Lebanese government returned to the objective that first motivated its public and definitive call for independence: access to, and control of, the revenues of the Common Interests (al-Masalih al-Mushtaraka). In December 1943, the Lebanese, Syrian, and French governments signed an agreement committing to the transfer of the Common Interests from French to Lebanese and Syrian control.[79] Yet it deferred specifying the mechanisms of transfer to subsequent protocols specific to each of the Common Interests' various components. The contours of the 1944–46 negotiations and transfers of the Common Interests reflected French and Lebanese rationales for this deferral. The agreement served French interests by permitting the High Commission to both control the sequencing of transfers and to maximize Lebanese concessions across multiple protocol negotiations. For example, the French delayed for as long as possible the transfer of the radio station, the telephone system, the railways, and—most particularly—the Special Troops. These infrastructures of communication, transportation, and security were critical to the ultimate balance of power between the High Commission and the Lebanese government. The French variously used the ongoing war or other contingencies to justify delaying the transfer of these institutions but were ultimately seeking to sign a formal treaty that would comprehensively safeguard French strategic, economic, and cultural interests.

On the other hand, the Lebanese government primarily sought to secure control of those institutions it viewed as critical to realizing its vision of governance. It prioritized negotiations over the customs administration (*idarat al-jamarik*) and the monitoring of the tobacco monopoly (*muraqabat hisr al-tabgh*), which generated a majority of the Common Interests' total revenue. The Lebanese government also sought better control over the mass media environment in Lebanon. To this end, it unilaterally assumed the functions of publications censorship (*muraqabat al-matbu'at*) and unsuccessfully prioritized the radio station in subsequent negotiations. According to some sources, the Lebanese government was reticent to take control of the Special Troops, in part due to their reluctance to take on the costs of the troops and their preferred reliance on the other internal security forces: the gendarmerie and police.

Popular groups closely followed, debated, and mobilized around the prolonged transfer of the Common Interests, treating it as a litmus test of elected officials' and government bureaucrats' commitment to national independence and sovereignty. They repeatedly emphasized "the patience" of "the Lebanese people" in the face of repeated French "delays" and "provocations."[80] They sometimes threatened to resume "struggle as before" (jihad kama fi al-sabiq) should the government or the French fail to fulfill expectations for full sovereignty.[81]

Between 1944 and 1946, the High Commission transferred some entities or functions to joint Lebanese-Syrian control, transferring others exclusively to one of the two states.[82] Initially the Lebanese and Syrian governments maintained the joint customs and monetary regimes. They created the Supreme Council for the Common Interests (al-Majlis al-A'la li-l-Masalih al-Mushtaraka) in 1944 to incorporate and jointly administer the customs, the monitoring of concessionary companies operating in both countries (e.g., the railway), and the management of the tobacco monopoly.[83] The Lebanese and Syrian governments' monetary policies and economic development strategies diverged after independence. One set of institutional outcomes of these divergences were the 1948 Franco-Lebanese monetary accord, the 1949 Lebanese monetary law, and the 1950 dissolution of the customs union with Syria. The first of these primarily involved mechanisms for the settling of France's overall debt to the Lebanese government and managing that settlement's potential impact on currency stability.[84] The second featured the issuance of a new Lebanese lira, distinct from the Syrian lira, delinked from the French franc, and pegged to the gold standard.[85] The third primarily involved the breakup of the Common Interests framework, most significantly the dissolution of the customs union, the erection of a trade barrier between Lebanon and Syria, and the pursuit of separate customs policies.[86] These new institutional arrangements were subjects of varying levels of elite and popular mobilizations.

The transfer of the Common Interests precipitated a significant expansion in the size, functions, and reach of Lebanese state institutions.[87] It offered the Lebanese government direct control over key revenue streams (i.e., customs and monopolies) and technologies of rule (i.e., radio, telephone, and telegraphy). The Ministry of Interior took control of the gendarmerie and police as well as the gunpowder monopoly. The Ministry of Post and Telegraph assumed administration of the telephone system. The Ministry of Public Works became responsible for monitoring Lebanon-based concessionary companies, managing the control of automobiles and related products, and conducting topographical studies. The Ministry of Education incorporated the units responsible for the supervision of antiquities, radio broadcasting interests, and foreign cultural institutions. Finally, the Ministry of National Economy took over the registration and enforcement of patents.

This assumption of new responsibilities by state institutions further consolidated the territorial encaging of governance within the boundaries of Lebanon that the French had inaugurated as part of their colonial rule. The creation of the Supreme Council for Customs (al-Majlis al-A'la li-l-Jamarik) in the Lebanese Ministry of Finance was the most notable example of this process.[88] It produced a new system for monitoring, documenting, and regulating the movement of goods across Lebanon's borders. Also important was the reorganization of the police and gendarmerie—collectively termed the Internal Security Forces (Quwwat al-Amn al-Dakhili) and the inauguration of a Directorate of General Security (Da'irat al-Amn al-'Am)—both under the aegis of the Ministry of Interior. The following year (1946), the cabinet established the Supreme Council for State Security (al-Majlis al-A'la li-Amn al-Dawla), headed by the minister of interior and made up of the public prosecutor of court of appeals, the Ministry of Interior's director general, the commander of the armed forces, the commander of the Internal Security Forces, the Police director, and the General Security director. Many of these institutions were directly shaped by their confrontation with and attempts to contain popular mobilizations. The decoupling of the Lebanese and Syrian components of the tobacco monopoly and railway administration was another important aspect.

The Régie Co-Intéressée Libano-Syrienne des Tabacs et Tombacs retained its concession for administering the tobacco monopoly in Lebanon and Syria after 1943. As part of the transfer of the Common Interests, the Supreme Council for the Common Interests initially assumed responsibility for monitoring the company. The 1950 breakup of the Lebanese-Syrian Common Interests precipitated a reorganization of the Régie into two companies, each with a concession specific to Lebanon or Syria.[89] In Lebanon, the newly formed Régie Co-Intéressée des Tabacs et Tombacs (al-Manfa'a al-Mushtaraka li-Hasr al-Tabgh wa-l-Tunbak) maintained its parent company's previous functional organization: general administration, cultivation, manufacturing, and marketing. Yet corporate management of the company and government supervision of its operations and of the Lebanese tobacco sector more generally were now wholly Lebanese affairs under the purview of the Ministry of Finance. The profit-sharing formula between the Lebanese government and the Régie was standardized on the basis of a 95 percent–5 percent split.[90] These institutional transformations provided the Lebanese bureaucracy with access to significantly greater revenues. They also afforded the Lebanese bureaucracy tremendous power in shaping the rural political economy, in which tobacco cultivation played an increasingly important role. The postindependence period featured a significant expansion in the total area of tobacco cultivation and the number of persons authorized to conduct such cultivation, both of which required Ministry of Finance approved permits.[91] While the Régie was required to purchase the entire authorized crop of tobacco leaf, its regional procurement committees assessed the crop grade and purchase prices of crop yields on the basis of formulas set by the Ministry of Finance. Tobacco farmers and tobacco workers, their supporters, and factions within elected officials repeatedly mobilized against the Régie throughout 1943–55.

Similar to the tobacco monopoly concession, the Société ottomane du chemin de fer de Damas-Hamah et prolongements (DHP, Sharikat Sikkat Hadid Sham Hama wa-Tamdidatuha) initially maintained its railway concession for Lebanon and Syria. Prior to independence, the DHP comprised four railway lines: Beirut-Riyaq-Damascus; Riyaq-Homs-Aleppo; Tripoli-Homs; and Hama-Aleppo.[92] The company's profitability declined after World War I, and the governments in both Lebanon and Syria agreed to subsidize the DHP in proportion to the length of track on each state's territory.[93] The DHP's annual budgetary deficit increased during the postindependence period.[94]

This was a function of declining passenger and freight traffic on the railways, which is attributable to upgrading and expanding Lebanon's road network and the increasing affordability of truck transportation.[95] In addition, reorganizing the railway system into two discrete entities and infrastructures was a more complicated and prolonged process than that of the Régie. In 1955, the government nevertheless initiated negotiations to purchase the components of the DHP on its territory, as the Syrian government had done earlier that year.[96] The interim period nevertheless featured repeated calls for the Lebanese government to invest in and enhance the capacities of the DHP.[97] DHP workers, reputed to have formed one of the first syndicates in the territories that constituted Lebanon during the late Ottoman period, repeatedly called upon the government to ensure timely salary payments and guaranteed pay raises and other benefits.

A more complicated development concerned the Naqura-Beirut-Tripoli railway line, which was part of the British-built and -administered Haifa-Damascus line constructed during 1941–42.[98] As World War II came to an end, and anticipation of the eventual evacuation of foreign troops intensified, a complex three-way struggle over the line's fate ensued between the Lebanese, British, and French governments. The British government had originally secured permission from the Free French to construct the railway on condition that the French had the first right of refusal to purchase it should the British decide to sell it. Yet when the British determined they wanted to dispose of the line, the circumstances had fundamentally changed. On the one hand, in 1944 the French began to press the British to permit them to exercise their option to purchase the line, part of their broader strategy to maintain influence and leverage in Lebanon. On the other hand, the postindependence Lebanese government rejected the idea of a French first right of refusal and sought to purchase the line itself. By 1946, the exigencies of diminished French influence, British strategic calculations, and local mobilizations—within the context of the shifting regional and global norms about infrastructural development—altered the negotiation terrain. The Lebanese government purchased the line from the British in 1947 and contracted the DHP to administer it starting in 1948.[99] By the end of 1955 the Lebanese railway system comprised three lines: the Naqura-Beirut-Tripoli line; the Beirut-Riyaq line; and the Riyaq-Ras Ba'albak line.

RETHINKING ECONOMY AND STATE

By 1955, Lebanon featured an open, laissez-faire, service-based economy.[100] The trade sector accounted for the largest share of national income, followed by agriculture, then manufacturing.[101] There was a concomitant prevalence of private sector firms and institutions (in terms of capital formation, employment, and output) across most sectors, including trade, agriculture, manufacturing, real estate, finance, tourism, transportation, and others.[102] Underpinning the consolidation of this economy was the deregulation of foreign exchange markets and foreign trade, which was largely accomplished between 1948 and 1952.[103]

For many scholars, Lebanon's postindependence consolidation of an open, laissez-faire, service-based economy represents a departure from the development model that underpinned the overwhelming majority of contemporary postcolonial states, whose governments pursued state-led development and organized closed economies based on either primary commodities or manufacturing.[104] Yet, existing narratives of Lebanon's postindependence economic development have often ignored or mischaracterized conflicts over the organization of the economy and the role of state institutions in shaping it. Contemporary champions of these policies, whose writings serve as the primary bases for most scholarly accounts, justified them through arguments combining geographic determinism and nationalist mythology.[105] Later critics of these policies, including scholars reflecting on the shortcomings and failures of Lebanon's open, laissez-faire, service-based economy, identified them as the function of elite consensus coupled with an intentional avoidance of government intervention in the economy.[106] Focusing attention on the state institutional arrangements that underpinned the transformation of Lebanon's postindependence political economy and the debates about it undermines such assumptions.

The politicians, businessmen, and economists who constituted Lebanon's elites vigorously debated the proper course of economic development. Some expressed their views through various interest associations like the Chamber of Commerce, Industry, and Agriculture of Beirut and Mount Lebanon (Ghurfat al-Tijara wa-l-Sina'a wa-l-Zira'a fi Bayrut wa-Jabal Lubnan, est. 1887) and the Association of Lebanese Industrialists (ALI, Jam'iyyat al-Sina'iyyin al-Lubnaniyyin, est. 1944). Still others worked through business consortiums like Société d'études et de réalisations industrielles, agricoles et commerciales (est. 1946). Also important were research institutions like Société libanaise d'économie politique (Jam'iyyat al-Iqtisad al-Siyasi al-Lubnani, est. 1943) and the Economic Research Institute (Ma'had al-Dirasat al-Iqtisadiyya, est. 1952). Central themes of the discourse produced by these organizations were the regulation of various economic sectors and actors, the appropriate levels of state investment in these sectors, and the potential redistribution of wealth across the regions and citizens of Lebanon.

The alliances and antagonisms informing these debates varied depending on the specific issue, its timing, and a host of both structural and contingent factors. For example, Société libanaise d'économie politique Director Gabriel Menassa and Economic Research Institute Director Albert Badre (1912–2010) shared many assumptions about the need to expand imports and transit trade, to develop the agricultural sector, and to reform budgetary practices and government services.[107] Both administrators viewed forms of indirect state intervention as necessary to coordinate the national economy. However, they—and the figures associated with their respective institutions—disagreed about the need for the establishment of a central bank.[108] Opinion in the Lebanese banking sector displayed a critical fault line around the issue of a central bank.[109] Banks allied with the Banque de Syrie et du Liban (BSL), the French-owned bank that continued to hold a Mandate-era concession granting it monopoly over bank note issue and government financial dealings, viewed a central bank as a threat to their dominance of the financial sector. Emerging rival banks, many of which were allied with US and Gulf financial institutions, recognized that such an entity was necessary if the state was to gain the upper hand in the money market. Despite these differences, both groups of banks supported proposals for state-sponsored development banks as an alternative to a central bank.[110]

ALI offers another example of how intra-elite alliances and antagonisms concerning the economy played out. Many historical narratives about this period are anachronistic, tending to project back into the late 1940s and early 1950s the sharp conflict between industrialists and traders that contributed to constituting the Lebanese political field from the 1960s forward. These narratives routinely describe "industrialists" as a self-contained group, whose economic interests are antithetical to the those of "traders," and whose marginalization represents the privileging of trade over industrialization (or even dependency over autarkic industrialization). A careful reading of ALI's public statements in the wake of independence reveals it to be much more conciliatory toward the emerging status-quo's privileging of the trade sector.[111] ALI certainly lobbied for a specific level of protection and support of local manufacturing. However, these measures remained squarely within the parameters of an open, laissez-faire, service-based economy. Rather than challenging the place of trade, ALI sought to divide the consumer market between imported and locally manufactured goods while simultaneously seeking the government's support for exporting manufactured goods. This strategy betrayed the reality that many of the founding members of ALI were cross-sectoral businesses whose origins were to be found in the trade sector, and thus had little to gain from reducing the volume or increasing the cost of imports. This business landscape reflected a strategy of diversification first adopted during the nineteenth-century collapse of the silk industry, and pursued much more broadly and intensely in the wake of the Great Depression and World War II's regulatory regime. The multisectoral nature of ALI membership during its first decade limits the plausibility that its function was to advance a program of privileging manufacturing over trade and agriculture. A more plausible alternative is that ALI served as a mechanism for self-regulation by members, offering a specialized forum to monitor sector-wide developments and cooperate on two critical fronts: preserving the oligopolistic structure of the local market and responding to the upsurge in labor militancy.[112]

Beyond elite circles, economic development was an object of great concern and vociferous criticism from popular groups. This is best exemplified by the frequency that calls for economic development and specific policies associated with it appeared in newspapers, political party platforms, petitions, and demonstrations. Workers debated and made demands concerning employment opportunities, job security, and wage levels.[113] Artisans and small manufacturers sought protection from imports and greater access to foreign markets.[114] Farmers lobbied for state-backed agricultural credit and state intervention to reduce the prices of fertilizers and mechanical equipment.[115] Urban residents demanded better quality of service and more affordable rates for public utilities like potable water and electricity.[116] Rural residents demanded the extension of such public utilities into their towns and villages. Across the country the prices of basic goods like bread, sugar, and fuel were discussed and protested.[117] At several junctures, diverse popular groups formed coalitions with one another and alliances with elite politicians to articulate their visions for the economic development of Lebanon. This was particularly the case for questions related to the regulation of commodity prices, the housing market, and the banking sector.[118]

The consolidation of Lebanon's open, laissez-faire, service-based economy was intimately connected to state bureaucratic expansion. Many scholars have explained the post–World War II development of Lebanon as a regional and global trading center as either a return to a presumptive prewar role or a combined function of the demise of Haifa's role as a regional port in the aftermath of the 1948 Nakba and the 1948–52 deregulation of foreign exchange markets and foreign trade. It was, however, equally, if not more so, the function of significant planning, regulation, spending, and other forms of state intervention occurring particularly under the aegis of the Ministry of Public Works, the Ministry of National Economy, and the Ministry of Finance.[119]

These ministries and successive Lebanese cabinets actively facilitated the development of the Beirut port. In some instances, this was done in collaboration with the Compagnie du Port, de Quais et des Entrepôts de Beyrouth (Sharikat Marfa' wa-Arsifat wa-Hawasil Bayrut). In other cases the port's development involved areas not covered by that company's concessionary agreements and thus under the direct control and supervision of the Lebanese state.[120] The government significantly enlarged customs, general, and private warehouses and introduced refrigerated and freezer storage.[121] The government also enlarged the surface area of the port's free zone by more than fourfold, made possible the establishment of a variety of industrial processing operations in that space, and improved the free zone's connections to the port's road and railway network.[122] The government furthermore expanded the port's overall links to land transportation systems, while also upgrading the national highway system and its connections to regional road networks. These developments made it faster and cheaper for merchants and governments in Iraq, Jordan, Saudi Arabia, and Syria to import goods through Beirut than other sea and land routes.[123] Expansions of the overall warehousing and transportation capacities of the port, including the free zone, also increased the ability of Lebanese merchants to selectively stockpile imported goods for longer periods, without paying import duties, to strategically manipulate local supplies and prices, and to make timely decisions about whether to sell goods in the domestic market or in other regional markets. The free zone greatly enhanced Beirut's evolving post–World War II role as entrepôt, amply demonstrated by the growing significance of reexport and transit trade in the economy's trade sector.[124] Such developments helped enrich Lebanese elites. They also raised the specter of nationalizing the port. In 1955 the argument for this move was informed by a normative understanding of development, and by the fact of the port company's increased profitability.[125]

Additionally, the government inaugurated an ambitious multistage and multiyear plan to develop the port of Tripoli, which became the site of intense local and foreign corporate competition for various design, construction, and operation contracts.[126] Certainly, the place of the Tripoli port in the national economy and regional trade paled in comparison to that of Beirut. It was nevertheless at the center of important debates and mobilizations about economic development. It also episodically served as a magnet for significant state-sponsored capital projects and foreign development proposals.[127] Such projects never fully addressed the host of popular grievances related to the state's economic neglect of Tripoli, its port, and its hinterland. They nevertheless produced a significant increase in port activity.[128] The concessionary agreements of the Lebanese government with the DHP and the Société des Travaux Maritimes et Urbains for operation of the wharves and the port, respectively, also meant that they featured in broader debates about foreign concessions, nationalization, and postcolonial development.

The Lebanese government further facilitated the growth of the trade sector through a series of legal measures. It amended the Lebanese commercial and maritime codes to attract foreign business operators and investors.[129] The Lebanese government also concluded a series of bilateral trade agreements, e.g., with Italy in 1950; with Egypt, Iraq, and West Germany in 1951; with Czechoslovakia, Jordan, and Syria in 1952; with East Germany and Yugoslavia in 1953; with the Soviet Union in 1954; and with China, France, and Turkey in 1955.[130] In addition, the Lebanese government took a leading role in the conclusion of the 1953 Arab Economic Treaty.[131] The commitment to concluding such agreements was institutionalized in two ways. First, the government established an intraministerial committee to negotiate and monitor the implementation of trade agreements in 1953.[132] Then, in 1954, the government decreed that imports from countries with whom Lebanon does not have a trade agreement would be subject to the maximum customs tariff rates (i.e., double the normal tariff rate).[133]

Rather than simply resuming its prewar levels of operation, the Beirut port experienced a dramatic increase in the volume and value of trade it facilitated. In 1954, for example, Beirut port workers processed approximately double the amount of cargo than they did in 1939.[134] This figure increased yet again by 25 percent in 1955.[135] Of particular significance in this overall expansion of trade is the regional role the Beirut port played. The 1951–55 period witnessed a dramatic increase in the volume of trade with regional states compared to the 1935–39 period.[136] Such trends challenge representations of Lebanon's postindependence economic policies as a return to pre–World War II colonial-era policies or to some notional Phoenician merchant past. The postindependence role of the Beirut port in the local, regional, and global economy is unimaginable in the absence of contemporary regional realities like the legacies of World War II policies, the infrastructures established by the Middle East Supply Centre, and the newfound commitment and autonomy to harness state institutional arrangements to plan, invest in, and regulate trading capacities and relations.

The consolidation of Lebanon as a tourism hub was similarly grounded in state institutional planning and bureaucratic expansion.[137] As part of its major public works programs, the Lebanese government improved routes between Beirut, summer resorts in Mount Lebanon, and other sites of touristic interest in the interior.[138] It drew on UN and other programs to plan and fund the redevelopment of key touristic sites in Ba'albak, Byblos, Sidon, Tripoli, and Tyre.[139] The Lebanese government episodically subsidized the transportation costs of visitors from Arab countries and, as part of its broader partnership with the BSL in the form of the Société de Crédit Agricole et Industriel du Liban (Sharikat al-Taslif al-Zira'i wa-l-Sina'i fi Lubnan, est. 1937), regularly facilitated state-guaranteed loans for hotel construction, renovation, and expansion.[140] In addition, the government supervised the planning, construction, and operation of the Beirut International Airport. When it unofficially began operating in 1951, 3,211 planes carrying 30,330 ordinary passengers and 28,100 transit passengers arrived.[141] The number of planes landing increased tenfold by 1955, carrying four times the number of ordinary passengers and triple the number of transit passengers.[142] Overall, the number of incoming tourists nearly doubled between 1951 and 1955, with an increasing share of Europeans and North Americans.[143]

In 1948 the government created the General Commission for Tourism and Summering (GCTE, al-Mufwadiyya al-'Amma li-l-Siyaha wa-l-Istiyaf) as an element of the Ministry of National Economy.[144] The precursor to the GCTE was the Tourism and Summering Service (Maslahat al-Siyaha wa-l-Istiyyaf, est. 1942).[145] The government decision to replace the service with a new commission followed a year in which some analysts claimed the tourism sector performed the worst it had in more than two decades.[146] This prompted investors and managers in the tourism industry to criticize the Lebanese government's allegedly inadequate promotion of tourism.[147]

The GCTE was the first public institution tasked with monitoring the tourism sector while also planning, regulating, and promoting it both within the country and abroad.[148] It established tourism information offices and a hospitality management school (al-Madrasa al-Funduqiyya), while facilitating the restoration of archaeological sites, developing a ski resort, and initiating the planning for the Casino du Liban.[149] The GCTE also established a tourism police force under its direct supervision, whose mandate was to ensure tourists' safety and enforce compliance with established regulations, including those governing prices.[150]

The commission thus facilitated Lebanon's emergence as a hub of Mediterranean tourism. It further institutionalized the complex relationship between summering (*istiyaf*) and tourism (*siyaha*) and actively facilitated the development of related infrastructure, all while seeking to combine representations of the mountain and the beach into a single totalizing narrative about Lebanon as a tourist destination for all.[151] The GCTE sought to make Lebanon part of the post–World War II international tourism industry while also mobilizing the Lebanese public to more consistently welcome visitors and provide them with desired goods and services.[152] The commission also guided Lebanon to membership in the International Union of Official Tourism Organizations in 1950.[153]

The GCTE was a key node in the bureaucratic expansion of state institutional arrangements, as it facilitated the drafting and issuing of several new regulations. These include the 1949 law regulating tourist guides and tourist agencies, the 1954 decree designating and regulating summer resorts, the 1955 formation of a tourism police force, and the initial legalization of gambling in 1950.[154] The commission also established standards for the construction, expansion, and renovation of hotels, restaurants, cafés, and bars, while setting price ranges for transportation, hotel accommodations, and entry fees.[155] It advocated the inclusion of tourism as part of the Ministry of Education's postindependence civics (*al-tarbiyya al-wataniyya*) curriculum.[156] The commission led the campaign known as Touristic Year (*sanat al-istiyaf*) in 1955, for which it helped organize the first Ba'albak International Festival, the Summer of Emigrants (*sayf al-mughtaribin*), and numerous commemorative publications.[157] The discourses and practices of the GCTE were central to further instantiating the intersecting notions of hospitality, tourism, economic development, state building, and national identity in Lebanon.[158]

The above survey of the intersection between the consolidation of Lebanon's open, laissez-faire, service-based economy and state bureaucratic expansion reflects the co-constitutive nature of these processes. Ideas about institutional design and development planning were critical to debates, mobilizations, policies, and outcomes concerning the economy. One of the clearest examples of this is the 1953 creation of the Economic Planning and Development Board (EPDB, Majlis al-Tasmim wa-l-Inma' al-Iqtisadi).[159] This twelve-person board, comprising holders of specific bureaucratic positions and cabinet-appointed economic experts, was the first instance of a Lebanese public institution to be tasked directly with national planning and economic development.[160] Poorly funded and limited to an advisory role, the EPDB nevertheless displayed a discursive commitment to planning and facilitated several subsequent institutional arrangements.[161] It also presaged the establishment in 1954 of the Ministry of Planning and Development (subsequently renamed the Ministry of General Planning), within which the EPDB was eventually subsumed.[162]

Before it was subsumed into the Ministry of General Planning, the EPDB recommended two major projects. One of them was the creation of a large-scale state-sponsored lending institution that would support development projects. Such a recommendation was in accord with episodic public demands for greater state funding of economic development and for the creation of a central bank.[163] The government took up this recommendation and eventually established the Bank for Agricultural, Industrial, and Financial Credit (BCAIF, Banque de Crédit agricole, industriel et foncier) in 1954.[164] The structure of the BCAIF—three autonomous departments of agriculture, industry, and real estate—each with its own mandated percentage of the banks' overall loans portfolio, reflected a compromise between advocates of a single institution and those desiring separate institutions for agriculture and industry.[165] The BCAIF's division of founding shares and loan capital reflected the triumph of the BSL and its allies in excluding international capital and designating the BSL as Lebanon's sole lender.

Another EPDB-recommended project was the creation of a national electricity and water company.[166] Parliament debated this proposal but ultimately approved a substitution, the Litani National Authority.[167] Parliament's opting for a project to develop the Litani River basin in the absence of a comprehensive electricity and water scheme was a reflection of the long-standing disagreements between competing visions of engineers and business interests vis-à-vis the question of development in general and electricity and water in particular.[168] The victor in this struggle was the camp allied with—and based in—the Ministry of Public Works. While a function of a variety of factors, this victory was in no small part also affected by the institutional power of this ministry. The Litani National Authority was the linchpin of a state-sponsored development scheme to enhance electricity generating capacity and expand rural water availability.[169] Unlike the BCAIF, the Litani National Authority facilitated the infusion of foreign capital in the form of Lebanon's first loan from the International Bank for Reconstruction and Development.[170] The specific conditions of the loan, including the requirement to sell the electricity produced exclusively to the Beirut Electricity Company, were a response to the shortage of electricity available in the capital at the time the loan was contracted.[171] These conditions also reflected the Beirut-centric nature of the Lebanese electricity sector and that sector's underdevelopment in smaller cities, towns, and rural areas.

Bureaucratic expansion was premised on increasing the volume of resources at the disposal of Lebanese state institutions. To this end, the Ministry of Finance was the locus of both increased revenue streams via customs, taxes, and fees as well as centralized control over distributing that revenue. Limited yet important fiscal reforms added additional revenue sources. For example, the government introduced an income tax in 1944, an inheritance tax in 1951, and a land tax in 1952.[172] These measures increased the contribution of direct taxes (in both absolute and relative terms) to the state treasury. They also formed one of the rationales for the formulation of a banking secrecy law by potentially subjecting elites' wealth to the tax collector's scrutiny.[173] Indirect taxes nevertheless remained the majority of state revenues in 1955: customs receipts accounted for the greatest share of public revenue, followed by the tobacco monopoly, duties on inflammables, and the income tax.[174]

This overall revenue structure helped reproduce class relations while restructuring economic sectors. The high proportion of indirect taxes meant that lower income groups contributed disproportionally to state finances.[175] The income tax compounded this inequity in several ways. It discriminated against persons who earned all or most of their income from one source (e.g., wages or salary) in favor of persons earning income from several sources (e.g., salary and business profits).[176] For example, an individual who derived all her income from a salary would pay more total income tax than another individual earning the same total income through a combination of salary and business ownership. Second, the tax rate on debts and equities was set at a flat rate of 10 percent, whereas that from business profits progressed from a minimum of 4 percent to a maximum of 42 percent. This effectively meant that, at a certain income level and above, an individual deriving income from debts and equities paid less in taxes than an individual earning income from operating a business. Finally, the size of tax brackets for enterprises increased at a slower rate than the relevant tax ratios in the lower brackets, but at faster rate than the relevant tax ratios in the higher brackets. Therefore smaller-earning businesses disproportionately contributed to the tax base relative to their larger-earning counterparts. The role of taxes in the reproduction of class relations was accompanied by limited opportunities for class mobility, most notably the education sector.

The Ministry of Finance also expanded the cadastral survey and land registry, both of which dated from the early Mandate. At the time of independence, less than half of the geographic territory of Lebanon had been surveyed and registered in the new system. The ministry accelerated this process between 1943 and 1955, yielding more accurate and efficient identification of state property. Bureaucrats laid claim to land, either as public domain or holding the promise of public utility (like water springs), either expropriating it or granting a concession for its use to private interests.

Due to its involvement in their financial affairs, the Ministry of Finance represented the primary means for bureaucratic centralization across all government ministries.[177] For example, all ministries' ordinary budgets were subject to review by the Ministry of Finance. The rapid and immense institutional growth of the state bureaucracy often required expenditures exceeding the amounts set by the routine ministerial budget estimates. The Ministry of Finance had the power to approve or reject all supplementary or extraordinary expenses; thus it was directly involved in almost every sphere of bureaucratic practice, shaping resource allocation within and across the state bureaucracy.[178]

The Ministry of Finance was one of many institutional arrangements that underpinned the open, laissez-faire, service-based economy that came to define Lebanon's postindependence period. This economy was not formed overnight. Some of its defining features took shape in the 1943–55 period, others date back to the Mandate era, and others would not be established until after the period on which this book focuses. The creation or reorganization of state institutional arrangements was a critical factor throughout the late twentieth century, as were the competing visions of Lebanon's postcolonial political economy and the differing capacities to realize those visions.

THE CIVIL SERVICE

As described above, the number of public sector employees more than doubled between 1943 and 1955. Such increases were spread across expanding ranks of both existing and new administrative units.[179] A new emphasis on the professionalization of the bureaucracy accompanied this increase in personnel. Between 1926 and 1952, the recruitment, organization, compensation, and conduct of civil servants were conditioned by a range of laws and decrees that created uneven terrain across different administrative units.[180] Entrance into the civil service nevertheless did entail a common set of minimal requirements. The prospective employee had to be eighteen years of age or older, capable of demonstrating relevant knowledge through documentation or examination, and free of any criminal convictions. Yet what constituted relevant knowledge, which documents could serve as evidence, and how the examination would be administered were all subject to the ad hoc decisions of any combination of officials in a given ministry. In addition, job classifications and salaries across ministries varied significantly enough to render difficult any general observations about the organization of the civil service.[181] Furthermore, salary scales had remained since the 1930s, only supplemented by wartime cost-of-living bonuses.

As part of the broader debates about state building, politicians, senior bureaucrats, and the public took aim at the existing civil service system almost immediately after independence. The result was a series of public lectures, newspaper articles, government committees, and foreign consultancies.[182] From 1953 to 1955, this process culminated in the passage of public administration and basic personnel laws.[183] These laws standardized and systematized employment across the entire state bureaucracy. They delineated recruitment, compensation, and disciplinary procedures, while articulating norms like recruitment by merit, political neutrality, and separation of office from officeholder. The government divided civil servants into two categories: a permanent cadre (*al-muwazzafun al-da'imun*) and temporary workers (*al-muwazzafun al-muwaqqatun*).[184] The cadre was made up of administrative and technical positions (*malak idari wa-malak tiqani*).[185] The organization and renumeration of these technical bureaucrats were often unique to each ministry. Yet administrative positions, which were subject to a standard classification system across all ministries, constituted the vast majority of the cadre. The government also unified the basic pay structure and various allowances (family, travel, etc.) of the administrative cadre. Henceforth, the salary ranges and accompanying allowances for any specific position were the same across the different ministries.

The government divided the administrative cadre into hierarchical categories (*fi'at*), that were subdivided into ranks (*rutab*), each with its own set of grades (*darajat*). The standardized positions (in ascending rank) were janitor, office boy and driver, secretary, clerk, chief of section, chief of department and inspector, director, chief of service, and inspector general, and director general. Applicants to all positions had to be Lebanese citizens, clear of any felony or "shameful misdemeanor" convictions (*ghayr mahkum 'alayh bi-jinaya aw junha sha'ina*), and free of disease and infirmity (*saliman min al-amrad wa-'ahat*). Entrants into the lowest two categories of the administrative cadre (i.e., as janitors, drivers, and office boys as well as secretaries and clerks) had to be between the ages of twenty and thirty-five years. Those entering higher category positions (i.e., as section, department, and service chiefs, inspectors and inspectors general, directors, and directors general) could be older. With the exception of janitors, drivers, and office boys (i.e., the bottom category), applicants required specific academic or vocational credentials. Those in the second-lowest category—secretaries and clerks—held a Baccalaureate I diploma or its equivalent. Administrators in higher categories held at least a university degree. Irrespective of category, all appointees to the cadre first served a one-year probationary period. They also had to sit for a position-specific qualifying exam, either at the time of application or before they would be removed from probation.[186] Successfully completing both the probationary period and the qualifying exam resulted in a permanent appointment (*tathbit*) into the civil service.

Once part of the permanent cadre, a state bureaucrat had guaranteed employment until the age of sixty-five—at which point they either retired (with a minimum of twenty years of service) or the government discharged them. Retirees received a pension for the remainder of their lives, whereas discharged bureaucrats received a dismissal indemnity.[187] Pension security and a range of other fringe benefits accompanied this position. Working hours averaged thirty-four per week in the fall, winter, and spring (i.e., 8 a.m.–2 p.m.) and thirty per week in the summer (i.e., 8 a.m.–1 p.m.). Bureaucrats were entitled to twenty days of paid annual leave, thirty days of paid sick leave, and an additional three months of paid maternity leave in the case of female cadre members. They also received an automatic raise to the next salary grade every two years—except when the raise meant a position grade promotion, in which case it was after a three-year period and only if other requirements were met.[188] Finally, the 1953–55 personnel laws also guaranteed a range of allowances for technical specialization, family dependents, overtime, travel, and disability.

Despite significant centralization and standardization, the 1953–55 restructuring of public administration and the civil service did not fully address many long-standing problems, as bureaucratic practices remained far removed from the principles set out in the personnel law.[189] Inadequate compensation was paramount among these issues. Total income for the rank and file of the bureaucracy was barely enough to provide subsistence for themselves and their families.[190] The new salary scales and allowance systems were significantly higher than those in place during the transition to independence, yet they failed to keep up with cost-of-living increases. Limited opportunities for promotion across categories compounded the situation.[191] While certain private sector jobs paid more than their public sector counterparts, the turnover rate in the public sector appears to have been minimal. Unstable employment prospects in the private sector, coupled with far fewer fringe benefits, particularly for those who worked as janitors, office boys, secretaries, and clerks, discouraged most from abandoning a government job.

Problems of qualifications and centralization also plagued the bureaucracy. Recruitment into the permanent cadre was effectively reduced to meeting the minimum requirements. Most applicants only submitted a photocopy of their identification card, police record, and educational degrees. There was neither an application form nor any other mechanism to demonstrate skills and experience. The salary scale compounded this issue by remunerating personnel on the basis of the official titles rather than their specific job responsibilities. At the same time, internal procedures required high-level approval for the most mundane decisions. This concentrated power among top-level bureaucrats, created high transaction costs and waiting times for those engaging the bureaucracy, and encouraged routine deferral to higher authority. Such practices echoed those of the French colonial period when the High Commission required Lebanese bureaucrats to refer all administrative decisions to the relevant French advisor attached to their ministry or office.

Sectarian allotments were another problem that disturbed the bureaucracy.[192] As a result of recruitment patterns prevalent during the French colonial period, Christians were overrepresented in the civil service. Furthermore, ministers and top-level bureaucrats sometimes gave preference to certain applicants as a way of demonstrating sectarian loyalty or inclusivity. Obviously, both of these motivations were in conflict with meritocratic hiring practices. In fact, an intense public debate erupted in 1953–54 around the sectarian distribution of public sector employment, particularly in top-level positions.[193] It culminated in the cabinet establishing a committee to investigate the issue.[194] No record of committee activities has come to light, suggesting that it probably went dormant shortly thereafter. Nonetheless, the underlying issue resurfaced periodically.[195]

Political interference and corruption also characterized the Lebanese state bureaucracy. The president, cabinet members, and parliamentarians frequently intervened in high-level appointments in the bureaucracy, to reward allies, restrain critics, or otherwise demonstrate their power. They also used the institutional and financial resources of certain ministries, attempting to facilitate their reelection or to personally enrich themselves.

Despite these long-standing problems, the structural experiences of public sector workers had significant effects in producing a degree of corporate consciousness. In contrast to relatively short-term ministerial positions, directors general and other top-level bureaucrats maintained institutional continuity and memory within their ministries. They also played a critical role in drafting and reforming various state initiatives and strategically negotiating opportunities to advance these initiatives vis-à-vis cabinet and parliamentary politics. Joseph Naggear (1908–2006) and Ibrahim Abd-El-Al (1908–59) exemplified these tendencies.[196] Both engineers with significant records of public service in the Ministry of Public Works, their names became synonymous with calls for statist development. In 1933 Naggear began serving as a consulting engineer for the Lebanese Ministry of the Interior and was appointed director of the Water Service in the Ministry of Public Works in 1938. He went on to serve in multiple state institutions, including the EPDB and the Litani National Authority. Abd-El-Al began his career in 1932 with the French High Commission's Hydraulic Studies Board, moving to the Ministry of Public Works Water Service in 1938, and then reaching the position of director general of the Ministry of Public Works in 1949, a position he held until his death in 1959. Other bureaucrats who played an important role in shaping state institutions during long-term public sector employment include Nadim Harfush (b. 1907) of the Ministry of Social Affairs, Anis Saleh (b. 1907) of the Ministry of Justice, Halim al-Rumi (1919–83) of the Lebanese Radio Station (Mahattat al-Idha'a al-Lubnaniyya), and Fu'ad Shadir (b. 1905) of the Customs Administration and Ministry of Public Works.[197] These bureaucrats' long-term career trajectories and horizons inclined many of them to advocate for a larger and more activist role for state institutions. Through media appearances, lectures, conference presentations, and book publications, they participated in public debates about the general role of state institutions and particular state-led projects.

Lower-level public sector employees also organized themselves and lobbied their superiors, the cabinet, parliament, and the public. Such efforts largely centered on demands for higher remuneration, better benefits, and—in the case of temporary workers—inclusion in the permanent cadre. The 1946 Labor Code recognized the right of workers to form unions, but excluded those in state institutions. The 1953–55 public administration and basic personnel laws introduced an explicit ban on the formation of public sector unions. These measures betrayed the reality of labor grievances and efforts by both the permanent cadre and temporary workers to organize around them. By 1956, a coalition of civil servants formed the Committee of Employee Rights to demand higher salaries and faster advancement across the pay scale.[198] Mobilizations of this nature inspired repeated revisions of the compensation paid to civil servants in 1957, 1959, and beyond, all the while maintaining the basic bureaucratic organization and normative assumptions introduced in 1953–55 through the public administration and personnel laws.[199]

In addition, workers in recently nationalized agencies like the Beirut Water Company or Beirut Electricity Company and semiofficial agencies like the railway company regularly sought recognition as part of the permanent cadre. The most notable example is the repeated mobilizations among the ranks of the Telephone Administration (Maslahat al-Hatif). The telephone system of Lebanon originated as part of the French military communication infrastructure. While access to the system was extended to civilians during the Mandate period, the Lebanese government did not secure control over it until after World War II. Despite significant upgrading and expansion of telephone infrastructure by 1952, the Lebanese government had incorporated only 904 individuals out of the 2,303-person staff into the permanent cadre.[200] That year, the mostly-women temporary workers of the Telephone Administration went on strike, initiating a perennial struggle to improve working conditions, increase benefits, and secure job permanency for all telephone employees.[201] Permanent workers in the administration frequently struck with the temporary workers, while the concomitant public debates articulated particular notions about the professionalism and loyalty of public sector workers and the responsibility of the government in cultivating and retaining them.

CONCLUSION

The period 1943–55 featured the expansion, strengthening, and centralization of state institutions. These dynamics were the function of top-down initiatives, bottom-up demands, or both, depending on the specific institutional arrangements in question. Throughout, state building and state institutions' centrality to the restructuring of political, economic, and social relations in Lebanon were defining features of discourses about legitimacy. Politicians, businessmen, party activists, and other Lebanese regularly invoked the idea of *al-dawla* in pursuit of their particular vision of the postcolonial. Yet their critiques, proposals, and mobilizations usually centered on specific institutional arrangements. In some cases, these institutions were indeed ministries and their various subdivisions. In most cases, however, they were much more microlevel arrangements such as laws or services. In the following chapters, I explore four examples of such institutional arrangements: the restructuring of the military and education systems, the introduction of a comprehensive labor law, women's suffrage, and electric utility services in Beirut. I highlight important historical legacies, normative understandings, and contingent events that contributed to the making of each.

Three

IN BARRACKS AND SCHOOLS

IN DECEMBER 1953, THE LEBANESE PARLIAMENT PASSED A LAW mandating military training (*al-tadrib al-'askari*) during the final two years of all public and private secondary and vocational education.[1] All students, fifteen years of age or older, were required to participate in this training. Official exemption was only possible with a decision from the minister of national education, accompanied by documentation from a military doctor that the student's health condition precluded their training. Failure to comply could result in expulsion from the school. While the mandatory training law primarily envisioned males, female students were also subject to it, albeit with the proviso that they only be trained in passive defense (*al-difa' al-salbi*).[2]

The details of the law revealed an intricate collaboration between two of the ministries—National Education and Defense—featuring some of the most dramatic changes during the 1943–55 period. The Ministry of National Education ensured that schools complied with the new requirement and was responsible for sharing student rosters with the Ministry of Defense and facilitating student attendance of both in-school training and summer training camps. It was also responsible for introducing a new physical training (*tadrib badani*) requirement into schools. While the ministry could decide the educational level at which to incorporate this new requirement, this incorporation had to occur prior to the final two years of secondary school and adhere to the Ministry of Defense's guidelines for physical training. The latter conducted the actual military training (but not the passive defense training), which covered morale, foot drill, and weapons training. The Ministry of Defense was empowered to recall students who completed their ordinary schooling and two years of mandatory military training for up to one month of additional training per year until they reached the age of thirty-five. During that same period, the ministry also had the authority to draft such persons into military service "to defend the safety of the homeland" (li-l-difa' 'an salamat al-watan).

The passage of the mandatory military training law was the culmination of an episodic and iterative public debate dating back to the 1943 struggle for independence. Repeated calls by student groups, political parties, women's organizations, and elite personalities, along with intense discussions in several parliamentary committees provided the bases of that public debate. The need stemmed in part from the exigencies of Lebanon's transition to independence and the realities of French and British colonial policies across the Middle East and North Africa. In addition, the partition of Palestine, the establishment of the State of Israel, and the expulsion of over 700,000 Palestinians were extremely significant in stimulating the demand for military training. Yet this perceived imperative also emerged logically from normative understandings of independence, sovereignty, and state building; the symbolic meaning of national armed forces and educational systems; and assumptions about the role that they both played in safeguarding sovereignty and promoting state building. To explore these dynamics, this chapter analyzes the processes, rationales, and institutional outcomes associated with the establishment and development of Lebanon's armed forces and the country's postindependence educational sphere.

NATIONAL VERSUS FOREIGN TROOPS

During the 1943–46 transition to independence, the French were most reluctant to transfer command of the Special Troops of the Levant, which was the only locally recruited military force that had formed a component of the French Army of the Levant since its founding in the Mandate era. The French military command had reorganized the Lebanese component of the Special Troops into a three-thousand-strong brigade in June 1943.[3] In the context of the piecemeal 1943–46 transfer of the Common Interests, the French Army replaced the French commander of the Lebanese brigade with Lebanese Colonel Fu'ad Shihab (1902–73).[4] During this period, Lebanese cabinet ministers and parliament members showed little initiative in pursuing the issue of the Special Troops. These officials appear to have been content with a June 1944 agreement for the French to place a few units of the Lebanese brigade under the control of the Lebanese government.[5] These units and their personnel actually numbered less than 20 percent of the ostensibly Lebanese component of the Special Troops. Nevertheless, French Delegate General and Commander in Chief of the Free French Forces in the Levant Étienne-Paul-Émile-Marie (Paul) Beynet (r. 1944–46) and Lebanese President Bishara al-Khuri seized the opportunity to a hold a military transfer ceremony in the Beirut Municipal Stadium (Mal'ab Bayrut al-Baladi, est. 1940).[6]

During the ongoing Lebanese-French negotiations, popular mobilizations played a critical role in keeping the immediate and complete transfer of the Special Troops at the center of discussions. Since November 1943, the Kata'ib, Najjada, League of Nationalist Action, and National Congress had been publicly demanding the Special Troops' transfer and the evacuation of all foreign military forces, as well as the establishment of a national army. These parties' mobilizations were echoed by those mounted by secondary and university students. Each group issued petitions and published pamphlets, flyers, and articles framing their demands as necessary prerequisites for genuine independence.[7] Aware that most politicians lacked interest in these issues, these constituencies addressed their demands directly to the Lebanese government by circulating petitions and staging demonstrations.

A student strike on January 29, 1945, and the general strike it precipitated the following day marked one high point of these mobilizations.[8] Using slogans like "No freedom or independence without the army" (la hurriyya wa-la istqlal illa bi-l-jaysh) and "Symbol and sole guardian of any independence" (ramz kul istiqlal wa-siyyajih al-wahid), demonstrations and the ensuing strike rocked Beirut and several other urban centers.[9] A broad coalition of students representing public and private schools and universities marched across the city, stopping at the Ministry of Foreign Affairs, Parliament, and Prime Minister's Office.

Students supplemented these street actions with letters to senior Lebanese and foreign officials. The Student Council of the American University of Beirut (AUB) sent one such letter to Prime Minister Abdul Hamid Karami (1890–1950).[10] The text announced the students' participation in the strike "in solidarity with all the students of Lebanon," and asked the government to "do all it can do and more to assume command of the Lebanese army."[11] A group of Lebanese, Syrian, Iraqi, Jordanian, and Palestinian students claiming to represent the student body (*hay'at al-talibat*) of the American Junior College for Women (AJCW) sent a similar letter to the British minister expressing their support for the Lebanese and Syrian governments' efforts to take control of the military forces of their countries.[12]

This student-led initiative brought the country to a standstill, a development that appears to have caught major political parties off guard. Despite some student calls to strike for a third day, several political parties held impromptu meetings on January 30, resulting in calls for the strike's end.[13] The Kata'ib and Najjada issued a joint statement asserting that the demand for a national army was "an age-old one among our ranks," recognizing the "students and the people's honorable stance" on the issue, committing to this goal, but also calling for a suspension of the strike.[14] The National Congress similarly called on "the Lebanese people" to "resume their regular occupations" and "leave the task of realizing national aspirations to national authorities."[15] Such sentiments echoed those expressed in a government statement issued on the morning of the second day of the strike. It thanked "the people, at the forefront of which were students," and asserted that "the cause now demanded that everyone disperse to their jobs and studies so as to give the government the opportunity to work in a calm atmosphere."[16]

The cabinet also took note of the strike's significance. It immediately dispatched a memo to the French High Commission.[17] This document constituted the first sincere attempt by the Lebanese government to demand the full and unconditional transfer of the Special Troops to its control. A few days later, the parliament unanimously passed a motion supporting the cabinet's efforts to secure control of the Lebanese brigade.[18] This action bought the government some time vis-à-vis potential protests. The French nevertheless continued to stall.

In May 1945 the issue erupted again, this time in response to two separate instances of French troop-carrying ships docking at Beirut.[19] It is not clear whether these were reinforcements or just replacements for other personnel rotating out.[20] Yet in response to official letters of protest from the Lebanese and Syrian governments, Beynet declared that French strategic interests necessitated the long-term maintenance of military bases in the Levant.[21] Returning to an issue the French had repeatedly attempted to discuss, he made the Special Troops' transfer to Lebanese control contingent upon completing an agreement that would safeguard those French interests.

Therefore, from May 18 to 21, 1945, many Lebanese took to the streets in support of a second general strike.[22] Three factors made this round of mobilization distinct from previous ones. The strike originated in Beirut on Friday, May 18, spread to Tripoli, Sidon, and Tyre on Saturday, and by Sunday included several provincial towns. Yet no known group's name accompanied the call or was subsequently recognized as spearheading the effort.[23] Most political parties held their first organizing meetings on the afternoon of the strike's initial day, indicating that they were responding to the mobilizations rather than leading them.[24] In addition, political party statements issued during the strike emphasized the need to maintain a united front and stand with the Lebanese government.[25] Such declarations betrayed leading party activists' sense of unease at how ubiquitous and decentralized strike actions had become. A final element unique to this mobilization was the broad-based call for the government to accept volunteers for a national guard that could be mobilized in the ongoing struggle against the French.[26]

Yet on Monday, May 21, 1945, the Lebanese government once again called for an end to a general strike.[27] Thus on the following Tuesday and Wednesday, businesses opened and schools resumed classes across the country.[28] Nevertheless, students staged a small march in Beirut echoing demands for the Special Troops' transfer and the creation of a volunteer-based national guard.[29] They marched across the city, stopping at several Arab diplomatic missions and concluding at the Presidential Palace. The next day, Thursday, May 24, Beirut residents struck again.[30] Notable among those participating were students from the Maronite Collège de la Sagesse (Kulliyyat al-Hikma), who had abstained from the January 1945 student strike.[31] They marched through the city's streets demanding that the government immediately form a national guard.[32] Furthermore, on that same day a delegation of female AUB students made a similar demand during a meeting with Prime Minister Karami.[33] Finally, later that day the Beirut Lawyers Syndicate (Naqabat al-Muhamiyyin fi Bayrut) announced a three-day strike beginning Friday, May 25.[34]

In the face of repeated, decentralized, and anonymously organized Beirut-wide strikes, the National Congress called for a general meeting of political parties and other popular organizations.[35] Representatives of the Kata'ib, League of Nationalist Action, Lebanese Communist Party, and Arab Women's Federation of Lebanon attended and made speeches in support of the Lebanese government. Of particular note was the attendance of the then-Maronite Archbishop of Beirut Ignatius Mubarak (1876–1958). He gave a profoundly conservative speech calling for an end to all strikes—claiming that they undermined the public good, disrupted the economy, and were a detriment to students' education. The meeting concluded with the issuance of a collective declaration calling for the end of the strike and justifying such demobilization efforts as allowing the government to "address the national cause in an atmosphere of utmost confidence."[36] The following Friday, May 25, Beirut residents resumed their normal work and school routines.

Nevertheless, the Lebanese government was under continuous pressure to deliver on the promise of independence. Thus it took more forceful action, claiming the mantle of popular protests and seeking to speak on their behalf.[37] The volatile nature of popular mobilizations in Syria further altered the calculations of Lebanon's government and leading political parties. During May 27–30, the French responded to the concurrent escalation of protests in Damascus, Hama, and Homs by shelling these urban centers.[38] On May 31, the British, fearing the total dissipation of their position in the Levant, ordered the French Army to stand down and return to their barracks.[39] The United States, under pressure from Lebanese and other Arab diplomats attending the United Nations Conference on International Organization (April–June 1945) and concerned about potential consequences, endorsed the British intervention and signaled its disapproval of French actions in the Levant.[40] In this context, President al-Khuri sought to bolster his domestic stature by announcing the popularly demanded establishment of a national guard, for which male citizens between the ages of eighteen and thirty-five could volunteer at designated recruitment centers.[41]

Political parties now took the lead, calling for another national general strike on Thursday, May 31, through Monday, June 4, 1945.[42] At this time they formed the Emergency Committee (Lajnat al-Tawari'), proclaiming it the sole legitimate leader of and speaker on behalf of the strike.[43] The Beirut and North Lebanon lawyers' syndicates joined by announcing that they would strike in solidarity.[44] The committee subsequently organized a march for Saturday, June 2, and reduced the length of the general strike, decreeing its end on Sunday.[45]

The shifting nature of regional and global politics reinforced the Lebanese (and Syrian) position. To break through the negotiation deadlock with the French, the Lebanese government now sought to leverage its multilateral relationships. Along with the Syrian government, it submitted a formal complaint to the Arab League (est. 1945), which subsequently passed a resolution condemning the French military presence in Lebanon and Syria as a violation of both countries' independence and sovereignty.[46] The league further called for the immediate transfer of the Special Troops and the evacuation of the French Army. A few weeks later (June 25, 1945), the United Nations Conference on International Organization concluded with the adoption of the UN Charter.[47] Understanding the conference's political significance vis-à-vis questions of sovereignty, French diplomats had attempted but failed to deprive Lebanon of participation.[48] While the UN Charter replaced the League of Nations Mandate system with the UN International Trusteeship System, it excluded from the latter system UN member states. As a participant in the founding conference and signatory to the charter, Lebanon's membership in the United Nations was a forgone conclusion and was formally confirmed in October 1945.[49]

In the interim between the Arab League decision and the conclusion of the UN conference, popular groups continued to mobilize. They now enhanced their demand to include the complete evacuation of French troops from Lebanon (and Syria). In turn, the National Congress declared the continued presence of French troops in Lebanon to be destabilizing the country.[50] The congress was particularly concerned about French control over the radio station, which they used to propagate their viewpoint, and over the telephone service, which they used to monitor and disrupt communications among and between political groups. Thus a group of political parties met and issued a joint statement echoing the now-ubiquitous call for the complete evacuation of French troops.[51] They buttressed this demand by emphasizing Lebanon's independence, its support for the Allied war effort, and its status as a founding member of the United Nations.[52] The list of signatories to the coalition's joint statement revealed the ever-widening networks that anchored mobilizations over the issue of evacuation. In addition to the groups that formed the Emergency Committee, the coalition now included—formally or informally—the League of Nationalist Action, the Vanguard Organization, the National Appeal Party, the Armenian Communist Party (Hizb al-Arman al-Shuyu'i), the Dashnak Party, the Ramgavar Party, the Armenian Renaissance Party (Hizb al-Nahda al-Armaniyya), the League Against Nazism and Fascism, the Student Committee (Lajnat al-Tullab), the Federation of Syndicates (Ittihad al-Naqabat), the Drivers' Syndicate (Jam'iyyat Ta'addud al-Sawwaqin), the Journalists' Association (Jam'iyyat al-Sahafa), the Arab Women's Federation of Lebanon, the Beirut Traders Association (Jam'iyyat Tujjar Beirut), and the Beirut and Mount Lebanon Chamber of Commerce, Industry, and Agriculture. Some of these organizations also issued individual statements.[53] In addition, popular groups in other states voiced their support. For example, Egyptian feminist Huda Sha'rawi (1879–1947) sent a telegram to the Arab League in the name of the General Confederation of Arab Women (al-Ittihad al-Nisa'i al-'Arabi al-'Am).[54] Sha'rawi protested French policies in Syria and Lebanon, arguing that they contradicted the Allied purpose of liberating Europe from tyranny. The telegram also asserted "the women of Egypt and the Arab world" were in solidarity with the women of Lebanon and Syria in their efforts to "defend the dignity of their countries."[55]

Several of these groups accompanied their demands for French military evacuation with actions challenging other French privileges in Lebanon.[56] The National Congress called on the government to dismiss all French citizens currently receiving salaries from state funds. Alternatively, the Najjada and Ghasassina petitioned the Municipality of Beirut to rename French-named streets after Lebanese "national figures." The municipality passed such a measure and established a committee to propose new names in consultation with Lebanese historians and writers. Furthermore, a group of secondary students at the Maqasid College announced their boycott of the French Baccalaureate exam in protest over French policies.

Mass protests, the emergence of a more radical popular consensus for the complete evacuation of French forces, and the Lebanese government's strategic use of the Arab League and the United Nations undermined French authority and prestige and fundamentally weakened the French negotiating position on the Special Troops. When the United States rejected a French proposal to establish an international commission of inquiry to investigate and recommend a solution to the impasse in Lebanon and Syria, French claims about the continuing applicability of their League of Nations Mandate in the Levant appear to have collapsed.[57] On July 8, 1945, France announced its readiness to transfer the Special Troops to Lebanese control.[58] By August of the same year, the Lebanese government had assumed control of the entire brigade, led by Colonel Shihab, whom it promptly promoted to general and appointed commander of the Lebanese armed forces.[59]

There still remained the matter of foreign troops' presence Lebanon. While the British had communicated a readiness to withdraw once the war ended, the French made no such commitments. In December 1945, they persuaded the British to support their plan for maintaining a military presence and deferring to the recently created United Nations for a final arrangement concerning the military security of the region.[60] The initial response of the Lebanese government was to secure assurances from the British government that its troops would not withdraw before their French counterparts.[61] Yet popular mobilizations once again spurred a more radical posture. Protesters not only railed against French and British policies, they also explicitly challenged the position of the Lebanese government, which they deemed accommodationist.

Many of the groups that mobilized supporting the Special Troops' transfer had simultaneously demanded the immediate and complete withdrawal of all foreign troops from Lebanon. Leading political parties reactivated the Emergency Committee, which had initially been formed in May 1945. The committee organized a general strike for Wednesday, January 2, 1946, which shut down the capital and significant parts of Tripoli, Zahleh, Riyaq, Sidon, Tyre, and Marja'yun.[62] In their memo to President al-Khuri announcing the strike, the popular organizations asserted that the committee represented the hopes and desires of the Lebanese people.[63] In fact, the memo's signatories embodied the further expansion of the coalition formally and informally working through the Emergency Committee. Most notable in this regard was the participation of the recently formed Union of Lebanese Women (Jami'at Nisa' Lubnan).[64] The memo also argued that the French-British agreement had "undermined Lebanon's sovereignty" and disregarded the UN Charter, "which was signed by fifty-five states with Lebanon among them."[65] It also addressed the Lebanese government, beseeching it to "not concede any of the country's rights" and "not abide by any agreement that harms the independence of Lebanon."[66] On the day of the strike, the executive body of the Emergency Committee sent a delegation to meet with the president, while party activists patrolled the streets of Beirut, coordinating the strike.[67]

Caught between popular movements demanding complete sovereignty and an intransigent foreign military presence, the Lebanese and Syrian governments turned to the inaugural meetings of the UN General Assembly and Security Council.[68] This new global stage provided the leverage that was lacking on the ground in the Levant.[69] It enabled the Lebanese and Syrian governments to deploy the tropes and concepts that the Allied powers asserted were the raison d'être of the new multilateral institution and the post–World War II international order. Speaking at the UN Security Council, Lebanese government representatives asserted that the presence of foreign troops violated the principle of national sovereignty and that the internal security of Lebanon was of concern only to the national government.[70] They also rejected the principle of negotiations and demanded an immediate and simultaneous withdrawal of French and British troops.

Mindful of the global forum, and seeking to balance between the legitimacy of Lebanese claims and fear of establishing precedents contrary to their interests and those of their allies, the United States submitted a resolution endorsing the principle of withdrawal yet stopping short of imposing it on France.[71] Recognizing this as an opportunity to undermine the credibility of Western powers while cultivating new relationships in the Middle East, the Soviet Union cast the first-ever veto at the UN Security Council, justifying it as an unqualified endorsement of the Lebanese and Syrian peoples' national sovereignty.[72] While no substitute resolution emerged, the strategy of turning to a global audience at the United Nations paid off. Within six weeks of the mid-February 1946 debate in the Security Council, Lebanon and Syria finalized agreements with France and the United Kingdom that committed to complete evacuation by December 31, 1946.[73] Throughout, popular mobilizations remained critical to pressuring the Lebanese, French, and British governments, who occasionally sought to stall negotiations or delay the finalization of an agreement.[74]

The Lebanese government marked the occasion by declaring December 31 a national holiday known as Evacuation Day (*yawm al-jala'*), seeking to inscribe this event within the broader nationalist narrative.[75] In addition, President al-Khuri presided over the installation of a commemorative plaque at the estuary of the Dog River (Nahr al-Kalb).[76] At that time, the site featured inscriptions about more than fifteen political regimes and military powers that had historically laid claim to the area, including Egyptian pharaohs, Neo-Assyrians, Romans, and Mamluks. More significantly, the site featured inscriptions by Emir Fakhr al-Din II (c. 1572–1635), Commander of the French Army of the Levant General Henri Gouraud (1920), and the Allied powers (1942). Al-Khuri spoke at the unveiling, thanking "the militant Lebanese at home and abroad since the beginning of Lebanese history to this day of our struggle."[77] Later that day, al-Khuri and other politicians laid wreaths at the Martyrs' Monument in downtown Beirut.[78] The Communists, the Najjada, and other popular groups participated in these official celebrations, while also organizing their own events.[79]

THE LEBANESE ARMED FORCES

The transfer of the Special Troops and the evacuation of French and British forces spurred numerous institutional developments within the Lebanese state. For example, in September 1945 the government created the Ministry of Defense as the institutional umbrella through which it would control the newly acquired Lebanese military units, the nucleus of the new Lebanese Armed Forces (LAF).[80] The LAF established its headquarters in Beirut, and distributed personnel across five military districts with command centers in Beirut (the capital), Tripoli (North Lebanon), Marja'yun (South Lebanon), Fiyyadiyya (Mount Lebanon), and Ba'albak (Biqa').[81] It also established a Lebanese military court, police force, and penal code.[82] Fiyyadiyya also became the site of a new military academy, replacing the former training facility of the Special Troops in Homs, Syria.[83] In addition to military subjects, cadets attended specialized nonmilitary courses covering Lebanese history, Lebanese geography, and the Arabic language.[84] The LAF also established several training facilities for enlisted men, including a physical training and combat school, a school for skiing and mountain warfare, and a flight school.[85] In 1949, the LAF created an air force, one equipped with a limited number of British training planes, British communications gear, and Italian bombers.[86] The air force received its first three (British) fighter jets in 1952 and added another four in 1954.[87] In 1953, the LAF also created a navy, which operated with borrowed boats until 1954, when it procured the country's first two (French) warships.[88]

The LAF command proceeded to Arabize the armed forces by mandating the use of Arabic and establishing a committee to ensure proper Arabic translations of military regulations and terminology.[89] It also sought to Lebanonize the armed forces. The LAF decommissioned the few Syrian nationals who had been attached to the units transferred to Lebanon and designed new uniforms and insignia.[90] The ministry also began publishing *al-Jundi al-Lubnani* (The Lebanese soldier), a monthly periodical for armed forces personnel.[91]

Soon after its creation, the LAF underwent significant transformations of its personnel, training, and equipment. Contemporary estimates put the number of the Special Troops transferred to Lebanon in 1945 at approximately 5,500 officers and soldiers.[92] Yet by the end of 1948, LAF personnel numbered an estimated three thousand persons, both officers and enlisted men.[93] Such a contraction in the overall number of troops reflected several trends. On the one hand, during the lead-up to the transfer of troops, many soldiers took one of four actions impacting the actual number of the Special Troops that the Lebanese government would eventually command: some deserted during World War II, some chose to remain in the service of the French Army, some accepted the transfer to Lebanese command, and some applied for discharge.[94] On the other hand, the Ministry of Defense organized at least four military recruitment drives during 1945–47 alone.[95] These and subsequent recruitment efforts appear to have been relatively successful.

Beginning in 1950, the LAF displayed continuous growth in its ranks, increasing from approximately 4,500 troops in 1950 to about 5,500 in 1951.[96] By early 1955, the LAF stood at 6,584 men and proposed expanding its numbers to 14,000 over the next three years.[97] Enlistment in the LAF was voluntary, lasted for a period of at least three years, and required enlistees to be literate, able-bodied, aged between eighteen and twenty-five, and unmarried.[98] These requirements were significantly more stringent than those governing service in the Special Troops during the French Mandate.[99] In fact, joining the LAF was a relatively competitive affair. In 1951, for example, the LAF accepted only 700 of 4,000 applicants for enlistment.[100] Recruitment patterns among enlisted men are difficult to ascertain using the extant sources. At the officer level, however, there seem to be some important continuities between the late-colonial Special Troops and the LAF's first ten years.[101] In the early postindependence period more than 75 percent of officers came from towns and villages rather than cities. Just over 40 percent of officers hailed from Mount Lebanon, whereas the rest were evenly divided between Lebanon's other four governorates. In addition, at least two-thirds of officers were Christian. Yet the period also featured a marked drop in the percentages of Druze and Armenians serving and a significant rise in those of Sunnis and Shi'is. Reflecting this degree of historical continuity across institutional contexts, Lebanon's initial (1950) military code recognized service in the Special Troops, in Faysal bin Husayn's Arab army, in the Mount Lebanon *mutasarrifiyya* gendarmerie, and in the Ottoman regular army when counting years of service toward promotion or retirement.[102]

Public debate about the potential for and merits of mass conscription was episodic in the aftermath of independence. It usually surfaced during times of perceived national crises like the 1943–46 controversy concerning the presence of foreign troops, the 1948 Palestine war, and the 1949 attempted Social Nationalist Party (SNP) revolt.[103] Public discussions of the potentially contentious issue of mandatory military training for students was similarly episodic,[104] eventually culminating in the 1953 law requiring military training during the final two years of secondary and vocational education.[105] The government implemented this law, which many celebrated as an initial step in the process of imposing mandatory military service, in stages. During the 1954–55 school year, for example, 2,500 students attending a total of 55 schools participated in military training courses.[106] The 1955–56 academic year featured 3,500 students at 62 schools.[107] This implementation was apparently restricted to male students in its first two years at least.[108]

The military's expansion was not limited to personnel. It also included military barracks, housing units, and officers' clubs previously used by French and British troops.[109] Many of these installations remained French-owned properties until the 1948 monetary accord between Lebanon and France. The Ministry of Defense developed these facilities between 1946 and 1955 through a series of renovation and expansion projects, while also establishing a military hospital and the previously mentioned training facilities.[110] Exemplary of such developments was the transformation of the Military Beach Club (al-Hammam al-'Askari) into a key socialization site for officers of the LAF and the Internal Security Forces, as well as their families, and a select group of civilians.[111] As the club ceased to be a symbol of French military exclusivity, it increasingly hosted school sporting events, meetings of various associational groups, and public lectures.

Such expansion of human and material resources necessitated the repeated reorganization of both LAF units and the Ministry of Defense.[112] A civilian cabinet minister presided over the ministry, which was divided into a general directorate and an armed forces command. The ministry standardized recruitment, compensation, promotion, retirement, discipline, and discharge guidelines, while also instituting a pension plan.[113] In addition, officers and enlisted men received a range of benefits in the form of health care and memberships in consumer cooperatives and leisure and recreation centers.[114] The armed forces therefore evolved into an important engine of public sector employment and one of the few means by which Lebanese could achieve upward social mobility.

The LAF established important relations with its European and US counterparts, which helped it to become an important node of Lebanese diplomatic, military, and cultural relations with the international community. To develop the LAF, General Shihab frequently contracted foreign military advisors to train or advise specific branches or units. In doing so, he drew on trusted French officers with whom he had personal relationships. But Shihab also took advantage of the postindependence context to be more selective when sourcing such advisors. For example, while French advisors supervised training at the ski school, Belgian advisors directed instruction at the military academy.[115] And while a French officer advised the Lebanese Navy, a long-term British Royal Air Force training mission helped organize, train, and supply the Lebanese Air Force. Lebanese officers and enlisted men attended various training courses or served in temporary assignments to the US and British armed forces.[116] At the same time, British and US military personnel benefitted from the use of various Lebanese resources, docking ships at the country's ports, visiting its military bases, and pursuing Arabic language study.[117]

Such military cooperation further enmeshed Lebanon within the imperial orbits and networks of the United Kingdom and the United States. It also helped transform the LAF from an exclusively Francophone institutional identity to one increasingly steeped in Anglo-American weaponry, organization, and training. This was evidenced by the fact that English proficiency was made a requirement for all officers by 1955, a goal that was facilitated by the British Council's English courses at the military academy and the US Point Four English courses conducted in each of the military districts.

Contemporary diplomatic and foreign intelligence assessments asserted that the LAF successfully instilled in its personnel a significant degree of enthusiasm, confidence, and discipline.[118] These assessments simultaneously praised the LAF as an efficient and effective instrument for internal security, the role that the US Embassy in Beirut, State Department, and Defense Department self-consciously understood, supported, and facilitated.[119] This appraisal was also borne out before, during, and after the inception of the Nakba in 1948, when the LAF largely restricted itself to assuming a defensive posture along the border with Palestine.[120] Its only offensive deployment was the half-day tactical assault on the Palestinian border villages of al-Malikiyya and Qadas on June 5, 1948. After preemptively seizing the two villages, the LAF handed control of them to the Arab Salvation Army (Jaysh al-Inqadh al-'Arabi) on July 8, 1948, and redeployed to the Lebanese side of the border.[121] It apparently later refused to support the Arab Salvation Army during Israel's fall offensives in northern Palestine, allegedly ordering the Arab Salvation Army to withdraw from the border region altogether. The Israeli forces subsequently conquered the remainder of northern Palestine, expelling the Palestinian population of al-Malikiyya. They subsequently advanced into Lebanon, occupying fourteen to twenty villages, including Houla, in which they massacred scores of villagers. The LAF declined to militarily engage the

Israelis occupying Lebanese territory, who remained until the March 1949 armistice agreement decreed their evacuation.

Such problematic wartime performance does not negate the fact that the LAF continued to expand its numbers, centralize its administration, and develop its capabilities during the 1945–55 period. Instead, this performance must be understood in the context of those processes, which were circumscribed by the developmental logic of establishing an internal security force that simultaneously served as a conduit for diplomatic, military, and economic relations. Presidents Bishara al-Khuri and Kamil Sham'un, the many prime ministers they appointed, and Commander of the Lebanese Armed Forces Shihab understood and operated on the basis of this logic. Throughout 1945–55 LAF soldiers' duties included border control, destroying hashish crops and combatting banditry in cooperation with the Ministry of Interior, and operations against illegal logging and quarrying in collaboration with the Ministry of Agriculture.[122]

EDUCATING CITIZENS

Until the end of the Mandate, geography and tier circumscribed public education, limiting it to primary schools and a small number of vocational schools.[123] By 1939 there was a total of 177 public primary schools enrolling 18,306 students.[124] In addition, there was the School of Arts and Crafts (Madrasat al-Sanayi' wa-l-Funun) and the Normal School (Dar al-Mu'allimin wa-l-Mu'allimat), which were a vocational school and teacher training school, respectively. The geographic distribution of public primary schools reflected the High Commission's perception of a division of labor between state institutions and mediating elites. Thus schools were concentrated in areas outside of Beirut where private schools were far fewer in number.[125] The overall number nevertheless paled in comparison to the 315 private primary schools (foreign and local) that enrolled 113,206 students.[126] Foreign missionaries and local groups had also established 71 private secondary schools that enrolled another 8,399 students.[127]

In the wake of independence, the Ministry of Education expanded access to public primary education for new towns and villages while also expanding their presence in major urban centers. By the 1955–56 academic year, Lebanon had a total of 967 public primary schools with a total enrollment of 80,567 students.[128] These numbers represent a more than fourfold increase in the number of public primary schools compared to 1943, and more than double the number of enrolled students. The number of private primary schools rose and fell cyclically in the early postindependence period, reaching 731 in the 1955–56 academic year. Yet the number of enrolled students remained relatively stable, estimated at 113,024.[129]

The private primary education system increasingly lost ground to the public schools, which accounted for 57 percent of all primary schools and 41 percent of all enrolled primary students in the 1955–56 school year.[130] Significantly increased government attention to, and investment in, public education was one reason for the relative stagnation of private primary school enrollment in this period. Also important were the financial difficulties private schools faced due to the postwar period's various economic crises. Relatedly, French private schools—representing over 80 percent of the number of foreign schools and their students in 1943—and French-allied local private schools lost the special privileges and subsidies they had previously received after the French High Commission was liquidated.[131] In the late 1940s, the Lebanese government began providing funding to local private schools. Yet in the opinion of these schools' administrators, it was never sufficient.[132]

In addition, the Ministry of Education inaugurated a public secondary school system in 1951. By the 1955–56 academic year, the system educated 6,494 students at 60 schools.[133] It would take several years for this system to catch up with private secondary education, which in 1955–56 operated nearly twice as many schools and enrolled three times as many students.[134] The ministry also further enhanced the existing public vocational school system. It added an agricultural track (1944) to the School of Arts and Crafts in Beirut, and in 1946 opened branches in Tripoli, Sidon, and Zahleh.[135] By 1955, the government had opened two new specialized vocational schools: the Commercial School (Madrasat al-Tijara) and the Hotel School (al-Madrasa al-Funduqiyya).[136] Consequently, public vocational school enrollments nearly doubled between the 1945–46 and 1953–54 academic years, when it reached 601 students.[137] As was the case with secondary education, private schools continued to dominate vocational education, operating approximately 15 schools and enrolling over 2,000 students.[138]

The presidencies of both Bishara al-Khuri and Kamil Sham'un, along with the multiple cabinets formed by them, deemed the expansion of public education an important factor in the production of loyal citizens, as well as a hallmark of the sovereign state.[139] For example, in his September 1943 ministerial statement, Prime Minister Riyad al-Sulh promised to "raise the youth with a proper national(ist) education" (tarbiyyat al-nishi' tarbiyya wataniyya sahiha).[140] Arabic as the national language, teaching Lebanese history and geography, and eliminating illiteracy were the pillars of educating "a single generation united in purpose, sentiment, and nationalism" (nishi' wahid muwwahhad al-hadaf wa-l-shu'ur wa-l-wataniyya).[141] Expanding public education imbued with such purpose also facilitated more effective recruitment into the growing civil service, the nascent armed forces, and various economic sectors.

Yet ministers, parliamentarians, and bureaucrats were also responding to public demands for new and increased state expenditures on education. Such demands dated back to the colonial period, but took on a new urgency with the postindependence drive for national development.[142] Women's organizations, political parties, neighborhood committees, and village delegations lobbied ministers of education, other cabinet members, parliamentary deputies, and presidents through articles, petitions, and demonstrations. Activists demanded increased access to public education and curricula better suited to a newly independent country. In some cases, mobilizations formed around demands to open a new public school in a specific neighborhood, village, or region.[143] In other cases, they manifested in support for broader claims about the need for more public schools, increased government funding, and improved teacher training and working conditions.[144] Public and private school teachers variously navigated their relationship to these demands, as did the administrators of private schools and universities.

The Ministry of Education anchored its expansion of public education in curricular reform. The 1946 national guidelines for kindergarten, primary, and secondary school instruction exemplified this change.[145] In structural terms, the new system divided public primary education into elementary (*ibtida'i*, grades 1–5) and complementary (*takmili*, grades 6–9) years, with an additional three grades (10–12) constituting secondary (*thanawi*) public education. The Certificate examination (*imtihan al-durus al-ibtida'iyya*) capped the elementary grades and served as a filtering mechanism, permitting passing students to begin the complementary grades or pursue an elementary vocational program in mechanics (four years) or weaving (two years) at the School of Arts and Crafts.[146] The Brevet examination (*imtihan al-durus al-ibtida'iyya al-'aliya*) was similarly a prerequisite for beginning secondary education, enrolling in the Normal Schools' two-year program, or entering the School of Arts and Crafts' recently established three-year secondary program in agriculture.[147] Students who entered secondary school chose between literary (*adabi*) and scientific (*'ilmi*) tracks, and sat for the Baccalaureate 1 examination at the end of the eleventh grade. Upon passage of that exam, students became eligible to take the Baccalaureate 2 examination at the end of the twelfth grade.[148]

In terms of academic content, the cumulative effect of the 1946 curricular reforms was the Arabization and Lebanonization of public education. Arabic became the language of instruction for all elementary-level courses, including mathematics and science. Students could now also choose between English and French as their foreign language. Complementary primary education was similarly Arabized, although students chose from Arabic, English, or French as their language of instruction and examination for mathematics and science. The government also reinforced the Arabization of the public-school curriculum through its standardized testing. Students were now required to pass a written Arabic language exam for both the Certificate (as of 1949) and the Brevet (as of 1953), whereas only an oral component had been required during the Mandate era.[149] Furthermore, in order to pass Arabic, students were required to make a higher score on an Arabic exam than they did on any other subject tests. A student failed any subject other than Arabic if they received a score of zero (0), but failed Arabic if they scored less than a two (2) on the Certificate and less than five (5) on the Brevet or Baccalaureate Part 1 or Part 2.[150]

The 1946 reforms Lebanonized the public school curriculum through several additional requirements. First, the history and geography (*al-tarikh wa-l-jughrafiyya*) components now presented Lebanon as a historically stable geographic, cultural, and national entity, a sharp break with the Mandate-era policy of blurring Lebanon's and Syria's histories.[151] Students were now taught "Lebanese history" from antiquity through the 1943–46 transition to independence, and were required to memorize the country's geographic features. Second, the curricular guidelines for primary education strongly emphasized civic education (*al-tarbiyya al-wataniyya*), which was grounded in a celebratory overview of Lebanon's constitutional, legislative, and judicial systems.[152] Civic education also used Lebanese historical figures and folklore to impart proper morals (*al-akhlaq*). Finally, the curriculum introduced a new subject to primary education: music.[153] Public schools now exposed students to composition, while offering singing and dancing activities that complemented the curriculum's geography, history, and civics components. In this way, music classes became key sites for the propagation of elite views of Lebanese national culture.

Cognizant of the persistent disparity between the numbers of public and private school students, the Ministry of Education simultaneously increased government control over the field of private education.[154] It defined private schools as any educational institution founded or administered by private individuals, associations, or missions, thereby abolishing Mandate-era distinctions and hierarchies between them. The ministry further required all new and existing private schools to secure a license from the government, while increasing the requirements for registration as well as who can direct schools and teach in them. Finally, it required all private schools to submit annual reports detailing the number and qualifications of their teaching staff and the number and demographics of enrolled students.

The measures imposed on private schools were not exclusively administrative in nature. The Ministry of Education also sought significant influence over private school curricula. Initially, it made the teaching of Arabic compulsory in all schools, whether public or private. The ministry established the principle that the curriculum of any private school, be it Lebanese or foreign, had to conform with its "national" curriculum. The ministry subsequently imposed all of the 1946 curricular guidelines on the private schools. It also established greater scrutiny over the selection of textbooks at private schools, requiring the use of a preapproved list of textbooks for teaching history, geography, and morals and civics. The same policy prohibited the use of ministry-banned textbooks in any subject.[155] In fact, to escape such a ban, textbooks now had to advance students' understanding of Lebanese national identity, national pride, and independence.[156] The inculcation of nationalist perspectives of history and geography was of such concern to the ministry that it made Lebanese citizenship a requirement for teaching history or geography in any school.

In addition to its curricular interventions, the Ministry of Education instituted a system of standardized testing and accreditation in the private schools. One provision of the system required students matriculating through private schools to sit for state-administered Certificate and Brevet examinations in order to advance to the next educational stage.[157] Furthermore, the government made admission into local universities, the civil service,[158] and the liberal professions (i.e., law, medicine, and engineering) contingent upon completion of the Lebanese Baccalaureate or its equivalent, as determined by a ministerial committee.

These forms of state intervention into the organization of, and teaching in, both public and private schools were unprecedented. They necessitated a dramatic increase in the budget, staffing, and political significance of the Ministry of Education. In the wake of independence, the ministry not only assumed the authority that the French High Commission had zealously guarded for itself through the Service de l'Instruction Publique (Department of Public Instruction).[159] It also significantly expanded public education and state control over private education. In addition, the ministry's reforms collectively effaced the privileged status that French language and culture enjoyed during the colonial era.[160] Furthermore, the state regulated private schools much more thoroughly. While it maintained the Department of Public Instruction's policy of allowing private schools to adopt their chosen "teaching methods," it no longer afforded these institutions such discretion in adopting curricula and textbooks.

To justify these reforms, Lebanese officials echoed the very justifications activists used to lobby the government for such changes. As the introduction to a 1946 compilation of the new elementary and complementary curricula and examination system expressed it, these changes constituted "a big step toward unifying education and directing it in a national direction" (tawhid al-ta'lim wa-tawjihuh tawjihan wataniyyan).[161] Foreign observers serving at embassies and participating in survey missions understood the potential consequences of realizing such a goal and lamented the private schools' resulting loss of autonomy.[162]

MOBILIZING EDUCATION

As previously noted, intense public debate and lobbying efforts spurred the Ministry of Education's administrative and curricular reforms. At issue were assertions about Lebanese sovereignty, national identity, and the state's proper role in instantiating both through education. As such, educators, party activists, and others mobilized to realize their visions of the educational domain and educational spaces in the wake of independence. The Najjada, for example, displayed particular interest in the issue of Arabic language education and the teaching of history. Women's organizations echoed such concerns, but also sought to increase the availability and improve the quality of girls' education. For their part, the Kata'ib primarily emphasized the need for more public schools and the state's responsibility to better facilitate the moral, intellectual, and physical development of youth. While such groups collectively participated in the production of a normative understanding of the state's expanded role in education, they did not necessarily agree on all substantive matters concerning the educational curriculum.

Local viewpoints and mobilizations around education were articulated in a regional and global environment that was also more actively taking up the question of education and its relationship to sovereignty and development. Throughout the 1940s and 1950s, regional states increasingly embarked on educational reform as part of their transition to independence. For example, the nationalist government in Syria initiated educational reform in 1943.[163] It restructured the Ministry of Education, the educational hierarchy, the curriculum, and the national examination systems. It also removed French language education from the primary school curriculum and established tighter controls over private schools. Furthermore, the Syrian government increased the number of primary and secondary public schools as well as enrollments, while also subsidizing the opening of new private schools.

Educational reform was also taken up at the regional level. During 1946, the Arab League ratified a convention on cultural cooperation.[164] In parallel the league organized a conference about the role of education in promoting Arab unity.[165] The conference established committees on Arabic language, the geography of Arab countries, Arab history, and national education. These committees in turn produced several reports detailing the status of education regionally, the obstacles to unifying the educational experiences of students, and strategies for overcoming these obstacles. The recommendations primarily addressed the establishment of a minimum common denominator between member states' differing curricula and collective efforts to improve the teaching of Arabic. The conference thus inaugurated ongoing collaboration between ministries and educators of different Arab League states (including Lebanon) addressing questions of education.[166]

The UN Educational, Scientific, and Cultural Organization (UNESCO) supported such efforts in furtherance of its global mission of promoting universal education. UNESCO's general conferences, its regional activities, and its country-specific engagements served as critical reference points for government officials, educators, and advocates of increased state commitments to education.[167] At the same time, participation in UNESCO activities offered the Lebanese government and its officials an important level of legitimacy vis-à-vis their international counterparts and the local population.[168] This was the context for Lebanon hosting the third general conference of UNESCO in late 1948, preparations for which included the construction of the UNESCO Palace in Beirut.[169]

The Ministry of Education formed various educational commissions intended to give shape to a postindependence national education system while also navigating the plethora of groups and views that constituted the debate about it. In the lead-up to the 1946 curriculum, the ministry formed a forty-person commission in 1944–45, and a twenty-eight-person one in 1945–46.[170] The very formation of the commissions appears to have been a point of contention, resulting in the repeated reconstitution of the commissions' membership and frequent delays of their meetings.[171]

At the commission's initial meeting (August 1944), Minister of Education Philippe Takla (1915–2016) informed commission members that they would be divided into three subcommittees to explore the development of a new unified secondary education curriculum, a new unified primary education curriculum, and the reform of the School of Arts and Crafts.[172] He then acknowledged the criticism of the commission's composition and skepticism about its ability to produce a new curriculum. Takla nevertheless foreshadowed much of the issues that the new curriculum would address. He asserted that educational curricula must provide an upbringing (*tarbiyya*) that was scientific, cultural, and capable of creating what the country needed in this era of independence and freedom (*'ahd al-istiqlal wa-l-hurriyya*), a patriotic spirit (*ruh wataniyya*). Accordingly, he identified reinforcing the national language of Lebanon (Arabic), teaching Lebanese history and geography, and strengthening the body through physical education as the pillars of such a curriculum.

The dearth of subsequent press coverage of these commissions' internal deliberations reflects the degree to which they featured polarized views that the organizers and/or members felt were too sensitive for public disclosure.[173] Episodic press reports lamented the slow pace of progress and expressed particular concern as each of the 1945–46 and 1946–47 academic years loomed without the announcement of a new curriculum.[174] Commission members' general reluctance to speak publicly during or about their deliberations contributed to this air of secrecy. Two exceptions were al-Maqasid College Principal Abdullah al-Mashnuq (1904–88) and private school teacher Munir Nsuli. Throughout 1945 and 1946, both gave lectures and published articles, at times directly responding to one another.[175] Al-Mashnuq and Nsuli's argument reveals several points of contention that animated the commissions' work for two years starting in August 1944. These four points were the commission's size and whether it was too large to reach consensus; the commissions' composition and whether representatives of Francophone educational institutions were dominant within them; the degree to which private schools should be subject to curricular guidelines beyond the teaching of Arabic, history, and geography; and French's status as a foreign language vis-à-vis English.

In October 1946, the Lebanese government issued the curricular reforms that collectively set new guidelines for public education, imposed those curricula on private schools, increased state control over private educational institutions, and reformed and expanded public vocational education. The content of these decrees and the statements that politicians and bureaucrats made when announcing them revealed the government's determination to transform Lebanon's educational landscape.[176] As demonstrated from the earlier description of this new landscape, in doing so, the Ministry of Education, the cabinet, and the president ultimately denied the pro–status quo wishes of the commissions' Francophone majority members, significantly transforming the educational field in the process.[177]

Perhaps most telling of the stakes involved in these early debates and reforms was the formation of two different coalitions of private schools. Sagesse College and several other Francophone private schools created the Cultural League for Free Education (al-Rabita al-Adabiyya li-l-Taʿlim al-Hurr).[178] They primarily objected to what its members viewed as infringements on both their autonomy and their Francophone and Phoenician-centric conceptions of the Lebanese nation. Alternatively, al-Ahliya School (Madrasat al-Ahliyya) and other Lebanese private schools collaborated with several of their US and British counterparts to create the Secondary Schools' Principals' Association (SSPA).[179] SSPA members' greatest concern was the requirement that graduates of their schools had to pass the Lebanese Baccalaureate (or its equivalent) to enroll in local universities, practice any of the liberal professions, or join the civil service.

Both organizations continued to function well into the 1950s, though their concerns remained distinctive. The Cultural League lamented the loss of private-school autonomy, framing it as an infringement on the human rights of Lebanese citizens and a problematic merging of cultural and political imperatives.[180] They also demanded greater government financial support for private schools, citing the allegedly significant historical role of private education in Lebanon and the sector's majority share of enrolled students.[181] Alternatively, the SSPA focused on the requirement of the Lebanese Baccalaureate or its recognized equivalent for entry into professional schools, practicing the liberal professions, and working in the higher echelons of the civil service.[182] The Ministry of Education's refusal to recognize a US or British equivalent (while recognizing the French Baccalaureate) meant that non-Francophone secondary schools had to tailor their curricula to the Lebanese Baccalaureate exam. When taking the exam, these schools' students also suffered a distinct disadvantage relative to their Francophone counterparts, despite the 1955 introduction of an English-language version of the Lebanese Baccalaureate exam.[183] After all, the Lebanese Baccalaureate exam was modeled on the French one, and the French-language version of the exam had been in place since 1929.

Both organizations sought to leverage various resources and networks when articulating their grievances and lobbying the Lebanese government. The Cultural League rallied figures like banker and Lebanese constitution coauthor Michel Chiha (1881–1954) and the Maronite Patriarch Antoine Butrus Arida (1863–1955), while also acquiring foreign allies becoming an official member of the Congress of Cultural Freedom (est. 1950).[184] The SSPA worked closely with the AUB and the British Council in Lebanon. It eventually secured a US Point Four Department of Education grant to survey private schools in Lebanon and analyze the effects of the existing Baccalaureate examination system on both students' education and their career trajectories.[185]

The major curricular reforms and other examples of expanded state intervention in the education sector during 1943–55 produced mixed outcomes. On the one hand, such intervention significantly reshaped the educational landscape. The attendant debates and conflicts displayed important continuities with those of the French colonial period and resulted in postindependence transformations less far reaching than those that occurred in Syria.[186] These changes nevertheless represented an unequivocal intensification of state intervention that undermined existing privileges, greatly empowered the Ministry of Education, and mobilized a range of personalities and groups across the divides that animated debates on education.

On the other hand, the efficacy of these reforms was rather uneven. Nearly ten years after the government introduced these reforms, less than 2 percent of public schools were teaching English as a foreign language (with most others teaching French).[187] This was, in part, a reflection of a broader problem with teacher training in Lebanon at the time. Government efforts at producing qualified teachers did not keep pace with the expansion of public education. Thus the Ministry of Education relied on a supply of teachers who were graduates of private schools in which French-language education was dominant.[188] According to a 1953–54 survey of the education sector, there were thirty-nine teacher training programs/schools in Lebanon.[189] Only three of these were public: the Mandate-era Normal School—one for males and another for females—and the Teachers' Institute (Ma'had al-Mu'allimin wa-l-Mu'allimat, est. 1951). These schools enrolled 208 of the total 843 students in teacher training programs/schools that academic year.[190] Yet even the private teacher training programs/schools could not keep up with public education's increasing demand for teachers. The overall shortage of teachers in Lebanon was a frequent complaint in educational surveys and media coverage.[191] According to the same 1953–54 study,

45 percent of schools had only one teacher on staff, 13 percent had two, and 6 percent had three.[192]

School building infrastructure also remained inadequate. The growing number of public-school buildings could not meet growing demand for enrollment, and many existing school buildings were overcrowded or otherwise inappropriate for their purpose.[193] According to the oft-cited 1953–54 study, 32 percent of public schools had only one classroom, 23 percent had two, and 13 percent had three.[194] Such figures reveal the scarcity of instruction in schools ostensibly meant to offer a range of educational grades (e.g., first through fifth, or sixth through ninth). In 1955, the Ministry of Education controlled approximately 1,100 school buildings.[195] Yet by its own admission, few were structurally sound or appropriate as sites for teaching.[196] In major urban areas, the ministry frequently rented homes and converted them into schools. In rural areas, the ministry often made use of dilapidated buildings donated by locals. It was not uncommon for extreme weather or otherwise unsafe building conditions to result in the temporary or long-term closure of schools.[197] Such underdeveloped infrastructure was due in part to the lack of proper funding, as the ministerial budget rarely provided for land purchases or building maintenance. It was also due to a lack of construction and engineering capacity. In one instance, the director general of the ministry argued that the building, maintenance, and renovation of school buildings should be the purview of the Ministry of Public Works, which he described as overwhelmed with other projects and unresponsive to the needs of the education sector.[198]

Of equal importance was the ways in which postindependence public education shaped gender and class dynamics. Public schools helped reproduce the gendered access to state institutions and normative division of labor and career trajectories of men and women. In 1953–54, only about 18 percent of public schools were exclusively for girls, with another 25 percent being coeducational.[199] Of total public-school enrollments, 37 percent were females, which accounted for 43 percent of all girls enrolled in both public and private schools, compared with public schools accounting for about 70 percent of all enrolled boys.[200] Broken down regionally, the percentages of female students in public schools were 57 in Beirut, 45 in Mount Lebanon, 33 in North Lebanon, 25 in South Lebanon, and 18 in the Biqaʿ.[201]

Expanded state intervention in education, whether in the form of curricular reform or administrative oversight, left intact French colonial policies that limited upward social mobility through education.[202] While postindependence governments significantly expanded public education, during the 1943–55 period they focused this expansion at the elementary level. During the 1953–54 academic year, nearly all public schools offered elementary education.[203] During the same period, only about 7 percent of public schools offered complementary education and less than 1 percent offered secondary education.[204] Such statistics reflect the attitude of key bureaucrats in the Ministry of Education. In a 1954 interview about education in Lebanon, Director General Najib Sadaka (1915–2011) acknowledged that the government was focused on primary education, that it had no specific plans for secondary education, and that private secondary schools provided adequate access to this level of education.[205] Sadaka further declared that most children should receive vocational training rather than attend secondary school. In this sense, Sadaka echoed French colonial bureaucrats who understood and used the education sector to shape class relations in both the material sense of who was allowed to pursue upward social mobility and the discursive sense of the futures Lebanese school children could imagine for themselves.[206]

In addition to effectively limiting its public education expansion to elementary education, the Ministry of Education also sought to limit the number of students entering secondary schools, universities, and the liberal professions. In this sense, the ministry continued the French colonial policy of ensuring the difficulty of official examinations and requiring said examinations to scale the educational and professional ladders.[207] The figures for May–June 1954 bear this out, as only 58.5 percent of the 14,071 Certificate candidates and 51 percent of 2,277 Brevet candidates passed their examinations.[208] That same season, the passing rates for Baccalaureate Part 1 and Part 2 were 14.3 percent of 1,960 candidates and 25.3 percent of 562 candidates, respectively.[209] These latter passing rates reflect a significant decline from the 1945 averages of just over 50 percent, despite a fourfold increase in the number of candidates.[210] Recall that educational reforms introduced during the 1946–55 period required students to pass the Lebanese Baccalaureate or the French (the only officially recognized equivalent) to enter university, practice the liberal professions, or enter the upper levels of the civil service. In 1955, it was estimated that only 6 percent of secondary school students were admissible to Lebanese universities due to the Baccalaureate requirement.[211]

Given its function as a gateway to upward social and economic mobility, the Baccalaureate examination's difficulty made it a frequent point of contention among students, teachers, bureaucrats, politicians, and the public. The 1943–55 period is replete with debates and mobilizations about the Baccalaureate exam.[212] For some, at issue was the ways in which the system privileged French education over Anglo-American education. Such complaints intersected with US policy objectives and Point Four activities in Lebanon, which helps explain the 1955 grant to study the efficacy of the Baccalaureate examination system mentioned earlier.[213] Additionally, the exam's difficulty incentivized some students to cheat and some teachers or bureaucrats to leak questions or discriminate in grading.[214] When these events became public knowledge, it prompted some critics to broaden their critiques to address the very purpose and efficacy of the educational system, if not the state itself.

Despite such mixed outcomes of the curricular reforms and the significant expansion of state intervention, schools were critical spaces for socialization, politicization, and mobilization during 1943–55. Education was one of the main issues underpinning popular and elite claims on state resources and was also a yardstick for measuring state conduct vis-à-vis visions of independence, sovereignty, and national identity. In addition, schools served as fertile recruiting grounds for various political projects. On the one hand, bureaucrats, politicians, and others viewed the school as a critical space for the disciplining of youth and inculcating them with particular sensibilities vis-à-vis nation, state, and the broader world. On the other hand, political parties and other associations recruited members and supporters from specific schools and mobilized those schools toward their broader goals.

STUDENTS AND TEACHERS AS STATE BUILDERS

As I have argued above, the educational sphere was an important issue around which people mobilized. It was also a site within and through which the public mobilized. Between November 1943 and late 1946, student and teacher mobilizations focused primarily on the struggle against the French (and their British allies) over the transition to independence. Students were a critical component of the November 1943 uprising and of subsequent mobilizations around the transfer of the Common Interests and the Special Troops, the evacuation of foreign troops, and the establishment of a Lebanese national army. Yet student mobilizations persisted well beyond the achievement of independence. They played a prominent role in protests and other forms of collective action. In fact, student demonstrations sparked some of the most dramatic popular mobilizations of the period. They were also critical components of other lesser-known mobilizations such as those protesting changes in the price of cinema tickets and tramcar fares. Furthermore, students were an increasingly important force in the expanding array of political parties. The ubiquity of student mobilization was not simply a function of the struggle over decolonization. It was also a reflection of Lebanese students' increasing capacity to mobilize. The most significant factor influencing this process was the expansion of primary, secondary, and university education. This expansion increased student opportunities—through producing shared experiences and characteristics—to form horizontal affiliations, whether conceptually or institutionally.[215]

The proliferation of student organizations was another important factor informing the capacity of students in Lebanon to mobilize. School-specific student organizations like student councils, committees, and clubs were one example of such organizations. There were also several attempts to organize students at multiple schools as a self-constituted interest group rather than as part of larger categories such as youth (*shabab*), neighborhood (*hayy*), or general organizational member (*'udow*). Initially, such efforts took institutional form through the Student Union Committee (SUC, Lajnat Ittihad al-Tullab).[216] Expansion in the committee's membership resulted in internal differentiation and the need for more specialized organization. In 1951, university students from the AUB, Saint Joseph University (USJ, Université Saint-Joseph), and the Lebanese Academy of Fine Arts (ALBA, Académie libanaise des Beaux-Arts) broke away from the SUC to form the Lebanese Federation of University Students (LFUS, Lajnat Ittihad al-Tullab al-Jami'iyyin). This move was in response to the frequency with which the SUC's secondary school student bloc outvoted the university student bloc.[217] To reflect this changed demography, the SUC subsequently renamed itself the

Student Union Committee of Secondary Schools (Lajnat Ittihad al-Tullab al-Thanawiyyin).[218]

It was common for students to be involved with, and take up leadership positions in, both organizations as they moved from secondary school to university. School administrations, the Lebanese government, and foreign embassies monitored these organizations and sought to influence their leadership structure and internal policies. For example, the Lebanese government twice prosecuted LFUS president and USJ law student Milhem Karam (1932–2010) for organizing two student strikes in 1953.[219] The USJ administration supported a group of students attempting to oust Karam as the law school representative and thus render him ineligible for membership in the federation's executive committee. At the same time, the US Embassy monitored Karam's activities, designating him as pro-Communist, and discussed his case with the Lebanese government. The membership of student organizations like the LFUS and SUC ebbed and flowed in response to a host of circumstances. For example, AUB students never officially joined the SUC even though they sometimes participated in the committee's campaigns.[220] Despite helping to draft the LFUS constitution and participating in its inaugural executive council, the AUB Student Council eventually withdrew from the federation.[221]

The third factor facilitating Lebanese students' capacity to mobilize was political parties' paying increasing attention to students and their activities.[222] In this period, the creation or reorganization of student sections was an important element of the Kata'ib, the Progressive Socialist Party, and the SNP strategies to expand membership. For example, these parties' publications began featuring columns or even entire sections dedicated to student affairs. In addition, the Communist Party supported the creation of the Student League of Lebanon (Rabitat al-Tullab fi Lubnan) as a framework for the mobilization of Communist and other leftist students.[223] The league affiliated with the International Union of Students (est. 1946) and sent delegates to its second World Student Congress (1950) held in Prague.[224] The Arab Nationalist Youth (al-Shabab al-Qawmi al-'Arabi), the original nucleus of what would become known as the Movement of Arab Nationalists (Harakat al-Qawmiyyun al-'Arab), was an altogether different example. In 1951–52, recent and soon-to-be graduates of the AUB formed the Arab Nationalist

Youth as a means to continue their activism through new modes of organizing.[225] They based most of their activities on the AUB campus but also recruited members and formed cells in several secondary schools, most notably those of the Maqasid system.[226]

One manifestation of the ubiquity of student mobilizations was the frequent marches and strikes protesting developments across the Middle East and North Africa region. In March 1951, secondary school students in Beirut, Tripoli, Sidon, and other urban centers issued public statements, sent telegrams to newspapers, and marched in the streets to condemn French violence in Morocco. The students unanimously supported Moroccan independence, with some demanding Lebanon sever all ties with France. In October of the same year, students from the Maqasid College for Boys, Maqasid College for Girls, and the Beirut school network of the Mission laïque française jointly marched in support of Egyptian Prime Minister Mustafa Nahhas Pasha's abrogation of the 1936 Anglo-Egyptian Treaty.[227] Security forces attempted to intercept them, but many of the students managed to reach Hamra Street and join AUB students who had broken open the campus's locked front gates. In January 1952, students at AUB marched in opposition to General Adib Shishakli's consolidation of authoritarian rule in Syria, which included the violent repression of student demonstrators in Aleppo. When AUB demonstrators attempted to march into the streets of Beirut, Lebanese security forces violently dispersed them, arresting more than fifty.[228] Those arrested were not released until students in Beirut, Tripoli, Sidon, and Tyre staged several days of solidarity strikes, including a hunger strike by thirty-five AUB students.[229] Around the same time, students of the Ja'fariyya College (al-Kulliyya al-Ja'fariyya) in Tyre held a demonstration condemning British policy in Egypt and French policy in Tunisia.[230] And in May 1953, students across Lebanon participated in the national day of action that several political parties organized to protest US Secretary of State John Foster Dulles's visit to Lebanon.[231]

In March 1954, security forces brutally dispersed an AUB student demonstration against the pending friendship treaty between Turkey and Pakistan, an Iraqi request for US military aid, questions around Lebanon's economic and military relationship to the United States, and the place of all these in the US-backed proposals for a "Northern Tier" strategy of containing the Soviet Union through agreements between pro-Western states.[232] This violent episode is one of the most well known of the early independence period, as it resulted in the death of one student demonstrator, the permanent paralyzing of another, the injury of twenty-six others, the arrest of a dozen more, and the suspension—and eventual dissolution—of the AUB student group al-'Urwa al-Wuthqa (The Indissoluble Bond, 1918–55).[233] Such incidents, however, were not confined to the AUB. When students first announced their intention to demonstrate, students from across the city were invited to participate.[234] The Lebanese cabinet declared all such demonstrations illegal and thus subject to the use of force. Cabinet members also asked the administrators of numerous schools to discourage their students from participating in the demonstration. Joint patrols of police and gendarmerie roamed the streets around Beirut schools. Several of the injured students were from schools other than the AUB: the USJ, Beirut Evangelical School (al-Kulliyya al-Injiliyya), Hawd al-Wilaya Public School (Madrasat Hawd al-Wilaya al-Rasmiyya), and Secondary Institute (al-Ma'had al-Thanawi).[235] In response to the public outcry against the government, security units were dispatched to multiple schools to prevent students from mounting a general strike.[236] Such efforts proved futile as a sufficient number of students boycotted their schools, compelling many administrators to declare an early beginning of spring break.[237] Students across the country struck for at least a week, including public primary school students in more remote locales like Hermel.[238]

Students also mobilized around issues of higher education policies and opportunities. In the wake of independence, Lebanese higher education was based in four institutions: the USJ, AUB, AJCW, and ALBA. French Jesuits established the USJ in 1875, eventually creating schools of medicine, engineering, law, and humanities.[239] The American Board of Commissioners for Foreign Missions established the Syrian Protestant College in 1866, which became the AUB in 1920.[240] By independence, the university featured schools of arts and sciences, medicine, dentistry, and pharmacy. It subsequently established schools of engineering (1951) and agriculture (1951). The AUB first permitted women to enroll in its professional schools in 1921. It began admitting women as members of the junior classes in the School of Arts and Sciences in 1927. In 1835, the American Board of Commissioners for Foreign

Missions also established the Beirut Female Seminary, which became the AJCW in 1927.[241] The AJCW initially offered a two-year associate's degree, soon enabling women to enter the AUB as juniors. It subsequently began offering a four-year bachelor of arts degree in 1949, precipitating a 1950 name change to the Beirut College for Women. In 1952, the AUB became fully coeducational, while in 1955 the Beirut College for Women began offering a bachelor of science degree. Finally, Alexis Butrous (1915–79) and the Association des Musiciens Amateurs (Association of Amateur Musicians) established ALBA in 1943, initially offering programs in architecture, music, and visual arts.[242] By 1955 ALBA was also offering programs in law, politics and economics, and the humanities.

Between 1943 and 1950, students periodically staged protests against the costs associated with attending these institutions of higher education. One peak in such protests occurred at the AUB from December 1949 through March 1950. The newly created 1949–50 Student Council led by President Abdul Halim Saidi, a twenty-four-year-old Syrian medical student, prioritized this issue in response to student-generated petitions and flyers.[243] They first demanded that meal plans be made optional (given the perceived overpricing of cafeteria food) and a reduction in tuition.[244] Impromptu student demonstrations led to the establishment of a Tuition and Fees Committee, which requested financial records from the university administration and met with then-President Stephen B. L. Penrose (r. 1948–54).[245] The AUB administration effectively stalled and sidetracked the issue.

Student cost-of-attendance mobilizations reached their dramatic apex at the USJ in January–March 1951. In the late 1940s, the elimination of High Commission subsidies and continuous inflationary pressures led the USJ administration to raise tuition several times, causing students to request government relief on a regular basis. Receiving no response, students initiated a strike on January 22, 1951.[246] Representatives from the USJ's medical, engineering, and law schools formed a strike committee and held a press conference on the following day.[247] ALBA students joined the strike, echoing the committee's demand for government subsidization of students' education costs. The AUB Student Council rejected a motion to endorse and join the strike, despite the fact that the AUB campus was the site of incessant debates about the cost of education.[248] The decision elicited criticism, but apparently not sufficient anger to inspire AUB students to join their USJ and ALBA counterparts in the strike.

During the first week, striking students refrained from rallies and marches. Yet the government's stalling tactics, coupled with its repeated demands that students end their strike, radicalized the USJ and ALBA students. On January 30 they organized a demonstration.[249] The police immediately surrounded the crowd and dispersed it with water cannons, sufficient escalation to make parliamentarians discuss the matter.[250] These deliberations focused on the maximum amount of support and the categories of students who would be eligible to receive it. The MPs appeared to be reaching a consensus that only low-income students should be offered assistance and that such support would be capped at 100,000 liras. The strike committee rejected this proposal, insisting on a larger subsidy that would be distributed to all Lebanese students irrespective of their family income level. The students reformulated their demands, insisting upon government scholarships totaling more than 100,000 liras for all university students and the establishment of a national public university that would offer free higher education.[251] They continually escalated their demonstrations from then on, staging more frequent demonstrations and delaying the ability of the universities to resume their business as usual.

The government responded by holding a series of meetings with the strike committee and by violently dispersing student demonstrations.[252] On February 2, high school students struck in solidarity with the USJ and ALBA students.[253] A few days later, the Lebanese cabinet passed a resolution to distribute a total of 100,000 liras in student aid and to open a public university by October 1952.[254] The strike committee initially rejected such gestures, demanding a larger figure for scholarships, while a USJ student assembly vote in support reinforced their resolve.[255] The cabinet responded by announcing its intention to secure 300,000 liras to fund the establishment of the public university. This decision divided striking students, with some feeling it was time to call off the strike, while others argued they should push further.[256] On February 12, ALBA students unilaterally ended their strike, which led USJ students to suspend their strike on the following day.[257] On that same day, parliament approved an appropriation of 300,000 liras for the founding of a public university.[258]

The January–February 1951 mobilization by USJ and ALBA students inaugurated several important changes in the landscape of higher education. First, it compelled the government to commit to the establishment of a public university. The seed of this new university was the Higher Institute for Teachers (Dar al-Mu'allimin al-'Ulya), which would promote the recruitment and training of secondary school teachers.[259] On the one hand, the measure advanced recruitment and training of teachers, which served the specific purpose of expanding public education at the secondary level. On the other hand, it constituted the nucleus of what the government inaugurated in 1953 as the Lebanese University—the country's first and only public institution of higher education.[260] For many years the project was limited to the Higher Institute for Teachers. Yet it was the 1951 government commitment and the institutional nucleus it created that served as the basis of future popular and elite mobilizations demanding the foundation of the university. In the interim, the student mobilization had also secured an annual government-funded university scholarship scheme that totaled 100,000 liras. Furthermore, for several subsequent years students periodically called strikes—or threatened to do so—to ensure the appropriation and disbursement of that sum.

Another important aspect of the educational landscape was the mobilization of teachers to improve their working conditions. In the wake of independence, private school teachers used the Private Schools Teachers' Syndicate (Naqabat al-Mu'limin li-l-Madaris al-Khassa, est. 1938) to seek the resolution of many grievances concerning salaries, job security, promotion, and end-of-service benefits that had not been addressed during French colonial rule and the 1942 law governing their profession.[261] In 1946, the syndicate submitted a draft law to the government.[262] Despite a series of meetings between the Teachers' Syndicate and the prime minister, speaker of parliament, and minister of education, private school teachers achieved few of their objectives during the 1940s.[263]

The election of a new executive committee in December 1949 and the promulgation of a new law organizing public school teachers in July 1950 prompted the syndicate leadership to change their tactics.[264] It became more assertive in organizing general membership meetings in order to define the most significant goals and mobilize the membership around them.[265] The syndicate formulated an eight-point agenda designed to significantly improve working conditions and living standards.[266] These demands included an increase in termination indemnities, the payment of an indemnities formula in the case of death or disability, the introduction of a retirement indemnity for twenty years of service, full tuition waivers for all teachers' children, and an increase in the monthly salary range from the current 25–135 to 50–350 Lebanese liras, with a classification system similar to that of public school teachers.

The syndicate framed these demands as a call on the government to fulfill its role as the guardian of youth education and guarantor of citizens' dignity. Private school teachers from across the country publicly supported these demands and the syndicate's performance. They attended general membership meetings, issued statements to the press, and liaised with different popular organizations.[267] All of these efforts ultimately bore fruit, as in November 1950 the minister of education submitted to the cabinet a draft law incorporating most of the syndicate's demands.[268]

Sensing the successful momentum of the teachers' syndicate, and equally alert to the shifting balance of power between the public and private education sectors, private school directors declared their support for the teachers, asserting that school administrations, teachers, and parents were united in their desire to preserve the quality of students' education while also finding a just solution to teachers' poor working conditions.[269] They nevertheless framed the issue as one of government responsibility to provide sufficient funds to meet teachers' demands, arguing that to do otherwise would undermine the financial viability of private schools. In an apparent attempt to assert a unified stance between schools and thereby shape the negotiations, fourteen schools announced the formation of a Conference of Private School Owners, Directors, and the Teachers' Syndicate (Mu'tamar Ashab wa-Ru'asa' wa-Naqabat Mu'allimi al-Madaris al-Khassa). The conference, whose primary purpose was lobbying the government for the necessary funds, declared itself the sole legitimate forum for addressing the grievances of private school teachers.[270] While the syndicate and its teachers participated in the conference and publicly acknowledged the administrators' position, they made clear that their priority was to secure their rights and they did not care whether the government or the private schools funded the new salaries and benefits they were seeking.[271]

Despite the private school teachers' early momentum, government officials (with back-channel coordination with private school administrators) employed various cabinet- and parliamentary-level stratagems to obstruct passage of the draft law. These officials and bureaucrats also introduced amendments to the draft legislation that made it less responsive to the demands of the teachers. At the same time, syndicate leaders held regular meetings to update teachers on developments while continuing to shuttle back and forth between the Ministry of Education, the Office of the Prime Minister, and relevant parliamentary committees. Students also mobilized in support of the private school teachers' campaign. From November 1950 onward, students from several private schools held organizing meetings to hear updates, deliberate on strategy, and issue statements in support of the teachers.

The syndicate issued several strike threats between December 1950 and February 1951. Sometimes the cabinet or a parliamentary committee moved the draft legislation forward at the last minute to avert a strike.[272] At other times, the teachers mounted a one-day strike that forced officials' hands.[273] On Friday, February 16, for example, private school teachers went on a one-day strike to protest proposed amendments to the law and the delay in its passage.[274] Many of the strikers gathered in the Grand Theater of Beirut, where speakers read aloud the statements of teachers from different parts of the country and the syndicate president explained the amendments proposed by the parliamentary committee on education. Those assembled agreed to resume their strike if the parliament failed to pass the law without amendment within one week and sent a delegation to meet with the prime minister and convey their decision.

One week later—on Friday, February 23—the syndicate held another public meeting to update its members on developments.[275] One report indicated that the parliament did not vote on the law in its Thursday meeting, wanting to permit the minister of education to negotiate with the education committee and thereby bring the final version closer to the teachers' demands. Thusly informed, the syndicate voted to postpone its strike until Wednesday, February 28, pending a parliamentary session scheduled for Tuesday. This decision proved unsatisfactory to the Tripoli contingent of teachers, who began an open-ended strike on Monday, February 26.[276]

Politicians read the apparent breakdown in syndicate discipline as a warning sign for the potential for a more radical constellation of teachers to assume leadership of the syndicate and its negotiation strategy.

On Tuesday, February 27, the parliament unanimously passed the new legislation with few changes.[277] The teachers secured a pay scale and promotion policy identical to those of their public school counterparts, expanded sick leave benefits, restricted school administrators' authority to discipline teachers, and introduced maternity leave and a retirement indemnity. The legislation nevertheless failed to fulfill all the syndicate's demands. Most notably, it required twenty-five years of service (rather than twenty) for retirement indemnity eligibility and excluded teachers working in free private schools (*al-madaris al-majjaniyya*) from the new law. The latter term designated private schools that did not charge tuition and were usually affiliated with religious orders and charitable networks, employers of a significant number of teachers. Overall, the passage of the new law represented a significant improvement on the status quo and constituted striking evidence of the syndicate's ability to mobilize resources for change.

The mobilization of Lebanon's private school teachers did not end in 1951. Their syndicate would subsequently participate in meetings with the Ministry of Education and representatives of private school administrations to finalize the details of the pension fund the new law required.[278] It would also frequently issue public statements or submit complaints to the government about the failure of some private schools to comply with the 1951 law. These lingering grievances and the election of a new president (1952) and parliament (1953) galvanized the syndicate to launch a campaign for a new and much more ambitious law.[279] They now turned their attention to expanding maternity leave benefits, introducing paid time off for marriages and the death of loved ones, decreasing the teachers' contribution to the pension fund, and limiting summertime service requirements.[280] The syndicate's mobilizations throughout 1954 and 1955 ultimately resulted in the new law's 1956 passage.[281] These actions included several strike threats and the adoption of a strategic plan for outreach to students' parents.[282] The further institutionalization of the student movement also meant that students were a more active component in this renewed campaign.

CONCLUSION

This chapter documents and analyzes the interaction of popular group mobilizations with the policies of incumbent politicians and the rapidly changing institutional framework of the armed forces and the education system. These accounts reveal how state officials and Lebanese citizens adapted ideas and practices as part of the broader imperative of state building. The armed forces and educational system emerged as critical sites for bureaucratic expansion in addition to the articulation of competing conceptions of independence, sovereignty, and state building. Both cases shed light on Lebanon's historically generated and evolving institutional landscape as well as the public discourse and popular mobilizations central to those changes. The subsequent chapters turn our attention from the more commonly understood sites of postcolonial state building to attend to the contingent yet critical sites that helped constitute the network of institutions that became the Lebanese state as well as the Lebanese political field itself.

Four

URBAN LABOR AND THE STATE

ON SUNDAY MAY 1, 1955, THE UNITED SYNDICATES OF WORKERS AND Employees (al-Naqabat al-Muttahida li-l-Mustakhdamin wa-l-'Ummal) held a celebration at their Beirut headquarters to mark International Workers' Day ('Id al-'Ummal).[1] Cosponsored with the League of Workers and Employees Syndicates (Jami'at Naqabat al-'Ummal wa-l-Mustakhdamin), the event had approximately three hundred workers attending. The Minister of Social Affairs Rashid Karami and the labor officers of the Argentine, British, and US diplomatic missions in Lebanon were also in attendance. Later in the evening, the Argentine and British embassies held sequenced receptions.

Three other federations organized their own celebrations that day: the Allied Independent Syndicates (Ittihad al-Naqabat al-Mustaqilla), the North Lebanon Federation of Labor Syndicates (Ittihad Naqabat al-'Ummal fi Shamal Lubnan), and the Federation of Workers and Employees' Syndicates (Ittihad Naqabat al-'Ummal wa-l-Mustakhdamin). The first two groups held closed events in their Beirut and Tripoli headquarters, respectively.[2] The latter group held its event in Casino Butrus in the northeastern suburban area of Dawra.[3] The casino event had upward of two thousand attendees, the crowd flooding the street in front of the building.

The Katai'b Party and the Progressive Socialist Party (PSP) also organized Workers' Day celebrations, choosing to hold multiple events around the country.[4] Heads of these parties attracted the lion's share of their membership attendance. The Kata'ib's Pierre al-Jumayyil spoke at Cinema Roxy in Beirut, where he criticized the government for not doing enough for workers. The PSP's Kamal Jumblatt spoke at Cinema Tanyus in 'Alay, where he criticized communism and championed his definition of socialism.[5]

State institutions also mobilized around International Workers' Day in 1955. On Saturday, April 30, the Supreme Council for State Security (al-Majlis al-A'la li-Amn al-Dawla) met to discuss and implement measures to "maintain security" throughout the day.[6] It put all security forces on alert, dispatched teams to each of the major non-Communist celebrations, and sought to confiscate any leaflets they claimed incited strikes or promoted Communism. Over the weekend, security forces arrested at least nine people for possessing or distributing such leaflets.[7] Government offices closed on Monday, May 2, in observance of International Workers' Day, though many government employees were not aware of the closure.[8] After all, it was only one year earlier that the Lebanese government first recognized May Day (*awwal ayyar*) as an official holiday. Government agencies typically did not close the day after an official holiday that landed on a Sunday. Yet a number of workers and syndicates had belatedly lobbied the government to do so in hopes of encouraging private-sector institutions to also close in observance.

Workers' Day celebrations were an annual feature of Lebanon's labor movement and the broader political landscape of the early independence period. For most of the colonial period, it was typical for a small set of labor activists to mark the day in a private home. This was primarily a function of the fact that early attempts at such celebrations were organized by Communist and other leftist intellectuals, workers, and syndicates. During the postindependence period, International Workers' Day increasingly became a public event, organized by workers, syndicates, and federations representing a range of political affiliations and orientations. They often times included government officials and diplomatic representatives. Furthermore, political parties across the spectrum joined or organized celebrations. These changes reflected important shifts in how the state recognized workers' rights in the context of increasing membership and numbers syndicates, the ubiquity of labor mobilizations, and the elaboration of a state bureaucracy to manage them.

LABOR AND THE STRUGGLE FOR INDEPENDENCE

By the eve of independence, workers, their varied organizations, and their mobilizations formed an important component of the political and social landscape of Lebanon.[9] The colonial period featured a dramatic expansion of the urban working class, whose origins date back to the late Ottoman period, and a concomitant emergence of a mass labor movement.[10] Despite an increasingly organized and mobilized labor movement, the French High Commission constantly refused to enshrine the rights and protections that workers in France enjoyed. It deemed such legislation unnecessary in the case of Lebanon, claiming workers lacked the necessary spirit of cooperation and that charity was the only appropriate remedy for their impoverished conditions.[11] At the same time, the High Commission regularly repressed labor organizing efforts.[12]

French colonial authorities were nevertheless forced to respond to at least some of the workers' demands related to unemployment, working conditions, and income—especially during the Great Depression (1929–c. 1939). Beginning in 1932, the annual French reports to the Permanent Mandates Commission increasingly recognized the formalization of workers' groups and their varied economic grievances.[13] The High Commission inaugurated a public works program (1933), explored import-substitution industrialization schemes (1933), set general standards for industrial hygiene and safety (1935), and placed safety restrictions on women and child workers (1936).[14] Labor activism secured an across-the-board pay increase in 1936 to compensate for the devaluation of the French franc and the first iteration of severance pay in 1937.[15] That the labor movement accomplished much of this agenda in the context of a suspended constitution reflected two dynamics: their determination and ability to build alliances with other groups around specific causes, and the desire of the High Commission to improve its rapport with workers before the resumption of constitutional life.

World War II intensified many of the dynamics that characterized the second half of the interwar period. On the one hand, the ranks of the urban workers expanded. On the other hand, workers experienced a range of economic hardships, including supply shortages and inflationary prices. The introduction of Allied troops into Lebanon and Syria in July 1941 and the incorporation of the area in to the Middle East Supply Centre further transformed the economy. The contraction in international trade coupled with an enlargement of the local market led British, French, and Lebanese authorities to partner with local businessmen in expanding local supply while reorienting the economy to satisfy domestic consumption through local production.[16]

Along with wartime economic changes, shifts in the balance of power during World War II altered the strategic opportunities for the Lebanese labor movement. Shortly after the outbreak of war in 1939, the High Commission again suspended the constitution and declared martial law. The July 1941 establishment of a Free French regime in the French Mandate for Syria and Lebanon created new possibilities. They lifted martial law in fall 1941, precipitating a wave of labor mobilizations in response to food shortages, price inflation, and inadequate wages. Between November 1941 and March 1943, the High Commission set or raised minimum wages, cost of living bonuses, and family allowances for civil servants and other parts of the public sector workforce.[17] Private-sector workers mobilized to extend those benefits to the private sector. Also in March 1943, the High Commission announced a 500,000-lira budget for disbursing state subsidies to workers' mutual-aid societies.[18]

Further indications of the political weight of workers manifested at the level of Lebanese state institutional arrangements. In January 1943 the government created the Social Affairs Service (Maslahat al-Shu'un al-Ijtima'iyya) to replace the Service for the Protection of Manpower (SPM, est. 1938).[19] The SPM was to recommend labor and other social policies around workers' needs. The Social Affairs Service incorporated the functions of SPM, yet its mandate was much broader—including the authority to monitor workers and adjudicate labor disputes. Workers had for some time demanded a specialized government agency with such powers, believing it would both provide recognition of their grievances and allow for a clear point of contact with the government and state institutions. There appear to have been additional, more nefarious, motivations for the creation of the service. Lieutenant Père André Victor Le Genissel (1899–1991), who headed the Social Section of the High Commission after 1941, proposed establishing the Social Affairs Service to the Lebanese government on the basis of his own experience monitoring and containing labor mobilizations in Lebanon.[20] He further recommended his

Lebanese protégé Joseph Donato (1918–2010) to help establish the service.[21] Such containment measures fell short, for now at least. In May 1943, labor mobilizations forced the local government to extend the wage increases and cost of living bonuses of public sector workers to those in the commercial and industrial wings of the private sector and introduced for the first time a family allowance scheme.[22]

Such developments belied the strength of the labor movement as well as both the High Commission and Lebanese government's desire to sway workers' opinion in the lead-up to the 1943 parliamentary elections. Workers' mobilizations formed part of a broader set of forces that transformed the French Mandate into a colonial welfare state.[23] They had put both the local government and nationalist elites on notice. Changes in how workers and their organizations marked International Workers' Day reflect much of the shifting nature and weight of the labor movement. Beyond two specific incidents in 1907 and 1925, there is little evidence of any public celebration of the day.[24] Colonial and local government repression rendered such activity illegal if not impossible. When labor groups organized events, they were for the most part the affair of a single group, held in private homes or offices. In 1933, the association for printing press workers held such a gathering in its office garden.[25] Leading members gave speeches on the status of workers in general and those of printing presses in particular. In 1942, labor organizations held three celebrations in private residences in each of Beirut, Tripoli, and Marja'yun.[26] In addition to various speeches by labor activists, singer and composer Iliya Bayda (1915–77) played music and Michel al-Qahwaji (1912–2011) recited a poem. Yet in 1943, a group of labor activists organized an International Workers' Day celebration at Café Parisienne in Martyrs' Square.[27] Attendance spilled out into the street and square, blocking traffic for approximately two hours. There is no indication that colonial or local authorities attempted to prevent or disrupt the event. On the contrary, a number of Lebanese notables and officials, including Prime Minister Sami al-Sulh, attended.

As constitutional life resumed in 1943, workers pressed on with their demands.[28] They also mobilized for the looming parliamentary elections and the ensuing struggle for independence. Workers frequently integrated anticolonial rhetoric and demands throughout the colonial period. Since some of the most spectacular workers' mobilizations were directed at foreign (primarily French-owned) concessionary companies, the labor movement was commonly understood to be a component of the nationalist struggle.[29] Workers also participated in broader instances of anticolonial resistance.[30] The role they played in the 1943–46 mobilizations against French colonial rule therefore built on previous precedents. The labor movement was a social force that could destabilize the colonial order. Many nationalist elites therefore selectively encouraged and legitimized it in the lead-up to independence.

On August 23, 1943, a coalition of syndicates of the printing presses, carpentry, upholstery, tailoring, textiles, tiling and construction, bakeries, and hotels, restaurants, and cafés issued a call to workers.[31] Identifying themselves as the Committee of Representatives of Workers' Syndicates and Associations (Lajnat Mumaththili Naqabat wa-Jam'iyyat al-'Ummal), they claimed workers could help shape the election outcome, encouraged workers to not abide by electoral lists, and called on them to instead vote for those candidates with nationalist (*al-wataniyya al-sadiqa*) and populist commitments (*yash'arun bi-alam al-sha'b wa-yudafi'un 'an khubzuh wa-thaqafatuh wa-hurriyatuh*). They appealed to solidarity across religious lines (*'ala ikhtilaf adyanihim wa-ajnasihim*), and encouraged vigilance against vote buying (*muharabat al-mutajara bi-l-aswat*). Not all labor groups supported the idea of a united front in the elections. The Drivers' Syndicate (Jam'iyyat Ta'addud al-Sawwaqin, est. 1929), for example, called for labor organizations to remain neutral and for workers to vote as individuals.[32]

The 1943 elections produced an ambiguous outcome for workers. Politicians allied with the Constitutional Bloc secured enough seats in parliament to elect Bishara al-Khuri to the presidency of the republic. Al-Khuri's tenure, various cabinets he helped form, and the parliament repeatedly disappointed workers with their socially conservative agenda. Yet workers' participation in the elections helped shape their debates, outcomes, and consequences of the elections.[33] In the short term, workers helped legitimate the elections. Several candidates and their lists explicitly recognized workers in their campaign literature. In the long run, workers directly participated in the 1943–46 struggle for independence that the coalition of electoral winners inaugurated. Workers helped challenge French power in the November 1943 uprising, amplified the demand for the transfer of control of various institutions, and joined the mobilizations for a complete French evacuation.

Workers were critical to the general strikes, marches, and rallies against French colonial rule.[34] Nationalist elites recognized this capacity and directly recruited workers into their anticolonial coalitions.[35] Labor activists and leaders Mustafa al-Aris (1912–81) and Sa'ad al-Din Mumneh were members of the National Congress (al-Mu'tamar al-Watani) established during the November 1943 uprising to serve as a national front bringing together otherwise politically disparate individuals and constituencies who shared in that moment a rejection of French colonial rule. Thus al-Aris and Mumneh's inclusion in the National Congress was as representatives of the labor movement and not the Communist movement, which they were certainly a part of. Workers thus formed a base of popular support in these various confrontations, further developing their own political weight.

During these instances and afterward, workers repeatedly couched many of their demands in the idiom of constitutional life (*al-hayat al-dusturiyya*) and national self-rule (*al-hukm al-watani*). They also noted their contributions to them. In one meeting with the president, prime minister, and minister of trade and industry, a delegation of workers from workshops and factories in Beirut and its suburbs topped their list of demands with "a new [labor] law, born of this independence era, to ameliorate our lives and those of our families" (qanun jadid walid hadha al-'ahd al-istiqlali li-siyanat hayatana wa-hayat ahalina).[36]

Workers' participation in the struggle for independence intersected in complex ways with their mobilizations to secure higher wages, better working conditions, and other benefits. Labor grievances against foreign corporations, especially those with public utility concessions, provided a potent medium to articulate anticolonial sentiments. How a politician, cabinet, or parliament responded to struggles between foreign companies and workers shaped their nationalist credentials. The unique terrain of labor laws, who they applied to, and what jurisdiction Lebanese courts had in adjudicating related disputes were also important.

The cumulative experiences of workers crystalized the need for a comprehensive labor law that would unify, standardize, and expands workers' rights. Passage of such a law, let alone its substantive nature, was not a forgone conclusion. Workers had intermittently called for such a law as early as the 1920s, though in earnest during the 1930s. The High Commission and both foreign and local employers rejected this demand. They preferred to avoid any standardization of wages and working conditions. Yet the onset of decolonization, the significant shift in the political weight of workers, and the legacy of temporary alliances with nationalist elites were not enough to realize this long-ignored demand. Workers needed to form a united front and apply significant pressure.

EARLY EFFORTS AT UNITY

Attempts at cross-syndicate coalition building were a key feature of the immediate postindependence period. Several syndicates constructed short-term alliances with one another throughout the colonial period. Some of the most robust examples manifested in the wake of the 1937–38 strike wave, when labor organizations made up of typesetters, carpenters, construction workers, and bakery workers formed the Federation of Syndicates Committee (Lajnat Ittihad al-Naqabat).[37] Wartime dynamics of martial law and Vichy rule disrupted these efforts.

Labor mobilizations around food supplies and wages after the Allied invasion of the Levant facilitated the resumption of efforts at unification. During the last quarter of 1942, seven syndicates representing workers in printing presses, carpentry, construction, bakeries, tailoring, shoemaking, and mechanics reconstituted the Federation of Syndicates Committee.[38] These syndicates and others drafted an eight-point petition and sent a delegation to meet with Prime Minister Riyad al-Sulh shortly after he formed a cabinet in October 1943.[39] The petition celebrated the return of constitutional life (described as democratic national rule) and asserted the role of workers in bringing it about. The workers framed their petition as a response to the recent ministerial statement. They claimed the conditions of workers were one of the most important national issues facing the cabinet and parliament. They demanded that the government recognize the right to organize (*al-i'itiraf bi-qanun al-tanzim al-naqabai*); legislate a law that protects workers and employees (*tashri' shamil yahmi al-'ummal wa-l-mustakhdamin*) and defines their relationship with employers (*yuhaddid al-'ilaqat baynahum wa-bayn ashab al-'amal*); lower the price of rationed goods (*takhfid as'ar al-i'asha*) for workers and those with limited income (*dhuwi al-madkhul al-mahdud*); distribute winter clothing; establish cooperative stores; increase wages in accordance with the cost of living; exempt workers, employees, and the poor from the vocational (*tamattu'*) tax; and establish sufficient public schools in rural areas.[40] The petition framed these demands as being in the service of national independence and their achievement as a sign of the dawn of a new era in the country.

Unity efforts took on a more broad-based and institutionalized form after independence in November 1943. By mid-January the following year, over fifteen labor organizations now formed the Workers and Employees' Syndicates Committee (Lajnat Naqabat al-'Ummal wa-l-Mustakhdamin).[41] The committee sent a delegation to deliver a petition in the name of workers to the prime minister.[42] It demanded an extension of the current rent-control law, the enforcement of decreed wage increases, and improved funding and staffing for the Social Affairs Service. In parallel with its mobilizations, the committee increasingly institutionalized itself. Its members formed an executive committee and elected al-Aris as president. The committee established its headquarters in Khandaq al-Ghamiq as well as branch offices in Tripoli and Zahleh. It organized meetings and activities in other parts of the country as well. By January 1946, the committee had renamed itself the Federation of Workers and Employees' Syndicates (FWES, Ittihad Naqabat al-'Ummal wa-l-Mustakhdamin) by the summer of 1945.[43] Throughout 1944–46, the coalition that would become known as the FWES expanded its number of affiliated syndicates and became the vanguard of the labor movement.

The federation regularly issued public statements and held meetings with government officials. It demonstrated tactical success in drawing energy from and helping leverage labor mobilization. For example, the FWES drew special attention to the topic of wages and cost of living as part of its broader platform since its earliest incarnation in 1944. The government's last wage increase was in May 1943. Yet the cost of living continued to precipitously rise as a function of deepening wartime shortages and inflation. Starting in May 1944, the federation elevated that topic above others. As parliamentary committees began drafting possible legislation, the FWES submitted comments on publicized details of the drafts. The increasing reach of the federation, combined with its technical expertise, forced the government to recognize the FWES leadership. Al-Aris appeared on the national radio station at least twice that year, in April and May 1944.[44] Prime Minister Habib Abi Shahla (1902–57) appointed him to represent workers in a committee the prime minister formed to review potential wage increases.[45] The government issued the new round of wage increases in September 1944, incorporating the FWES's two most important demands: that increases be relative to wages paid on December 31, 1943, and that workers would receive five months of retroactive wage increases.[46]

The federation took an active role in worker mobilizations in different sectors, including facilitating the formation of workers' committees and syndicates, supporting ongoing strike actions, and mediating between workers, employers, and government officials. An intensification of strike action across different sectors and companies provided the field within which the FWES expanded its reach, formalized its relationships, and demonstrated its ability to further workers' goals. Some strikes lasted for a few days. Many of them went on for over a week. In 1944, these included workers in carpentry, upholstery, tanneries, soap production, tailoring, baking, and shoemaking.[47] In 1945, workers at beer, mattress, and glass factories went on strike.[48] Textile workers demonstrated a significant increase in their militancy throughout 1945. This included a strike by workers at Zumikyan Stocking Factory in Dawra (February and June), Yusif al-Ashqar and Tawfiq Dumit's silk factory in Dbayyeh (April), the Arida Brothers cotton-spinning factory in Bihsas (July), and the Sabbagh-Yanni factory in Beirut (September).

The most spectacular of these strikes was at the National Wool Company (Ma'mal al-Aswaf al-Wataniyya) in Hazmiyya, which lasted for four months (July–November 1945).[49] Owners and managers had refused to implement mandated wage increases and family allowances. They also intervened to disrupt the attempts of seven hundred workers to form an association to represent them with the company and the government. Workers initially struck when company guards beat a worker and management fired several others. Workers expanded their demands after police attempted to break up the strike, resulting in several injuries and arrests among the workers. They now demanded the reinstatement of dismissed workers, the release of those arrested, the prosecution of the police captain who supervised the raid, an official permit authorizing the workers' association, implementation of all laws related to wages and family allowances, one week paid annual leave, a bonus worth one month of wages, and severance for women workers who leave work to marry. The workers eventually secured most of their demands, with the notable exception of reinstating three of their dismissed colleagues (who were nevertheless paid their owed severance).[50] Critical to the success of the strike was the perseverance of the company workers, the developing threat of a general strike in support of them, and a cabinet reshuffle.

Such strike actions were rooted in the specifics of workplace dynamics, yet they also highlighted commonalities faced by most urban workers, contributed to a sense of collective struggle, and formed the material basis for linkages across different groups of workers. Throughout the 1944–45 strikes and beyond, workers demanded different combinations of higher wages, an eight-hour working day, a weekly day off, sick leave, paid vacation, and appropriate severance and pension pay. None of these were legally established rights, and workers had been making many of these demands since the early twentieth century. Wages figured most prominently. In some cases, workers demanded the implementation of wage increases, cost-of-living bonuses, and family allowances the government had decreed. In other cases, they opted for different strategies of augmenting their income. These included annual bonuses and interest-free loans. Many workers pointed to wages and benefits enjoyed by other groups of workers to justify their demands. These mobilizations cumulatively normalized such demands and created opportunities for solidarity and coordination among workers. The FWES facilitated this process by linking these strikes to underlying deficiencies in the economy and state policy. It also helped institutionalize linkages among syndicates and between itself and those syndicates.[51]

TOWARD A COMPREHENSIVE LABOR LAW

As discussed above, the late colonial period and the transition to independence featured important gains for the labor movement in Lebanon. Yet the state continued to deny workers as a corporate identity. It did, however, recognize several others corporate interests through laws governing chambers of commerce (1910), patents (1924), foreign corporations (1926), contracts (1932), and commercial transactions (1942). The lack of a labor code meant that labor interests were subjected to the Ottoman Law of Associations (1909)—legislation too broad to regulate labor relations. As a result, labor was legally invisible as a collective interest even as the ranks of wage earners in general and urban workers in particular increased significantly. Many workers viewed this status quo as the basis for many of their struggles, both to organize as workers and to secure better wages, working conditions, and job security. The simultaneous invisibility, growing ranks, and precarity of workers mobilized a labor movement that coalesced around the issue of securing a comprehensive labor code that protects workers and employees and defines their relationship with employers.[52]

The FWES began a concerted campaign to secure a comprehensive labor law in the summer of 1945. It organized a series of open meetings for workers and syndicates, issued multiple statements and petitions, and linked the demand for a labor law with ongoing strikes. Workers increasingly called for such a law, stressing the need to both standardize labor practices and enable workers to more effectively call on the state to defend their rights. The combination of multiple strike actions, the work of the FWES, and the emerging consensus among workers pressured the government into initiating the process.

In October 1945, the cabinet announced it was ready to introduce draft legislation to parliament.[53] The FWES protested the lack of transparency on preparing the legislation and insisted on the opportunity to review and comment on the draft law prior to its introduction to parliament.[54] By the end of February 1946, the FWES had given feedback on two different drafts.[55] It organized a members' meeting both times to circulate, discuss, and establish consensus vis-à-vis the drafts. It subsequently issued a formal memo to the relevant parliamentary committee and organized a public event to present its findings. These meetings and the memo were part of a broader flurry of federation activities around the country during the first three months of 1946.[56] It had succeeded in establishing itself as both the vanguard of the labor movement and the leading force in support of revising and passing the draft labor law.

It is in this context that a number of labor syndicates not formally part of the FWES began to coalesce around what came be to be known as the Labor Front (Jabhat al-ʿAmal, est. 1946).[57] The founding meeting of the front coincided with a public meeting by the FWES to discuss developments related to the draft labor law. Farid Jubran (1911–95) of the Syndicate of Commercial Employees (Jam'iyyat Mustakhdimi al-Tijara) called for the meeting, which was attended by the syndicates of bank employees; hotel, restaurant, and café employees; drivers; and employees and workers of the Régie, as well as the Alumni Association of the School of Arts and Crafts (Jam'iyyat Khariji Madrasat al-Sanayi' wa-l-Funun).[58] The front was the product of several dynamics. Many of its founders were critical of the popularity and dominance of al-Aris within the FWES and the labor movement more generally. Some of these individuals or their labor organizations held anti-Communist views or were affiliated with anti-Communist parties. In addition, the front featured a majority of labor organizations made up of white-collar workers—as distinct from the blue-collar workers that constituted the majority of the FWES.[59]

Government consideration of a draft labor law and labor mobilizations to shape it provided an opportunity for founders of the Labor Front and their organizations to form an alternative coalition of syndicates beyond the framework of the FWES. In seeking support for such endeavors, the front elected Henri Far'un (1905–93) its honorary president.[60] While this was reflective of the dominance of the drivers' syndicate (for whom Far'un was the patron), it also belied the general proximity to power that some of the front's founders cultivated.[61] In fact, the front frequently framed its role as one of bridging the divide between employers and their workforces. In this sense, it represented the gradualist non-Communist (perhaps even corporatist) sentiment among some in the labor movement and the political parties that supported them.

These factors might account for what appears to be a more conservative approach of the Labor Front to general labor politics. For example, the front had little to say as part of the public debates in 1946 around the Supreme Council for State Security's February assertion that it could repress any strike it deemed to threaten national security and the mass layoffs of Lebanese workers by French and British armed forces as part of the evacuation throughout the year. Despite forming committees, it made few demands and instead appealed to the benevolence of companies and the government.[62] More importantly, the front recommended a minimal set of revisions to the draft labor law and generally focused its public statements on supporting passage of the law rather than demanding it be more responsive to the needs of workers.[63]

Yet the picture is more complex. While the drivers' syndicate and the alumni association were constant members of the front, the participation of the other labor organizations was much more volatile. In some cases, these syndicates broke ranks with the front and participated in general meetings, protests, or strikes called for by the FWES. In other cases, the front served as an important source of advocacy for the passage of a labor law—though not its improvement. Nevertheless, its overall effect appears to have been to counter and contain the influence of the FWES.[64] It was for this reason that al-Khuri took an interest in the front and apparently supported it.

The government delayed taking decisive action on the labor law. It regularly stalled the drafting process, convening multiple ad hoc committees it claimed were necessary to further develop the draft. It sometimes justified the delays as a function of the government's focus on negotiating the complete evacuation of all foreign troops. Seeking to manage expectations, the president, prime minister, and relevant cabinet members continued to receive labor delegations and include worker representation on ad hoc committees.[65] The government complemented such stalling and patronizing tactics with repeated shows of force. In February 1946, the Supreme Council for State Security asserted the government's right to stop any labor strikes that threatened the security of the country.[66]

These tactics emboldened employers, who frequently rejected the demands of workers. They regularly sought to discipline workers. In some cases, employers transferred suspected organizers to isolate them from potential recruits. In other cases, they fired workers for organizing meetings or strikes. They also brought in the police or gendarmerie to intimidate or forcibly remove workers during meetings, demonstrations, and sit-ins. The ubiquity of repressive strategies led worker mobilizations to increasingly adopt the right to organize as a key demand.

The situation of workers in concessionary companies is particularly instructive of the complex intersection between the demand for a labor law, the context of specific workers, and the role of state institutions. They were at the center of critical developments during April–July 1946 that pressured the government to move forward with a comprehensive labor law. Workers at the Société ottomane du chemin de fer de Damas-Hamah et prolongements (DHP, Sharikat Sikkat Hadid Sham Hama wa-Tamdidatuha), Régie, electricity companies of Beirut and Tripoli, and Beirut Water Company had episodically struck since December 1943. At issue was the uneven terrain of wages and cost of living bonuses, and legal jurisdiction resulting from the multiple sources of authorities during the war.[67] Both the High Commission and the Lebanese government issued wage increases during the war. In its wage laws (issued between November 1941 and March 1943), the High Commission specifically identified all enterprises under its direct control, all public service enterprises operating on the basis of a concession, and all enterprises enjoying a monopoly. Between December 1941 and May 1943, the Lebanese government's wage laws specifically excluded those enterprises covered by the High Commission's wage increases. Yet its most recent wage law of September 1944 did not reference laws decreed by the High Commission. Instead, it substituted previous exemptions with new ones: domestic workers (*al-khadam*), public sector workers and employees (*'ummal wa-mustakhdami al-dawa'ir wa-l-sulutat al-rasmiyya*), and workers whose employers voluntarily raised wages (provided they met the minimum established for a forty-eight-hour work week).[68]

Workers in the concessionary companies recognized an opportunity in the shifting circumstances and demanded the application of the 1944 wage increases. Their employers rejected such demands. This context set up a showdown between workers and companies, one that exposed the complex intersections between decolonization and labor militancy. These workers increasingly coordinated their efforts in 1946.[69] They initially pursued their demands through a series of joint meetings and petitions vis-à-vis the government, including the president, prime minister, cabinet, relevant ministries, and the parliament.[70] Some of these demands were general to all workers across the different companies. Other demands were specific to each set of workers.

The cabinet was unwilling to force the companies to accede to the demands, even those related to the application of existing laws. Instead, it established a committee composed of representatives of the workers, the companies, and the cabinet itself.[71] The government facilitated stop-gap measures that fell far short of what workers demanded.[72] These included paying bonuses and converting previously disbursed loans to grants. While such remedies addressed some of the worker's demands, they did little to address one of the underlying structural issues defining their lived experiences: inadequate wages.

The government further committed itself to repressing existing and potential workers' grievances. It mobilized army, gendarmerie, and police units to take up positions around Beirut on April 8, 1946.[73] Fearing a coordinated strike by workers of the concessionary companies the following day, they occupied the Beirut electricity plant, the Dbayyeh water plant, and all railway stations. The cabinet promptly issued a statement warning of strict enforcement of laws prohibiting strikes and the firing of anyone who missed three consecutive days of work.[74]

On April 13, 1946, Beirut Electricity Company (EDB, Sharikat Kahruba' Bayrut) workers began a strike that changed the terms of struggle.[75] For twenty-one consecutive days, they reported to their job sites but refused to perform their duties. Their physical presence prevented the company from discharging them on the basis of work absence. It also obstructed EDB efforts to find other ways to operate the tramcars, as drivers guarded their tramcars at the main depot. The striking workers also formed a special committee to ensure the provision of electricity in cases of emergencies. This helped demonstrate to the public that they intended to secure their objectives without risking the safety or lives of others who might be affected. The EDB workers demanded pay raises, job permanency after one year of employment, paid sick days, annual vacation days, and a personnel policy that guaranteed opportunities for promotion.[76] A comprehensive labor law and the cessation of retaliation against workers were also key demands.

Minister of Interior Emil Lahud (1897–1954) was the government's public face during this strike.[77] He claimed the government could not force the EDB to raise wages without also allowing it to raise prices. Lahud asserted that the government lacked the legal mechanisms to force the company to accede to workers' demands. In doing so, he maintained a division between the wage increases of the High Commission and those of the Lebanese government. Workers and commentators seized on this point: the government, they argued, had abdicated its role in consolidating independence and asserting the sovereignty of Lebanese law.[78] The public increasingly supported the EDB workers, sending telegrams and letters. Some parliamentarians saw an opportunity to criticize the cabinet and bolster their nationalist credentials. Politicians critical of the president or cabinet and/or supportive of workers used the strike to publicly challenge the government's competence in and commitment to establishing a new postindependence order. Those in parliament successfully passed a law on April 25 that explicitly extended the Lebanese government's wartime wage increase to all enterprises in Lebanon without exception.[79]

As the EDB strike entered its third week, negotiations between the workers, the company, and the government intensified. By the end of April, the parties signed an arbitration agreement to submit the case to a special tribunal, while workers continued with their strike.[80] Workers put forward the case of Hasan al-Bizri. A married man and father of four children, al-Bizri had worked at the company since at least 1939 and had his fourth child in 1944. Between 1941 and 1943, the EDB implemented wage increases in accordance with the High Commission. It subsequently voluntarily raised al-Bizri's wages. The workers believed his situation provided the ideal testing ground for their legal claims. They filed the case with the tribunal on April 30 alleging al-Bizri was owed back pay as well as a wage increase. The EDB countered with three claims: (1) that it followed the High Commission laws, (2) that the Lebanese government's wage increases exempted the company, and (3) that the Lebanese civil procedure code affirmed the jurisdiction of mixed courts in cases involving foreign joint-stock companies. The tribunal issued its ruling on May 3.[81] It asserted its jurisdiction and sided with al-Bizri. The tribunal ordered the company to pay him 397 liras in back pay and raise his monthly wages (including family allowance) from approximately 219 to 240 liras. Workers and their supporters immediately hailed the decision as vindication for their years of struggle. The EDB announced plans to abide by the ruling and apply the Lebanese government's wage increases to its workforce. The strike ended that day, and tramcars circulated as scheduled the following day.

The May 3, 1946, ruling emboldened many other workers to take on a more militant stance.[82] They issued a flurry of ultimatums throughout the month, threatening indefinite work stoppages if their employers did not increase their wages accordingly. Workers directed these demands at both their employers and the government. For example, a committee representing workers of petroleum companies demanded that the government force their employers to implement the wage increases and threatened to strike within a week if the companies stalled. The FWES also mobilized. Sensing a political opportunity, it called for an open-ended general strike beginning Monday, May 20, if the parliament did not pass the latest draft labor law along with its recommended amendments.[83]

From printing presses of Beirut, to factories of major cities, and throughout several smaller towns, workers of different sectors and provinces struck on May 20, 1946.[84] However, the success of the general strike or its ability to last longer than a day is not clear. On the one hand, the parliamentary committee and the president were concerned about the potential reach of the strike. They each met with the FWES on May 17 and 19, respectively.[85] Some accounts claim al-Khuri offered to facilitate any FWES transportation and communication needed to call off the strike.[86] Yet other reports indicate al-Aris agreed to call off the strike on condition of receiving written assurances that the current parliamentary session would pass the labor law.[87] Both the parliamentary committee and the president declined to do so. On the other hand, significant segments of the labor movement did not adhere to the general strike.[88] These included workers of most concessionary companies as well as of hotels, restaurants, and cafés. The resignation of the cabinet the day before the strike day could have changed the strategic calculations of certain workers. The limited scope of the strike also reflected the organizational limits of the federation. While the FWES was an impressive coalition of syndicates, it was not representative of all syndicates or workers. It ultimately called off the strike at the end of the first day. It claimed success, insisting the government provided enough assurances to satisfy its concerns.

Parliament began discussing the labor law in late May, and voted on approximately the first thirty articles by June 7.[89] This represented an important victory for the labor movement, as the government had stalled for several years. However, the newly formed cabinet also filed an objection to the labor tribunal ruling in the Bizri case on May 31.[90] The previous cabinet had signed an arbitration agreement with the EDB and its workers to seek the adjudication of the labor tribunal. The new cabinet claimed the ruling caused the government undue hardship since the application of the law to

DHP and Régie workers would affect the state budget.[91] This development emboldened most employers and reinforced their lack of responsiveness to workers' grievances. Workers heightened militant activity as the FWES mobilized and supportive lawyers volunteered to represent them.[92]

Concessionary company workers took the lead this time, in contrast to their lack of participation in the general strike. Régie workers struck first on June 11, with those of the warehouses at the forefront.[93] Unlike other concessionary companies, women made up a significant portion of the Régie workforce and their mobilizations.[94] Workers in the EDB (June 15), DHP (June 15), and Beirut port (June 22) followed.[95] Each set of workers struck for implementation of the tribunal ruling as well as other demands specific to their contexts. Yet they were not equally successful. As a general policy, Minister of Interior Sa'ib Salam (r. May–December 1946) ordered companies to withhold strike pay, refused to negotiate with striking workers, and insisted on awaiting the tribunal's decision on the government's objection.[96]

The strike by EDB workers was the shortest, lasting six days.[97] The start of the strike on June 15 coincided with powerline failures that plunged much of the city into darkness and brought tramcars to a halt for more than four days.[98] Other impositions such as the suspension of telephone service, disruptions to hospital services, and the risk posed to perishable goods in refrigerated storage centers compounded the effects of the power failure.[99] Salam initially detained tens of EDB repairmen and threatened them with imprisonment if they did not restore power.[100] They informed him power could temporarily be provided by activating old generators in the company's Beirut power plant. This belied the company's earlier public statements that the failure would necessitate reduced electric supply for several weeks while it identified and repaired the source of the problem. The EDB apparently hoped the public pressure to restore electricity would strengthen its negotiating position with the workers. Facing a crisis of confidence, Salam threatened the company with seizing its facilities if it failed to restore power immediately.[101] The EDB did so within hours and subsequently settled with its workers. It granted them most of their demands, including implementation of the wage increases (irrespective of the forthcoming tribunal decision), raises for workers not covered by the ruling, and a combination of grants and loans.

The Régie and DHP workers did not fare as well despite much longer strikes. The legacy of labor activism in their companies and the perseverance of workers were important reasons for this staying power. The settlement between the EDB and its workers also encouraged them. Several factors nevertheless mitigated against similar success. Salam's experience with the EDB emboldened his use of coercion. On the one hand, his threats of imprisonment and seizure produced immediate and tangible results. On the other hand, the settlement between the EDB and its workers highlighted the potential domino effect of any further strike victories. The Régie strike created a shortage of cigarettes and skyrocketing prices, while cigarette sellers reported several robberies and lootings.[102] The DHP strike caused delays in the importation of wheat and its distribution through the rationing system.[103] In this context, Salam escalated the government's confrontation with the Régie and DHP workers, seeking to break their strikes. He refused to allow for strike pay to be part of any settlement, and threatened to arrest the workers of both companies.[104] Salam then arranged for military vehicles to transport cigarettes and wheat from Syria and around the country, and dispatched the gendarmerie to force open cigarette warehouses and distribute to merchants.[105]

The escalation with the Régie workers proved fatal.[106] On June 27, a group of primarily women workers used their bodies to disrupt the government's efforts to move tobacco and cigarette supplies between Régie facilities in Bikfayya, Mar Mikhayil, and Furn al-Shubbak. At the later location, the gendarmerie opened fire on the workers, killing eighteen-year-old Warda Butrus Ibrahim, seriously injuring a man and a woman, and wounding at least twenty-seven other people.[107] The incident initially galvanized Régie workers and the public at large.[108] The press and numerous politicians roundly condemned Salam and his approach. Other political calculations shielded Salam from the pressure of individual resignation. Confrontations between the Syrian government and workers in the railways, electricity companies, and the Régie buttressed state violence in Lebanon.[109] The combination of a prolonged strike and dramatic escalation took its toll on workers. Strategic disagreements surfaced. For example, the DHP strike committee resigned after workers rejected a solution it supported despite falling far short of the initial demands.

July 11 was a turning point. The tribunal announced its decision in favor of the government's objection.[110] It reduced the backpay awarded to al-Bizri from 397 to 92 liras and restored his pre-ruling monthly income of 219 liras in wages and family allowance (instead of the 240 it initially ruled he should receive). This decision did not affect EDB workers, whose wage increases were no longer tied to the tribunal. Salam then threatened both the Régie and DHP workers with arrest. Workers in the two companies sought out the intervention of former prime minister Riyad al-Sulh. In the face of the government's and companies' obstinance, they wanted to end the strikes while ensuring strike pay (*daf' 'ujur ayyam al-idrab*).[111] Both sets of workers secured far less than what they demanded, and in some cases might have lost more than they gained.[112] The Régie workers settled for a grant worth six weeks of wages, a loan in the amount of two months of wages, and other administrative benefits. The DHP workers primarily received a grant worth two weeks of wages.

The June–July 1946 strikes by concessionary company workers helped further publicize the need for a standardized system of wages, working conditions, and other relations. Workers in other sectors also contributed to this process, including those that struck in August at the Banque de Syrie et du Liban, the Orient Fertilizer Company, and the Jallad factories.[113] These and other mobilizations maintained pressure on the government to deliver on its promise of a comprehensive labor law. Also important was the limited but consistent public support given by notable politicians such as Muhyi al-Din al-Nsuli and those of his status.[114] Workers' mobilizations during 1946 were destabilizing to the point that they forced the cabinet, parliament, and president to shift strategies. Rather than obstruct or delay passage of the labor law, they now sought to promulgate it as a means of mitigating labor conflict.[115]

There were important detractors from the government's new strategy because they believed the proposed law was either too radical or would otherwise disincentivize capital investment. The previous nine months featured a string of public opposition to the labor code, including by small employers, directors of concessionary companies, and an ad hoc group of businessmen that identified themselves as a "defense association."[116] Others voiced and resolved their disagreements through back-channel negotiations. For example, as late as June 1, 1946, Foreign Minister Philippe Takla (1915–2006) believed the draft labor code "went too far in favour of workers" and claimed the cabinet was intent on making amendments that would "correct this."[117] Prior to that representatives of the Iraq Petroleum Company, Royal Dutch Shell, and British government provided extensive feedback, soliciting the Lebanese government's "appreciation" for their "collaboration."[118] Similar views and efforts were underway through the US Legation in Beirut. In early May, the US commercial attaché conveyed to Deputy Prime Minister Gabriel al-Murr that the draft law's "extreme provisions are strongly opposed" by the Beirut representative of the Socony-Vacuum oil corporation.[119] Murr apparently shared these views and had tried to amend the draft law in the cabinet before its introduction to the parliament. The parliament passed 82 of the labor code's 114 draft articles with little actual discussion and without amendment. This included the entire chapter on syndicates, which had been single-handedly authored by Joseph Donato.[120] While politicians proposed amendments for the remaining 32 articles, only 22 of them passed. These include the exemption of public sector workers and employees and the addition of a government representative to the labor arbitration councils. The parliamentary debate and amendment process ultimately rendered the law more conservative. This was unsurprising given the proclivity of cabinet and parliament members and the outside pressures they experienced.

The president signed the labor law on September 23, 1946, nearly a month after the parliament debated and voted on the final set of articles.[121] The outcome was the inauguration of a new labor regime that redefined the relationship between workers, employers, and the government. While it incorporated rights workers secured in the colonial era, the law also introduced a new set of rights. These include a forty-eight-hour work week, overtime compensation, paid sick leave, and fifteen days of annual vacation. The law also mandated forty days of paid maternity leave. It further established the ability to form worker-only syndicates, as distinct from associations and separate from employers. The law created a new system of labor arbitration councils, one for each governorate. These new rights were the culmination of intense struggles and clearly articulated demands on the part of workers throughout the early independence period, which built on the legacies of the colonial period while at the same time making use of the context of decolonization. The 1946 Labor Law served as the framework for all subsequent Lebanese labor legislation in the postcolonial era.

The labor law nevertheless left unaddressed or introduced a different set of challenges for workers.[122] It excluded public sector workers, domestic servants, family establishments, and agricultural workers whose products were not tied to the manufacturing or trade sectors. The labor law also limited many of the social safety provisions (e.g., maternity leave, dismissal and retirement indemnities, and survivors' benefits) to those workers who served one employer for a minimum time period. In addition, the law limited work-accident compensation to nine specific types of jobs, excluding most of those in manufacturing, trade, and other sectors. Furthermore, the family allowance provision was applicable only to the lowest earners: it was not applicable to anyone whose wages exceed the sum total of the minimum wage plus the amount of the allowance they would be due given their family size.

Strikes continued to occupy an ambiguous legal position. On the one hand, the new labor law made no mention of strikes, their legitimacy, or their illegality. On the other hand, the 1943 Penal Code prohibited strikes by government employees (Article 340) and others in transportation, communication, electric utilities, and water supply sectors (Article 342).[123] It also banned work stoppages that sought to "pressure public authorities or protest a decision or measure issued by such authorities" (Article 341).

The labor law also required all syndicates to apply for a license from the Social Affairs Service. Such decisions were not subject to appeal by workers and were reached in consultation with the Ministry of Interior. Syndicates remained nonlegal entities until the Social Affairs Service published its approval decision in the government's official gazette (*al-Jarida al-Rasmiyya*). Furthermore, the law subjected all syndicates to a standardized set of requirements for the internal organization of syndicates and how to join them. While the law allowed for non-Lebanese with work permits to join syndicates, it forbade them from running or voting in their elections.

Independence and the passage of the labor law did not bring an end to labor mobilizations. Rather, these transitions marked the beginning of a new phase in the continuing struggles between labor and capital, within the working class, and between workers and the state. The labor law is therefore best viewed as a reform of state institutional arrangements that was necessary to contain and manage labor conflict—which had reached an unprecedented level of polarization by the summer of 1946. The labor law provided important new rights and guarantees. Yet it endowed state institutions with their enforcement.

URBAN WORKERS IN THE SHADOW OF INDEPENDENCE

Between 1946 and 1955, the urban wage-earning population of Lebanon continued to expand. Several factors undergirded this process. Primary among them were increasing levels of urbanization due to accelerated rural-to-urban migration and new capital flows into Lebanon. These dynamics reflected an intensification of late colonial patterns colored by post–World War II local, regional, and global developments. On the one hand, the neglect of rural areas and eventual collapse of the agricultural sector pushed larger numbers of people to seek work in the cities.[124] On the other hand, domestic wartime profits and savings, migrant remittance flows, and capital flight from Palestine and Syria—albeit for very different reasons—helped expand the local economy during the postindependence period—in particular starting in the late 1940s.[125] Booms in manufacturing, construction, tourism, and banking followed.[126]

A 1955 government-sponsored census of 1,861 urban "manufacturing establishments" in Lebanon employing five or more persons provides insight into the structural features of this expansion.[127] Businesspersons created 827 of these establishments in Lebanon between 1946 and 1955.[128] This accounted for approximately 45 percent of the surveyed manufacturing establishments operating in Lebanon during 1955. The largest expansion occurred in textiles (including footwear and apparel), food manufacturing (including beverages), and wood manufacturing (including furniture). Such trends were consistent with those of the late colonial period. The specific nature of this expansion and concomitant employment patterns shaped the dynamics of the postindependence labor movement.

The same 1955 survey identified 35,031 workers engaged in the 1,861 manufacturing establishments. Textiles, food, and wood manufacturing employed 27.7, 21.5, and 10.1 percent of workers, respectively.[129] They combined to account for 59.3 percent of the workforce in the surveyed establishments. Such employment was dispersed. Out of the total 1,861 manufacturing establishments with 5 or more workers, more than 55 percent (1,031) employed between 5 and 9 persons, while another 31 percent (581) employed between 10 and 24 persons.[130] Eight percent of establishments (149) employed between 25 and 49 people, while another 3 percent (60) employed between 50 and 99.[131] Only 2 percent (40) of industrial establishments employed 100 persons or more.[132]

These urban manufacturing establishments and their workers were geographically concentrated. Approximately 53 percent of them were located in the Beirut governorate, while another 25 and 13 percent were located in the Mount Lebanon and North Lebanon governorates, respectively.[133] The Biqa' and South Lebanon governorates accounted for a combined 7 percent.[134] The regional distribution of the workers paralleled that of industrial establishments. Beirut, Mount Lebanon, North Lebanon, Biqa', and South Lebanon accounted for approximately 43, 36, 14, 2, and 2 percent of industrial employment, respectively.[135] In Beirut, the port, Ashrafiyya, Mazra'a, Sayfi, and Rmayl neighborhoods featured the largest concentrations of industrial establishments, accounting for 60 percent of those in the city.[136] Those of North Lebanon were concentrated in Tripoli (90 percent), whereas those of Biqa' and South Lebanon were in Sidon (89 percent) and Zahleh (73 percent), respectively.[137] Mount Lebanon presents a particularly complicated case of disaggregating geography. The Ba'abda and Matn districts accounted for 36 and 52 percent of the governorate's industrial establishments.[138] However, more than half of the establishments in those two districts were located in the Beirut Metropolitan Area—the urban agglomeration comprising the Beirut Governorate and adjacent municipalities of the Mount Lebanon Government.[139]

A small number of enterprises also dominated certain urban production sectors through monopolies, ownership of key establishments, significant concentrations of urban workers, or relatively large amounts of capital formation. For example, the Régie owned and operated all three tobacco establishments (Hadath, Bikfayya, and Khinshara) in Lebanon during 1955—making it the exclusive employer of the 1,743 workers in the sector.[140] At the same time, the Iraq Petroleum Company and the Trans-Arabian Pipeline company owned and operated the only two oil pipeline systems and refineries in the country (located in the Tripoli and Zahrani oil export terminals, respectively). The Iraq Petroleum Company was one of the single largest employers in Lebanon throughout the 1946–55 period.[141]

Workers in nonmanufacturing sectors represented an equally important component of the urban labor landscape. As Lebanese and other investors increasingly turned to real-estate speculation and development, the construction sector featured a near continuous expansion throughout the early postindependence period.[142] Between 1945 and 1955, the annual number of building permits issued for Beirut tripled, while the built-up area of the city quadrupled and its commercial floor space increased tenfold.[143] Major infrastructural projects, including Beirut and Tripoli ports expansion, the Khalde airport construction, the highway system creation, and the inauguration of the Trans-Arabian Pipeline system, were also relevant sites.[144] Those tracking labor statistics regularly assessed construction workers as one of the largest single constellations of urban workers.[145] Yet they also noted that, because of the temporary nature of specific construction jobs, workers in this sector were limited to daily wages and not entitled to many of the benefits the labor law provided for workers who remained with a single employer for more than a year.

Workers in transport, commerce, and education further made up an important component of urban wage earners. As road networks expanded, automobile importation increased, and Beirut consolidated itself as a post–World War II regional and global hub for shipping, air traffic, and tourism, the number of people working as drivers mushroomed. These included taxi and service drivers, private and public bus line drives, and truck drivers (some driving for a specific company and others for hire).[146] In parallel, the growth in trading houses and banks as well as hotels, restaurants, and cafés increased the number of workers and employees in these sectors. Both the number of banks and tourists doubled between 1943 and 1955. While there was little expansion in private education during the same period, approximately six thousand persons worked as private school teachers of various ranks.[147] To these examples of urban laborers we can add the expanding cadre of public sector workers, whether in security (military, gendarmerie, and police), education (primary and secondary school teachers), or in ministries and municipalities (including clerks and cleaners).[148] Workers in these sectors were regular protagonists in the newspaper coverage of labor mobilizations across the period.

Most primary sources on workers, their conditions, and their mobilizations during the 1943–55 period do not distinguish between male and female workers.[149] Nevertheless, it is clear that women constituted a critical—even if difficult to identify—part of the landscape of urban labor in this period. The 1955 industrial census indicates that women made up 22 percent of the of the 35,013 workers and employees identified.[150] Over 90 percent of these women worked in the Beirut and Mount Lebanon Governorates.[151] Other sources show that women workers were particularly concentrated in tobacco and textile manufacturing, sometimes constituting nearly half (if not more) of the workforce in a given establishment.[152] Depending on the particular factory, women also appear to have been a significant part of the workforce in certain parts of food-processing and match-making industries.[153]

Women also constituted an important (and sometimes growing) share of nonmanufacturing urban jobs. They were well represented among the ranks of public and private school teachers.[154] Women also increasingly took up work as typists, stenographers, secretaries, and clerks in private offices, commercial enterprises such as banks, and government offices.[155] Both dynamics were intimately tied to expanding women's access to education at the elementary, vocational, and university levels. Alternatively, we know very little about the status of domestic workers. Their explicit exclusion from the 1946 Labor Law indicates they formed an important component of the urban workforce.[156] According to one of the few government statistics that included them, there were at least eighteen thousand domestic workers working in Lebanon during 1947.[157] A not insignificant portion of them were from rural Lebanese backgrounds and often return-migrated annually to their villages.[158] While sex work was technically legal and women's organizations episodically mobilized to criminalize or eliminate it, we know even less about sex workers than we do about domestic workers.[159]

The urban workers of Lebanon in the 1940s and early 1950s therefore represented a diverse and heterogenous spectrum. They labored in a variety of sectors, and were further differentiated by geographic location, capital intensity, and workforce size. Beirut, Tripoli, Sidon, and Zahleh served as the primary centers of urban employment. Some worked for foreign-owned enterprises, while others worked for local ones.[160] They were also segmented by age and gender. Most workers earned a daily wage and were paid weekly. Wage differentials were critical, whether across regions, enterprises, skill level, or genders. The statistics for 1949 are particularly telling in this regard.[161] A skilled male worker averaged 1.08 Lebanese liras per hour at the EDB as opposed to 1.5 liras per hour at the Beirut port company. Unskilled male workers averaged 0.6 Lebanese liras at the DHP in contrast with 1 lira per hour at the Beirut port company. Women's wages were almost always equivalent to half or less of their male counterparts. For example, daily wages at the Régie were 2.5 Lebanese liras for skilled women workers as opposed to 4.5 liras for men. The discrepancy slightly increased with respect to the daily wages of unskilled workers at the Régie that same year: women earned 1.7 liras whereas their male counterparts earned 3.5 liras. It is worth noting that these figures represent some of the best-paying companies vis-à-vis manual jobs, the total take-home pay of which ranged from just above the minimum wage (last adjusted in 1945) to well below.

Any discussion of workers in the postindependence period must account for the impoverishment of the majority of them and the precariousness of employment. One of the salient features of post–World War II period was the continued increase in the cost of living. Despite important mobilizations during 1943–46 calling for subsidizing the price of bread, a minimum wage, family allowances, and cost of living bonuses, workers' incomes did not keep pace with the rising cost of living.[162] Of particular concern was the cost of food, which continued to rise during 1945–1953, only stabilizing in 1954–1955. Throughout, the majority of the average worker's income was spent on food. Cabinet officials and those of relevant ministries continuously refused to increase the default minimum wage set by the 1946 Labor Law, despite a specific clause that empowered them to do so without parliamentary legislation. This effectively meant that despite increases in the cost of living between 1946 and 1955, the minimum monthly salary and daily wage (as well family allowances) for private sectors workers remained constant across the 1943–1955 period.

The persistence of chronic unemployment compounded the issue of wages.[163] Its initial impetus was the end of the Allied war effort and evacuation of all foreign troops. These featured the closing of military bases and production facilities, the end of military orders with civilian-owned enterprises, and the reduction in the size of the local market.[164] The resumption of import trade and foreign competition was also a contributing factor.[165] Continued rural-urban migration aggravated the situation.[166] Despite the expansion of local enterprises throughout the postindependence period, their ability to absorb the growing ranks of urban workers was highly uneven across regions, sectors, and businesses. Unemployment was a ubiquitous concern commented on by the local press and foreign observers.[167] Between 1948 and 1955, estimates of the number of unemployed Lebanese ranged between thirty thousand and fifty thousand. These deflated estimates did not include women or working-age men who were not head of their households. Rising unemployment also drove wages down, particularly among unskilled workers earning hourly or daily wages.

Regional, international, and environmental developments frequently intensified socioeconomic distress. The creation of the State of Israel in 1948 disrupted exports to Palestine.[168] The breakup of monetary and customs union with Syria presented a host of other challenges in 1950 related to currency and trade. For example, the ʻAsayli-owned Filature de Coton in Jdaydeh on the outskirts of Beirut dismissed four hundred workers between January and December 1950.[169] This represented over 30 percent of its 1,200-person workforce, and was in response to the loss of the Syrian market. Both the Korean War (1950–53) and the 1954 US recession caused temporary spikes in local food prices.[170] Furthermore, the deepening of import-substitution industrialization in Syria, Jordan, Iraq, and Egypt resulted in further fluctuations. Episodic drought and blight would cause a spike in the price of specific food items.

Such dynamics, coupled with indifference on the part of most government officials, business owners, and workplace managers, meant that labor mobilizations persisted throughout the early postindependence period. For example, worker strikes in 1949 took place at the Beirut tramway, DHP, and several textile factories. In 1951, carpenters in the Gemayel-Harfush Manufacturing Company and bakery workers in Tripoli struck. Work stoppages in 1953 included those of Beirut municipal street cleaners, Beirut port longshoremen and day laborers, and public school teachers. In 1955, workers at the EDB, Régie, and Telephone Administration, as well as those across fourteen banks, struck. Throughout these years workers also issued many more strike threats, which were often treated as seriously as actual strike actions.

Labor mobilizations between 1946 and 1955 reveal several trends. Workers believed the postindependence era (with its new labor law) should offer a system of rule that better incorporated the interests of labor. They therefore regularly challenged their status, while also seeking relief from government officials and state institutions. Throughout, worker-led mobilizations occupied an intrinsic place in broader questions of state building and economic development. At the same time, these workers routinized a culture of labor contestation.

Some workers mobilized through preexisting syndicates. Others relied on ad hoc committees, which sometimes laid the foundation for the creation of new syndicates. Most syndicates grouped workers and employees across enterprises within a specific trade or profession (e.g., the Syndicate of Bank Employees and the Syndicate of Printing Press Workers). Some syndicates were enterprise specific (e.g., the Syndicate of the Régie Workers and Employees, and the Syndicate of Iraq Petroleum Company Workers and Employees). By 1955, the Lebanese government officially recognized at least sixty-two syndicates. The labor law required all previously existing labor organizations to reapply for licensing, which means that the officially recognized syndicates in 1955 had all applied for and secured their licenses after 1946. While these syndicates accounted for approximately twenty thousand to twenty-five thousand workers and employees, that figure represented an estimated 20 percent of the entire manufacturing and commercial workforce. Most workers and employees were unaffiliated with a syndicate and very well might have been laboring in a trade or profession that did not yet form a syndicate. The transportation sector featured the highest percentage of syndicate membership, specifically those of the DHP, automobile drivers, and EDB-operated tramway staff. The Beirut port featured a more complicated if telling picture. Long-term workers and employees of the port company constituted one syndicate, and longshoreman constituted another. Yet the day laborers of the port did not form any formal organization. While not representing as high a membership percentage as syndicates of the transportation sector, the Syndicate of Hotel, Restaurant, and Café Workers and the Syndicate of Printing Press Workers nevertheless featured enough members to be effective in their mobilizations. This was also the case with shoe shop and bakery workers, even if to a lesser extent.

Urban workers most frequently sought to address the matter of income. In some instances, they sought to ensure timely payment of wages and salaries. In others, they specifically demanded raises. Workers also pursued diverse ways to supplement their wages. This typically manifested in demanding an annual bonus, yet also included other strategies such as family allowances, cost of living bonuses, interest-free loans, and conversion of such loans into grants. In many instances, workers also demanded better working conditions, an eight-hour limit to daily working hours, days off, and accident insurance. Depending on circumstances, workers without job security sought ways to either further secure their employment or better buttress their inevitable dismissal. In understanding these demands, workers sometimes framed them in reference to the labor law and expectations that the government enforce it more effectively. In other instances, they recognized the limitations of the labor law—whether in terms of its application to their particular situation or in its insufficient guarantee of rights and protections.

The outcome of specific labor mobilizations ranged depending on a combination of structural, strategic, and contingent factors. In some cases, workers successfully secured all of their major demands. In other cases, they were unable to secure more than stop-gap measures. Most mobilizations frequently involved disciplinary action on the part of employers and coercive violence on the part of security forces. Whether the punishment, dismissal, or prosecution of workers remained in effect also varied in relation to the workers' level of success at pressuring employers and governments while also securing support of other workers, the public more generally, and politicians in particular.

Workers also regularly mobilized around broader demands. They primarily called for better implementation of the labor law. Recognizing the relationship between such a demand and state institutional capacities, workers also frequently called for increased funding and bureaucratic expansion of the Social Affairs Service (1943–51) and then the Ministry of Social Affairs (est. 1951). Labor mobilizations also called for the establishment of a social security system. This resulted in the introduction by government agencies of at least three draft laws (May 1949, November 1949, and June 1952).[171] The government withdrew each of these proposals after workers articulated strong objections to their shortcomings. Workers nevertheless continued to call for a social security system through petitions, public meetings, and the formation of joint committees.[172]

Furthermore, workers demanded affordable and adequate housing. Their advocacy took several forms. On the one hand, workers were an intrinsic part of the perennial mobilizations around rent control laws (s. *qanun al-ajarat*). They either participated as individuals in the Tenants' Defense Committee (Lajnat al-Difa' 'an al-Musta'jirin) or as syndicates producing their own proposals or supporting those of the committee. On the other hand, workers frequently demanded a government-sponsored program of public or low-income housing. In doing so they sought to address rising rents and property prices as well as the inadequacy of existing housing.[173] The latter primarily took the form of overcrowding in either very old buildings or informal settlements. While the government constituted several committees and hired multiple consultants, a low-income housing project would not be realized during this period.[174]

LABOR COALITION POLITICS

Cross-syndicate coalition building and rivalry was an important feature of postindependence labor mobilizations. As demonstrated from the earlier discussion about the labor law, the FWES emerged from the collective action of 1944–46 as the leading coalition of labor syndicates. It was headed by al-Aris, and anchored in a number of Communist-affiliated blue-collar labor syndicates (including al-Aris's Syndicate of Printing Press Workers). The FWES functioned as the vanguard of the labor movement in the struggle for a labor law while also facilitating the formalization and mobilization of labor organizations across sectors and geography.

Beginning in fall 1946, the FWES sought to consolidate and expand its role through three strategies. First, the FWES continued to issue statements and send delegations to meet with government officials in the name of the labor movement in general and specific groups of workers when particular struggles emerged.[175] Second, the federation sought to facilitate cross-syndicate deliberations and unified positions. It initially did so in October–November 1946 through preparatory meetings for holding a national conference of workers. However, the government prohibited the conference. Alternatively, the FWES organized a series of meetings in 1947 for syndicates to discuss specific topics, including laxed enforcement of the labor law, the inadequate staffing of the arbitration councils, and the perceived coordinated attack on workers by workplace managers and owners.[176] The third strategy of the FWES was to push more aggressively for its official licensing by the government, earlier attempts of which had failed.[177] To this end, the FWES drafted a basic law and submitted a formal request for licensing in 1947.[178] The government does not appear to have issued a decision, and the FWES continued to function without a license.

Despite its critical role in 1944–46 and continued mobilizations during the late 1940s, the size, role, and effectiveness of the FWES as a federation was increasingly reduced. This trajectory was in part due to the internal machinations of the FWES leadership. It was also—and more importantly—a function of the government's growing capacity to repress organized labor and other popular movements. In 1948–49 alone, the government had on three separate occasions raided the FWES headquarters, confiscated its documents, and imprisoned its leadership for operating an unlicensed organization. By early 1953, the FWES held only clandestine meetings and overwhelmingly limited itself to issuing leaflets.[179] By 1954, those syndicates previously the core of the federation were identified as independent Communist syndicates.[180] The FWES had effectively ceased to exist. While Communist-affiliated syndicates continued to coordinate their efforts, they were much less effective than they had been during the heyday of the FWES. There were eight such syndicates by 1955, estimated to represent three thousand members, including those working at printing presses; hotels, restaurants, and cafés; carpentry shops; tanneries; and construction.[181]

The repression of the FWES was paralleled with the active facilitation of a new rival federation. Elite and government support for the establishment of the previously discussed Labor Front in February 1946 represented an early iteration of this approach. Farid Jubran (1911–95) of the Syndicate of Commercial Employees headed the front, and it was anchored in a set of primarily non-Communist white-collar syndicates. However, it was dominated numerically by the historically anti-Communist Drivers' Syndicate and patronized by a leading politician. In contrast to the FWES, the Labor Front secured a government license on May 1, 1946—less than three months after its formation. The front's organizational membership appears to have been initially smaller and less stable than that of the FWES. For example, the front claimed to include the Régie workers and employees from early on, but there is no evidence indicating its membership after July 1946. By early 1947 the Labor Front consolidated itself as the largest federation, consisting of the syndicates of drivers; commercial employees; hotel, restaurant, and café workers; bank employees; and DHP workers and employees.[182] This prominence, however, was rather short lived; the front was no longer operating in 1949.

One potential explanation for the Labor Front's disappearance is the formation of a second anti-Communist labor federation, with a greater degree of elite and government support. Four syndicates that withdrew from the FWES in 1946 established the League of Workers and Employees Syndicates (Jami'at Naqabat al-'Ummal wa-l-Mustakhdamin) later that year. Primary among them was the Syndicate of Private Car Drivers headed by Muhammad al-Masri (b. 1899). Despite his decades-long involvement with the Communist-affiliated labor movement, Sa'ib Salam successfully retained al-Masri as part of his own bid to contain the labor movement and advance his following within its ranks.[183] Salam first facilitated al-Masri working for General Security as a confidential informant. It would appear that the 1946 withdrawal of the four syndicates was coordinated between al-Masri and General Security. Salam then worked with al-Masri to establish the League during his tenure as Minister of Interior (May–December 1946). By 1949, the League designated Khalil Bishara al-Khuri (b. 1923) as its honorary president.[184] Its proximity to the top echelons of power and avowedly anti-Communism belied both the corruption of al-Masri and the league's gradualist and reformist approach to labor issues. The number of League-affiliated syndicates ebbed and flowed. In 1955, there were fifteen such syndicates, estimated to represent six thousand workers and employees, including commercial employees, pharmacy assistants, tobacco salesmen, theater and film actors, taxi drivers, bakery workers, and cooks.[185]

The fall of Bishara al-Khuri's regime in September 1952 created the conditions for three more federations to form. In 1952, syndicates of the workers and employees of the Beirut port, EDB, DHP, and Régie along with the Syndicate of Bank Employees established the United Syndicates of Workers and Employees (al-Naqabat al-Muttahida li-l-Mustakhdamin wa-l-'Ummal).[186]

Several of these organizations applied to do so in 1949 but were denied by the government.[187] It instead pressured them into joining the league. After al-Khuri fell, the new government approved a new application for licensing by these syndicates. This change in policy reflected the Sham'un regime's desire to legitimate itself as reformist while also dealing a blow to the league, which had become of a pillar of al-Khuri's social base. The member organizations of the United Syndicates represented some of the oldest, most institutionalized, and largest groupings of organized workers and employees. The five-member composition of this federation remained constant through 1955, representing an estimated six thousand workers and employees.[188]

Two additional federations formed in 1953. Former League president Abdel Majid Mehyu led a group of seven syndicates to defect from the league and establish the Allied Independent Syndicates (Ittihad al-Naqabat al-Mustaqilla).[189] Defection and reaffiliation between these two federations reflected the fluid and contingent nature of coalition politics. Like the league, the Allied Independents was openly anti-Communist and its membership fluctuated. Despite some delay, the government ultimately licensed the Allied Independents in 1954.[190] The following year, there were six affiliated syndicates, estimated to represent approximately three thousand workers and employees, including those of mechanics shops, printing and bookbinding establishments, and customs clearing.[191]

Several syndicates based in Tripoli and the surrounding region established the North Lebanon Federation of Labor Syndicates (Ittihad Naqabat al-'Ummal fi Shamal Lubnan). The formation of this federation reflected both the concentration of urban workers in Tripoli and the very different socioeconomic standing of its workforce as compared to Beirut. While the federation leadership declared themselves anti-Communist, several of its member syndicates were led by Communist labor activists. The federation functioned under the patronage of Rashid Karami (1921–87), who served first as the minister of social affairs (August 1953–September 1955) and then as prime minister (September 1955–March 1956) during the federations' founding, licensing, and early expansion. In 1955, there were at least ten affiliated syndicates, representing over two thousand workers and employees (primarily in Tripoli), including those of bakeries, commercial establishments, and machine shops.[192]

By 1955, the landscape of organized labor featured almost seventy licensed syndicates (and an unknown number of unlicensed syndicates), at least forty-five of which were organized into five federations (including the unlicensed FWES).[193] These federations established permanent offices. In some instances, they issued internal bulletins or more public periodicals. In other instances, they relied on the newspapers of politicians or political parties they were allied with. Despite ideological, organizational, and other differences, these federations served as critical nodes for cross-syndicate collective action in the form of joint positions and solidarity strikes. The federations also provided fora for deliberations on state institutional arrangements, including existing policies, potential reforms, and more. Thus federations played a key role in mobilizations demanding the establishment of a ministry of social affairs, organized labor's representation in the process of drafting social security legislation, and the designation of International Workers' Day as an official paid holiday.

The development of the labor movement and shifting landscape of coalitions politics was shaped by several factors. The leadership styles, personal proclivities, and petty rivalries of labor activists were not negligible. The FWES appears to have been most vulnerable to infighting during extended absence by al-Aris when traveling or imprisoned. In addition, changes in the League leadership and the movement of syndicates between it and the Allied Independents often pivoted around specific personal disagreements with the presidents of both federations.

National and local political developments also intervened to shape the course of the labor movement. Political elites of various persuasions sought to bolster their power in the emerging postindependence order by building and evidencing mass followings across different social sectors. The roles of Far'un, Karami, and Salam discussed above are but three examples. Other notable politicians during this period include Habib Abi Shahla and Sami al-Sulh. Similarly, political parties across the ideological spectrum contributed to labor mobilizations and their internal fault lines. The Lebanese Communist Party is a prime example of this effort. It cultivated links with and contributed to the expansion and organization of workers as far back as the late 1920s. The Kata'ib, the PSP, and—to a lesser extent—the Social Nationalist Party provide three later examples. Beginning in the early 1950s, these organizations increasingly developed links with, and sought to influence, syndicates and federations. In some instances, electoral competitions within syndicates and federations reflected party rivalries.[194] Political parties also selectively championed specific strike actions, syndicates, and federations based on their existing or hoped-for relationship to these groupings. By developing ties with and helping organize urban workers, these politicians and political parties buttressed workers as a corporate interest while selectively amplifying their demands and capacities.

International labor politics reinforced local efforts at championing, organizing, or otherwise shaping labor mobilizations in the early postindependence period. The FWES was a founding member of the World Federation of Trade Unions (WFTU, est. 1945).[195] Lebanese delegations participated in its first (1945) and second (1953) conferences, and al-Aris was a member of its first executive committee.[196] Reflecting its anti-Communist commitments, the League was a founding member of the International Confederation of Free Trade Unions (ICFTU, est. 1949), organized in opposition to the WFTU by the US Congress of Industrial Organizations (est. 1935) and the UK Trade Union Congress (est. 1868).[197] The League sent a representative to each of the ICFTU annual conferences through 1955.

Both the WFTU and ICFTU reflected the ubiquity of urban labor activism across the world, the emergence of an international labor politics, and its ideological and organizational divisions. These two organizations also supported their Lebanese affiliates. The WFTU called on UNESCO in 1948 to investigate the Lebanese government's campaign of repression against the FWES.[198] In 1950, it directly petitioned the Lebanese government on the same matter. The ICFTU sent a delegation to Lebanon in 1953 to inquire into the defection of Mehyu from the League and subsequent establishment of the Allied Independents. In 1955, the ICFTU opened its first regional office in Beirut.

The International Labor Organization (ILO, est. 1919) also played a role in the development of the labor movement in Lebanon. It served as an international forum that legitimated the Lebanese state in general and its approach to labor in particular. Lebanese delegations to ILO conferences privileged bureaucrats working in the government agencies that managed labor. For example, in 1951 the delegation representing Lebanon comprised Director General of the Ministry of Social Affairs Nadim Harfush, the ministry's

Joseph Donato, President of the Syndicate of Commercial Employees Michel Abi Ghanim, and private businessman Rashid Jabir.[199] Through the *International Labour Review*, the ILO facilitated the publication of several articles on Lebanon and the Middle East that celebrated the Republic of Lebanon's approach to labor.[200] It was therefore not surprising that the ILO Committee on Freedom of Association dismissed a complaint it received in 1953 from the Trade Unions International of Postal, Telegraph, Telephone, and Radio Workers (est. 1949) on behalf of the Beirut Telephone Administration workers.[201]

US imperialism was a further factor shaping the labor movement and the shifting terrain of coalition politics. The US diplomatic mission in Beirut began monitoring and reporting on labor relations in Lebanon as early as 1946.[202] A labor attaché and labor reporting officer anchored this activity. The CIA also contributed. Such close observation was part of a larger policy of both applying US Cold War containment logic to the field of labor while promoting a politically reliable and compliant labor movement.[203] By 1955, the US Embassy had built up a close and effective relationship with key elements of organized labor. It had cultivated personal relationships between embassy staff and specific labor leaders and syndicate members. In some cases, these workers or employees served as informants. The embassy selectively shared what information it gathered with the Lebanese government, whose labor policy it generally viewed in favorable terms. US policy also provided funding to syndicates and federations through the Point Four program and sponsored delegations and training trips to the United States.[204] Syndicates and federations variously navigated this US approach to labor, at times engaging in a tacit competition to gain favor with the United States. Such policies and effects were part of a global US approach to organized labor, which it coordinated with the United Kingdom. In fact, the British Embassy in Beirut carried out many similar activities to that of the US Embassy.[205] UK efforts were nevertheless much smaller in scale.

The final, and perhaps most important, factor shaping the contours of the labor movement in Lebanon was the role of state institutions. By the end of 1955, these featured a significantly elaborated set of arrangements and repertoires for the management and containment of labor mobilizations. These tools were premised on—but went significantly beyond—relevant provisions of 1946 Labor Law and the 1943 Penal Code. Within two years of legislating the

Labor Law, the government established a labor arbitration council (*majlis tahkimi*) in each of the five governorates (as mandated by the law). The number of cases processed by the Beirut arbitration council indicates a steady growth from 1947 (888) to 1955 (1,856).[206] Reflective of the primacy of job insecurity in the labor market, the vast majority of these cases involved "dismissal compensation."[207] Initially, labor arbitration councils were final and not subject to appeal. However, revisions to the labor law (the only revisions for the 1946–55 period) made cases involving a minimum amount of money subject to appeal.[208] The parliament also revised the Penal Code to institute penalties for refusal to carry out the decisions of the labor arbitration council.

The efficacy and autonomy of state institutional capacities to address labor issues was of concern to workers, employers, and state officials alike—albeit for different reasons and toward different ends. It will be recalled that in January 1943, the Lebanese government created a Social Affairs Service in what would subsequently come to be known as the Ministry of National Economy. This service was responsible for studying labor issues, supporting the drafting of relevant decrees and legislation, and monitoring the implementation of applicable laws concerning the conditions of workers and employees. The 1946 labor law gave the service the power to license and monitor syndicates and supervise the labor arbitration councils. Between 1946 and 1950, workers regularly protested what they viewed as the inadequacy of the service's capacities.[209] They demanded that the government improve funding and staffing for the service. As an illustration of the its limited capacities, the service apparently relied on several associations, including the Juveniles Protection Union (Ittihad Himayat al-Ahdath, est. 1936), to supplement its own efforts in monitoring and reporting on labor. Such dynamics in the context of persistent labor mobilizations resulted in several institutional enhancements of the service during 1948–49, including its internal reorganization and the addition of six labor inspectors.[210] Important as they were, these enhancements proved insufficient in the face of ongoing labor mobilizations. In 1950, the Social Affairs Service created a specialized Syndicates Section. Rather than facilitating the development of organized labor, the section was specifically meant to undermine it.[211]

In 1951, the Lebanese parliament established the Ministry of Social Affairs.[212] This new institutional arrangement was the culmination of three intersecting dynamics. Workers and employees consistently argued for more robust government attention and intervention into their labor conditions. Some went so far as to explicitly call for the establishment of such a ministry. In addition, those within the Social Affairs Service sought autonomy from both the Ministry of National Economy and other cabinet ministers and parliamentarians that frequently intervened in the policies and practices of the service.[213] Furthermore, there was a growing recognition by successive parliaments and cabinets of the need for a more specialized as well as better funded and staffed state institution to manage labor mobilizations.

This 1951 measure inaugurated the elevation of monitoring, managing, and containing labor mobilizations to a ministerial level of government attention akin to that of other fields such as the armed forces, education, health, agriculture, and the national economy. Upon its creation, the ministry comprised four services: labor, social affairs, syndicates, and monitoring companies.[214] This represented not only an upgrading of the administrative units responsible for labor and social affairs (relative to their previous status as departments within a services). It also featured the elevation of the unit responsible for syndicates to be on par with that of labor and social service. The raison d'être of the new ministry was to address "all the issues arising from the labor law."[215]

State institutions in Lebanon monitored, regulated, adjudicated, and intervened into labor relations through a variety of methods. Both the Ministry of Social Affairs and Ministry of Interior kept close tabs on the labor movement through a combination of surveillance and bureaucratic procedures, including applications for licenses, membership roster submissions, and certification of election results. Both ministries coordinated to delay or withhold licensing from syndicates and federations deemed politically undesirable.[216] In some instances, they encouraged the formation of rival syndicates within a trade or profession. While this primarily manifested around Communist-affiliated syndicates and federations, it also affected avowedly non-Communist groups like the above-discussed United Syndicates between 1949 and 1952. Providing financial support was also important. This initially took the form of an annual subsidy to the League. By 1955, the government was disbursing subsidies to all four licensed federations and sixteen syndicates.[217] The amount of the subsidy had less to do with the size or effectiveness of the labor organization and more to do with the political expediency such funding provided. For example, the government subsidy to the League accounted for the majority of the federation's revenue, thus maintaining its ability to function while also building up a dependency on the government. Subsidies would also be given to incentivize certain behavior. This was the case with syndicates of the film distribution companies' workers and transport and travel agencies' employees, who immediately affiliated with the League upon receiving the funds. But it was also the case with Communist-affiliated syndicates of printing press workers and those of hotels, restaurants, and cafés. To these various tools at the disposable of the government, one must recall the lack of proper enforcement of the rights enshrined in the labor law and frequent deployment of the coercive force of the state to break up meetings and strikes; arrest, prosecute, and imprison labor activists; and otherwise repress worker and employee mobilizations.

The above-discussed factors worked to shape labor relations in general and to mitigate against a strong labor movement that could improve labor conditions. They were nevertheless always responding to the reality of workers and employees that understood their circumstances, had a desire to improve them, and mobilized accordingly. By 1955, the ranks of urban labor, the number of labor organizations, and the relative share of organized labor had all expanded significantly. Repeated and regular mobilizations by workers and employees secured important gains while also reflecting the power of employers and that of state institutions. In doing so, they normalized a culture of labor contestation and shaped state institutional expansion to contain them. These mobilizations helped establish workers and employees as constituent element of the political field. It was in this context that by 1955 International Workers' Day was an official holiday, marked by several public events, organized by workers, syndicates, and federations representing a range of political affiliations, and featuring government officials and diplomatic representatives.

CONCLUSION

Relations between labor and the state and between labor and capital in the postindependence period were critical components of the political field. The transition to independence liberated workers and employees from the antilabor approach and policies of the French High Commission. Yet it also featured an ultimate break in the alliance between national elites and organized labor that had underpinned that transition. Workers and employees sought to improve their labor conditions by building on legacies, adapting to new realities, and navigating contingencies. Alternatively, officials and bureaucrats sought to centralize state authority, consolidate independence, and chart a strategy for economic development and international alliances. Doing so involved expanding the capacity of state institutions to more effectively manage labor mobilizations and increasingly intervene into all aspects of labor politics. Episodically, the labor movement secured important gains from employers and the state, whose intervention in their struggle with the former they regularly invited. The organized labor movement ultimately consolidated an increased relevance to local and national politics.

Five

WOMEN AND SUFFRAGE

IN MARCH 1953, THE LEAGUE OF WOMEN'S ORGANIZATIONS IN Lebanon (Jami'at al-Hay'at al-Nisa'iyya fi Lubnan) held a public celebration at Cinema Roxy in Beirut under the patronage of First Lady Zulfa Tabet Sham'un.[1] The event marked the attainment of women's suffrage in Lebanon. It also honored the Executive Committee of Women's Organizations in Lebanon (al-Lajna al-Tanfidhiyya li-l-Hay'at al-Nisa'iyya fi Lubnan), a nine-woman ad hoc committee that orchestrated a three-year campaign to secure women this right. Lamya Bayhum welcomed the audience in the name of league president Laure Tabet, who was representing Lebanon at an international women's conference. Former president and prime minister Alfred Naqqash gave the first speech, detailing his view of the history of the "women's cause" (qadiyyat al-mar'a) that led to the present moment. According to Naqqash, women's engagement with "parliamentary life" (al-hayat al-niyabiyya) would expand freedom of expression and elevate the country's morale. Najjada founder and Arabic daily *Bayrut* (Beirut) publisher Muhyi al-Din al-Nsuli urged women to embrace education in order to fully realize their aspirations at home and in society. He also cautioned them against forgetting "the home that she entered with her life partner" (al-bayt alladhi dakhalathu ma' rafiq hayatiha). Then came the reading aloud of congratulatory telegrams from President of the General Confederation of Arab Women

Ibtihaj Qaddura and Fayza al-Sulh, wife of deceased former prime minister Riyad al-Sulh. Najla Sa'b then spoke on behalf of the Executive Committee, extolling women for persevering until victory, refusing anything short of their complete suffrage rights (*haqquha al-siyassi*). Sa'b declared this day the beginning of a "national era for women . . . building together a nationalist entity whose foundation is justice" (*'ahd al-mar'a al-qawmi . . . sanabni ma'an ba'd al-yawm kiyanan qawmiyyan assasahu al-'adl*).

The campaign that succeeded in securing Lebanese women the vote emerged out of a broader context of women's associational activities. This context featured complex tensions and negotiations of class relationships. While the campaign and its context have their origins in the late Ottoman and French colonial periods, the postindependence period featured unique local, regional, and international developments that both expanded the Lebanese women's movement and advanced the cause of suffrage. Women and their organizations were critical actors in popular mobilizations and thus shaped Lebanon's trajectory of state formation. To explore these phenomena, this chapter analyzes the processes, rationales, and relationships that informed the women's movement in 1943–55 in relation to state institutional arrangements in general and women's suffrage in particular.

POSTCOLONIAL EXPANSION OF THE WOMEN'S MOVEMENT

A self-conscious women's movement was a signal feature of Lebanon's postindependence political landscape. Anchored in a diverse array of groups with various levels of institutionalization and politicization, the women's movement included heterogenous and contentious networks of leading women, their organizations, and their activities. Participants in the women's movement were concerned with numerous and varying issues. Some focused on charity, providing the needy with clothing and food, as well as managing orphanages.[2] Others emphasized girls' education. They established or managed private schools at kindergarten and elementary levels, administered literacy programs, and offered financial support to female students.[3] Social reform constituted the third set of issues. Women's organizations called for criminalizing and abolishing sex work, reforming prisons, and the economic development of rural areas.[4] Finally, other women were focused on promoting and expanding the national economy. They championed local industry, encouraged the consumption of local products, and called for measures to protect local producers from the impact of imported goods.[5]

The Lebanese women's movement displayed important internal faults. First, women's organizations were unevenly distributed across space and time. Despite their geographic reach, most were anchored in Beirut. As one moved further from the capital, women's organizations and the range of issues around which they mobilized declined in number. Yet the specific distribution of organizations, issues, and resources unpredictably shifted over time, depending on both the exigencies of a particular moment and the strategic visions of the women who led these organizations. Second, many of the women's organizations were religiously based. Some primarily serviced specific sectarian or religious communities, while others merely drew most of their members from such communities. Finally, the leadership and active membership of most women's organizations hailed overwhelmingly from upper- and middle-class strata. Despite increasing inclusion of women from different backgrounds, those who would rise through the ranks of their organizations, in particular, followed practices that privileged elite norms.

One might question whether it makes sense to refer to this array of women's organizations as a women's movement. Neither these organizations' class basis nor the issues of primary interest to them comport with what some consider the defining features of a women's movement, by which they mean a feminist movement that explicitly addresses the structural subordination of women. In fact, many politically active women did not publicly identify as or define themselves thusly. Nevertheless, the organizations these women joined served as important spaces for women to break out of the confines of family structures, congregate with other women, and collectively engage the broader political, social, and economic contexts in which they and others lived. Furthermore, these women perceived and represented their heterogenous organizations and activities as constituting a collective culture and political identity, a key element of which was the desire to improve the position of women in Lebanon. Almost all of the women involved in this effort self-consciously referred to their organizations' collective existence as "the women's movement in Lebanon" (al-haraka al-nisa'iyya fi Lubnan). In this sense, they were located on an arc stretching back to the interwar period, and which propelled upper- and middle-class women in Lebanon and the region away from discursive references to a "women's awakening" (al-nahda al-nisa'iyya) and toward claiming roles in a "women's movement."[6] The activities of most women's organizations were dominated by social welfare provisioning. Yet it was the leadership, members, and networks linking these organizations that also mobilized to challenge various patriarchal structures throughout the postcolonial period, as they had under French rule. These mobilizations variously demanded women's suffrage (*huquq al-mar'a al-siyasiyya*), women's right to work and receive equal pay (*haq al-'amal wa-l-tasawi fi al-'ujur 'inda al-tasawi fi al-'amal*), and various elements of the personal status system.

Despite their differences in terms of membership, activities, and geographic locations, many of these organizations' memberships and activities overlapped. Many women were involved in more than two organizations, each of which focused on a different issue and operated in a different community. In addition, many of these organizations formed both informal and formal coalitions. Some of these coalitions were based on a specific geographical location or activity, like the League of Beirut Districts Women's Welfare Associations (Rabitat al-Jam'iyyat al-Khayriyya al-Nisa'iyya li-Ahya' Beirut), composed of several Beirut-based neighborhood associations.[7] Others were based on a shared activity irrespective of geography. The Lebanese Union of Child Welfare Societies (al-Ittihad Ri'ayat al-Tufl al-Lubnani), for example, included eighteen member organizations identified as "women's societies" in 1954.[8]

In certain instances, women's organizations formed alliances with, or lent support to, other social movements like labor unions, student organizations, or political parties. In 1946, the Arab Women's Federation in Lebanon (AWFL, al-Ittihad al-Nisa'i al-'Arabi fi Lubnan), the Union of Lebanese Women (Jami'at Nisa' Lubnan), and the Women's Awakening Society (Jam'iyyat al-Nahda al-Nisa'iyya) joined other associations and political parties in petitioning the government to do more to reduce the cost of living.[9] Between 1949 and 1954, several women's organizations joined forces with the likes of the Dentists' Syndicate, the Islamic Youth Movement, the Orthodox Youth Movement, the Teachers' Syndicate, and various university alumni associations to form the Conference on Non-Government Organizations in Lebanon.[10] In 1950, the conference elected Jamal Karam Harfush (head of Lebanese Union of Child Welfare Societies) president, Mary Hananiyya (president of the Beirut College for Women Alumnae Association) treasurer, and Alice Nakkash (of the Juveniles Protection Union), Janet Tadrus (of the Union of Lebanese Women), Munira Shehadi (of the Zahleh Women's Society [al-Jam'iyya al-Nisa'iyya fi Zahleh]), Adilaid Rishani (of the Women's Awakening Society), and Edma Bayouth (of the YWCA) at-large members of the conference executive committee.[11]

Many women's organizations in Lebanon actively spurred the creation of state institutions. This was certainly the case when many of their members actively participated in the November 1943 uprising and the subsequent mobilizations to transfer the Common Interests and force the evacuation of French troops. Yet the most frequently recurring form of such mobilizations was campaigns to establish public schools in specific neighborhoods. No less significant was their participation in debates about price controls, food rationing, and mandatory military training in schools.[12] Women's organizations participated in, broadened, and amplified public deliberations while also lending their mobilizational capacities to help shape outcomes. Between 1953 and 1955 several women's organizations participated in the formation of the National Conference of Parties and Organizations (al-Mu'tamar al-Watani li-l-Ahzab wa-l-Hay'at), which issued a program of administrative, political, economic, and social demands, and episodically mobilized in response to regional developments.[13]

One of the most tangible examples of how women's mobilizations intersected with state formation is the role the Association for the Protection of Juveniles (Jam'iyyat Himayat al-Ahdath, est. 1936) played in establishing and supporting the Juvenile Delinquency Court (Mahkamat al-Ahdath, est. 1948). The founding of the court inaugurated a special judicial jurisdiction, process, and set of outcomes for children accused of violating the law.[14] This juvenile delinquency system authorized the prosecution of persons sixteen years of age and older as adults while defining children between the ages of seven and fifteen as responsible for their actions but requiring a specialized judicial process.[15] In 1955, the court processed no fewer than eight hundred cases.[16] The Association for the Protection of Juveniles had a team of six social workers and one lawyer who represented and advocated for children who were unable to secure their own legal representation. Yet the relationship between the association and the court was much more complex.[17] The social workers prepared reports on all cases before the court, investigating the background and conditions of the child in question while also making suggestions for "treatment." In exchange, the association received an annual subsidy from the government, with which it supplemented individual and institutional membership dues received from the association's supporters.

The women's movement of the early postindependence period (1943–55) was not simply a remnant from the late Ottoman and colonial periods. During this era women's organizations expanded numerically, geographically, and topically. For example, between 1920 and 1939 more than thirty-six women's groups registered with the Lebanese state, the vast majority of them in Beirut.[18] Yet early to mid-1950s reports on the women's movement variously listed more than double that number of groups.[19] At least three of these groups traced their origins back to the late nineteenth century (1880–85).[20] According to one study, fifty-five women's organizations were located in Beirut, twenty-two were in Tripoli, and at least one was in 'Alay, 'Amyun, Batrun, Bayno, Bayt Shabab, Ihdin, Sidon, Suq al-Gharb, Zahleh, and Zgharta.[21] These latter cities and towns spanned the entire geography of Lebanon, and included the regions of Mount Lebanon, North Lebanon, South Lebanon, and the Biqa'. The expansion of the women's movement in the aftermath of independence was certainly uneven in time, space, and issue. Different women (and sometimes existing organizations) took the lead in forming new organizations in response to a range of factors in a variety of ways.

One example of a new organization created by women is the Union of Lebanese Women (Jami'at Nisa' Lubnan). Between December 1943 and January 1944, Hunayna Tarsha, Najla Sa'b (1908–71), Eva Badr Malik (1914–88), Ibtihaj Qaddura (1893–1967), Jamal Karam Harfush (1914–2000), and Rose Shahfa (1890–1955) submitted a request to officially register the union.[22] This organization originally took shape in November 1943 as the Lebanese Women's Strike Committee (Lajnat al-Idrab al-Nisa'iyya al-Lubnaniyya), which was discussed in chapter 1. In the strike's aftermath, committee members determined to institutionalize the relationships and the revolutionary spirit they forged during the eleven-day general strike that led to French recognition of Lebanese independence.[23] These women also sought to create an organization focused on what they considered women's roles in an independent Lebanon.

The union's most significant project was the establishment of a monthly magazine in 1945. Titled *Sawt al-Mar'a* (The Voice of Women),[24] the publication originated as the one-page daily bulletin of the same name created by the strike committee.[25] Tarsha was the publication's managing editor during its first ten years. Teacher and radio presenter Edvick Juraydini Shaybub (1918–2002) and Nazik Sarkis were also regularly involved during that time. In addition, at least eight other women rotated through various editorial and managerial roles in publication's initial ten years. *Sawt al-Mar'a* was reaching a significant number of readers by 1948.[26] Its circulation reached government and commercial offices and the workplaces of lawyers, doctors, and other members of the professional middle class. Its largest circulation, however, was to private homes. One of the leading publishers in Lebanon at the time, Dar al-Kitab, produced and promoted the magazine, which featured advertisements targeting middle- and upper-class consumers and promoting various urban and rural industries. Initially priced at fifteen liras for a domestic (Lebanese) individual annual subscription, the fee structure evolved relatively quickly to include foreign individual subscriptions (ten US dollars) as well as an institutional rate (twenty-five liras) for government, commercial, and other establishments.

Sawt al-Mar'a regularly featured profiles of different women's organizations and those who led them. It also provided a platform for women to share their opinions about contentious issues like the Arabization of school curricula, mandatory military service, press censorship, public utilities, urban poverty, and rural development. The magazine, which featured regular content on home economics, literature, and the arts, served as Lebanon's only women's publication during the early postindependence period. This fact is particularly significant given that, due to a host of practical, strategic, and political factors, the initial 1920s florescence of the women's press ended in the early 1930s.[27]

Other new women's organizations formed as result of the growth and institutionalization of what began as committees within existing organizations. With time, the work of these committees and the number of women involved in them increased sufficiently as to justify establishing a separate organization. This was the case with the Child Welfare Society (Jam'iyyat Ri'ayat al-Tufl). The Women's Committee (al-Lajna al-Nisa'iyya) of the Islamic Orphanage (Dar al-Aytam al-Islamiyya) first established a child welfare outreach program in 1946. By 1949, the work of the program had expanded significantly enough for its members to reconstitute themselves as an independent organization,[28] whose first president was Na'mih Baydun Qurunful (b. 1917).[29] By 1955, the Child Welfare Society boasted ninety members, a monthly meeting, and an annual budget that combined private donations with national and municipal government subsidies.[30] Its activities primarily focused on the treatment and prevention of disease among poor children. The Child Welfare Society managed three centers—Basta, Horsh, and Ras Beirut— in the capital. In addition to a mobile center in rural areas, it also managed three village centers: Bshitfin (just north of Dayr al-Qamar in the Shuf District), Qar'un (just east of the lake in the Biqa'), and Hanniya (in the Tyre District). These centers served as nodes for interaction between members of the organization, volunteer doctors, local and national governments, and various private institutions. The clinic in Hanniya is particularly telling of this nature: it was the product of a collaboration between the UN Reliefs and Works Agency and the Child Welfare Society. The former provided an on-duty nurse and medical supplies for Palestinian refugees, while the latter secured the building and provided medical supplies for Lebanese patients.[31]

Some women created organizations out of a desire to parallel or compete with existing organizations. In 1948, for example, Habiba Sha'ban Yakun (b. 1918) established the Young Muslim Women's Society (Jam'iyyat al-Shabbat al-Muslimat).[32] This organization was effectively the women's wing of the Young Muslim Men's Association (Jam'iyyat al-Shabab al-Muslimun), and modeled its activities on those of the YWCA, which was founded as a Lebanese branch of the World Alliance of Young Christian Women's Associations in 1920.[33] Within a year of its establishment, the Young Muslim Women's Society boasted seven hundred members spread across Beirut, Tripoli, and Sidon, and was organizing public lectures, literacy campaigns, sewing workshops, homemaking tutorials, and language training.[34]

Changing socioeconomic conditions and ideas about development served as the bases for other women's organization-building activities. In 1951 writer Eveline Bustros (1878–1971) collaborated with Druze Orphanage

(Dar al-Aytam al-Durziyya) board member Anissa Rawda Najjar (1913–2016) to found the Village Welfare Society (VWS, Jam'iyyat In'ash al-Qarya).[35] Several women's organizations had previously worked in the countryside, but the VWS was the first instance of a Lebanese organization dedicated solely to "raising the economic standards of village women" by working exclusively in rural areas. This reflected broader ideas about the need to uplift rural communities, notions that were circulating as part of post–World War II debates on development. It also mirrored a broader concern with what was, in hindsight, the collapse of the rural economy in Lebanon. The VWS established schools, centers, and programs focused on literacy and food production. It established a girls' school in Maymis (near Hasbayya in South Lebanon), serving approximately 55 students from a community where the estimated illiteracy rate was 75 percent.[36] In doing so, the VWS actively sought to emulate the local public elementary boys' school, which offered first-, second-, and third-grade schooling for almost 80 students. In Munsif (between Jbayl and Batrun in Mount Lebanon), VWS established a school that enrolled 115 students, 25 of whom were boarders at the school, drawn from seven surrounding villages.[37] The VWS also established a canning program in Bshitfin, which at the time included 140 families and a total population of 900.[38]

Lebanon's new status as an internationally recognized sovereign state prompted women to exploit new and different possibilities. Throughout the colonial period, the Red Cross operating in Lebanon was technically a branch of the French Red Cross. Therein, Lebanese women participated as junior partners, structurally subordinated to French leadership. In 1945, Najla Sa'b and other Lebanese women took advantage of the new postindependence reality and established the Lebanese Red Cross Society (Jam'iyyat al-Salib al-Ahmar al-Lubnani).[39] In addition to setting up clinics and providing various services in major cities, the society inaugurated a fleet of mobile clinics that operated across Lebanon, serving approximately forty-five villages that lacked access to physicians.[40] The society played a pivotal role in relief efforts for Palestinian refugees expelled to Lebanon by Zionist conquest during the 1948 Nakba. Soon thereafter it supported government efforts to consolidate relief facilities into seventeen official refugee camps and several informal settlements. Providing these services gave the organization greater prominence, thus increasing its fundraising opportunities and enhancing its infrastructure.[41]

The expansion of the women's movement also meant increased coordination between organizations. In the colonial period, a number of women's organizations joined forces to establish the Women's Federation of Lebanon (al-Ittihad al-Nisa'i fi Lubnan).[42] The federation was the institutional framework through which a cross-sectarian women's movement coordinated their demands for increased state-sponsored social welfare and for women's political, social, and personal status rights.[43] The Women's Federation of Lebanon affiliated with the International Women's Suffrage Alliance (est. 1902) in 1930.[44] By 1931, the federation claimed approximately twenty member organizations, whose activities took the form of regular meetings, publishing a magazine, submitting petitions—and to a lesser extent—holding demonstrations.[45] The federation also organized more than seven major conferences during this period.[46]

In 1944, the Women's Federation in Lebanon formally renamed itself the Arab Women's Federation in Lebanon (AWFL, al-Ittihad al-Nisa'i al-'Arabi fi Lubnan) and renewed its coordinating activities after a brief period of dormancy. Between 1944 and 1949, it established committees on education, political rights, and international peace, complementing the work of the committees it created during the colonial period: health, moral standards, and prison reform.[47] The federation, which officially claimed twenty-three member organizations between 1949 and 1951,[48] regularly sent delegations to visit and confer with member organizations across Lebanon,[49] and ultimately participated in numerous regional and international conferences about social and cultural affairs, as well as other issues of concern to women and children.

The discrepancy between the small number of AWFL members relative to that of all women's organizations highlights the degree to which the Lebanese women's movement lacked cohesion. In fact, the women's movement experienced a range of factional strains. In 1947, a number of women's organizations splintered from the AWFL, joining with other independent groups to form Women's Solidarity (al-Tadamun al-Nisa'i),[50] a schism that endured for approximately five years. Beyond the fact that most women who remained in the AWFL identified as Muslim, and those who created Women's

Solidarity were primarily Christian, we know very little about the internal issues underlying this split. However, the two groups merged in November 1952 to form the League of Lebanese Women's Organizations (Jami'at al-Hay'at al-Lubnaniyya al-Nisa'iyya). By 1955, when the league's membership had reached 103 organizations, the league was affiliated with both the International Alliance of Women and the International Council of Women.[51] It held monthly meetings and organized its activities around committees devoted to political rights, economics, education, youth, emigration, and publicity.

Several factors facilitated the above-described expansion of Lebanese women's organizations during the early postindependence period. First, mobilizations related to the November 1943 uprising, the transfer of the Common Interests, and the evacuation of French troops, not to mention the wartime and post–World War II socioeconomic fluctuations, intensified activities within the women's movement. Activist women's participation in the struggle for independence politicized Lebanese women more generally. It also further demonstrated the efficacy of women's collective action. At the same time, the transition to independence raised a host of new questions and new possibilities for state, market, and citizen formation. These questions included the organization of electoral politics in general and women's suffrage in particular, public education, mandatory military training and service, and the government's foreign policy orientation. Many women joined or created new organizations in order to participate in the attendant debates and participate in the new institutional arrangements that would emerge from them. The postindependence period also witnessed the return of education as a central concern of women's mobilizations. Women's increasing access to elementary, secondary, and college education was simultaneously an important driving force behind the expansion of the women's movement and a shared objective of most women's organizations, both old and new.

Women across the Middle East resumed their prewar coordination and succeeded in building or enhancing their institutions, a process in which Lebanese women and their organizations played a central role.[52] Their gatherings were spaces in which to share experiences and cement solidarities. In the most significant example, Huda Sha'rawi (1879–1947) and other women active in the Egyptian Feminist Union hosted the Arab Women's Congress (al-Mu'tamar al-Nisa'i al-'Arabi) in Cairo, December 12–16, 1944.[53] Sha'rawi and her co-organizers held some of their preparatory meetings in Lebanon as part of a regional tour to promote a conference to inaugurate a regional confederation of women's organizations.[54] The Arab Women's Congress conference included delegations from Egypt, Iraq, Lebanon, Palestine, Syria, and Transjordan, whose total attendance nearly doubled that of the most recent (1938) Arab women's conference, also held in Cairo.[55] One-fifth of the women present had attended that previous regional conference. The writer and activist Rose Shahfa led the Lebanese delegation of twenty-nine delegates to the congress,[56] which passed fifty-one resolutions designed to improve the status of women, including several on women's suffrage and personal status reform, and also endorsed the Arab League, then still in formation. More importantly, the delegates established the General Confederation of Arab Women (al-Ittihad al-Nisa'i al-'Arabi al-'Am), and elected Sha'rawi its president. The confederation provided an important institutional space for strategic learning, moral support, and the establishment and expansion of solidarity networks. Upon returning home from Egypt, Lebanese women held events and published articles highlighting the conference's resolutions and the establishment of the confederation. Less than a year after Sha'rawi passed away in 1947, the confederation held its second congress in Beirut in 1949.[57] The delegates elected as Sha'rawi's successor Lebanon's Ibtihaj Qaddura, who moved the confederation's headquarters to Beirut, thereby empowering Lebanon's growing women's movement. Thus in 1954, Qaddura hosted and presided over the confederation's third congress in Beirut.[58]

During the postwar period, changing international norms and the creation of the UN and other multilateral institutions buttressed women's local and regional organizing efforts. In February 1946, for example, the UN established a subcommission on the status of women under the supervision of the Commission on Human Rights. The decision was the product of decades of women's international lobbying, first at the League of Nations and subsequently at the inaugural meeting of the UN General Assembly.[59] In response to demands to further elevate women's status and improve their living conditions, the UN upgraded the body in June 1946, establishing the Commission on the Status of Women (CSW).[60] Its mandate was to report and make recommendations to the UN Economic and Social Council on the promotion of women's political, economic, social, and civil rights. The CSW would be an important resource in the struggle for Lebanese women's suffrage, and would legitimize the creation, activities, and inclusion of women's organizations more generally.

The CSW also lobbied the UN successfully, advocating for the use of women-inclusive language and minimal use of the word *man* as synonymous with *human being* in the Universal Declaration of Human Rights. The CSW also normalized the presence of women's organizations in the sessions of various UN commissions and councils. Furthermore, the CSW ensured that Lebanese women played a role in their government's contribution to creating the United Nations and its subsidiary organizations. Angela Jurdak Khoury (1915–2011) served as the Lebanese delegate on the UN's original (1946) seven-person subcommission. Khoury was also the Lebanese delegate to the CSW during the 1950 and 1951 sessions, at which she was elected as one of its officers, the rapporteur,[61] making her one the first Arab women to serve on an international body of that magnitude.[62] Laure Tabet (1896–1981) succeeded Jurdak Khoury as the Lebanese delegate to the CSW sessions from 1952 to 1955.

The growing number of international affiliations among women's organizations in Lebanon was one indication of local, regional, and international trends. As previously described, the AWFL was affiliated with the International Alliance of Women and International Council of Women, while the YWCA was an official branch of the World YWCA headquartered in Geneva. In addition, the Lebanese Red Cross was an official member of the League of Red Cross Societies. Likewise, the Lebanese Medical Women's Association was affiliated with the International Medical Women's Association, while the Lebanese University Women's Association (Jam'iyyat al-Lubnaniyyat al-Jami'iyyat) and Federation of Lebanese University Women (Jam'iyyat Ittihad al-Jami'iyyat al-Lubnaniyya) affiliated with the International Federation of University Women. The Village Welfare Society affiliated with the Associated Country Women of the World, and the Association for the Protection of Lebanese Girls affiliated with the International Association of Catholic Nuns for the Protection of Young Girls. Finally, the Union of Child Welfare Societies affiliated with the International Council of Child Welfare.

A final dynamic undergirding the postindependence expansion of women's organizations in Lebanon was the acceptance of women as official members of existing political parties. There is little evidence that women either formed or joined political parties prior to independence. Yet the late 1940s and early 1950s featured important developments in this regard. Three primary examples are the Committee for Women's Rights (CWR, Lajnat Huquq al-Mar'a), the Kata'ib Women's Organization (KWO, al-Munazzama al-Nisa'iyya al-Kata'ibiyya), and the Women's Branch of the Progressive Socialist Party (Fir' al-Nisa'i li-l-Hizb al-Taqaddumi al-Ishtiraki). We know very little about this third group, except that several petitions circulating in the 1950s bore its endorsement.

A group of leftist women—Thurayya Khatib 'Adra (d. 1995), Emily Faris Ibrahim (1914–2011), Alvira Khuri, and Mary Thabit chief among them—established the CWR in 1946–47.[63] The committee demanded the recognition of women as "complete human being[s], equal to men in rights and duties."[64] This recognition applied to suffrage and women's pay, but it also entailed abolishing sex work and allowing women to freely express their political views. Although little is known about the CWR's early years,[65] its leaders appear to have been experienced organizers, members of the Lebanese Communist Party or sympathetic to it, connected to the wider leftist milieu, and to have had access to Soviet material support.[66] The CWR affiliated with the Women's International Democratic Federation (est. 1945), sending delegates to that organization's conferences and congresses.[67] In fact, the federation's third congress (Copenhagen, 1953) elected Layla Khalil and Mary Thabit of the CWR to the federation's new council.[68] The CWR also appears to be the first women's organization in Lebanon to publicly celebrate International Women's Day (Yawm al-Mar'a al-'Alami, March 8).[69]

These and other of the CWR's early activities caught the attention of the leftist and other opposition presses, thus attracting the attention of General Security (al-Amn al-'Am), which appears to have surveilled the committee for an extended period of time,[70] just one of the times its mobilizational activities aroused the unwelcome interest of the authorities. In 1949, for example, the government denied the CWR a permit to celebrate International Women's Day at the Grand Theater of Beirut (Tiatro al-Kabir).[71] In response, the organization held the event at a private home, from which it organized a march of approximately sixty women,[72] who demanded political rights for women, equal pay for equal work, civil liberties (*huquq dimuqratiyya*), and more. Despite the police intercepting and dispersing this march,[73] the CWR mounted follow-up events a week later in Tripoli and Zahleh. And in 1950, the group organized coordinated rallies and marches commemorating International Women's Day in Beirut and Tripoli. We know little of what transpired on this occasion in Tripoli, but at least twenty-seven women were detained during the Beirut march.[74] Despite such state repression, the CWR persisted in publicly celebrating International Women's Day by issuing statements and holding events. In 1955, for example, the committee sent a delegation to participate in such a celebration in Damascus,[75] then subsequently organized its own events in Beirut, Tripoli, and Ayn Harsha (Biqa').[76]

Another significant group was the KWO, which the Kata'ib Party officially established as an affiliate in March 1941.[77] The KWO began recruiting members and organizing public events in March–April 1948.[78] From that point forward, May Joseph Fayyad, attorney and activist Laure Nasr (1929–97), and Sonya Latif hosted meet and greets, presented public lectures, and conducted neighborhood visits to stimulate support for the organization. The KWO organized its membership along regional and neighborhood lines like its male counterparts in the Kata'ib Party. In 1950, the group created its first neighborhood chapter in Burj al-Barajna, followed by others in Dikwana, Furn al-Shubbak, and Harat Hrayk.[79] The KWO's stated objective vis-à-vis women was equipping them to "carry out their national duties."[80] In fact, women's suffrage was not an element of the KWO's 1941 founding documents, nor was it part of the group's initial (1948–49) program of activities. Yet beginning in 1950, the organization increasingly addressed the issue of suffrage, as did its parent organization, the Kata'ib Party.[81]

The emergence of the CWR and KWO marked a turning point in the Lebanese women's movement and in popular politics more generally. Political parties began to offer women a mechanism to mobilize and become more politicized by incorporating them into party activities. These parties increasingly dedicated sections and columns of their publications to women and women's issues. In some cases, parties facilitated the emergence of new women's movement leaders through the creation of women's auxiliary formations or by recruiting women as party members. The poet Emily Faris Ibrahim and Laure Nasr's involvement in the CWR and KWO, respectively, are indications of this development. Their class origins, professional backgrounds, and ideological orientations differed from one another as well as from many leaders of the women's movement. Most significantly, the pair played decisive roles in organizing Lebanon's successful campaign for women's suffrage.

Party-affiliated women's organizational activities drew on existing party methods of public engagement, recruitment, and vetting. Linda Matar (1925–2023) exemplified this tendency.[82] In response to an invitation, Matar and a friend attended a CWR protest—Matar's first—near both her home and the St. George Church in Beirut's 'Ayn al-Rummana neighborhood. A week later, Edma Ghulam and Evelin 'Uqays knocked on Matar's door and asked her to accompany them collecting petition signatures from residents of her neighborhood. Within a week, the CWR's 'Ayda Maqdisi also reached out to Matar to help establish a committee branch in 'Ayn al-Rummana. Matar headed this branch, becoming a full CWR member in 1953, soon thereafter being elected general secretary of the organization.

SUFFRAGE REVISITED

In the entire history of the Lebanese women's movement, perhaps no issue is as celebrated as the securing of female suffrage in 1953. This victory was the culmination of a long-standing struggle, and the function of changes in Lebanese, regional, and international politics. Prior to independence, groups of women had episodically organized to secure what they defined as equal political rights (*huquq siyasiyya mutasawiyya*). Women from Beirut and elsewhere in the territories that would become Lebanon first lobbied for suffrage via a 1919 petition to Faysal bin Husayn demanding equal rights for women in the future Arab state. There is no evidence that this attempt elicited any official response, or that it was part of a broader pro-suffrage movement.[83] Women next attempted to secure suffrage through male allies in post–World War I representative institutions. The first such case occurred in April 1920 during the constitutional deliberations of the Syrian National Congress (SNC),[84] and subsequently in May 1924 as part of a motion to permit women to vote in the elections for the Representative Council of the State of Greater Lebanon.[85] Both SNC delegate Ibrahim al-Khatib and Representative Council member Yusuf al-Khazin framed their respective proposals with the concept of "educated women." A not insignificant diversity of personalities, including urban notables, religious scholars, and judges, supported al-Khatib's and al-Khazin's proposals. Conservative—and mostly landowning—politicians led the opposition to women's suffrage. It is worth noting that the debate in 1924 also featured a preponderance of Francophone and Mandate-supporting politicians opposing suffrage. Despite heated debate at both events, neither proposal succeeded, and discussion ceased at the SNC when several delegates walked out of the meeting, causing the quorum to collapse. The body eventually approved a constitution for Faysal's kingdom that did not grant female suffrage. Discussion of the topic ended in the Representative Council when only three representatives declared their support for removal of the male referent in the electoral law. This outcome, which was more definitive than the ambiguous deliberations of the SNC, left leaders of the women's movement devastated.[86]

The Representative Council subsequently ratified the 1926 Constitution of the Republic of Lebanon, whose Article 21 states "Every Lebanese citizen who has completed his twenty-first year and fulfills the conditions laid down by the electoral law is an elector."[87] Article 24 of the constitution explicitly references the electoral law of March 8, 1922, which determined the conditions for electing representatives to the Chamber of Deputies.[88] While this article also enabled the chamber to enact new electoral legislation should it so decide, women's appeals to the government on two separate occasions in the 1930s failed to produce electoral laws that did not specifically define the electorate as men.

Thus women failed to secure suffrage in the colonial period. Despite the presence of some important male allies, most Lebanese men viewed women's suffrage as incompatible with their conservative, masculine vision of anticolonialism. In addition, women's suffrage would necessitate a new electoral law, which would open the door to other alterations that might undermine the power of incumbent (male) politicians. They owed their positions to the existing system, which the French High Commission deliberately crafted to favor specific social groups. At the same time, the failure to secure female suffrage in Lebanon paralleled similar developments across the Middle East and North Africa, France, and other parts of the world.[89]

Such early setbacks combined with the reduction of women's access to public spaces during the 1930s.[90] In response, many women leaders and their organizations adapted to a new ideological and strategic premise that acquired prominence in that decade: "patriotic motherhood."[91] They increasingly championed "domestic duties and charity work as national service, and advanced demands for women's civil and social rights in order to accomplish this service."[92] In this way, women mirrored trends in other national women's movements, like those of Egypt and India. Patriotic motherhood also served more immediate strategic goals: broadening the movement's appeal, increasing recruitment of members, and helping nationalist parties enter government to secure the political and social rights for which the women's movement had struggled during the interwar era. Not all women approved of this general strategic trend, but it nevertheless defined the broader contours of women's activism until the dissolution of the French Mandate.

Independence offered new opportunities to raise the issue of suffrage, as women had been crucial to anticolonial mobilization and the consolidation of political independence in 1943–46. Thus, throughout the pages of Lebanon's periodicals, women argued that the political equality of the sexes was a sign of genuine independence and progress.[93] As the issue gained currency, smaller-scale discussions also occurred in many sites. One example was the American University of Beirut (AUB) Debating Team's examination of the question of whether Arab women should exercise political rights.[94] Several women's groups also submitted petitions demanding suffrage to the government—the AWFL in 1943, Women's Union in 1944, and AWFL again in 1947.[95] Despite sympathetic statements from a number of politicians, nothing came of such efforts initially. Critics of the petitions appealed to tradition and religion, and stressed women's domestic duties as their primary and necessary contribution. Women like Emily Faris Ibrahim, Laure Nasr, and author and teacher Salwa Mahmasani Mumneh (1908–57) countered by publishing various articles that praised their allies and called out their detractors.[96] While many women held firm to the principle that they should share equally in the rights and responsibilities of suffrage, women's organizations rarely mobilized for that specific goal during the immediate postindependence period.[97] With the exception of the CWR and the KWO, most women and their organizations confined their advocacy of suffrage to the publication of editorials.[98]

For several reasons, 1949 was a watershed in the long-term struggle for suffrage. It immediately followed the UN General Assembly's December

1948 proclamation of the Universal Declaration of Human Rights.[99] Despite its limitations, many women in Lebanon and beyond viewed the declaration as endorsing long-standing grievances as well as recurrent demands made to both national governments and foreign powers. Of course, the declaration's multiple assertion of the equal rights of men and women were of particular relevance to the women's movement in Lebanon.[100] The CSW had guided the General Assembly in this direction, explicitly making equal political rights a pillar of its agenda in 1947 and passing resolutions specifically endorsing women's political rights in 1948 and 1949.[101] In 1950–51, the CSW initiated, drafted, and debated the Convention on the Political Rights of Women.[102] These multilateral efforts enshrined "women's political rights" as international norms of governance while simultaneously providing one of the most consistent definitions of these rights.

Upon the invitation of Lebanon's UN Ambassador and the UN Economic and Social Council's Charles Malik (1906–87), the CSW held its 1949 session between March 21 and April 4 at the UNESCO Palace in Beirut. The invitation was more about the broader strategy of Lebanese international diplomacy than a governmental commitment to women's rights. Nonetheless, convening the session in Beirut strengthened links between international norms of governance and local women's mobilizations.[103] This was not without its complications, as the discussions during the CSW's Beirut session revealed critical fault lines on the issues of Palestine, the political rights of married women, and the international competition between the United States and the Soviet Union.[104] The session nevertheless energized the Lebanese women's movement on the issue of suffrage.

In the lead-up to the CSW gathering, several women's organizations successfully petitioned to participate in the session.[105] In keeping with emerging UN practices, a number of Lebanese women's organizations arranged their attendance by securing the consultative status accreditation available to nongovernmental organizations.[106] Other Lebanese organizations and individuals participated as representatives of their international affiliates.[107] Another group of women formed an official, government-sponsored delegation of women known as the Women's Committee of Lebanon (WCL, Lajnat Shu'un al-Mar'a al-Lubnaniyya). It included Jumana Ahdab, Farida Bisar, Eveline Bustros, Jamal Karam Harfush, Najla Kfuri, Ibtihaj Qaddura, Najla Sa'b, Laure

Tabet, and Zahiyya 'Usayran.[108] The committee hosted a reception for CSW delegates at the Normandy Hotel and organized Sunday excursions outside of Beirut. Such activities enabled members of the Lebanese women's movement to enhance their political and social capital vis-à-vis the government and the public, while simultaneously offering a platform to inform the public about their work and garner support for it.

The local, regional, and US-European press also amplified CSW events and dynamics. *Al-Bayraq*, *Bayrut*, *al-Hayat*, *Le Jour*, *al-Nahar*, *Revue du Liban*, and *Telegraph*—in addition to the Arab News Agency, *Vatan* (Turkey), Agence France-Presse, the *Christian Science Monitor*, and the Telegraph Agency of the Soviet Union (TASS), among others—gained access to meetings by registering with the CSW press office.[109] *Le Jour* and *al-Nahar* in particular provided semiregular coverage of events and debates, and the Lebanese Broadcasting Station featured interviews with two delegates of the CSW session. The local press did not focus on women's issues relative to their detailed coverage of the plight of Palestinian refugees, UN mediation of Arab-Israeli negotiations, and the aftermath of the March coup d'état in Syria. Nonetheless, the coverage was sufficient to contribute to the normalization of women's rights as a topic of conversation. The local press did this by highlighting the active participation of Lebanese women, the tacit support of key Lebanese officials, and the increasing centrality of women's rights to international norms of governance.

Building on the publicity surrounding the Universal Declaration of Human Rights and in anticipation of the 1949 CSW session in Beirut, women planned for a regional women's conference to immediately follow the CSW's closing session on April 4, 1949. Several CSW delegates, including Bustros and Harfush, attended and addressed the regional conference. In addition, Lebanese Foreign Minister Hamid Frangieh spoke to the conference, praising the women's movement in Lebanon and endorsing their bid for equal rights, including suffrage. Frangieh's presence perfectly captured the doublespeak of several postindependence cabinets in which certain members offered support as individuals but rarely used their positions of power to take action.

The Women's Committee of Lebanon used the opening of the regional conference to present and amplify a petition addressed to both the United Nations and Lebanese government.[110] In this petition, the WCL declared itself the representative of all licensed women's organizations in Lebanon,[111] and urged the CSW to investigate the changing conditions impacting the family, the fundamental unit of society. The document then called on the Lebanese government to enact specific reforms in the realms of political, educational, and economic rights, and called for revising the Lebanese constitution by inserting "both men and women" after its first reference to Lebanese citizens. The petition also proposed amending the electoral law to reflect equal voting and candidacy rights and enforcing the constitutional provision granting all Lebanese citizens, without discrimination, the right to hold public office. On the educational front, the petition called for the free and mandatory education of both sexes up to the age of twelve, unifying the primary education curricula for boys and girls, and raising the standard of education in public and private schools. On the economic front, it called for equal pay for equal work. Such a combination of demands reflected the spectrum of the women's movement's long-standing goals in Lebanon as well as newly articulated assertions for said demands, with suffrage at their forefront.

The new Syrian electoral law passed in September 1949 was another event designating that year as a turning point.[112] Article 7 of this law defined the electorate as men and women who were eighteen years or older, with the proviso that women voters must have completed their primary education. This law, which followed the second of three 1949 military coups, responded to the long-standing women's mobilizations in Syria. This was the first official recognition of women's suffrage in any Arab state, and only the second in the Middle East (after Turkey). Several women writing in support of suffrage in Lebanon reflected on this development for most of the second half of 1949 and throughout 1950.[113]

The confluence of these events produced a renewed focus on the issue of women's suffrage in the public sphere during 1949. *Sawt al-Mar'a* published several articles that documented support for women's suffrage across the leadership of the women's movement.[114] In addition, various women's organizations individually endorsed the WCL's petition to the UN and the Lebanese government.[115] Habiba Sha'ban Yakun of the Young Muslim Women's Association, then an AUB student, published an article in *al-'Urwa al-Wuthqa*, a leading venue for anticolonial and Arab nationalist writings, and the journal of the AUB student organization of the same name.[116] Furthermore, several students at the American Junior College for Women held a panel discussion on women's activism and the question of political equality.[117] Jamal Karam Harfush gave an invited lecture entitled "A Testimony on Women" at the Cénacle Libanais (al-Nadwa al-Lubnaniyya), perhaps Lebanon's premier public forum for discussing contemporary politics. Therein Harfush asserted the righteousness of the demand for women's political rights and praised the conduct of Lebanese women at the CSW conference.[118] Soon, male allies like the leftist intellectual George Hanna began to express support for women's suffrage publicly. In fact, Hanna published an Arabic book-length "scientific defense" of women's political, economic, social, and cultural equality during the critical year 1949.[119] While the women's movement focused less on the issue of suffrage in the 1930s than it had in the 1920s, there was now a renewed and broad interest in publicly discussing and agitating on behalf of the issue.

THE SUFFRAGE CAMPAIGN

Several women's organizations joined forces in March–April 1950 to form the Executive Committee of Women's Organizations in Lebanon (al-Lajna al-Tanfidhiyya li-l-Hay'at al-Nisa'iyya fi Lubnan). The committee's exclusive purpose was representing women's collective interest in the right to vote.[120] Nine women comprised the Executive Committee: May Joseph Fayyad, Emily Faris Ibrahim, Najla Kfuri, Jamal Karam Harfush, Laure Nasr, Ibtihaj Qaddura, Alin Rihan, Najla Sa'b, and Laure Tabet. These nine figures represented an intergenerational, cross-sectarian, and politically inclusive coalition of women activists.

The Executive Committee was formed as a working group whose sole purpose was the design and implementation of a plan for securing women's suffrage. They first crafted a petition addressed to the president, cabinet, and parliament.[121] Three features of this petition are particularly notable. First, it specifically identified amending the current electoral law as the means by which "women can practice their political rights as citizens, in absolute equality with men."[122] This wording reveals that the Executive Committee understood women's suffrage as a legislative matter rather than one requiring a constitutional amendment. A second notable feature of the petition is the number (fifty-three) of women's organizations endorsing it. The

Executive Committee issued the petition in the name of these organizations after securing their support in a mass public meeting held on June 15, 1950.[123] The signatories spanned the spectrum of issues that defined the women's movement: education, health care, child welfare, and women's social and political rights. They included religiously affiliated organizations of the Armenian, Maronite, Orthodox, and Sunni communities. They were also based in several of Lebanon's cities: Beirut, Sidon, Tripoli, Zahleh, and others.

The petition justified the demand for women's suffrage through explicit reference to several sources of legitimacy. It listed Article 7 of the Lebanese constitution, which asserted the equality of all Lebanese citizens with respect to political and civil rights. It also identified the Charter of the United Nations, the Universal Declaration of Human Rights, and the resolutions of the second and third sessions of the UN Commission on the Status of Women. The petition sought to secure the very same rights women lobbied for in the 1920s, 1930s, and 1940s, yet it also revealed an unprecedent degree of coordination across the women's movement within a context of newly legitimizing international norms.

The Executive Committee waged a thirty-month-long campaign to secure women's suffrage. They experienced an early defeat and acquired a new rallying cry when parliament passed the electoral law of August 10, 1950, which retained the historic restriction of suffrage to men by exclusively using the male referent when referring to voters and candidates. This new law energized and focused the efforts of the Executive Committee, who continued to express the necessity of amending Article 21 of the law by adding the female referent to the passage that defined voters and candidates. The Executive Committee's range of activities reflected a complex strategy that operated on multiple levels. The Executive Committee itself met regularly, sometimes as often as three times a week. In these meetings the nine women crafted their collective strategy, divided tasks among themselves, and reported back to one another.

The Executive Committee met with or sent memos to the president, prime minister, speaker of parliament, and the parliamentary committee on administration and justice. It also organized a series of general meetings for representatives of women's organizations, unaffiliated women, and the public more generally.[124] In these meetings—held in Beirut, Tripoli, Sidon,

Tyre, Zahleh, and elsewhere—the Executive Committee updated their constituencies on recent developments, mobilized them for sending telegrams or other types of campaigns, and issued statements to the press. It also encouraged, facilitated, or participated in raising the issue of women's suffrage in various fora, in addition to holding meetings with potential allies and taking advantage of the increasing frequency of popular mobilizations in opposition to government policies. For example, in January 1951, the Executive Committee concluded a meeting with several labor unions by issuing a joint telegram in support of women's suffrage.[125] In February 1952, the Executive Committee hosted a meeting with six political parties, including the National Bloc, the Mandate-era parliamentary faction that was the chief adversary of President Bishara al-Khuri's Constitutional Bloc.[126] The other participating parties represented more populist elements of society, including the Kata'ib Party, the Progressive Socialist Party, the National Appeal Party, the National Organization, and the National Congress. Like the array of women's organizations that signed the petition, this combination of political parties cut across sectarian affiliations, regional allegiances, and standard ideological orientations. What the parties shared was an opposition to the current government (both the president and cabinet), their relative exclusion from a parliamentary base, and their increasing participation in street demonstrations. The six parties reached agreement with the Executive Committee on three key points: recognizing women's suffrage as a national—rather than exclusively a women's—issue, unequivocally supporting the Executive Committee's goal of securing women's suffrage, and committing to meet regularly and collectively organize in support of the suffrage campaign.

The women of the Executive Committee introduced several tactics not previously used in mobilizations for Lebanese women's suffrage. First, they identified and publicly praised male supporters among Lebanese politicians, businessmen, journalists, and intellectuals. The Union of Lebanese Women's *Sawt al-Mar'a* was particularly active in this regard, highlighting these men's views.[127] In the 1951 elections, the Executive Committee also pledged support to those candidates who included women's suffrage in their platforms. At the same time, they publicly named and criticized candidates who did not. Such support was not simply a matter of private commitment. The Executive Committee drafted a pledge for candidates to sign that included a commitment, upon election, to "raise the cause of granting women their complete political rights and to support said cause."[128]

Another novel tactic employed by the Executive Committee was the inauguration of a women's week on January 8–11, 1951.[129] The program featured a series of public rallies and other activities. The week opened with a press conference in Beirut, followed by events in 'Alay, Ba'albak, Sidon, Tripoli, and Zahleh. The lead-up to the women's week featured an active flyer distribution campaign conducted by the Executive Committee and several women's organizations. They also issued press releases and placed ads in the cinemas. The week's program culminated in a large event at the Roxy Cinema in downtown Beirut. Contemporary reports describe a standing-room-only audience and crowds overflowing into Martyrs' Square.[130] Ibtihaj Qaddura served as emcee, while the speakers included Emily Faris Ibrahim on the current status of women in Lebanon and Laure Nasr on how Lebanese women should be at the vanguard of "Eastern women's" liberation. Reflecting the campaign's broader strategy, the event was organized under the patronage of First Lady Laure al-Khuri, and also featured speeches by MP Habib Abi Shahla on parliamentary support for women's suffrage, by the attorney and legal scholar Subhi Mahmasani (1909–86) on Islam's injunctions about women's equality, and by Prime Minister Abdullah al-Yafi, who spoke in support of women's equal political rights.

Despite this impressive array of campaigning, alliance building, and popular mobilizations, the Executive Committee continued to face obstacles to granting women suffrage. Opponents in government regularly engaged in stalling tactics. Cabinet members and parliamentarians initially insisted that any legislation on the matter be preceded by discussion in the parliamentary committee on administration and justice. It was not until February 1951 that this committee publicly confirmed there was no constitutional impediment to parliament legislating women's suffrage, a fact widely known at the beginning of the campaign The parliamentary committee then sent the issue to the legislative committee, which did not issue a statement until March of that year. The statement proposed an incremental approach to granting women's suffrage, starting with the upcoming municipal elections and subsequently revisiting the issue with regard to parliamentary elections. Several observers noted that government officials were stalling, and perhaps even attempting to pacify and silence the suffrage movement prior to the upcoming 1951 parliamentary elections.[131]

This situation prompted a fierce debate within the Executive Committee and the women's movement more generally. Such disagreements largely remained internal matters. That said, some activist women took to the press to criticize the Executive Committee,[132] whose nine members ultimately voted in favor of accepting the government's decision to allow women to participate in the upcoming municipal elections, then pressed on with their campaign. To demonstrate their resolve in the face of stalling tactics like the incremental approach, the Executive Committee mobilized its base and increasingly resorted to protests. In response to this escalation, the US Embassy in Beirut inaugurated its own reporting on the women's movement in Lebanon.[133] On March 20, 1951, the Executive Committee staged a demonstration whose participants gathered outside of parliament and attempted to force their way into one of its sessions.[134] Soon, women in other parts of Lebanon joined the Executive Committee, sometimes as official signatories and other times through autonomously demonstrating in support of women's suffrage. For example, the gendarmerie dispersed a protest of three hundred women in Mashghara, in the Biqa' Governorate.[135]

CONTINGENCIES MATTER

A key turning point in the campaign for women's suffrage was the September 1952 downfall of President Bishara al-Khuri. The women's movement had maintained an ambiguous relationship with al-Khuri, for while many of his political allies either publicly opposed women's suffrage or simply declined to support it, al-Khuri made a number of supportive statements about the women's movement in general and women's rights in particular. In addition, his wife Laure patronized a number of women's organizations and publicly supported the suffrage campaign.

Elite and popular opposition to the Khuri regime and its policies steadily increased throughout the late 1940s and early 1950s. As a formal political opposition coalesced, it incorporated key reformist demands, women's suffrage among them. This was largely the result of the Executive Committee's outreach to certain labor unions and political parties, both of which represented significant components of the opposition. The opposition's adoption of women's suffrage confirmed that women's right to vote had become a core element of visions of a postcolonial Lebanon as well as a resource in the struggles to realize those visions.

The Lebanese parliament elected Kamil Sham'un as successor to al-Khuri. In exchange for a promise to hold early parliamentary elections in 1953, Sham'un secured temporary legislative powers for his four-person technocratic cabinet headed by Khalid Shihab. On November 4, 1952, the cabinet issued a new electoral law that restricted female suffrage in the upcoming parliamentary elections to educated women.[136] As with previous iterations of the gradualist approach—most notably women's participation in municipal elections—the Executive Committee, the broader women's movement, and other interested parties fiercely debated the proposed electoral law.[137] The Executive Committee ultimately issued a statement describing the proposal as "a step in the direction of progress, despite falling short of securing the citizenship rights of uneducated women—an issue that will have a lasting effect among women."[138] A few days later, the Executive Committee called on newly eligible women voters to secure official documentation confirming completion of the necessary level of education prior to the upcoming elections.

The Executive Committee mobilized to eliminate this barrier to women's full voting rights. On November 20, 1952, it published an open letter to President Sham'un declaring its intention to persist with the suffrage campaign until all Lebanese women secured the right to vote.[139] The Executive Committee also organized a general meeting of the women's movement and its supporters for November 25, 1952.[140] After updating those present on the campaign's current status and pledging to press on, committee members invited supporters to send telegrams to the government protesting the conditions placed on women's voting rights. Furthermore, the committee asked the president and prime minister to attend a joint meeting with the Executive Committee to explain the decision to limit suffrage.[141]

Members of the Executive Committee made use of a wide array of networks to express opposition to the decision, attracting the support of many women's organizations, various political parties, and many independent politicians. Such intensified criticism was concurrent with the purging or defection of key elements of the coalition that had brought Sham'un to power.

Many of those individuals and factions now joined the newly coalescing opposition in launching a multipronged media attack on cabinet ministers, chairs of various parliamentary committees, and the speaker of parliament.

In this context of increasing opposition to Sham'un, and more notably the potential collapse of his cabinet, the government increasingly turned to women's political rights as a means of acquiring greater legitimacy. A legislative decree of February 18, 1953, removed the educational requirement for the upcoming parliamentary elections.[142] All women, as long as they met the same requirements imposed on men, were eligible to run for office and to vote in the elections. In short, Sham'un and his cabinet sought to consolidate their tenuous positions by endorsing women's suffrage and thereby making new allies and claiming status as progressive reformers. This decision presaged the president and the cabinet's other attempts to shore up their political legitimacy. One such attempt was the decision to establish provisional control over the French-owned Beirut Electricity Company, which is discussed in the following chapter. Nevertheless, the Executive Committee's three-year campaign and the broader legacy of the women's movement rendered women's suffrage a legible metric of reform, independence, and legitimacy. The Executive Committee met a final time on March 18, 1953, concluded that it had achieved its purpose and fulfilled its mandate, and resolved to disband.[143]

BEYOND POLITICAL RIGHTS

Emily Faris Ibrahim was the only woman to run for parliament in the July 1953 elections, despite initial indications that Ibtihaj Qaddura and Laure Tabet would do so as well. Ibrahim ran and lost as an independent in the Zahleh electoral district. While realistic about her prospects, Ibrahim argued that women should not absent themselves from the first electoral contest in which they would be eligible to participate.[144] As she put it, "I do not see in the probability of my loss a cause to avoid the battle. . . . If I only succeed at creating a new movement among the ranks of women—based on faith in their right and duty to practice it—then that is worth it."[145]

The period between February and July 1953 featured a wide range of responses to women's electoral participation. These revealed broader dynamics at play within the women's movement and society more generally. First, the achievement of women's suffrage appears to have mobilized conservative and reactionary voices in the public sphere. The opening editorial of the June 1953 issue of *Sawt al-Mar'a* identified and responded to the "violent, arbitrary campaigns against women waged by a team of our literati and journalists."[146] Unsurprisingly, such criticisms focused on Lebanese women's alleged neglect of their domestic duties. In response, the *Sawt al-Mar'a* editorial rebuked anyone who claimed the Lebanese woman was deviating (*tanharif*) from her primary duties (*wajibatuha al-ra'isiyya*). This exchange highlights the perseverance of conservative, gendered notions of citizenship and national duty. Yet it also reveals another reality: the women's movement had rarely challenged such gendered conceptions openly. The strategy of patriotic motherhood adopted in the 1930s remained an integral discursive component of the women's movement despite the suffrage campaign and its victory. Such continuities do not diminish the radical nature and transformative potential of women's mobilizations in the postindependence period. They nevertheless highlight the persistence of different-order phenomena that were not necessarily a central concern of the movement. The June 1953 editorial acknowledged that some women had indeed abandoned their putative domestic duties and thus deviated from what the editorial's authors viewed as normative behavior. They argued, however, that these "deviants" represented a tiny minority of Lebanese women. This minority, the editorial continued, was smaller than the number of men who deviated from their primary responsibilities, and implied that some of these offenders could be among the movement's critics.

A second set of responses emerged from within the ranks of the suffrage campaign and the women's movement. Women on the Executive Committee and in the broader movement it represented encouraged women both to participate as voters and to take their political rights and responsibilities seriously. Yet they diverged on the question of women as candidates for office. Laure Nasr was pessimistic about the prospects of women running in, let alone winning, parliamentary elections.[147] She identified the novelty of the experience and the limited financial resources available as the primary obstacles. Laure Tabet attributed her decision not to run to two factors: Lebanese women's lack of adequate preparation for the exercise of their full rights, and men's inability to view women as legitimate partners in the political process.[148] In this context, women published a critical mass of articles and opinion pieces in the pages of *Sawt al-Mar'a*, and the press more generally, that reflected on the efficacy and possibilities of women's participation in the July 1953 parliamentary elections. While most such publications focused on proposing ways for women to educate themselves and identify the principles underlying their voting decisions, others took on the critics among the women's movement more forcefully. For example, Emily Faris Ibrahim characterized Tabet's explanation for not running as tantamount to asserting that the government moved too quickly in giving women the vote, a position that Tabet actually opposed during her work with Executive Committee.[149] Ibrahim deplored Tabet's claims about Lebanese women's lack of preparedness, especially because they were coming from the current president of a major women's organization. Such variations in viewpoints reveal important differences between the leading personalities of the women's movement in Lebanon, and the extent to which the Executive Committee provided a temporary framework in which to unify their message on the question of suffrage.

Electoral campaigns featured a third set of responses to women's recently secured right to participate in parliamentary life. For the first time, many election pamphlets and candidate speeches addressed both women and men voters (*al-nakhibat wa-l-nakhibin*).[150] Several candidates endorsed or otherwise highlighted the equality of men and women, defined in various ways. They accomplished this most notably by inserting the clause "of both sexes" (min al-jinsayn) after the reference to "every citizen" (kul muwatin).[151] However, not all candidates did so. Others continued to exclusively use the male referent for voters, some even referring to the electorate as the "sons of" (abna') the electoral district.[152]

We lack reliable empirical date about women's participation in the 1953 parliamentary elections. The government did not publish any official statistics that differentiated between women and men voters. Those commenting from within the women's movement viewed women's participation in positive terms.[153] They claimed that women's turnout reached as high as 60 percent in some districts, also noting the unprecedented spectacle of women standing in line to vote, many of whom were elderly and/or dressed up for the occasion.[154]

Beyond the immediate responses to Lebanese women's 1953 victory in securing suffrage, developments within the movement produced several longer-term legacies during the early postindependence period (1943–55). Ibrahim's 1953 electoral loss prompted many activists within the women's movement to publish editorials attempting to explain women's inability to break into parliamentary office. The failure of every other woman to succeed in such an effort until 1992 inspired attempts to analyze and ameliorate the problem.[155] With rare exceptions, such inquiries would revisit the 1953 elections as the first of many failures, while simultaneously celebrating the accomplishment of securing the right to vote.

Another legacy of the suffrage victory was the invention of a new campaign repertoire among the women's movement. The use of ad hoc committees to advance a specific cause—first inaugurated for the 1950–53 suffrage campaign—afforded the opportunity to engage in more intense and detailed strategizing, coordination, and adaptation, capacities that longer-term extant organizations lacked. It also enabled the formation of alliances and the development of protest tactics that individual organizations might have been reticent to endorse officially. Women in Lebanon repurposed the model of the 1950–53 Executive Committee to pursue numerous subsequent campaigns, including those focused on matters of inheritance (1959), citizenship (1960), the freedom to engage in foreign travel (1974), and reproductive rights (1983). For example, a group of women met on June 17, 1954, to lay the foundations for a campaign to award women equal inheritance rights.[156] Subsequent meetings, consultations, and mobilizations established the Committee for Inheritance Equality (Lajnat al-Musawat bi-l-Irth), which secured a 1959 law granting Christian women the right to equal inheritances in cases with no last will and testament. Today little is known about the factors informing the decision to, at least initially, focus on Christian women's rights. At least in part, the 1959 law was a response to Christian personal status courts applying the Hanafi Sunni formula for inheritance, which was a common practice throughout the colonial and early postindependence period.

A final legacy of the early postindependence period is the creation of institutions and organizations that would survive, thrive, and play significant roles in Lebanon's subsequent history. Included among these are numerous elementary schools that had initially been established by women's organizations and were subsequently incorporated into the expanding network of public schools. It also includes the creation of organizations that continued to serve as powerful vehicles for women's collective action in Lebanon. One example is the previously mentioned Committee for Women's Rights (CWR), which was established in 1947. Its Communist leanings and affiliations prevented the organization from securing official recognition until the post-1967 licensing of previously unrecognized organizations. Yet the CWR secured official registration in 1969–70, played a major role in Lebanon's participation in the UN Decade for Women (1975–85), and helped mobilize society around a range of women's issues in the post–civil war period. A second example is the 1952 founding of the League of Women's Organizations in Lebanon (Jami'at al-Hay'at an-Nisa'iyya fi Lubnan), which bridged the division in the women's movement revealed by the differences between the AWFL and Women's Solidarity. The league's leadership rotated annually between Muslim and Christian women (specifically Ibtihaj Qaddura and Laure Tabet, 1953–66). After changing its name to the Lebanese Women's Council (al-Majlis al-Nisa'i al-Lubnani) in the 1960s, it organized a series of panels across the country calling on various political parties, militias, and government officials to de-escalate the increasingly polarized political environment. The council maintained its unity throughout the civil war period (1975–90) and was the only formal national coalition of women's organizations in Lebanon until the late 1990s.

CONCLUSION

The women's movement of Lebanon experienced significant expansion during the early postindependence period. The organizations that made up this movement, its leaders, and the rank-and-file members were significant participants in the popular mobilizations occurring during 1943–55. This dynamic was both reflective, and constitutive, of women's increasingly more salient presence in the public realm. The postindependence movement displayed important ideological, organizational, and strategic continuities—as well as breaks—with its colonial-period predecessor. Significant in this respect were the opportunities for politicization, mobilization, and resources that the new context of independence and shifting terrain of regional and international women's politics made possible. Women therefore persisted in their Mandate-era role of debating and mobilizing about state formation. Yet both movements adapted to the changing nature of state formation and increased opportunities for local, bottom-up participation in that process. This was most notable in the sphere of voting rights, which the women's movements succeeded in securing voting rights in 1953. This accomplishment transformed electoral politics while also raising new questions about the meaning of equality, the institutional constraints placed upon it, and contending visions and strategies for expanding both.

Six

THE BEIRUT ELECTRICITY COMPANY

THE PUBLIC UTILITIES SYSTEM THAT PROVIDED ELECTRIC CURRENT in Beirut—like many other such services across the Levant—has its origins in the last century of the Ottoman Empire. As discussed in chapter 1, the nexus of late Ottoman developmentalism, the fiscal limits of imperial and local governments, and the availability of private capital produced an incentive structure for concessions as a vehicle to fund and administer infrastructural development projects.[1] The result was a complex edifice of concessionary agreements and joint-stock companies underpinning the operation of ports, railways, tramlines, urban lighting, and potable water in various combinations across imperial domains.[2]

In 1905 Salim Ra'ad established the first company to obtain an electricity-related concession for Beirut. Ra'ad, his son-in-law Najib Malhama Pasha, the latter's two brothers Philippe Effendi and Habib Effendi, and a group of Belgian investors constituted the majority shareholders of the Ottoman Beirut Tramway and Electricity Company (OBTEC, al-Sharika al-Mughaffala al-'Uthmaniyya li-l-Tramway wa-l-Kahruba' fi Bayrut).[3] The Ottoman Ministry of Public Works granted OBTEC a ninety-nine-year concession for a Beirut tramway system in 1906.[4] The company intended to build an electric plant to power the trams, and also expand into supplying electricity for lighting and manufacturing.[5]

Ibrahim and Elias Sabbagh headed a rival business family in Beirut.[6] They bought the Malhamas out of OBTEC in 1907.[7] The Sabbaghs were majority shareholders in the Ottoman Beirut Gas Company (OBGC, al-Sharika al-Mughffala al-ʿUthmaniyya li-l-Ghaz fi Bayrut, est. 1887), which held the concession for gas lighting in the city and thus risked losing ground to OBTEC.[8] They also controlled the Beirut Water Company (Sharikat Miyah Bayrut, est. 1909).[9] Their buyout of the Malhamas therefore became part of their broader pattern of seeking to monopolize Beirut's utilities concessions.[10] In 1911, the Malhama family sold off its shares in the Beirut tramway and gas companies to primarily Belgian investors.[11]

Construction on the electric tramway system began in 1908, with service beginning fifteen months later in 1909.[12] By the eve of World War I, OBTEC was operating the tramlines and providing current for mechanical power, while the OBGC was supplying lighting services through gas as well as electricity.[13] However, the post-Ottoman reformulation of concessionary arrangements featured the 1922–24 reestablishment of the rights and properties of both those companies under the purview of the Beirut Tramway and Light Company (BTLC, Sharikat al-Tramway wa-l-Inara fi Bayrut, est. 1922).

The French High Commission drew on late Ottoman precedents in order to oversee the development of infrastructure while also providing investment opportunities for French capital. The High Commission neither issued new concessions nor renewed existing concessions until after the 1923 Treaty of Lausanne and the 1924 French Mandate concession law. The former guaranteed the maintenance of concessionary contracts entered into before the war. The latter established a new mechanism for the request, negotiation, grant, and (later) amendment of new concessionary contracts under the purview of the High Commission.[14]

Three dynamics characterized the political economy of concessions during the Mandate period.[15] First, "the High Commission held tight but indirect control over the major concessions and their ownership and operation."[16] While a new local concession-granting authority was established—drawn first from municipal authorities and eventually also including representatives of the "national" government—the High Commission had to approve each concession request. This ensured that the realm of possible outcomes was in accordance with French administrative preferences. The litmus test for a concessionary bid hinged on Lebanese-Syrian applicants having already contracted out the financial and technical aspects of operating the concession to French business interests.[17] Second, "this configuration led to an ownership structure for major concessions that sometimes featured Syrian-Lebanese directors or involved some Syrian-Lebanese capital, but was supervised by French engineers and dominated by French capital and its investors."[18] The determination to secure French economic privileges in the realm of concessions highlighted the collusion between—and thus exposed the thin veneer allegedly separating—French administrative and business interests both in the Mandate and the metropole. Third, French business interests "won" the lion's share of concessionary contracts. Consequently, those companies providing services and earning profits in Lebanon were exempt from local tax laws even if they featured capital input from Lebanese-Syrian and other interests.[19] The reform and restructuring of the concessionary agreements concerning the provisioning of electric current and tramway service for the city of Beirut is illustrative of these dynamics.

The devastation of World War I and the economic crises that persisted into the 1920s undermined both the fiscal integrity of the OBTEC-OBGC and the quality of their services.[20] Both companies are reported to have been unable to fulfill their responsibilities regarding the provisioning of tramway services and electricity for lighting and mechanical power due to the dilapidated conditions of the installations, increased demand that could not be met, and near bankruptcy. In February 1922, shareholders of the Ottoman tram and gas companies transferred their concessions and properties to a new company, the BTLC. The High Commission approved the transfer in June 1923, and all parties completed the process in May 1924.[21]

Founders established the BTLC on January 3, 1923, with the explicit intention of buying out both OBTEC and the OBGC as part of a broader investment strategy rooted in concessions for the provisioning of public utilities in Beirut and its vicinity. Reflective of a broader trend during the Mandate period, French capital was dominant in the BTLC, even though the company featured limited Belgian and Lebanese-Syrian participation. While the 1922–24 transfer involved a considerable investment, it represented only the transfer of the still-valid Ottoman concessions and not the granting of new Lebanese-Syrian concessions. The High Commission did the latter between 1925 and 1929 when the BTLC secured concessions for the following public utilities services:[22] construction and development of an electric tramway network in the city of Beirut (June 4, 1925);[23] public distribution of electrical energy (for all purposes) in the city of Beirut and its surrounding districts (June 4, 1925);[24] construction and development of a high-voltage electrical energy network for the city of Beirut (August 26, 1925);[25] construction and development of a hydroelectric power plant on the Safa River (Nahr al-Safa) as an energy source for the second and third concessions listed above (June 4, 1929);[26] and public distribution of electrical energy (for all purposes) both to and within the Lebanese population centers of Ba'abda, Bdadoun, Shuwayfat, Hadath, Kfarshima, and Wadi Shahrur (July 27, 1929).

These five concessions constituted renewals, adaptations, or expansions of the original tramway, electricity, and gas lighting concessions for Beirut during the late Ottoman Empire. Like other public utility concessionary arrangements of the Mandate period, the BTLC concessions were contractual agreements between the local government and the company in question. In reality, however, they ultimately reflected the high commissioner's preferences vis-à-vis which companies were granted particular concessions. The 1924 concession law asserted the right of states and municipalities (depending on the situation) to grant concessions.[27] The law also imposed an array of monitoring and controlling mechanisms for the High Commission. The validity of any concession was conditioned upon certification of the High Commission.

In 1935, the BTLC (Société des Tramways et Éclairage de Beyrouth) changed its name to the Beirut Electricity Company (EDB, Société de Électricité de Beyrouth).[28] The name change was a strategic calculation by shareholders and/or managers. It distanced the company from a legacy of popular mobilizations throughout the Mandate period.[29] Beirut residents organized boycott campaigns lasting four weeks or more during 1922 and 1931.[30] Company workers struck for several weeks at a time in 1924 and 1926. Such mobilizations highlight the dual importance of public utilities and struggles around their provisioning, both to the making of Lebanon's colonial political economy as well as to the everyday lives of its urban populations.

The name change also reflected how during the Mandate, electricity—as opposed to tramlines—came to represent the overwhelming majority of the company's capital investment, physical infrastructure, consumer market, and profit generation. The tramway system reached structural limits in terms of users during the Mandate. The company made few equipment upgrades to the tramway system. Additionally, the colonial period featured a significant increase in automobile transportation's availability and use in the form of private cars as well as various taxi and bus services. This set up a long-standing struggle between the automobile transport drivers and the EDB tramway system—one that carried into the postindependence period. A critical element was the episodic debate about replacing the trams with buses.[31]

Electricity, on the other hand, became increasingly a part of everyday life—even if unevenly so. The growing use of electric lighting and home appliances reflected this, as did the proliferation of technologies such as telephones, radios, and cinemas.[32] The number of hospitality establishments such as hotels, restaurants, and cafés significantly increased.[33] Electricity production for the city of Beirut quadrupled between 1925 and 1939.[34] Similar trends emerged with respect to subscribers. In 1920 there were approximately eight hundred domestic and commercial electricity subscribers in Beirut.[35] By 1938, the number of subscribers reached approximately fourteen thousand.[36] In sum, there was more than a seventeenfold increase in the number of electricity subscribers between the establishment of the French Mandate in Lebanon (1920) and the eve of World War II (1939). While specific figures for industrial subscribers are unavailable, they accounted for 37 percent of electricity consumption in Beirut by 1942.[37] These statistics speak to a significant increase in electricity's use and to the EDB's centrality in technological advancements, economic development, and social change in Lebanon. The EDB represented the primary French investment in the public utilities sector. Company profits increased eightfold between 1923 and 1930, reaching an annual total of 5.6 million French francs.[38] The EDB was an influential, lucrative, and successful business venture for its shareholders. This dominant role reveals the significance of public utilities as a site of shaping daily life, and the claims people would make about their collective lives, the economy, and the state.

ELECTRICITY AT INDEPENDENCE

Lebanon's transition to independence coincided with important developments in the country's electricity infrastructure. Two companies anchored electricity production in 1943. The first was the Beirut-based EDB. The second was the North Lebanon Electricity Company (Sharikat Kahruba' Shamal Lubnan, est. 1924).[39] In addition to supplying the two largest cities (Beirut and Tripoli), these companies provided electric current to the majority of surrounding towns. There were at least another ten electricity-generating companies and double as many distribution companies in the country during the early postindependence period.[40] Many of these, like the Zahleh Electricity Company (Sharikat Kahruba' Zahleh), date back to the French colonial period. The Lebanese government also issued a number of new concessions during 1943–55.[41] Some of these reflected the expansion of electrification into new regions. Others were meant to shore up supply for the existing network. The EDB and Qadisha combined to produce over 95 percent of electric power in 1943. They would more or less maintain that share through 1955. Their dominant position was a function of two factors. One was the urban bias of French colonial development. The other was the preference for foreign and local capital to take advantage of economies of scale in the two major cities.

Both the EDB and Qadisha were primarily foreign-owned and -managed companies whose concessions dated back to the Mandate period. Yet there were important differences between the two. In 1951, the EDB was capitalized at nearly three times the capital of Qadisha. The gap between the two amounts reflected other differences. Electric consumption in Beirut accounted for two-thirds of all consumption in the country. The EDB had three times the number of subscribers as Qadisha, including twelve subscriber bases in nearby towns (as opposed to Qadisha's two). In sum, the EDB produced more than twice as much electricity as Qadisha. The proximity of the EDB to centers of power and opposition in the capital was also important. These differences combined with other factors to produce a very different trajectory of mobilizations around electric utilities in Beirut than obtained in Tripoli.

The larger size of the EDB in terms of capital, infrastructure, subscribers, and geographic reach masks other important developments that contributed to the making of a major postindependence crisis. The company's electricity production prior to World War II was more than sufficient to satisfy demand. Wartime import-substitution industrialization and rural-urban migration altered this equilibrium. By 1945 there was a deficit in electricity production despite a 68 percent increase relative to 1939. The deficit, due to increases in both the total number of subscribers and average subscriber consumption levels, manifested in power outages in Beirut and several of the towns it supplied or sold electricity to.[42] Wartime conditions in general and Middle East Supply Centre trade restrictions in particular deferred plans and expectations for infrastructural expansion.

The coincidence of the end of World War II with Lebanon's transition to independence featured several important dynamics alluded to in previous chapters. The government's postindependence development strategies undermined the agriculture sector. The rate of rural-urban migration continued to grow, and Beirut's population further mushroomed. Contrary to wartime expectations, the manufacturing sector also expanded—albeit in a modified fashion relative to the consolidation of Lebanon's postcolonial political economy. Wartime savings, renewed global trade in consumer goods, and the new US-linked commercial networks combined, leading to a dramatic increase in the use of household electrical appliances among middle- and upper-class households. According to one estimate, the number of home refrigerators increased from eight hundred to six thousand between 1946 and 1951. Statistics for importation or purchase of radios, irons, and heaters exhibited similar trends.

The EDB took advantage of the new boom in electricity demand as a financial opportunity. It more than doubled its subscribers between 1946 (28,000) and 1951 (58,000). The EDB increased its capital by 900 percent between 1946 and 1950. It installed four new diesel turbines, replaced dilapidated high-voltage transmission cables, and expanded the electrical grid. Yet the EDB was unwilling to keep pace with demand and pursued strategies to manipulate consumption patterns. It imposed contractual conditions on individual subscribers, limiting the total amount of electric consumption or creating specific time-slots for the use of home electrical appliances. It enforced these conditions through disconnecting service when subscribers violated them. Even when supplying electricity, the voltage regularly fell well below the promised 110 volts. This is to say nothing of the increasing frequency of power outages in Beirut and other urban centers dependent on EDB electric power generation. The EDB accompanied these deficiencies in the quality of service with various revenue-maximizing schemes. These included account deposits, meter rentals, inspection fees, and a reconnection charge after service disruption.[43]

The transition to independence also featured important shifts in the regulatory framework of electricity companies. For most of the Mandate period, a specific division within the Common Interests monitored concessionary arrangements. The High Commission exclusively transferred the monitoring of the EDB and the Beirut Water Company to the Lebanese government on January 5, 1944.[44] This transfer did not abrogate existing agreements between the Lebanese state and the EDB, but simply removed the High Commission as an intermediary between the two. The transfer only involved responsibility for the concession granting and monitoring authority established under the 1924 concessionary law.

The 1948 Franco-Lebanese accord reinforced the constrained nature of the 1944 transfer of prerogatives. As discussed in chapter 2, the accord primarily dealt with fiscal and monetary issues related to currency reserves, debt servicing, and trade. However, it also committed the Lebanese government to negotiate any modifications to existing French-related concessionary arrangements. The accord further stipulated that until such modifications are negotiated, the status quo on January 1, 1944, would remain in force. The Lebanese government thus committed itself to both the colonial-era arrangements and the principle of negotiations and mutual agreement for the modification of concessionary agreements.

The EDB was initially subject to the supervision of the Department for Monitoring Concessionary Companies (Mudiriyyat Muraqabat al-Sharikat dhu al-Imtiyyazat), which was adjoined to the Ministry of Public Works when the Lebanese section was transferred from the Common Interests in 1944.[45] In 1949, the Lebanese government moved the department into the Ministry of National Economy.[46] It reported directly to the minister of national economy, and was responsible for the financial, economic, and technical monitoring of all concessionary companies as well as public limited companies. As such, it was empowered to penalize companies for violating laws, agreements, and contracts. The monitoring department also had the authority to review the accounts and budgets of concessionary companies, as well as control the pricing scheme—including the study of any requests for changing them.

THE 1951–52 PROTEST CAMPAIGN

Throughout 1949–51, home consumers, commercial stores, and manufacturing plant owners increasingly took to the newspapers and the streets protesting the quality and cost of the EDB's electricity services.[47] While the broader context was a production deficit, the proximate spark appears to be the company's decision to increase its electric utility rates in late 1949.[48] Other factors contributed to collective outcry. The price increase, production deficit, and public outcry manifested within a broader and longer history of struggle between local engineers and investors about how to develop Lebanon's power (and water) sector.[49] The 1946–51 period featured the consolidation of three competing camps.[50] The struggle between these camps involved an intense public debate that manifested in lectures, newspaper articles, books, and the lobbying of Lebanese and foreign governments. The Litani River featured heavily as an object of analysis and linchpin of their proposals. Furthermore, the Lebanese government invited the US Bureau of Reclamation to research the potential uses of the Litani River in power and water development. The bureau's first mission lasted from April to December 1951 and would lead to a second mission in 1952–54 culminating in a major report.[51]

The EDB and the government clearly understood the potential for protest campaigns that would demand better and more accountable public utility services. Small-scale protests had become episodic around the country. During 1950–51, the national government and local municipalities negotiated with electricity companies to lower their prices in specific places like al-Damur, Dayr al-Qamar, and Tripoli.[52] There were also increasing calls for revaluating foreign concessions and agreements. These included local struggles calling for the nationalization of the Beirut Water Company and the cancellation of the tobacco monopoly.[53] Regional developments also impinged, most notably the nationalization of the railroads in Syria, opposition in Egypt to the military treaty with Britain, and increasing calls for the nationalization of the Anglo-Iranian Oil Company. The onset of the Korean

War (1950–53) and its economic reverberations further increased the cost of living in Lebanon as elsewhere. These dynamics would later feed into the 1951–52 protest campaign. Until then, most politicians and economists in Lebanon, state officials among them, were largely silent on the EDB.

The EDB was sensitive to these developments and hyperaware of the growing alienation of a number of political figures and movement from President Bishara al-Khuri. This was evident in June 1950 when the company formally requested assurances from al-Khuri that the government would not lower electric utility rates and that it would defend the company "against any demagogy threatening the equilibrium the future depends on."[54] It appears that al-Khuri gave the EDB such promises.[55] On this basis, they agreed to begin constructing the Zouk Mkayel power plant in 1951.[56] The plan included four turbines that would allegedly resolve the short- to medium-term electric energy supply issues facing the country.[57] In the interim, the EDB contracted with the Phoenician Hydroelectric Power Company of the Ibrahim River (Société Phénicienne des forces hydro-électriques de Nahr-Ibrahim, est. 1929) to provide additional power to its system. Nevertheless, these measures were not enough to assuage EDB customers' grievances. In December 1951, a full-fledged campaign against the company was underway.

The archival record is not definitive on who initiated the protest campaign or when it actually begun. There are two plausible narratives of who called for the 1951–52 campaign. One dates the campaign's origin to November 1951, when opposition parliamentarian 'Abdallah al-Hajj (1899–1975) suggested customers withhold payment until either the EDB or the government changes the company's policies.[58] Another narrative highlights several individual subscribers and factory owners taking small-scale initiatives.[59] This makes sense given the increasing frequency of public complaints and the escalating modes of protest. For example, residents of the Uppermost Matn region (al-Matn al-A'la) began a payment-strike campaign in late 1949 against the Matn Electricity Company (Sharikat Kahruba' al-Matn). Nearly eight months into the mobilization, the company, which had a concession to distribute power to more than twelve villages, experienced such duress that that it sought to sell or rent its concessionary rights.[60] The Union of Textile Factory Owners threatened to do the same, but appear to have stopped paying their electricity bills without announcing a formal campaign.

It is most likely that these two scenarios overlapped, and by late December 1951, a formal campaign had a broad support base that transgressed the popular-elite divide and brought together varying economic interests. On December 29, 1951, the Katai'b Party and the National Organization—which at the time were two populist political parties largely operating outside the realm of formal politics—announced the formation of a joint committee to explore the idea of a Beirut-wide boycott campaign.[61] They encouraged those already boycotting by not paying their bills to continue doing so, indicating they would provide an inclusive list of demands to rally the city. The involvement of the Kata'ib and the National Organization forced the government's hand. Up until then, both cabinet members and parliamentarians overwhelmingly avoided taking up the EDB's case. They resorted to legal arguments about jurisdiction and precedent. Only a few days after the political parties formed their joint boycott committee, the government formed an ad hoc panel to study the complaints of Beirut residents against the EDB.[62] These developments marked a turning point of sorts. Sensing a shifting political terrain, the EDB issued its first public statement to defend itself against the litany of complaints.[63] It outlined its infrastructural expansion projects since 1946 and ultimately blamed undisciplined, uninformed consumers for the power outages and outcry against electric utility rates and fees.

On January 2, 1952, the Kata'ib and National Organization officially launched a city-wide, open-ended campaign to boycott bill payments to the EDB.[64] Their thirteen demands included reductions in electricity rates, the elimination of additional fees, consistency in the supply of 110 volts to subscribers, enough supply to meet demand, branch offices in each of the major neighborhoods, judicial preapproval for service disconnection, and payment of income tax by the company. The announcement of the campaign marked a turning point in the public mobilizations against the EDB. It mobilized people on the streets and brought together disparate political groupings. As the campaign progressed, constituencies based in different Beirut neighborhoods and other urban areas declared their participation or the launch of a similar campaign against the different company operating therein. In addition, other organizations increasingly endorsed the campaign against the EDB. The campaign held regular public meetings to give updates on the state of the campaign.[65] Other political parties, labor syndicates, and associations regularly attended these meetings and participated as speakers.[66]

The protest campaign against the EDB officially ran from December 1951 to July 1952. During this time, the struggle over the EDB proceeded in four phases: initiation, escalation, stalemate, and turning point, culminating in a government-issued reduction in electric utility rates. It was shortly after that reduction that the central protest committee formally ended the campaign. However, such a price reduction—government imposed, no less—was by no means a guaranteed outcome. The course of the campaign featured stiff resistance on the EDB's part, a high degree of government collusion with the company, and various ebbs and flows in securing campaign victories. It was the combination of the campaign's discipline, the increasing polarization of the Lebanese political field, and various external contingencies that produced the eventual outcome. That the primary tactic of the campaign was to refuse payment of electric utility bills revealed a strategic adaptation on the part of Beirut residents. Electricity was much more integral to everyday life in 1951 than it was during the 1922 and 1931 electricity boycotts. Residents therefore insisted on access to electricity, but rejected the terms imposed on them by the EDB and the legacy of colonial state formation.

The initial phase (December 1951–January 1952) featured two important events. The first was the EDB's distribution of a pamphlet justifying the company's electric utility rates.[67] This document echoed the standard company line with respect to issues of production costs, planned capacity development, and the EDB's fiscal integrity. The second event was the establishment of an ad hoc commission alluded to above. Its mandate was to investigate the cost of electricity production and recommend lower electric utility rates.[68] The committee very quickly submitted its report, and the government in turn announced its intention to negotiate with the EDB to lower prices.[69] Both the pamphlet justifying electric utility rates and the committee of inquiry on prices reflect how seriously the EDB and the government took the protest campaign. By late January 1952, the EDB claimed that approximately 50 percent of Beirut subscribers were not paying their electricity bills.[70] This development resulted in major revenue losses for the company. By end of April 1952, the protest campaign had deprived the EDB of approximately 2.25 million liras in owed revenue.[71]

The campaign's second phase lasted from February through March of 1952. Escalation characterized this period. The campaign expanded to include a broader spectrum of tactics and participants as increasing number of political parties joined and street protests became more frequent.[72] The Kata'ib and National Organization provided phone numbers for people to call in case the EDB disconnected service for nonpayment.[73] They established technical teams to restore electricity to city residents disconnected for lack of payment.[74] The protest committee invited citizens to join the campaign and placed advertisements for technical assistance contacts in newspapers and cinemas.[75] The EDB identified the Rivoli and Opera cinemas as particularly willing to show prescreening advertisements.[76] On another level, some individuals and groups vandalized EDB offices and installations.[77] The campaign against the EDB furthermore inspired similar campaigns around the country. On February 3, 1952, for example, residents of Bahmadun formed a twenty-five-person preparatory payment strike committee.[78] Their demands echoed those of the Beirut campaign. The campaign also increasingly drew in new constituents. On March 14, 1952, the Syndicate of Hotel, Restaurant, Café and Employees held a general conference where one of their resolutions was the endorsement of the campaign.[79]

The EDB responded to this escalation in several ways that both recognized the threat posed by the protest campaign and sought to bolster its position. It indicated to the government a willingness to reduce rates, provided that the Lebanese state covered the loss of revenue.[80] The EDB also solicited affidavits of support from experts and professionals in the global electricity industry. These experts variously endorsed the EDB's claim that it alone had the right to modify electric utility rates, and that its current pricing scheme was commensurate with its resources and those of Lebanon. These included, among others, representatives of Electricity of France (est. 1946), Electricity of Strasbourg (est. 1899), and the British Electricity Authority (est. 1947). Furthermore, top managers at the Beirut office of the EDB began a months-long series of trips between Beirut and Paris as they consulted with their corporate headquarters.[81] It was in this context of escalation that the government and the EDB began official negotiations.[82]

Three additional developments took place during the escalation phase. First, in late February the committee of inquiry into the EDB pricing scheme presented its findings.[83] It concluded that EDB justifications for its existing pricing structure were sound and that a price reduction would invariably increase the demand for electricity while undermining the finances needed to further develop the production capacities of the company. The committee's report began by presenting a brief survey of the history and installations of the EDB, highlighting an 18-percent average annual increase in the demand for electricity between 1946 and 1951. Much of this survey echoed the position of the EDB as manifested in the above-mentioned pamphlet it distributed to the public toward the end of December 1951, justifying its prices on the basis of the nature of electricity consumption as well as the financial and technical aspects of increasing production.

The second development during this escalation phase was a series of meetings between representatives of the government and the EDB that inaugurated formal negotiations.[84] The company showed willingness to reduce the electric utility rates for the lowest consumption level of domestic subscribers.[85] On all other issues, the EDB and the government agreed to seek arbitration. Thus, the company rejected most of the protest campaign's demands, while the government revealed itself to be more conciliatory than antagonistic toward such a position.

The final development during this escalation phase was the cabinet forming the ad hoc Supreme Committee of Inquiry for Concessions (Lajnat al-Tahqiq al-'Ulya li-l-Imtiyazat).[86] The decree establishing the committee directly referenced the "approval of the parliament," and set a six-month period for the investigation of concessionary companies so as to suggest "recommendations, projects, and amendments to the [contractual] specifications needed to secure the public good."[87] The EDB protested the creation of the committee, indicating that it accepted the premise of renegotiating the existing agreement but rejected the idea that new institutions had the authority or expertise to determine whether the company was conducting itself appropriately.[88] Since late December 1951, members of the formal opposition had regularly called on the government to review all concessionary companies.

Stalemate characterized the third phase from March through May of 1952. On the one hand, the government announced that it had forced the EDB into certain concessions and that this was only the first victory of many it was pursuing.[89] These claims were far from reality. As mentioned above, records reveal the government's conciliatory posture toward the EDB and its pliancy in agreeing on arbitration on matters that EDB was unwilling to compromise on.[90] There is little indication that the government was at that point either exerting meaningful pressure on the EDB or pursuing alternative avenues for addressing the protestors' grievances. In fact, the government's collusion with the EDB went so far as to deploy security forces to accompany electricity bill collectors. Still the EDB expressed its frustration that the government was not doing enough to stand with the company.[91] The protest campaign for its part perceived the government as at best stalling and at worst supporting the EDB. It issued the government a warning, setting a ten-day deadline to deliver meaningful resolution to the standoff with the EDB.[92] This tactic did not yet translate into any tangible gains from the government or the EDB. However, it does appear to have constrained the company's responses. As one report put it, "The company is not able to take measures normally available to electric distribution systems around the world—that is, to deprive those who refuse to pay for the benefits of distribution—as the movement is too large to take such measures."[93]

The period of stalemate featured the publication of two documents that effectively cleared the EDB of any wrongdoing and legitimated the status quo. The first was a letter from the Supreme Committee set up to investigate concessionary companies. The committee cleared the EDB, claiming that the company had conducted itself in accordance with its obligations under the contracts and specifications of its concessions.[94] The company would go on to cite this letter in subsequent negotiation meetings and public statements as a means of legitimating its position.[95] The second document was a more comprehensive report authored by two Dutch consultants.[96] The government and the EDB had jointly commissioned the "international experts" as external reviewers, and their findings corroborated those of the committee of inquiry. After a comprehensive technical and economic survey of the EDB, the "Dutch report"—as it came to be referred to—concluded that "these prices are based on sound economic principles and can satisfy the needs of the clients."[97] The report went on to recommend a rate reduction for monthly domestic consumption levels that did not exceed twenty kilowatt-hours. It did so on the basis of what it termed a "social [rather than economic or legal] perspective." Thus, it strongly discouraged any other rate reductions and deferred to the EDB to "elaborate a pricing system that incorporates this special reduction without changing other prices."[98] The Dutch report reinforced the EDB's position in its meetings with the government. This third period of the protest campaign ended with a divergence between the protesters and the government. On the one hand, records of back-channel negotiations between the government and the EDB indicate that by the end of May 1952 the government was moving even closer to the company's position. On the other hand, around the same time, the central protest committee rejected the findings of both the committee of inquiry and the Dutch experts.

A turning point in the protest campaign against the EDB began in late May and early June. This would not have been possible without the protestors' persistence in the face of the EDB's unresponsiveness, government inaction, and the reports validating the EDB. However, the turning point was also a function of increasing polarization of the Lebanese political field. Various segments of society organized protest campaigns of their own. These included strikes by the telephone and postal workers, the railroad workers, as well as the syndicates of vegetable merchants, furniture builders, and barbers. These strikes were part of a series of protests that had effectively paralyzed the government.[99] While the protest campaign against the EDB was certainly the longest lasting, it was part of an expanding repertoire of contentious politics of the early independence period in general and the last year of the Khuri presidency in particular.

The formal opposition also drew on the EDB protest campaign in escalating their attacks against al-Khuri.[100] In what appears to be a major escalation in Patriotic Socialist Front (PSF, al-Jabha al-Ishtirakiyya al-Wataniyya) discourse and accusations, MP Kamal Jumblatt published an article titled "The Foreigners Put Them In, So Let the People Get Them Out."[101] He explicitly argued that al-Khuri, his inner circle and associated cabinets, and the economic interests they all represented had forsaken the cause of independence and failed to represent Lebanese citizens. In retaliation for the article, the government closed Jumblatt's newspaper (*al-Anba'*), eventually suspending it for eight months, and referred Jumblatt to the Ministry of Justice for prosecution. In addition, the government suspended six other papers for one month for republishing Jumblatt's article after his newspaper was suspended.[102]

In this general context, the protest campaign appears to have gained the upper hand. Two particular developments hint at this shift. First, EDB correspondence with the government featured a change in tone. Prior to the end of May 1952, the company justified its existing rates with reference to rights under concession terms: the "fiscal balance" of the corporation and the notion that, absent a capacity to increase supply, a decrease in the electric utility rates would result in increased demand and consumption and additional power outages.[103] However, the company now began to frame rate reductions as threats, not simply to the company itself, but to ongoing projects to expand electric production capacity and meet electricity needs across the country.[104] The second indication that the protest campaign was gaining the upper hand is the government's decision to negotiate directly with the central protest committee and exclude the EDB from these meetings. Government officials increasingly made public statements sympathetic to the protest campaign. They acknowledged many of the campaign's grievances. More importantly, government officials began to reverse the previous official position that changes in electric utility rates could only be implemented with EDB consent. On several occasions, both the minister and director general of public works put forth proposals that were clearly unacceptable to the EDB. The problem, they now claimed, was EDB intransigence: the only solution was forcing the company to accept the proposals.

Such statements represented both the government's shift in public position on the campaign's demands and its attempts to claim the mantle of popular representation that was at the core not just of the campaign, but also of the formal opposition's critique of government policy on the EDB. The minister of public works, in particular, claimed that it was the government's proposal, rather than that of the central protest committee, that provided the solution. He further argued that the government had always been acting in the interest of the people. Such statements reflected a broader conflict between the government and the central protest committee, which had its roots in the months of struggle between the two—despite the fact that the government was now more responsive to the committee than the EDB. This conflict, however, was for the most part put aside in an attempt to reach a final decision that the government would announce and the central protest committee would accept by calling for the end of the campaign.[105] As the second week of July began, various newspapers suggested the potential end of the "conflict over electricity" and went on to speculate on the campaign's final accomplishments.[106]

Surely enough, on Thursday, July 10, 1952, the government issued a reduction in electric utility rates.[107] The decree listed nearly all the major EDB-related laws and agreements with the exception of the 1948 monetary accord. Throughout the protest campaign, the EDB drew on the monetary accord to establish the basis for its claims that any changes to the relationship between the company and the government (including the authority to set prices) necessitated negotiations. The government had initially accepted this as a basis for negotiations. However, the protest campaign's mounting pressure and the EDB's steadfastness forced the government to abandon the goal of a consensual agreement with the company. More importantly, the reductions lowered the maximum applicable rates by 21 percent from 21 to 16.5 piasters for lighting (domestic use), by 22 percent from 13.25 to 10.25 piasters for low voltage mechanical power, and by 37 percent from 13.25 to 8.5 piasters for high voltage mechanical power. The reductions also set a standard discounted rate for lighting at 6.5 piasters, making all subscribers of lighting power with a monthly consumption above a certain level eligible. These discounted consumption levels were drastically lower than the EDB's previous pricing scheme. This reduction reflected actual electric energy type (ten-ampere versus seventy-ampere meters) rather than types of establishments (homes versus restaurants). The new rates were effective as of January 1, 1952, thus retroactive to the protest campaign's early period.

The official protest campaign against the EDB ended on July 11, 1952, when the central protest committee called for its end.[108] On that day, the government also issued a letter to the EDB formally informing the company of the rate reductions.[109] However, this was not the end of the conflict. The EDB for its part protested the rate reductions and argued that it was entitled to government compensation for revenue lost due to the new policy. Additionally, many factories and cinemas continued to refuse paying electric utility bills—claiming that the rate reductions did not go far enough in addressing their specific circumstances.[110]

As the Khuri regime continued to face ever-expanding and disruptive political opposition, it sought to mitigate against the situation by announcing a series of reforms. The government claimed that these reforms addressed the grievances of various protesters, the formal opposition, and the regime's defectors. Two additional reductions in electric utility rates were important components of these alleged reforms. The government issued a second rate reduction on August 19, 1952, specifying discounted rates for low-voltage and high-voltage mechanical power consumption above a certain level.[111] These modified rates were available to all subscribers irrespective of the type of establishment, and represented significantly lower rates on all levels than those previously offered by the EDB. This second reduction also established on-peak hours for each month of the year. The government issued the third and final reduction on September 5, 1952, affirming the universal rate for lighting electricity while also providing additional instructions regarding off-peak versus on-peak usage for mechanical power.[112] These reductions satisfied enough factories and cinemas to definitively end their organized protest campaign.

However, the additional electric utility rate reductions solicited a dramatic reaction from the EDB. On September 5, 1952, the company instituted its first formal electricity-rationing program. It justified the program on the basis that rate reductions had caused an "artificial inflation of demand."[113] The EDB claimed it was unable to meet this inflation given existing constraints on capacities and finances. By then, however, the Khuri regime was paralyzed. The country soon became entangled in an open confrontation between al-Khuri and his loyal parliamentarians on the one hand, and the PSF and a range of mobilized parties and protesters on the other. The two-day general strike of September 15–16, 1952, culminated in al-Khuri's resignation and the eventual election of Kamil Sham'un as president. After this point, debates and struggles over the EDB would take on an entirely new set of dynamics. Rather than responding to bottom-up mobilization or intervening on behalf of protesters, the Sham'un regime dramatically shifted the government's approach toward the EDB as well as the broad constituencies of protesters who sought to assure access to infrastructure.

KAMIL SHAM'UN, NATIONALIZATION, AND THE POLITICS OF COALITION BUILDING

The start of Sham'un's presidency overlapped with a parliament whose majority sided with al-Khuri until the very last moment.[114] More specifically, the PSF had vigorously attacked this majority as part of the opposition campaign to mobilize pressure on the incumbent government and eventually force the resignation of al-Khuri. However, rather than basing his first cabinet on PSF parliamentarians—which identified themselves as "a popular majority even if not a numerical majority"—Sham'un opted to carry on with the al-Khuri regime strategy of designating the PSF as a minority bloc and thus according it minimal cabinet representation. This immediately caused a rift between Sham'un and the core of the PSF, which Jumblatt represented and from which the National Bloc increasingly distanced itself.[115] Thus in its first few months, the Sham'un regime was characterized by a reformist mandate while undergirded by an antireformist alliance. It was in this context that the next major round of mobilizations around the EDB unfolded. Rather than bottom-up mobilizations, this new round featured the presidency and cabinet as the driving force of a dynamic that—though unplanned—would lead to nationalization.

The events that led to the nationalization of the EDB proceeded in four phases: negotiations, escalation, and polarization, culminating in the government-imposed provisional control of the company. It was almost one year after the imposition of this control and the French government's subsequent filing of a case with the International Court of Justice that all parties reached agreement on a government buyout of the concessions and facilities of the EDB. However, such a trajectory was neither a preestablished goal of the Sham'un regime nor an inevitable outcome of the negotiations between the government and the company. Rather, it was the combination of contingent developments in domestic coalition politics as well as the legacies of popular mobilizations against the EDB that produced the eventual outcome.

The initial phase (October 1952–February 1953) featured a new round of negotiations between the EDB and the government. This is indicated by an exchange of letters in which both parties called for negotiations while defining the issues at stake.[116] The negotiations were to conclude with agreement on expanded production capacity, a revisiting of the current electric utility rates, and general principles for amendment of concessionary agreements. The EDB highlighted the impact on company finances of the government-imposed price reductions, specifically noting a 26 percent drop in revenues.[117] The company further noted that many factories had in fact persisted in refusing to pay their electric utility bills despite the decreed retroactive reductions. For its part, the government responded by highlighting the "exceptional circumstances" of recent developments that "forced the government to find a means of coping with the difficulties it faced."[118] The government also acknowledged the "financial and infrastructural efforts" of the company throughout 1952, and pledged to support the company through "collaboration . . . in the spirit of understanding and on the basis of common interests."[119]

The negotiation phase lasted until the end of February 1953. Unable to reach agreement through the first round of exchanges, the EDB sent a letter to the government warning that failure of negotiations undermined the confidence of the company in its own financial future.[120] Consequently, the company argued, it was able neither to make dividend payments to its shareholders nor to continue construction of the Zouk Mkayel power plant.[121] Such a conclusion to the negotiation phase should not obscure its key features. First, the electricity price reductions had a significant impact on the profit margins of the EDB. Second, some sectors of Lebanese society—most notably industrialists—pressed for additional reductions through continuing to refuse to pay their electric utility bills. Most important, the government made no indication of seeking to nationalize the company and in fact sought to deescalate the dynamic with the EDB by deflecting responsibility for the reductions on to the protest campaign, the political opposition, and the instability they combined to produce.

Despite such conciliatory gestures, the initial phase of negotiation gave way to one of escalation. This phase lasted throughout the month of March 1953. It was during this period that the remaining elements of the PSF intensified their opposition to the government, declaring that their grace period for Sham'un to deliver on his promises of reform had ended without anything more than half-hearted attempts. Members of the PSF consequently presented an ultimatum to the president, asking him to distance himself from the failed policies of the four-person technocratic cabinet headed by Khalid Shihab (r. September 30, 1952–April 30, 1953). The PSF claimed Shihab "was fit for normal circumstances but not for revolutionary circumstances."[122] One of the issues the PSF raised was the continuing electricity problems, and most notably the rationing that the company had put into effect as of September 5, 1952.[123] Soon enough, the PSF launched a multipronged media attack on various members of the government, including cabinet ministers, chairs of various parliamentary committees, and the speaker of parliament.[124]

It was in this context of increasing opposition to Sham'un, and more notably the impending collapse of his appointed cabinet, that the government escalated its dynamic with the EDB. On March 2, 1953, the government issued a letter to the EDB demanding that the company resume construction on the Zouk Mkayel power plant and threatening to "ensure proper service by all means."[125] The EDB responded by pointing out that this was the first time in several months that the government had directly mentioned the Zouk Mkayel plant despite repeated attempts by the company to prioritize reaching agreement on the issue.[126] Indeed, this fact is borne out in the exchange of letters between the two parties that constituted the negotiation phase. The EDB ended its letter by invoking its right to arbitration. It was at this juncture that both the government and company seem to have entrenched themselves even deeper into their divergent positions. Seeking to avoid compromising on the Zouk Mkayel plant, the government proposed that the EDB temporarily purchase electric power from the Nahr al-Bared Electricity Company so as to ensure an adequate supply of electric current to its subscriber base while negotiations on the Zouk Mkayel power plant continued.[127] The EDB rejected the proposal, insisting that the government agree to compensate the company for any purchases made from Nahr al-Bared.[128] Faced with a rapidly escalating opposition that sought to undermine the basis of Sham'un's mandate, the government on March 19, 1953, established provisional control over the EDB.[129] Such an act was limited to the production and distribution of electricity in Beirut and its suburbs. The provisional control did not apply to the Nahr al-Safa power plant, high-voltage transmission system, or the distribution of electric current to certain mountain towns.

Such measures thus reflected a poorly planned symbolic gesture rather than an intentional strategy to nationalize the company. Two facts in particular justify such a reading. The first is the seizure of EDB offices without the seizure of all of its production and distribution facilities. Given that such provisional control excluded both the operational Nahr al-Safa plant and the unfinished Zouk Mkayel plant, the seizure would have little effect in terms of a coordinated production increase. Second, the government apparently made no preparations for the seizure of EDB offices. Only five days after implementing provisional control, the government sent a telegram requesting technical assistance from the EDB in the management of the relevant facilities.[130] The EDB responded within the week expressing its willingness to provide such technical assistance, noting that such cooperation did not constitute recognition of provisional control.[131] According to the documentary record, neither the government nor the EDB interpreted the March 19, 1953, institution of provisional control as an attempt toward nationalization. While they continued to publicly criticize one another, letters exchanged subsequent to the initiation of provisional control indicate that negotiations toward resolving the deadlock over the construction of the Zouk Mkayel project was a priority for both parties. Such goals and expectations, however, were subject to change.

Polarization characterized the fourth phase (April–September 1953) of the dynamics between the government and the EDB. The opposition to Sham'un developed to include direct attacks on the president, going so far as to claim that he had failed to deliver on his promise of reform by not even replacing a single manager in a single department. The government moved to demonstrate otherwise. On April 4, 1953, the government extended its provisional control to all electricity-related concessions of the EDB.[132] Thus state officials seized control of all EDB production, distribution, and construction facilities. They also froze the financial assets of the company. This represented a significant shift from the initial implementation of provisional control. It was in this latest phase that the government issued a pamphlet to the public justifying its seizure of EDB facilities.[133] The document outlined a litany of well-known problems with the company's provisioning of electric current to its subscribers. Most importantly, the pamphlet claimed in its introduction that genuine political independence and real economic development rendered existing concessional agreements with the EDB obsolete and necessitated a redefinition of the relationship between the country and the company.

EDB managers and shareholders seem to have understood the implications of this juncture of the standoff with the Lebanese government and—by extension—the Lebanese population. Subsequent public statements and letters on behalf of the company make no references to seeking to continue negotiations. Instead, they focused on how the EDB had acted within its rights under the concessionary agreements signed with the government.[134] On August 14, 1953, the French government filed a case with the International Court of Justice on behalf of the EDB.[135] In its filing, the French government claimed the Lebanese government had violated its concessionary agreements with the company, which the two parties concluded during the Mandate period and which were recognized by the 1948 monetary accord. There are no documented exchanges between the EDB and the Lebanese government subsequent to the filing of the case. However, the International Court of Justice discontinued the case exactly one year later upon the request of the French government.[136] A review of the Lebanese archival record indicates that on March 26, 1954, the Lebanese government—represented by the prime minister and minister of public works—and the EDB—represented by the president of its board of directors—concluded an agreement for the reclamation by the government of all EDB concessionary rights and their associated facilities.[137] The Lebanese parliament ratified the agreement on July 3, 1954, and thus authorized the disbursement of 23,500,000 Lebanese liras owed to the EDB as settlement for the buyout.[138]

CONCLUSION

There were a number of long-term legacies of the nationalization of the EDB. It set a precedent that emboldened critics of foreign concessions to demand greater state intervention in, if not nationalization of, other public utility companies in Beirut and around the country. Populist groups and opposition parliamentarians also used the example of the EDB to demand a better share of profits from the two major oil pipelines in Lebanon: the Iraq Petroleum Company and Trans-Arabian Pipeline. These campaigns animated the 1950s and extended into the 1960s and 1970s.

The establishment of new state institutions is another legacy. On July 7, 1954, parliament created the Electricity and Common Transport Service (ECTS) to administer the nationalized offices, infrastructure, and services of the EDB. The service was officially attached to the Ministry of Public Works. Yet the ECTS constituted a new type of state institution: the public corporation. It had legal personality as well as administrative and financial autonomy. The government utilized this model of state institutional arrangements to incorporate nearly all remaining public utility services into the state bureaucracy during the postcolonial period.

A final legacy of the nationalization of the EDB more directly impinges on the broader trajectory of electric public utilities in Lebanon. The ECTS would take up the mantle of increasing electricity production in the country. It did so by inaugurating the Zouk Mkayel power plant in 1956. More importantly, the ECTS was the institutional foundation for the government's 1964 establishment of the national state-owned company, Electricity of Lebanon (Kahruba' Lubnan). Once created, Electricity of Lebanon had the exclusive authority to initiate new electricity projects in Lebanon. It was also tasked with incorporating other electricity-generating and distribution companies when their concessions expired or they otherwise sought to sell their rights, infrastructures, and services to the state. Electricity of Lebanon eventually became notorious for being administratively constrained and at the helm of a fundamentally unintegrated national electricity system. The roots of both of these dynamics lay in the fact that Electricity of Lebanon was simply the ECTS with a national rather than Beirut-specific mandate.

Conclusion

WHERE IS THE STATE?

HOW SHOULD THE POSTCOLONIAL HISTORY OF LEBANON BE PERIODIZED? Some consider the period from 1943 to 1975 to be a single unit. This approach sees little fundamental change across these years,[1] or collapses it into a teleology: a series of external shocks leading inevitably to the Lebanese Civil War (1975–90).[2] Others identify the three-month rebellion or civil war of 1958—the terminology varying with the author's analytic preference and political worldview—as a pivot separating the early years of independence from the period presumably leading to the 1975–90 Civil War.[3] This rebellion, and the US military intervention to contain it, undermined incumbent office holders of the late-Mandate-era political elite, leading to the presidential election of Commander of the Lebanese Armed Forces General Fu'ad Shihab, the crystallization of a new political formation around him, and the restructuring of the relationships between existing political organizations and state institutions. Scholars have conventionally identified the presidencies of Shihab (r. 1958–64) and his successor Charles Helou (r. 1964–70) as the period when Lebanon temporarily, and ineffectively, followed regional trends in state building, economic development, and social policies.[4]

This book offers several challenges to the dominant periodization. One challenge is to emphasize that popular mobilizations and state formation are ongoing processes. Different members of elite and popular social groups regularly make claims on government; use public performances like petitions, speeches, demonstrations, and strikes to do so; draw on existing repertoires of collective action and invent new ones; forge selective alliances with status-quo forces and subaltern groups; exploit political opportunities; and use a combination of institutional and extrainstitutional channels to advance their claims. While the nature of popular mobilization varies across time, space, constituency, and issue, it is a constant feature of modern politics.[5] State institutions, practices, and capacities, alternatively, emerge to realize visions of incumbent politicians, placate allies and would-be allies, and contend with elite and popular dissent. The network of state institutions is fundamentally asymmetrical, reflecting varying levels of importance, attention, and capacity.[6] As the nature of popular mobilizations shifts, state institutions are in turn selectively reinforced, reformed, and restructured. In other words, there is no period in the modern history of Lebanon that was not simultaneously a period of state formation and popular mobilization.

This brings us to the issue of how to periodize state formation and popular mobilization. Some scholars of Lebanon emphasize the 1950 dissolution of the customs union with Syria as a key juncture.[7] Others highlight changes in the financial regulatory regime, like the establishment of a central bank in 1964.[8] This book is grounded in the assumption that the 1943–55 period represented a particular phase in the relationship between state formation and popular mobilization. The overlap of this period with that of decolonization—however imprecise—endowed Lebanese state institutions with a fluid quality. Incumbent elites were liberated from certain decision-making constraints and popular groups were similarly freed from mobilizational constraints inherent to direct colonial rule. The context in which Lebanon transitioned to independence is also significant, as it was defined by the conclusion of World War II, the reconfiguration of a new regional order and international system, and the consolidation of US global hegemony.

The 1943–55 period also featured unique patterns of conflict occurring within structural, institutional, and intellectual environments quite different from those that followed. Patterns of conflict shape opportunities for elite and popular mobilizations, determine the interests around which to organize, and make available forms of organization to such groups in very specific ways. The immediate aftermath of independence in Lebanon featured fluctuations in the local, regional, and global balances of power, and in the institutional arrangements reflecting these power relations. Under these conditions, elite and popular groups in Lebanon did not necessarily have "one set of clear, fixed interests or strategies." The patterns of conflicts and alliances in Lebanon between 1943 and 1955 were not "scripted processes pitting sharply articulated categories" of ideologically or socially constituted collective actors operating against one another within clear strategic contexts and institutional settings. Rather, they reflected an "essentially indeterminate process" that, while bounded, occurred within an ambiguous environment that "provided considerable scope for improvisation."[9]

The year 1955 marks a critical turning point in the dynamics of state formation and popular mobilization. The features most clearly associated with the Lebanese postcolonial political economy were institutionalized by 1955: open, laissez-faire, and service based. That year also capped a multiyear effort to permanently concentrate Palestinian refugees receiving services from the UN Relief and Works Agency for Palestine Refugees (UNRWA) into seventeen official refugee camps and several informal settlements. UNRWA then began its project of replacing tents with prefabricated shelters and cinder block dwellings. In December 1955 the Abu Ali River flooded in Tripoli, killing over a hundred residents and destroying tens of homes, shops, and historical sites. In March 1956 a multishock earthquake struck Lebanon, the epicenter of which was at the intersection of the Shuf and Jizzine districts. This quake killed over a hundred people, destroyed entire villages, and displaced thousands. The Lebanese government's grossly inadequate responses to these natural disasters fundamentally altered the residents' relationship to the state and served as new loci around which political organizations mobilized vis-à-vis the cabinet and relevant ministries. At the regional level, the US attempt to isolate Egypt's Gamal Abdel Nasser (1918–70), the September 1955 Soviet bloc weapons sales to Egypt, and the 1956 Suez Crisis combined to establish Nasser as the region's preeminent anti-imperialist figure.[10] Nasserism subsequently emerged as the newest and most dominant ideological pole within the Arab nationalist landscape.[11] The July 1958 Free Officer coup in Iraq and 1958–61 union between Egypt and Syria further affected the meaning of Arab nationalism and of its organizational manifestations. To these developments must be added the emergence of the United States as the unrivaled Western imperial power in the Middle East, especially after 1956—reflecting both the eclipse of British and French power and the progressively deeper level of foreign intervention into local Lebanese politics.[12] The long-term institutionalization of particular patterns of economic development, political representation, and ideological positions, combined with a rapid succession of events starting in late 1955, transformed local, regional, and global dynamics in ways that radically shifted the array of available strategic choices and possible outcomes.

These are the transformations that recalibrated political stakes, created and hardened new fault lines, and altered imaginative possibilities in Lebanon. While the late 1950s and subsequent periods featured many of the same individual and collective actors highlighted in this book, they would experience important shifts in the models of political organization they aspired to; the visions of state and economy they pursued; the local, regional, and international alliances they made; and the resources at their disposal relative to the 1943–55 period. This becomes crystal clear starting in 1958.

The post-1958 array of Lebanese political parties offers an important reflection of the transformations just described. There were short-term shifts like the alliance between the Kata'ib Party and the Syrian Social Nationalist Party in defense of President Kamil Sham'un in 1958. Yet longer-term changes prevailed. The National Bloc reestablished its political prominence, regularly participating in cabinets throughout the 1960s and 1970s.[13] Alternatively, the Kata'ib Party began to participate in cabinets and established itself as a party of the new status quo.[14] In addition, Sham'un formed the National Liberal Party (Hizb al-Ahrar al-Wataniyyin) to facilitate his political career beyond the presidency of the republic.[15] At the same time, the Lebanese branch of the Arab Socialist Ba'th Party (Hizb al-Ba'th al-'Arabi al-Ishtiraki, est. 1947–52) expanded its membership base to become a mass party that competed with the Progressive Socialist Party and the Lebanese Communist Party.[16] Around the same time, the Arab Nationalist Youth firmly consolidated itself as both a regional political party and a force outside its traditional area of operation, the American University of Beirut. It also renamed itself the Movement of Arab Nationalists (Harakat al-Qawmiyyun al-'Arab), engaged in organizational restructuring, and began to display internal fissures around the question of socialism.[17]

The post-1958 period and the inauguration of the Shihabist project featured important continuities with the period under study in this book. Banking reform, the nationalization of public utilities, the creation of the social security system, and the state-led rejuvenation of the agricultural sector have their origins in debates and struggles that long preceded 1958. Some initially emerged in the 1943–55 period, while others date back to the Mandate era. Thus, many policies associated with the Shihabist period cannot be reduced to the ideological preferences of a particular presidential regime or to the emulation of regional trends. They were part of a longer history of local debates and mobilizations over the trajectory of state formation.

By the end of the Lebanese Civil War (1975–90), Lebanon had become "synonymous with a failed state."[18] This was itself a remarkable transformation from its representation in international media and Western academic writings throughout the 1960s and early 1970s.[19] There is a tendency to view the civil war as the logical culmination of Lebanese history, with the preceding period(s) posited as explanatory. Some highlight the protracted fifteen-year civil war as exemplifying Lebanon's allegedly weak national identity, state institutions, and economic development compared to other countries in the region. The predominant characterizations of the civil war are, first, as a violent manifestation of irreconcilable sectarian and ideological differences overlaid with multiple forms and sources of foreign intervention and, second, as the complete breakdown of national authority and with it the network of state institutions.[20]

The multiple and overlapping crises that manifested in the post–civil war period—especially after the 2005 assassination of former prime minister Rafiq al-Hariri (r. 1992–98 and 2000–2004)—reified the narrative of Lebanon as a failed state. At the political level, the efficacy of the electoral system was exposed to severe strains and subjected to major questions. On the one hand, elections in postwar Lebanon failed to bring about any reasonable response to the needs and aspirations of the residents of the country. On the other hand, the formal political field became polarized. The March 14 and March 8 coalitions, both founded in the wake of Hariri's assassination and Syria's subsequent military withdrawal, remained at odds after an escalating series of cabinet crises culminating in the political system's total gridlock. Incumbent politicians had a dubious mandate after the 2009-elected parliament extended its constitutional four-year term of office by an additional five years. They also postponed the 2022 municipal elections for three years. Legislators were unable to elect a president by simple majority in 2014–16 and 2022–25. Caretaker cabinets with limited powers governed Lebanon during both of these "absent" presidencies. The only exception to the zero-sum game dynamics between political factions occurs when a threat to the political system that makes both their incumbency and gridlock possible appears to be existential.

At the fiscal level, the Lebanese state budget has run a deficit every year since the end of the civil war. Simply put, expenses have far outpaced revenues on an annual basis. A regressive tax system is one explanation for this problem.[21] More important is the burden of public debt. Successive postwar Lebanese governments relied on public debt rather than taxation to fund reconstruction projects and finance public expenditures. Lebanon's public debt is one of the largest in the region (and world) relative to GDP. The terms of that debt "imposed a high debt-servicing burden on the state," leaving it with relatively little money in the long term to spend on actual expenses.[22] Between 1993 and 2019, debt servicing accounted for nearly a third of overall state expenditures.

Lebanon has also experienced a developmental crisis in the postwar period. Successive governments have pursued an economic development model that has benefitted the privileged few. Throughout the 2000s, poverty, unemployment, and underemployment rates rose while purchasing power decreased. Between 2005 and 2014, the richest 10 percent of Lebanon's population received 55 percent of the total national income.[23] This is due, in part, to the same patterns that characterized other regional states in the 1990s and 2000s, particularly the combination of policies that liberalized trade; privatized state properties, enterprises, and services; and cut various social provisions.[24] It is also due to the historically constituted links between bankers and the state.[25] The Lebanese banking sector holds more than 50 percent of gross public debt, with the most politically connected banks holding more public debt than the banking sector average.[26] Lebanon's development model showed signs of strain in 2019 when foreign exchange supplies dried up and the Lebanese pound's exchange rate of 1,507 to the US dollar collapsed. Thus by the summer of that year, the black-market rate was 15,000 to 1. Since then, the Lebanese pound has lost more than 98 percent of its value.[27] The foreign currency crisis hampered the importation of luxury goods *and* staples. Banks introduced ad hoc and illegal capital controls on dollar deposits, making it difficult for depositors to access cash at its current value.[28] By 2023 most people in Lebanon were struggling to survive.[29]

Equally important is Lebanon's infrastructural crisis. The waste management and electricity sectors have collapsed, while other sectors like water and transportation have remained in crisis.[30] These infrastructural failures and the political crises that accompany them should not be underestimated. On the one hand, they have brought to light endemic corruption in several state institutions. On the other hand, the breakdowns reflect an intensification of political factions' conflict over domestic sources of revenue, as external sources increasingly disappeared in the context of the 2008–9 global financial crisis and the 2020–23 COVID-19 pandemic.

The violence and destruction of the civil war, along with the multiple and overlapping crises of postwar Lebanon, loom large in our understanding of Lebanese politics. Many activists, journalists, and scholars working in or on the country have consequently emphasized state weakness, dysfunction, and failure as the starting points for research and analysis of both historical and contemporary politics in Lebanon. Viewing such dynamics through the prism of state failure reflects a normative bias whereby state institutions only matter when they promote specific political, economic, and social development.[31] In turn, the Lebanese state is understood in terms of what it lacks rather than what it has.[32] This leads to a misunderstanding of how politics work and how state institutional arrangements can change and yet still retain their significance.

There has been renewed scholarly interest in narrating and analyzing popular mobilizations in Lebanon during the last fifteen years. Inspired in part by the Arab uprisings but more directly by the episodic outbreak of mass popular mobilization in Lebanon (including the 2019 uprising), scholars, journalists, and activists are revisiting some of the most important episodes in postwar popular mobilizations. These include well-known and specific instances like the 2015 garbage protests and the 2016 mobilizations for municipal elections.[33] Equally important are longer-term movements like those to protect the Dalieh in Beirut or to support the drafting of a civil personal status law.[34] Still others have a much longer trajectory, including the Committee of the Families of the Kidnapped and Disappeared in Lebanon (Lajnat Ahali al-Makhtufin wa-l-Mafqudin fi Lubnan, est. 1982) and the Lebanese Union for People with Disabilities (al-Ittihad al-Lubnani li-l-Ashkas al-Mu'awwaqin Harakiyyan, est. 1981).[35] This is to say nothing of a myriad of labor mobilizations that take shape in the public and private sectors.[36] Much of the writings on these popular mobilizations have viewed them as a response to state weakness and failure or have otherwise analyzed them in isolation from their context, the terrain of state institutions. But as the episodes and stories featured in this book demonstrate, focusing on just one or the other could be an analytic dead end. State formation and popular mobilization are co-constitutive and, as such, feature powerfully interactive—even if highly contingent—qualities. Moving beyond the conventional narrative about Lebanon necessitates taking seriously this dynamic, not as something limited to a romanticized period in time or a privileged set of issues, but as an iterative process of reconstituting politics.

Notes

This study is primarily based on documents from the Archive Section of al-Furat Bookshop in Beirut, the Archives and Special Collections Department of the American University of Beirut (AUB), the Sophia Smith Collection of Women's History at Smith College, the UK National Archives (TNA), and the US National Archives and Records Administration (NARA), as well as numerous issues from primarily the following Lebanese Arabic periodicals: *al-'Amal*, *al-Anba'*, *al-Nahar*, and *Sawt al-Sha'b*. At al-Furat, I looked at flyers, pamphlets, and booklets issued by political parties and coalitions. The AUB was particularly rich in sources. Therein I explored the Eveline Bustros Collection, the Iliya Harik Collection, the Asad Jibrail Rustum Collection, and the Linda Sadaka Archival Collection. At Smith College, I made use of the Ruth Frances Woodsmall Papers. At the TNA, I made use of files from the Records of the Foreign Office (FO) and the records of departments responsible for labor and employment matters and related bodies (LAB). At NARA, I primarily looked at the Records of the Foreign Service Posts of the Department of State (Record Group 84), particularly correspondences between the US Legation/Embassy in Beirut and the Department of State. I also virtually accessed the International Labour Organisation (ILO) Institutional and Open Access Repository, the UN Archives, and the World Bank Group Archives.

Introduction

1. For example, see Leila Tarazi Fawaz, *Merchants and Migrants in Nineteenth-Century Beirut* (Harvard University Press, 1982); Jens Hanssen, *Fin de Siècle Beirut: The Making of an Ottoman Provincial Capital* (Oxford University Press, 2005); Ussama Makdisi, *The Culture of Sectarianism: Community, History, and Violence in Nineteenth-Century Ottoman Lebanon* (University of California Press, 2000); Kais Firro, *Inventing Lebanon: Nationalism and the State Under the Mandate* (I. B. Tauris, 2003); Elizabeth Thompson, *Colonial Citizens: Republican Rights, Paternal Privilege, and Gender in French Syria and Lebanon* (Columbia University Press, 2000); Raghid El-Solh, *Lebanon and Arabism: National Identity and State Formation* (I. B. Tauris, 2004); Theodor Hanf, *Coexistence in Wartime Lebanon: Decline of a State and Rise of a Nation* (I. B. Tauris, 1993); Elizabeth Picard, "The Political Economy of Civil War in Lebanon," in *War, Institutions, and Social Change in the Middle East*, ed. Steven Heydemann (University of California Press, 2000), 292–322; James R. Stocker, *Spheres of Intervention: US Foreign Policy and the Collapse of Lebanon, 1967–1976* (Cornell University Press, 2016).

2. For example, see Helena Cobban, *The Making of Modern Lebanon* (Westview, 1985); Samir Khalaf, *Civil and Uncivil Violence in Lebanon: A History of the Internationalization of Communal Conflict* (Columbia University Press, 2002); Caroline Attié, *Struggle in the Levant: Lebanon in the 1950s* (I. B. Tauris, 2004). Such trends also betray a particular understanding of violence that eschews more subtle or structural forms of violence. For an exception that takes such forms of violence seriously, see Michael Gilsenan, *Lords of the Lebanese Marches: Violence & Narrative in an Arab Society* (I. B. Tauris, 1996).

3. For example, see Irene L. Gendzier, *Notes from the Minefield: United States Intervention in Lebanon and the Middle East, 1945–1958* (Columbia University Press, 1997).

4. On cultural production, see Christopher Stone, *Popular Culture and Nationalism in Lebanon: The Fairouz and Rahbani Nation* (Routledge, 2008); Robyn Creswell, *City of Beginnings: Poetic Modernism in Beirut* (Princeton University Press, 2019); Zeina Maasri, *Cosmopolitan Radicalism: The Visual Politics of Beirut's Global Sixties* (Cambridge University Press, 2020). On various aspects of social transformation, see John Gulick, *Social Structure and Cultural Change in a Lebanese Village* (Johnson Reprint Corp., 1971); Michael W. Suleiman, *Political Parties in Lebanon: The Challenge of a Fragmented Political Culture* (Cornell University Press, 1967); Hicham Safieddine, *Banking on the State: The Financial Foundations of Lebanon* (Stanford University Press, 2019).

5. Makdisi, *Culture of Sectarianism*; Max Weiss, *In the Shadow of Sectarianism: Law, Shiʿism, and the Making of Modern Lebanon* (Harvard University Press, 2010).

6. Ilham Khuri-Makdisi, *The Eastern Mediterranean and the Making of Global Radicalism, 1860–1914* (University of California Press, 2010); Thompson, *Colonial Citizens*; Malek Abisaab, *Militant Women of a Fragile Nation* (Syracuse University Press, 2010); Betty S. Anderson, *The American University of Beirut: Arab Nationalism and Liberal Education* (University of Texas Press, 2012).

7. Akram Khater, *Inventing Home: Emigration, Gender, and the Middle Class in Lebanon, 1870–1920* (University of California Press, 2001); Andrew Arsan, *Interlopers of Empire: The Lebanese Diaspora in Colonial French West Africa* (Oxford University Press, 2014); Stacy Fahrenthold, *Between the Ottomans and the Entente: The First World War in the Syrian and Lebanese Diaspora, 1908–1925* (Oxford University Press, 2019).

8. Maya Mikdashi, *Sextarianism: Sovereignty, Secularism, and the State in Lebanon* (Stanford University Press, 2022); Safieddine, *Banking on the State.*

9. For example, see Kamal Salibi, *Crossroads to Civil War: Lebanon, 1958–1976* (Caravan Books, 1976); Farid al-Khazen, *Breakdown of the State in Lebanon, 1967–1976* (Harvard University Press, 2000).

10. For example, see Attié, *Struggle in the Levant*; Dylan Baun, *Winning Lebanon: Youth Politics, Populism, and the Production of Sectarian Violence, 1920–1958* (Cambridge University Press, 2021).

11. Safieddine, *Banking on the State.*

12. For example, see Kamal Salibi, *A House of Many Mansions: The History of Lebanon Reconsidered* (University of California Press, 1988); Albert Hourani, *Political Society in Lebanon: A Historical Introduction* (Center for Lebanese Studies, 1989).

13. For example, see Lara Deeb, Tsolin Nalbantian, and Nadya Sbaiti, eds., *Practicing Sectarianism: Archival and Ethnographic Interventions on Lebanon* (Stanford University Press, 2022).

14. For example, see Clovis Maksoud, "Lebanon and Arab Nationalism," in *Politics in Lebanon*, ed. Leonard Binder (John Wiley & Sons, 1966); Youssef Chaitiani, *Post-Colonial Syria and Lebanon: The Decline of Arab Nationalism and the Triumph of the State* (I. B. Tauris, 2007).

15. Sara Pursley, *Familiar Futures: Time, Selfhood, and Sovereignty in Iraq* (Stanford University Press, 2019), 24, 58–69.

16. For example, see Carolyn L. Gates, *The Merchant Republic of Lebanon: Rise of an Open Economy* (I. B. Tauris, 1998); Kamal Dib, *Warlords and Merchants: The Lebanese Business and Political Establishment* (Ithaca Press, 2004).

17. For two of the few exceptions, see Safieddine, *Banking on the State*; Fawwaz Trabousli, *al-Tabaqat al-Ijtima'iyya wa-l-Sulta al-Siyasiyya fi Lubnan* (Dar al-Saqi, 2016).

18. For example, see Brinkley Messick, *The Calligraphic State: Textual Domination and History in a Muslim Society* (University of California Press, 1993); World Bank, *Unlocking the Employment Potential in the Middle East and North Africa: Toward a New Social Contract* (World Bank, 2004); Nora Barakat, *Bedouin Bureaucrats: Mobility and Property in Ottoman Empire* (Stanford University Press, 2023); Oliver Schlumberger, ed., *Debating Arab Authoritarianism: Dynamics and Durability of Nondemocratic Regimes* (Stanford University Press, 2007); Kevan Harris, *A Social Revolution: Politics and the Welfare State in Iran* (University of California Press, 2017).

19. Timothy Mitchell, discussing this dynamic with respect to the discipline of political science, has identified these two approaches as "statist theories" and "systems theories," respectively. Timothy Mitchell, "The Limits of the State: Beyond Statist Approaches and Their Critics," *American Political Science Review* 85, no. 1 (1991): 77–96.

20. Compare, for example, Daniel Lerner's *The Passing of Traditional Society: Modernizing the Middle East* (Free Press, 1958) and Roger Owen, *State, Power and Politics in the Making of the Modern Middle East* (Routledge, 2006).

21. Richard Peet and Elaine Hartwick, *Theories of Development: Contentions, Arguments, Alternatives* (Guilford, 2009); Zachary Lockman, *Contending Visions of the Middle East: The History and Politics of Orientalism* (Cambridge University Press, 2004).

22. For example, see Steven Heydemann, *Authoritarianism in Syria: Institutions and Social Conflict 1946–1970* (Cornell University Press, 1999), 1–29, 206–18.

23. Scholars have, to a lesser extent, drawn on the works of Pierre Bourdieu, *On the State: Lectures at the Collège de France*, 1989–1992 (Polity, 2020); Antonio Gramsci, *Selections from the Prison Notebooks*, ed. and trans. Quintin Hoare and Geoffrey Nowell Smith (International, 1989); Michael Mann, *The Sources of Social Power* (Cambridge University Press, 1986); Joel S. Migdal, *Strong Societies and Weak States: State-Society Relations and State Capabilities in the Third World* (Princeton University Press, 1988); Charles Tilly, *Coercion, Capital, and European States, A.D. 990–1990* (Blackwell, 1990); James C. Scott, *Seeing Like a State: How Certain Schemes to Improve the Human Condition Have Failed* (Yale University Press, 1999).

24. Max Weber, *Economy and Society: An Outline of Interpretive Sociology*, ed. G. Roth and C. Wittich, vol. 2 (Bedminster, 1968), 956–1005.

25. Michel Foucault, "Governmentality," in *The Foucault Effect: Studies in Governmentality*, ed. G. Burchelle, C. Gordon, and P. Miller (Harvester/Wheatsheaf, 1991), 87–104.

26. For example, see Khaled Fahmy, *All the Pasha's Men: Mehmed Ali, His Army and the Making of Modern Egypt* (American University in Cairo Press, 1997); Donald Quartaert, *The Ottoman Empire, 1700–1922* (Cambridge University Press, 2005); Afshin Marashi, *Nationalizing Iran: Culture, Power, and the State, 1870–1940* (University of Washington Press, 2008).

27. For example, see Reeva Spector Simon and Eleanor H. Tejirian, *The Creation of Iraq, 1914–1921* (Columbia University Press, 2004); Matthew H. Ellis, *Desert Borderland: The Making of Modern Egypt and Libya* (Stanford University Press, 2018); Jordi Tejel, *Rethinking State and Border Formation in the Middle East: Turkish-Syrian-Iraqi Borderlands, 1921–46* (Edinburgh University Press, 2023). The remainder of this paragraph (and my summary of the border making process) draws in particular from Sara Pursley, "'Lines Drawn on an Empty Map': Iraq's Borders and the Legend of the Artificial State (Part 1)," *Jadaliyya*, June 2, 2015, https://www.jadaliyya.com/Details/32140.

28. I am drawing on Steven Heydemann and Marc Lynch's definition of the term. See their "Introduction," in *Making Sense of the Arab State*, ed. Steven Heydemann and Marc Lynch (University of Michigan Press, 2023), 4.

29. Heydemann and Lynch, "Introduction," 4.

30. For example, see Heydemann, *Authoritarianism in Syria*; Tariq Tell, *The Social and Economic Origins of Monarchy in Jordan* (Palgrave Macmillan, 2013).

31. For example, see Marsha Pripstein Posusney and Michele Penner Anrist, eds., *Authoritarianism in the Middle East: Regimes and Resistance* (Lynne Rienner, 1995); Jillian Schwedler, *Protesting Jordan: Geographies of Power and Dissent* (Stanford University Press, 2022).

32. For example, see Bassam S. A. Haddad, *Business Networks in Syria: The Political Economy of Authoritarian Resilience* (Stanford University Press, 2011); Hesham Sallam, *Classless Politics: Islamist Movements, the Left, and Authoritarian Legacies in Egypt* (Columbia University Press, 2022).

33. For example, see Clement Henry and Robert Springborg, *Globalization and the Politics of Development in the Middle East* (Cambridge University Press, 2010).

34. This is a point made by several scholars, including Eugene Rogan, *Frontiers of the State in the Late Ottoman Empire: Transjordan, 1850–1921* (Cambridge University Press, 1999); James L. Gelvin, *Divided Loyalties: Nationalism and Mass Politics in Syria at the Close of Empire* (University of California Press, 1999); Michael Provence, *The Last Ottoman Generation and the Making of the Modern Middle East* (Cambridge University Press, 2017).

35. I am drawing on and inspired by Sara Pursley's description of her own methodological approach in *Familiar Futures*, 27.

36. I am drawing on Hicham Safieddine's description of the relationship between the institutions he studies and sectarian politics. See Safieddine, *Banking on the State*, 6–7.

37. Safieddine, *Banking on the State*, 6.

38. For example, see Albert Hourani, "Lebanon: The Development of a Political Society," in *Politics in Lebanon*, ed. Leonard Binder (Wiley, 1966), 13–29; Edmond Rabbath, *La formation historique du Liban politique et constitutionnel: Essai de syntheses* (L'Université libanaise, 1973), Hanf, *Coexistence in Wartime Lebanon*, 71–74.

39. For a standard scholarly narrative of the National Pact, see Farid el-Khazen, *The Communal Pact of National Identities: The Making and Politics of the 1943 National Pact* (Centre for Lebanese Studies, 1991).

40. Bishara al-Khuri, *Haqa'iq Lubnaniyya*, vols. 1–3 (Awraq Lubnaniyya, 1960–61).

41. Emil Bustani, *"al-Mithaq al-Watani" wa-Lubnan al-Mustaqbal* (Beirut: n.p., 1958).

42. Jonah Schulhofer-Wohl makes a similar argument about the pact in his *Quagmire in Civil War* (Cambridge University Press, 2020), 58–68. One indication for this is the complete absence of the National Pact from studies on Lebanese politics produced in the 1940s and early 1950s. For example, see Albert Hourani, *Syria and Lebanon: A Political Essay* (Oxford University Press, 1946); Pierre Rondot, *Les institutions politiques du Liban. Des communautés traditionnelles à l'État moderne* (Institut d'Études de l'Orient contemporain, 1947), Nicola A. Ziadeh, *Syria and Lebanon* (Ernest Benn Limited, 1956).

Chapter 1

1. For example, see Auguste Pasha Adib, *Le Liban après la guerre* (Imp. P. Barbey, 1919); Yusuf al-Sawda, *Fi Sabil Lubnan* (Dar Lahad Khater, [1919] 1988); Phillip Hitti, *Lebanon in History* (Macmillan, 1957); William R. Polk, *The Opening of South Lebanon 1788–1840* (Harvard University Press, 1963); Kamal Salibi, *The Modern History of Lebanon* (Praeger, 1965); Iliya Harik, *Politics of Change in a Traditional Society* (Princeton University Press, 1968).

2. Ussama Makdisi, *The Culture of Sectarianism: Community, History, and Violence in Nineteenth-Century Ottoman Lebanon* (University of California Press, 2000), 28–50; Alessandro Olsaretti, "Political Dynamics in the Rise of Fakhr al-Din, 1590–1633: Crusade, Trade, and State Formation along the Levantine Coast," *The International History Review* 30, no. 4 (2008): 709–40; Carol Hakim, *The Origins of the Lebanese National Idea, 1840–1920* (University of California Press, 2013), 99–194.

3. See Sara Pursley, *Familiar Futures: Time, Selfhood, and Sovereignty in Iraq* (Stanford University Press, 2019), 47–48, 65–68; James L. Gelvin, *Divided Loyalties:*

Nationalism and Mass Politics in Syria at the Close of Empire (University of California Press, 1999), 136–37, 260; Eugene Rogan, *Frontiers of the State in the Late Ottoman Empire: Transjordan, 1850–1921* (Cambridge University Press, 1999), 253–55; Rosie Bsheer, *Archive Wars: The Politics of History in Saudi Arabia* (Stanford University Press, 2020), 20–59. Also see Michael Provence, "Ottoman Modernity, Colonialism, and Insurgency in the Interwar Arab East," in "Relocating Arab Nationalism," special issue, *International Journal of Middle East Studies* 42, no. 2 (2011): 205–25.

4. Jane Hathaway, *The Arab Lands Under Ottoman Rule, 1516–1800* (Routledge, 2008).

5. The following discussion of several transformations adopts and modifies the framework of James L. Gelvin as presented in his in-class teaching and published work. See James L. Gelvin, 105C: The Middle East, 1500–Present (class lectures on "Defensive Developmentalism," "Imperialism," and "The Great Nineteenth-Century Transformation," University of California, Los Angeles, Fall 2008); James L. Gelvin, *The Modern Middle East: A History*, 3rd ed. (Oxford University Press, 2011).

6. I am drawing on the concept of the "modern world system," a historical model for the organization of the international system in the modern period of world history. See Immanuel Wallerstein, *World-Systems Analysis: An Introduction* (Duke University Press, 2004).

7. Engin Akarli, *The Long Peace: Ottoman Lebanon, 1861–1920* (University of California Press, 1993), 102–46; Makdisi, *Culture of Sectarianism*, 5–95; Jens Hanssen, *Fin de Siècle Beirut: The Making of an Ottoman Provincial Capital* (Oxford University Press, 2005), 55–83, 113–90.

8. Akram Khater, *Inventing Home: Emigration, Gender, and the Middle Class in Lebanon, 1870–1920* (University of California Press, 2001), 19–47; Malek Abisaab, *Militant Women of a Fragile Nation* (Syracuse University Press, 2010), 1–16; Kristen Alff, "Levantine Joint-Stock Companies, Trans-Mediterranean Partnerships, and Nineteenth-Century Capitalist Development," *Comparative Studies in Society and History* 60, no. 1 (2018): 150–77.

9. Roger Owen, "The Study of Middle Eastern Industrial History: Notes on the Interrelationship Between Factories and Small-Scale Manufacturing with Special References to Lebanese Silk and Egyptian Sugar, 1900–1930," *International Journal of Middle East Studies* 16, no. 4 (1984): 475–87; Kais Firro, "Silk and Agrarian Changes in Lebanon, 1860–1914," *International Journal of Middle East Studies* 22, no. 2 (1990): 151–69; Akram Fouad Khater, "'House' to 'Goddess of the House': Gender, Class, and Silk in 19th-Century Mount Lebanon," *International Journal of Middle East Studies* 28, no. 3 (1996): 325–48.

10. Khater, *Inventing Home*, 21–22.

11. Abisaab, *Militant Women*, 12–13; Kristen Alff, "The Business of Property: Levantine Joint-Stock Companies, Land, Law, and Capitalist Development around the Mediterranean, 1850–1925" (PhD diss., Stanford University, 2019), 16, 89, 94.

12. For example, see Tamara Chalabi, *The Shi'is of Jabal 'Amil and the New Lebanon: Community and Nation-State, 1918–1943* (Palgrave Macmillan, 2003), 17–28.

13. Stanford J. Shaw, "The Origins of Representative Government in the Ottoman Empire: An Introduction to the Provincial Councils, 1839–1876," in *Near Eastern Round Table, 1967–1968*, ed. R. Bayly Winder (Near East Center and the Center for International Studies, New York University, 1969), 53–142; Hanssen, *Fin de Siècle Beirut*, 37–52, 70–73.

14. Hanssen, *Fin de Siècle Beirut*, 142–44; Alixa Naff, "A Social History of Zahle: The Principal Market Town in Nineteenth-Century Lebanon" (PhD diss., University of California Los Angeles, 1973), 417–33.

15. Stanford J. Shaw, "The Central Legislative Councils in the Nineteenth Century Ottoman Reform Movement before 1876," *International Journal of Middle East Studies* 1, no. 1 (1970): 73–84; Hanssen, *Fin de Siècle Beirut*, 19.

16. Stanford J. Shaw, "The Ottoman Census System and Population, 1831–1914," *International Journal of Middle East Studies* 9, no. 3 (1978): 325–38; Kemal H. Karpat, "The Ottoman Adoption of the Statistics from the West in the 19th Century," in *Studies in Ottoman Social and Political History: Selected Articles and Essays*, ed. Kemal H. Karpat (Brill, 2002); Sa'id B. Himadeh, "Fiscal System," in *Economic Organization of Syria*, ed. Sa'id B. Himadeh (American Press, 1936), 340–43; Stanford J. Shaw, "The Nineteenth-Century Ottoman Tax Reforms and Revenue System," *International Journal of Middle East Studies* 6, no. 4 (1975): 421–59; Metin M. Coşgel, "Efficiency and Continuity in Public Finance: The Ottoman System of Taxation," *International Journal of Middle East Studies* 37, no. 4 (2005): 567–86; Caesar Farah, *The Road to Intervention: Fiscal Politics in Ottoman Lebanon* (Center for Lebanese Studies, 1992); Akarli, *The Long Peace*, 102–31; Glen W. Swanson, "The Ottoman Police," *Journal of Contemporary History* 7, no. 1/2 (1972): 243–60; Nadir Özbek, "Policing the Countryside: Gendarmes of the Late 19th-Century Ottoman Empire (1876–1908)," *International Journal of Middle East Studies* 40, no. 1 (2008): 47–67.

17. Gültekin Yıldız, "Ottoman Military Organization (1800–1918)," in *The Encyclopedia of War*, ed. Gordon Martel (Blackwell, 2012); Benjamin C. Fortna, *Imperial Classroom: Islam, the State, and Education in the Late Ottoman Empire* (Oxford University Press, 2002); Hanssen, *Fin de Siècle Beirut*, 116–37; Carla Eddé, *Beyrouth: Naissance d'une Capitale 1918–1924* (Actes Sud. Sinbad, 2009), ch. 6. Also see Michael Provence, *The Last Ottoman Generation and the Making of the Modern Middle East* (Cambridge University Press, 2017), 9–55.

18. I am drawing on Michel Foucault's definitions of these terms. See his *The History of Sexuality*, vol. 1, *An Introduction*, trans. Robert Hurley (Vintage Books, 1990).

19. V. Necla Geyikdaği, *Foreign Investment in the Ottoman Empire: International Trade and Relations, 1854–1914* (I. B. Tauris, 2011), 29–73.

20. For example, see Jacques Thobie, "French Investment in Public and Private Funds in the Ottoman Empire on the Eve of the Great War," in *East Meets West: Banking, Commerce, and Investments in the Ottoman Empire*, ed. Philip L. Cottrell, Monika Pohle Fraser, and Iain L. Fraser (Ashgate, 2008), 140–42.

21. Hanssen, *Fin de Siècle Beirut*, 84–112.

22. Charles Issawi, "British Trade and the Rise of Beirut, 1830–1860," *International Journal of Middle East Studies* 8, no. 1 (1977): 91–101; Hanssen, *Fin de Siècle Beirut*, 25–54, 87–92; Naff, "Social History of Zahle"; Leila Fawaz, "Zahle and Dayr al-Qamar: Two Market Towns of Mount Lebanon during the Civil War of 1860," in *Lebanon: A History of Conflict and Consensus*, ed. Nadim Shehadi and Dana Haffar Mills (I. B. Tauris, 1988), 49–63.

23. Yaşar Eyüp Özveren, "The Making and Unmaking of an Ottoman Port-City: Nineteenth Century Beirut, Its Hinterland, and the World-Economy" (PhD diss., State University of New York at Binghamton, 1990), 63–105.

24. Hanssen, *Fin de Siècle Beirut*, 84–112.

25. Naff, "Social History of Zahle," 250–470.

26. Chalabi, *Shi'is of Jabal 'Amil*, 26–27; Hanssen, *Fin de Siècle Beirut*, 33–35.

27. See James A. Reilly, *The Ottoman Cities of Lebanon: Historical Legacy and Identity in the Modern Middle East* (I. B. Tauris, 2016).

28. Fuad I. Khuri, *From Village to Suburb: Order and Change in Greater Beirut* (University of Chicago Press, 1975), 21–32; Leila Tarazi Fawaz, *Merchants and Migrants in Nineteenth-Century Beirut* (Harvard University Press, 1982), 28–60; Hanssen, *Fin de Siècle Beirut*, 193–263; Toufoul Abou-Hodeib, *A Taste for Home: The Modern Middle Class in Ottoman Beirut* (Stanford University Press, 2017), 7–15, 21–24, 56–58; John Gulick, *Tripoli: A Modern Arab City* (Harvard University Press, 1967), 18–30.

29. Alixa Naff, *Becoming Arab American: The Early Arab Immigrant Experience* (Southern Illinois University Press, 1985), 76–117; Khater, *Inventing Home*, 48–70; Stacy Fahrenthold, *Between the Ottomans and the Entente: The First World War in the Syrian and Lebanese Diaspora, 1908–1925* (Oxford University Press, 2019), 14–30. On emigration to French West Africa, see Andrew Arsan, *Interlopers of Empire: The Lebanese Diaspora in Colonial French West Africa* (Oxford University Press, 2014), 23–39, 47–60.

30. Khater, *Inventing Home*, 110–14.

31. Khater, *Inventing Home*, 108–90.

32. Hakim, *Origins of the Lebanese National Idea*, 170–77; Fahrenthold, *Between the Ottomans and the Entente*, 31–84; Graham Pitts, "The Ecology of Migration: Remittances in World War I Mount Lebanon," *Arab Studies Journal* 26, no. 2 (2018): 102–29.

33. Khater, *Inventing Home*, 179–90; Abou-Hodeib, *A Taste for Home*.

34. I am drawing on the work of James L. Gelvin, who argues that the late Ottoman period was a critical juncture in the inauguration of a new political sociability such that "the significance of vertical ties of dependence within the overall context of social relations declined" and "the organization of power among non-elites increasingly followed horizontal lines." See James L. Gelvin, "The Social Origins of Popular Nationalism in Syria: Evidence for a New Framework," *International Journal of Middle East Studies* 26, no. 4 (1994): 646.

35. Gelvin, *Divided Loyalties*, 14–16, 51–86; Makdisi, *Culture of Sectarianism*, 51–145; Ilham Khuri-Makdisi, *The Eastern Mediterranean and the Making of Global Radicalism, 1860–1914* (University of California Press, 2010), 135–64; Abou-Hodeib, *Taste for Home*, 15–21, 29–48.

36. Elizabeth Thompson, *Colonial Citizens: Republican Rights, Paternal Privilege, and Gender in French Syria and Lebanon* (Columbia University Press, 2000), 92–94; Melanie S. Tanielian, *The Charity of War: Famine, Humanitarian Aid, and World War I in the Middle East* (Stanford University Press, 2018), 47–49. Also see Lisa Pollard, "Egyptian by Association: Charitable and Service Societies, circa 1850–1945," *International Journal of Middle East Studies* 46, no. 2 (2014): 239–57; Murat C. Yıldız, "Strengthening Male Bodies and Building Robust Communities: Physical Culture in the Late Ottoman Empire" (PhD diss., University of California Los Angeles, 2015), 69.

37. Yusuf Ziya Karabıçak, "The Development of Ottoman Government's Policies towards Greek Associations, 1861–1912" (MA thesis, Boğaziçi University, 2012), 41.

38. Mass politics also manifested across the local and diasporic divide. See Andrew Arsan, "'This Age Is the Age of Associations': Committees, Petitions, and the Roots of Interwar Middle Eastern Internationalism," *Journal of Global History* 7, no. 2 (2012): 166–88.

39. Tanielian, *Charity of War*, 46–49.

40. Peter Hill, *Utopia and Civilization in the Arab Nahda* (Cambridge University Press, 2020), 30–46. This includes the Syrian Scientific Society (al-Jam'iyya al-'Ilmiyya al-Suriyya) in its various iterations (1846–69).

41. Katherine Kalemkerian, "Being an Otto-Man: Entangling Identities in Beirut and Beyond 1860–1914" (PhD diss., McGill University 2018), 155; William McClenahan, "Lebanese Sports from a Basketball Perspective" (MA thesis, American University of Beirut, 2007), 109.

42. Eliezer Tauber, *The Emergence of the Arab Movements* (Frank Cass, 1993); Hratch Bedoyan, "Armenian Political Parties in Lebanon" (MA thesis, American University of Beirut, 1972), 74–75.

43. Dorothee Sommer, *Freemasonry in the Ottoman Empire* (I. B. Tauris, 2015).

44. Donald Quatert, "Economic Climate of 'Young Turk Revolution' in 1908," *The Journal of Modern History* 51, no. 3 (1979): D1147–D1161; Hanssen, *Fin de Siècle Beirut*, 105–9. Beirut's first general strike, featuring port, railway, and gas company workers, took place in October 1908. The 1893 Beirut port workers strike is the earliest recorded occurrence of a collective labor strike in Lebanon.

45. Emily Faris Ibrahim, *al-Haraka al-Nisa'iyya al-Lubnaniyya* (Dar al-Thaqafa, 1966), 26–28; Thompson, *Colonial Citizens*, 93; Ellen Fleischmann, "The Other 'Awakening:' The Emergence of Women's Movements in the Modern Middle East, 1900–1940," in *Globalizing Feminism, 1789–1945*, ed. Karen Offen (Routledge, 2010), 174–81.

46. Bedross Der Matossian, "Formation of Public Sphere(s) in the Aftermath of the 1908 Revolution Among Armenians, Arabs, and Jews," in *"L'veresse de la liberté" La révolution de 1908 dans l'Empire ottoman*, ed. Francois Georgeon (Peeters, 2012), 189–219.

47. Karen M. Kern, *Imperial Citizens: Marriage and Citizenship in the Ottoman Frontier Province of Iraq* (Syracuse University Press, 2011), 89–113.

48. Rashid Ismail Khalidi, "The 1912 Election Campaign in the Cities of Bilad al-Sham," *International Journal of Middle East Studies* 16, no. 4 (1984): 461–74; Hasan Kayali, "Elections and the Electoral Process in the Ottoman Empire, 1876–1919," *International Journal of Middle East Studies* 27, no. 3 (1995): 265–86; Akarli, *Long Peace*, 82–101; Hanssen, *Fin de Siècle Beirut*, 64–70, 138–62.

49. "Qanun al-Jam'iyyat (29/Rajab/1327 & 13/Aughustus/1325) and "Qanun al-Ijtima'at al-'Umumiyya (20/Jamadı/1327)," both in Republic of Lebanon, Ministry of Justice, *al-Majmu'a al-Haditha li-l-Qawanin al-Lubnaniyya* (Maktabat Sadir, 1954).

50. Linda Schilcher, "Famine in Syria, 1915–1918," in *Problems of the Middle East in Historical Perspective: Essays in Honour of Albert Hourani*, ed. John P. Spagnolo and Albert Hourani (Ithaca, 1996); Leila Tarazi Fawaz, *A Land of Aching Hearts: The Middle East in the Great War* (Harvard University Press, 2014), 81–120; Graham Pitts, "Fallow Fields: Famine and the Making of Lebanon" (PhD diss., Georgetown University, 2016); Tanielian, *Charity of War*, 51–78.

51. Pitts, "Fallow Fields," 119–60; Graham Auman Pitts, "'Make Them Hated in All of the Arab Countries': France, Famine, and the Creation of Lebanon," in *Environmental Histories of the First World War*, ed. Richard P. Tucker, Tait Keller, J. R. McNeill, and Martin Schmid (Cambridge University Press, 2018), 175–90.

52. Alff, "The Business of Property," 234–47.

53. Abisaab, *Militant Women*, 13.

54. On why and how Mount Lebanon was more affected than surrounding areas, see Pitts, "Fallow Fields," 35–45.

55. For a comparative assessment see Tariq Tell, "Guns, Gold, and Grain: War and Food Supply in the Making of Transjordan," in *War, Institutions, and Social Change in the Middle East*, ed. Steven Heydemann (University of California Press, 2000), 33–58.

56. For example, George Antonius, *The Arab Awakening: The Story of the Arab National Movement* (J. B. Lippincott, 1939), 13–242; Antun Yamin, *Lubnan fi al-Harb: Aw Dhakirat al-Hawadith wa-l-Mazalim fi Lubnan fi al-Harb al-'Umumiyya 1914–1919*, vol. 1 (al-Matba'a al-Adabiyya, 1919).

57. For example, Tawfiq Yusuf 'Awwad, *al-Raghif: Riwaya* (Dar al-Makshuf, 1939); *Safar Barlik: 1914*, dir. Henry Barakat (Phoenicia Films, 1967); "Fi Mithl Hadha al-Shahr min Sanat 1915," *Awraq Lubnaniyya* 8 (1955); Yusuf Ibrahim Yazbek, *Mu'tamar al-Shuhada': al-Mu'tamar al-Ladhi Adha' al-Amani al-Qawmiyya wa-Jarra A'da'ahu ila al-Mashaniq* (Matba'at Jaridat al-Yawm, 1955).

58. Pitts, "Fallow Fields," 79–80; Pitts, "'Make Them Hated,'" 188–90. Calls to enlarge the administrative territory of Mount Lebanon to encompass more food-producing regions date back to the 1840–61 period. Such proposals were premised on Mount Lebanon as an Ottoman semiautonomous subprovince, not an independent state. See Hakim, *Origins of the Lebanese National Idea*, 53–64, 85–87.

59. Gelvin, *Divided Loyalties*, 27; Thompson, *Colonial Citizen*, 39.

60. Susan Pedersen, *The Guardians: The League of Nations and the Crisis of Empire* (Oxford University Press, 2015).

61. Hakim, *Origins of the Lebanese National Idea*, 231–60.

62. Gelvin, *Divided Loyalties*; Thompson, *Colonial Citizens*, 40–41; Hakim, *Origins of the Lebanese National Idea* 215, 233–35.

63. For examples of local mobilizations directed at the commission, see "List of Delegations Received by the Committee, August 1919"; "Petition of the 'Workers' Association,' 1919"; "Petition from Professional Societies in Lebanon, 1919"; "Petition from the Notables and Landowners of Tripoli, 1919"; "Petition from Beirut, Supporting the French"; and "Petition against the French Government, 1919," all in King-Crane Digital Collection, Oberlin College Archives, Oberlin, Ohio; James L. Gelvin, "The Ironic Legacy of the King-Crane Commission," in *The United States in the Middle East: A Historical Reassessment*, ed. David W. Lesch (Westview, 1995), 13–29; Chalabi, *Shi'is of Jabal 'Amil*, 65–69; Hakim, *Origins of the Lebanese National Idea*, 242–51, 259.

64. Fahrenthold, *Between the Ottomans and the Entente*, 85–111; Simon M. W. Jackson, "Mandatory Development: The Political Economy of the French Mandate in Syria and Lebanon, 1915–1939" (PhD diss., New York University, 2009), 392–458.

65. Hakim, *Origins of the Lebanese National Idea,* 231–60.

66. "Arrêté no. 299 (3/8/1920)" and "Arrêté no. 318 (31/8/1920)," in *Recueil des actes administratifs de Haut-commissariat de la République Française en Syrie et au Liban,* vol. 1, *Année 1919–1920* (Imp. Jeanne d'Arc, n.d.), 113–14, 132–34.

67. Hakim, *Origins of the Lebanese National Idea,* 209–11.

68. Hakim, *Origins of the Lebanese National Idea,* 209–11.

69. Hakim, *Origins of the Lebanese National Idea,* 235.

70. Hakim, *Origins of the Lebanese National Idea,* 242–45, 255–59.

71. League of Nations, "French Mandate for Syria and the Lebanon," *American Journal of International Law* 17, no. 3, Supplement: Official Documents (1923): 177–82.

72. Hakim, *Origins of the Lebanese National Idea,* 260. In this sense, the forces undergirding the creation of Greater Lebanon paralleled the establishment and repeated reorganization of the Syrian state(s) under French rule and the separation of Transjordan from Palestine under British rule. See Philip Shukry Khoury, *Syria and the French Mandate: The Politics of Arab Nationalism, 1920–1945* (Princeton University Press, 1987), 57–60, 136–41; Tariq Tell, *The Social and Economic Origins of Monarchy in Jordan* (Palgrave Macmillan, 2013), 55–71.

73. Gérard D. Khoury, *La France et l'Orient arabe: naissance du Liban moderne, 1914–1920* (Armand Colin, 1993); Hakim, *Origins of the Lebanese Idea,* 213–23.

74. I am drawing on the work of Manu Goswami, who analyzes the centrality of the territorial consolidation of Indian state structures through a variety of practices. See Manu Goswami, "From Swadeshi to Swaraj: Nation, Economy, Territory in Colonial South Asia, 1870 to 1907," *Comparative Studies in Society and History* 40, no. 4 (1998): 609–36.

75. I am drawing on the work of Sara Pursley, who challenges us to eschew an assumed applicability of the analytical models that treat British colonial rule in India and Egypt as paradigmatic of colonialism and colonial state formation. See Pursley, *Familiar Futures,* 31–33. On the centrality of security to French colonial policies in the Levant, see Daniel Neep, *Occupying Syria under the French Mandate: Insurgency, Space and State Formation* (Cambridge University Press, 2012); Jean-David Mizrahi, *Genèse de l'État mandataire: Service des renseignements et bandes armées en Syrie et au Liban dans les années 1920* (Éditions de la Sorbonne, 2020).

76. Elizabeth Thompson provides what is to date the most thorough rendering of the nature of the colonial state in Lebanon. The following discussion draws on her tripartite framework and modifies it on the basis of my own reading of the scholarship and primary sources of the period. See Thompson, *Colonial Citizens,* 39–90, 229–46.

77. In 1925, the French High Commission officially ended military rule in Lebanon (and Syria) that had been established shortly after the invasion in 1918. It nevertheless maintained several exceptions that permitted the direct intervention of the French Army of the Levant and its subsequent incarnations throughout the colonial period.

78. Humbert du Hays, *Les armées françaises au Levant, 1919–1923*, 2 vols. (Service historique de l'armée de Terre, 1978–79); Maurice Albord, *L'armée française et les États du Levant, 1936–1946* (CNRS Éditions, 2000).

79. The French military reorganized and expanded the diaspora-recruited Légion d'Orient (est. 1916) and locally recruited Syrian Legion (est. 1919) into the Auxiliary Troops of the Levant (Troupes Auxiliaires du Levant) in 1923 and reinforced them during the 1925–27 revolt with irregular recruits organized as the Supplementary Troops of the Levant (Troupes Supplétives du Levant). The High Commission constituted the Special Troops in March 1930 by merging and reorganizing the various remnants of these local forces. See discussion of military forces in République Française, Ministère des affaires étrangères, *Rapport à la Société des nations sur la situation de la Syrie et du Liban*, 15 vols. (Imprimerie Nationale, 1925–1939) [henceforth cited as *Rapport à la Société*]; N. E. Bou-Nacklie, "Les Troupes Spéciales: Religious and Ethnic Recruitment, 1916–46," *International Journal of Middle East Studies* 25, no. 4 (1993): 645–60.

80. *Rapport à la Société* (1927), 56; *Rapport à la Société* (1928), 36–37; *Rapport à la Société* (1937), 45–47; *Rapport à la Société* (1938), 45–47; Aziz Ahdab, *Jaysh Lubnan wa-Munaqibiyatuhu al-'Askariyya* (Beirut: n.p. 1975), 68–79.

81. See discussion of gendarmerie and police in annual editions of *Rapport à la Société*, especially *Rapport à la Société* (1939), 138. Lebanon featured 1,248 gendarmerie and 545 police personnel by 1939. For example of a newly introduced unified command and control structure, see "Arrêté no. 336 (1/9/1920)," in *Recueil des actes*, 1:141–50; "Arrêté no. 366 (20/9/1920)," in *Recueil des actes*, 1:167–70. Also see Nicola Nasif, *Sirr al-Dawla: Fusul fi Tarikh al-Amn al-'Am 1945–1977* (al-Mudiriyya al-'Amma li-l-Amn al-'Am, 2013), 20.

82. "Arrêté 1964 (25/5/1923)," in *Recueil des actes*, 4:69–71; "Marsum 2640 (17/1/1928)" and "Marsum 3795 (21/9/1928)," both in Republic of Lebanon, *Majmu'at Qawanin wa-Marasim*, vol. 1, *Min Shahr Ayyar Sanat 1926 ila Shahr Kanun al-Thani Sanat 1929* (Matba'at al-Adab, 1930), 295–306, 280–88. Also see relevant sections of *Rapport à la Société*.

83. "Qarar 1061 (5/1/1921)" and "Qarar 1768 (19/2/1923)," in The State of Greater Lebanon, *Majmu'at al-Muqarrarat li-Dawlat Lubnan al-Kabir: Min Awwal Aylul Sanat 1920–31 Kanun al-Awwal 1923* (Matba'at al-Adab, 1925), 264–69, 294–296; "Marsum 3308 (19/5/1928)," Republic of Lebanon, *Majmu'at Qawanin*, 1:325–58, "Marsum

Ishtira'i 341 (1/3/1943)," *al-Jarida al-Rasmiyya* (March 17, 1943): 10945–55. Also see Nasif, *Sirr al-Dawla*, 21–25.

84. Thompson, *Colonial Citizens*, 58.

85. Norman Burns, *The Tariff of Syria 1919–1932* (American Press, 1933), 12; *Rapport à la Société* (1931), 49, Annex 8; *Rapport à la Société* (1939), 44, Annex 6.

86. Burns, *The Tariff of Syria*, 12.

87. "Qarar Numero 86," *Majmu'at al-Muqarrarat 1920–1922*, 2–9. These were first organized as departments of internal affairs, justice, finance, public works, post and telegraph, public education, economic affairs, public health, and the gendarmerie.

88. For example, see *Rapport à la Société* (1939), 44, Annex 6.

89. Thompson, *Colonial Citizens*, 50–66.

90. Jacques Weulersse, *Paysans de Syrie et du Proche Orient* (Gallimard, 1946), 90–115; Doreen Warriner, *Land Reform and Development in the Middle East: A Study of Egypt, Syria and Iraq* (Oxford University Press, 1962), 71–101; Masoud Daher, *al-Judhur al-Tarikhiyya li-l-Mas'ala al-Zira'iyya al-Lunbnaniyya 1900–1950* (Manshurat al-Jami'a al-Lubnaniyya, 1983), 35–63; Haim Gerber, *The Social Origins of the Modern Middle East* (Lynne Reinner, 1987), 95–101; Christian Velud, "Syrie: Etat mandataire, movement national et tribus (1920–1936)," *Monde arab Maghreb-Mashrek* 147 (January–March 1995): 66–67; Michael Gilsenan, *Lords of the Lebanese Marches: Violence and Narrative in an Arab Society* (University of California Press, 1996), 79–94; Thompson, *Colonial Citizens*, 77–79, 166–67.

91. Thompson, *Colonial Citizens*, 61, 63, 77–80.

92. Thompson, *Colonial Citizens*, 60–61.

93. Thompson, *Colonial Citizens*, 78.

94. Gilsenan, *Lords of the Lebanese Marches*, 84–5.

95. Michael Johnson, *Class & Client in Beirut: The Sunni Muslim Community and the Lebanese State 1840–1985* (Ithaca, 1988), 11–96; Kais Firro, *Inventing Lebanon: Nationalism and the State under the Mandate* (I. B. Tauris, 2003), 71–125.

96. Omri Nir, *Lebanese Shi'ite Leadership, 1920–1970s: Personalities, Alliances, and Feuds* (Palgrave Macmillan, 2017), 36–39; Johnson, *Class & Client*, 60–67; Firro, *Inventing Lebanon*, 179–86.

97. Firro, *Inventing Lebanon*, 90–91.

98. Pitts, "Fallow Fields," 119–44; Alff, "The Business of Property," 220–38.

99. Gilsenan, *Lords of the Lebanese Marches*, 79–94.

100. Gilsenan, *Lords of the Lebanese Marches*, 11–12, 22.

101. Iliya Harik, *Man Yahkum Lubnan* (Dar al-Nahar, 1972), 51; Iliya Harik, "Political Elite of Lebanon," in *Political Elites in the Middle East*, ed. George Lenczowski (American Enterprise Institute, 1975), 208–10.

102. For the text of the constitution, see League of Nations, *Organic Law for Syria and the Lebanon* (League of Nations, 1930), 3–13.

103. See Cyma Sami Farah, "From the Grand Serail to the Great Revolt: Constitutionalism and Revolution in Lebanon, 1925–27" (PhD diss., Rice University, 2023).

104. Elections during French colonial rule were regulated by a 1922 and then a 1934 electoral law. See "Qarar 1307 (10/3/1922)" and "Qarar 2 (2/1/1934)" in Republic of Lebanon, Chamber of Deputies, "Qawanin al-Intikhabat," https://www.lp.gov.lb/ViewPublications.aspx?id=7. The most significant change between the 1922 and 1934 electoral laws was the abandonment of the two-stage indirect election process—in which eligible voters in the first stage elected secondary voters, who in turn voted for the actual deputies of parliament. In some instances, an electoral law deferred the confessional distribution of seats—both in total and within electoral districts—to a separate but related law.

105. These amendments were passed primarily on October 17, 1927; May 8, 1929; and March 18, 1943. The most significant changes were the restructuring of the legislature from a bicameral legislature (with an elected lower house and a mixed elected-and-appointed upper house) into a single assembly since known as the Chamber of Deputies and the election of the entire assembly. See *Majmu'at Qawanin wa-Marasim Hukumat al-Jumhuriyya al-Lubnaniyya*, vol. 3, *Min Shahr Kanun al-Thani Sanat 1929 li-Ghayat Kanun al-Awwal Sanat 1930* (Matba'at al-Dabbur, 1933), 1–40; "Qarar 129," in "Qawanin al-Intikhabat."

106. Contrary to popular misconceptions about the colonial period, the archival record is replete with various types of decrees by the High Commission, the state government, and local municipalities that sought to regulate almost every aspect of life in colonial Lebanon. In doing so, they regularly affirmed the applicability of specific Ottoman-era laws and explicitly replaced or otherwise voided them.

107. "Part V.—Provisions relating to the Mandatory Power and the League of Nations" in "Constitution of the Lebanese Republic."

108. "Qarar 2825 (30/8/1924)," "Qarar 15 (19/1/1925)," and "Qanun (27/5/1939)," all in Lebanese University, Markaz al-Abhath wa-l-Dirasat fi al-Ma'lumatiyya al-Qanuniyya, "al-Nusus al-Qanuniyya," http://77.42.251.205/LegisltaionSearch.aspx. Also see *Rapport à la Société* (1926), 44–45.

109. The constitution did not establish the principle of sectarian distribution of seats within the legislature. Laws governing each election cycle stipulated the precise confessional distribution of seats. Consequently, the drafting and decreeing of such laws were especially contentious throughout the colonial period.

110. I am drawing on the work of Maya Mikdashi, who identifies this modality of power and names it "sextarianism." See Maya Mikdashi, *Sextarianism: Sovereignty, Secularism, and the State in Lebanon* (Stanford University Press, 2022), 1–23.

111. Rania Maktabi, "The Lebanese Census of 1932 Revisited: Who Are the Lebanese?," *British Journal of Middle Eastern Studies* 26, no. 2 (1999), 219–41; Mikdashi, *Sextarianism*, 21–29.

112. Thompson, *Colonial Citizens*, 113–54; Max Weiss, *In the Shadow of Sectarianism: Law, Shi'ism, and the Making of Modern Lebanon* (Harvard University Press, 2010), 92–125. Thompson and Weiss show the complex ways that the post-Ottoman personal status system in Lebanon differed from both the *millet* system and late Ottoman practices of governance. As Weiss and Mikdashi argue, personal status court practices are more productive of sectarian identities than they are reflective of them. See Weiss, *Shadow of Sectarianism*, 157–85; Maya Mikdashi, "Sex and Sextarianism: The Legal Architecture of Lebanese Citizenship," *Comparative Studies of South Asia, Africa, and the Middle East* 34, no. 2 (2014): 279–93.

113. League of Nations, "The French Mandate for Syria and Lebanon," 179.

114. Thompson, *Colonial Citizens*, 94–100, 117–54, 238–43, 272–76.

115. Amin Mashhur, *Majmu'at al-Nusus al-Qanuniyya al-Khassa bi-l-Tashri' al-'Iqari wa-bi-Nizam al-Mulkiyya al-'Iqariyya fi Suriyya wa-Lubnan* (Matba'at al-Nijma, 1945).

116. "Law Regulating Chambers of Commerce and Industry, dated 13 June 1910," in Iraq, Ministry of Justice, *Translation of the Ottoman Constitutional Laws* (Baghdad: n.p., 1921), 68–71; "Qarar 2385 (17/1/1924)," in *al-Majmu'a al-Haditha*; "Qarar 'Adad 96 (20/1/1926)," in Republic of Lebanon, Ministry of Justice, *Majmu'at al-Qawanin* (Matba'at al-Jumhurriya al-Jadida, 1948); "Qanun al-Mujibat wa-l-'Uqud," in *al-Majmu'a al-Haditha*; "Marsum Ishtira'i 304: Qanun al-Tijara," in *Majmu'at al-Qawanin*.

117. "Qanun al-Jam'iyyat (29/Rajab/1327 & 13/8/1325)," in *al-Majmu'a al-Haditha*.

118. "Qarar 294 LR (20/1/1934)," in *al-Majmu'a al-Haditha*.

119. "Marsum 5 (31/5/1926)," in *Majmu'at al-Qawanin*.

120. Walter H. Ritsher, *Municipal Government in the Lebanon* (American University of Beirut, 1932); "Qanun (13/1/1928)," in *Majmu'at Qawanin wa-Marasim*, 1:221–34; "Marsum Ishtira'i 5 (3/2/1930), jadwal (a)," in *Majmu'at Qawanin wa-Marasim*, 3:221–41; *Rapport à la Société* (1937), 168–70.

121. Thompson, *Colonial Citizens*, 63.

122. Thompson, *Colonial Citizens*, 59–66.

123. Sa'id B. Himadeh, *Monetary and Banking System of Syria* (American University, 1935), 61–72.

124. Himadeh, *Monetary and Banking System of Syria*, 24–60.

125. Himadeh, *Monetary and Banking System of Syria*, 73–96, 102–12; Hicham Safieddine, *Banking on the State: The Financial Foundations of Lebanon* (Stanford University Press, 2019), 24–25.

126. "Ittifaq Tarikh 23 Kanun al-Thani Sanat 1924 bayn Hukumat Suriyya wa-Lubnan wa-Jabal al-Druz wa-bayn Bank Suriyya wa-Lubnan," in *al-Majmu'a al-Haditha*; Safieddine, *Banking on the State*, 23–25.

127. Burns, *Tariff of Syria*, 12–51.

128. Himadeh, "Fiscal System," 333–402.

129. Safieddine, *Banking on the State*, 31.

130. Jackson, "Mandatory Development," 200–391.

131. See "Qarar 251 (20/3/1924)," in *Majmu'at al-Muqarrarat li-Dawlat Lubnan al-Kabir: Awwal Kanun al-Thani Sanat 1924–31 Kanun al-Awwal Sanat 1925* (Matba'at al-Adab, 1927), 482–83.

132. See Jackson, "Mandatory Development," 200–323.

133. The Compagnie du Port originated as an Ottoman-registered joint-stock company, the primary shareholders of which in 1926 successfully reregistered the company as French as a result of the Treaty of Lausanne. See "ICJ Pleadings, Case concerning the Compagnie du Port, des Quais et des Entrepôts de Beyrouth and the Société Radio-Orient (France v. Lebanon)," 5.

134. "The Ottoman Tobacco Industry," *Journal of the Society of Arts* 42 (1893–1894): 733–34; Shaw, "Nineteenth-Century Ottoman Tax," 447–8; Elias Gannagé, *L'imposition des tabacs au Liban* (Paris: Librairie générale de droit et de jurisprudence, 1956), 76–90.

135. "Qarar 'Adad 16/LR (30/1/1935)," in *Majmu'at al-Qawanin*. The Régie was established by four investor groups: French, Franco-Swiss, Lebanese-Syrian, and Anglo-American Egyptian. See "Pour le Haut Commissionnaire le Compagnie Libano-Syrienne de Tabacs," March 14, 1934, carton 866, Archives of the French Foreign Ministry (MAE), Nantes, France. The interim period between 1929 and 1935 is known as the "banderole" system. Therein, the state monopoly ended, effectively privatizing the tobacco industry. See Abisaab, *Militant Women*, 19–29.

136. Himadeh, *Monetary and Banking System*, 137–63; Safieddine, *Banking on the* State, 15–34.

137. "Ittifaq Tarikh 23 Kanun al-Thani Sanat 1924 Bayn Hukumat Suriyya wa-Lubnan wa-Jabal al-Druz wa-bayn Bank Suriyya wa-Lubnan," in *al-Majmu'a al-Haditha*. This agreement was for a fifteen-year period, and in 1937 was extended for another twenty-five years as of the date of expiry by a new (and slightly amended agreement). See "al-Ittifaq wa-Tabadul al-Murasalat bayn al-Hukuma al-Lubnaniyya wa-Bank Suriyya wa-Lubnan al-Kabir."

138. Bassim A. Faris, *Electric Power in Syria and Palestine* (American Press, 1936), 125–34; "Qanun (11/1/1951)," in *Majmu'at al-Qawanin*; Edward F. Nickoley, "Transportation and Communication," in *Economic Organization of Syria*, ed. Sa'id B. Himadeh (The American Press, 1936), 180–85.

139. Raja S. Himadeh, *The Fiscal System of Lebanon* (Khayyat, 1961); Elias S. Saba, *The Foreign Exchange Systems of Lebanon and Syria 1939–1957* (American University of Beirut, 1961).

140. Thompson, *Colonial Citizens*, 54.

141. The exception to this is those French officials assigned by the High Commission as "administrators" in the Common Interests or "advisors" in the local state bureaucracies.

142. Decree no. 1945 of May 12, 1928 "concerning the constitution and working of the management account for the receipts and expenses of the services of common interest to the States under mandate." Cited in "Decree of the High Commissioner of the French Republic, no. 3115 of May 14, 1930, promulgating the organic regulation of the 'Conference of Common Interests,'" in League of Nations, *Organic Law for Syria and the Lebanon*, 31–33.

143. *Rapport à la Société* (1939), 60–67; Mohammed Amine El-Hafiz, *La Structure et la politique économiques en Syrie et au Liban* (Imprimerie Khalife, 1953), 130–31.

144. George Hakim, "Fiscal System," in *Economic Organization of Syria*, ed. Sa'id B. Himadeh (The American Press, 1936), 385. In relative terms, trade tariffs accounted for more than 80 percent of the Common Interests' annual revenue during most of the mandate period.

145. See relevant sections of *Rapport à la Société*.

146. Hakim, "Fiscal System," 335, 391–94.

147. In relative terms, Lebanese share of trade tariffs revenue accounted for no less than 40 percent of ordinary annual state revenue during most of the mandate period. See Hakim, "Fiscal System," 381–82.

148. Hakim, "Fiscal System," 338–86.

149. Andre Tueni, "al-Muwazana wa-Nizam al-Dara'ib fi Lubnan," *Muhadarat al-Nadwa*, no. 5–6 (1950): 76–99. Himadeh, *Fiscal System of Lebanon*, 1–2; The High Commission inaugurated the process of unifying all the taxes and duties in Lebanon, recognizing those in force in the province of Beirut at the end of Ottoman rule. However, the actual process was both slow and uneven.

150. Hakim, "Fiscal System," 386–91.

151. Albert Hourani, *Syria and Lebanon: A Political Essay* (Oxford University Press, 1946), 184–85; Nicola A. Ziadeh, *Syria and Lebanon* (Ernest Benn, 1957), 194–95; Michael W. Suleiman, *Political Parties in Lebanon: The Challenge of a Fragmented*

Political Culture (Cornell University Press, 1965), 250–52; Labib Zuwiyya Yamak, "Party Politics in the Lebanese Political System," in *Politics in Lebanon*, ed. Leonard Binder (John Wiley & Sons, 1966), 155–56.

152. On the proliferation of such spaces, see Samir Kassir, *Beirut*, trans. M. B. Deveoise (University of California, 2010), 267.

153. Nickoley, "Transportation and Communication," 192–95; Elizabeth Thompson, "Engendering the Nation: State-Building, Imperialism and Women in Syria and Lebanon, 1920–1945" (PhD diss., Columbia University, 1995), 216–17.

154. Kassir, *Beirut*, 273–74, 285–86, 303–4.

155. Muhammad Darkub, *Judhur al-Sindiyaniyya al-Hamra': Hikayat Nushu' al-Hizb al-Shuyu'i al-Lubnani, 1924–1931* (Dar al-Farabi, 2007); Sana Tannoury Karam, "The Making of a Leftist Milieu: Anti-Colonialism, Anti-Fascism, and the Political Engagement of Intellectuals in Mandate Lebanon, 1920–1948" (PhD diss., Northeastern University, 2017), 50–88.

156. Republic of Lebanon, Ministry of Information, *The Case of the Nationalist Party* (Beirut: 1949), 9–14; Labib Zuwiyya Yamak, *The Syrian Social Nationalist Party: An Ideological Analysis* (Harvard University Press, 1969), 53–61.

157. Al-Kata'ib al-Lubnaniyya, *al-Qanun al-Asasi* (Beirut: n.p., 1937), Linda Sadaka Collection, Archives and Special Collections, Nami Jafet Library, American University of Beirut, Lebanon (henceforth Sadaka Collection); F. S., "Al-Kata'ib al-Lubnaniyya: Tarikh wa-A'mal," booklet reproducing the contents of an article published in *al-Manara* (September–November 1943); John P. Entelis, *Pluralism and Party Transformation in Lebanon: Al-Kata'ib, 1936–1970* (Brill, 1974), 43–59.

158. Munazzamat al-Najjada, *al-Qanun al-Asasi* (Beirut: n.p., 1937), Sadaka Collection.

159. These parties originated as clandestine Armenian political movements seeking to establish an independent Armenian state during the late nineteenth and early twentieth centuries. They underwent significant strategic, ideological, and territorial transformation during World War I, the collapse of the Ottoman Empire, and the establishment of the postwar settlement. While some historians trace the first Huntchak and Dashnak formations in Beirut to the early twentieth century, it was in the 1920s—in the wake of the Armenian Genocide, and its attendant displacement of Armenians and their eventual mass settlement in Lebanon (and Syria)—that all three parties formally established national branches therein. Some, like the Tashnaq, initially created joint Lebanese-Syrian central committees only to separate them into distinct branches in the 1930s. See Bedoyan, "Armenian Political Parties in Lebanon," 3–90; Razmik Panossian, *The Armenians: From Kings and Priests to Merchants and Commissars* (Columbia University Press, 2006), 200–27; Tsolin

Nalbantian, "Fashioning Armenians in Lebanon, 1946–1958" (PhD diss., Columbia University, 2011), 32–34; Zaven Messerilian, *Armenian Participation in the Lebanese Legislative Elections 1934–2009* (Hagazian University Press, 2014), 17–27.

160. For a recent attempt at conceptualizing these organizations in relation to the French colonial order and its global context, see Dylan Baun, *Winning Lebanon: Youth, Politics, Populism, and the Production of Sectarian Violence, 1920–1958* (Cambridge University Press, 2020), 22–48.

161. Najib B'ayni, *Rijal min Biladi* (Mu'assassat Dar al-Rihani li-l-Tiba'a wa-l-Nashr, 1984), 199–213; Shafiq Juha, *al-Haraka al-'Arabiyya al-Siriyya (Jama'at al-Kitab al-Ahmar) 1935–1945* (Dar al-Furat, 2002), 33–39; Raghid al-Solh, *Lebanon and Arabism: National Identity and State Formation* (Centre for Lebanese Studies, 2004), 27–31.

162. Thompson, "Engendering the Nation," 372–83; Thompson, *Colonial Citizens*, 95.

163. Jacques Couland, *al-Haraka al-Naqabiyya fi Lubnan 1919–1946*, trans. Nabil Hadi (Dar al-Farabi, 1974), 95–290; Iliyas al-Buwari, *Tarikh al-Haraka al-Naqabiyya wa-l-'Ummaliyya fi Lubnan* 1908–1946 (Dar al-Farabi, 1979).

164. See *Qanun Naqabat al-Sahafa* (al-Matba'a al-Adabiyya, 1927); Naqabat Muharriri al-Sahafa al-Lubnanyya, *Dalil al-Sahafa al-Lubnaniyya wa-Ba'd al-A'mal al-Naqabiyya wa-l-Sahafiyya* (Beirut: n.p., 1943); Basim Jisr, "Waqi' al-Sahafa al-Lubnaniyya," *Mahadir al-Nadwa* 10, no. 3 (1956): 149–85; Naqabat al-Mu'allimin, *al-Nizam al-Dakhili: Nabdha Tarikhiyya* (Beirut: n.p., n.d.), 3–5; Juha, *al-Haraka al-'Arabiyya al-Siriyya*, 115–19.

165. Qadri Qal'aji, "Risalat al-'Usba," *al-Tariq* 1, no. 1 (December 20, 1941): 1, 22; "Mu'tamar Mukafahat al-Fashistiyya," May 6–7, 1939, Beirut, Sadaka Collection; Abdalla Hanna, *al-Haraka al-Munahida li-l-Fashiyya fi Suriyya wa-Lubnan: 1933–1945* (Dar al-Farabi, 1975); Sana Tannoury-Karam, "The Making of a Leftist Milieu: Anti-Colonialism, Anti-Fascism, and the Political Engagement of Intellectuals in Mandate Lebanon, 1920–1948" (PhD diss., Northeastern University, 2017), 132–75.

166. Sana Tannoury-Karam, "This War Is Our War: Antifascism Among Lebanese Leftist Intellectuals," *Journal of World History* 30, no. 3 (2019): 421–29; Thompson, *Colonial Citizens*, 191–96; Gotz Nordbruch, *Nazism in Syria and Lebanon: The Ambivalence of the German Option, 1933–1945* (Routledge, 2009), 14–80; Jennifer M. Dueck, *The Claims of Culture at Empire's End: Syria and Lebanon Under French Rule* (Oxford University Press, 2010), 118–41.

167. Kamil al-Da'uq, *Thawrat Bayrut 'ala Sharikat al-Kahruba' wa-l-Tram 1931–1959* (Matba'at al-Bayan, n.d.); Jackson, "Mandatory Development," 233–50, 286–318; Carla Eddé, "La mobilisation 'populaire' à Beyrouth à l'époque du Mandat, le cas des boycotts des trams et de l'électricité," in *France Syrie et Liban 1918–1946:*

Les ambiguitiés et les dynamiques de la relation mandataire, ed. Nadine Meouchy (IFEAD, 2002).

168. Bou-Nacklie, "Les Troupes Spéciales," 647–49; Simon Jackson, "Diaspora Politics and Developmental Empire: The Syro-Lebanese at the League of Nations," *Arab Studies Journal* 21, no. 1 (2013): 171–74; Simon Jackson, "Global Recruitment: The Wartime Origins of French Mandate Syria," in *France in an Era of Global War, 1914–1945: Occupation, Politics, Empire and Entanglements*, ed. Ludivine Broch and Alson Carrol (Palgrave MacMillan, 2014), 133–51.

169. Fahrenthold, *Between the Ottomans and the Entente*, 85–111, 137–59; Jackson, "Diaspora Politics," 174–78; Reem Bailony, "From Mandate Borders to the Diaspora: Rashaya's Transnational Suffering and the Making of Lebanon in 1925," *Arab Studies Journal* 26, no. 2 (2018): 44–73.

170. To this end, the role of al-Shimali and Sa'ada in establishing the Communist Party of Syria and Lebanon and the Syrian Nationalist Party, respectively, is instructive. Both men emigrated from Lebanon and spent significant time in the diaspora. Both men also established their parties relatively soon after their return. On al-Shimali's early life, see Karim Mruweh, *al-Shuyu'iyyin al-Arba'a al-Kibar fi Tarikh Lubnan al-Hadith* (Dar al-Saqi, 2009), 16–18. On Sa'ada, see Yamak, *Syrian Social Nationalist Party*, 53–54.

171. Thompson, *Colonial Citizens*, 71–90.

172. Thompson, *Colonial Citizens*, 91–111, 155–70.

173. See Hourani, *Syria and Lebanon*, 230–40; Ziadeh, *Syria and Lebanon*, 62–65.

174. Hourani, *Syria and Lebanon*, 242, 252, 371–72, 378–81.

175. General Georges Albert Julien Catroux (1877–1969) commanded the Free French Forces who invaded the Levant in 1941. He also served as the first delegate-general in Lebanon and Syria, assuming the title a few weeks after the allied invasion.

176. Aviel Roshwald, "The Spears Mission in the Levant: 1914–1944," *The Historical Journal* 29, no. 4 (1986): 897–919. The British liaison mission to the Free French Forces came to be known as the Spears Mission, since it was Major-General Sir Edward Louis Spears (1886–1974) who established and oversaw it.

177. Roshwald, "Spears Mission," 903. In addition to his continued role heading the liaison mission, in March 1942 Spears inaugurated a new official position, minister of state to Syria and Lebanon.

178. I am drawing on the work of Elizabeth Thompson, who argues that the 1930s featured a transformation of the civic order, such that "paternalistic social aid once bestowed by France through it collaborating with intermediaries was gradually

transformed into social rights claimed directly upon the state itself." See Thompson, *Colonial Citizens*, 167.

179. On the development of welfare as a right of citizenship in colonial Lebanon, see Elizabeth Thompson, "The Climax and Crisis of the Colonial Welfare State in Syria and Lebanon During World War II," in *War, Institutions, and Social Change in the Middle East*, ed. Steven Heydemann (University of California Press, 2000), 59–99.

180. The British government first established MESC in April 1941 to manage the supply and demand of the civilian population in Egypt, Palestine, Transjordan, and Cyprus. It continuously expanded its area of operation through April 1943, at which time it covered seventeen states/territories. Martin W. Wilmington, *The Middle East Supply Centre* (State University of New York Press, 1971); Robert Vitalis and Steven Heydemann, "War, Keynesianism, and Colonialism: "Explaining State-Market Relations in the Postwar Middle East," in *War, Institutions, and Social Change in the Middle East*, ed. Steven Heydemann (University of California Press, 2000), 100–48; Sherene Seikaly, *Men of Capital: Scarcity and Economy in Mandate Palestine* (Stanford University Press, 2016), 77–126.

181. MESC incorporated Lebanon (and Syria) into fields of operation in July 1941, and carried out its work therein through the Economic Section of the Spears Mission, which in turn worked through the French Commission supérieure de ravitaillement. In March 1944, British, French, US, Lebanese, and Syrian government representatives established a Joint Supply Council for the Levant States to take over MESC activities in the area in the wake of the termination of the Spears Mission. See US Foreign Economic Administration, *The Middle East Supply Center (MESC)* (n.p., 1944), 25. On specific policies that fundamentally reorganized the Lebanese economy, see Carolyne L. Gates, *The Merchant Republic: Rise of an Open Economy* (I. B. Tauris, 1998), 36–50.

182. I am drawing on the work of Robert Vitalis and Steven Heydemann, who argue that Allied regulatory practices in Egypt and Syria during World War II were critical to the consolidation of new public norms and institutional capacities concerning economic development. Vitalis and Heydemann, "War, Keynesianism, and Colonialism."

183. Gates, *Merchant Republic*, 53.

184. Gates, *Merchant Republic*, 53.

185. Gates, *Merchant Republic*, 50.

186. Gates, *Merchant Republic*, 51.

187. Gates, *Merchant Republic*, 51.

188. Gates, *Merchant Republic*, 52.

189. Gates, *Merchant Republic*, 52.

190. Gates, *Merchant Republic*, 51–52.

191. Several historians identify the 1930s as a critical turning point in the organization of mass politics in Lebanon and the relationship between the colonial state and the local population. In particular, see Jackson, "Mandatory Development," 17, 287–89; Thompson, *Colonial Citizens*, 155–224; Eddé, "La mobilisation."

192. On January 29, 1943, the Algiers-based French Committee of National Liberation agreed to reinstate the constitutions of Lebanon and Syria. Then on March 18, 1943, General George Catroux (r. 1941–43) reinstated the Lebanese constitution.

193. "Qarar 'Adad 312/FC (31/7/1943)," in "Qawanin al-Intikhabat." Despite frequent changes in the total number of deputies, electoral districts, and the former's distribution across the latter, all subsequent parliamentary elections through the Lebanese Civil War (1975–90) shared these two characteristics.

194. G. W. Furlonge (Beirut) to Edward Spears, "Lebanese Elections," August 21, 1943, FO 226/240-9/649/43, TNA; Richard Casey to Foreign Office, October 16, 1943, FO 371/35182-E 6220/27/89, TNA; George Wadsworth to Department of State (henceforth DoS), 2663 September 3, 1943, 890E.00/160, in Walter L. Browne, *The Political History of Lebanon*, vol. 3 (Documentary Publications, 1980), 409–12; Thompson, *Colonial Citizens*, 248–52.

195. Spears to Foreign Office, September 8, 1943, FO 371/35181-E5421/27/89, TNA; Furlonge to Spears, "Lebanese Presidency," September 10, 1943, FO 226/240-9/502,610/43, TNA; Spears to Casey, September 21, 1943, FO 226/240-9/641/43, TNA; Spears to Foreign Office, September 20, 1943, FO 226/240-9/645/43, TNA; Wadsworth to DoS, 284, September 29, 1943, 890E.00/165, in Walter L. Browne, *The Political History of Lebanon*, vol. 2 (Documentary Publications, 1977), 414–15; Thompson, *Colonial Citizens*, 248–52. For cabinet composition, ministerial statements, and parliamentary vote of confidence, see Yusuf Quzma Khuri, ed., *al-Bayanat al-Wizariyya al-Lubnaniyya wa-Munaqashatuha fi Majlis al-Nuwwab 1926–1984*, vol. 1, *1926–1966* (Mu'assasat al-Dirasat al-Lubnaniyya, 1986), 125–36.

196. US Consul (Beirut) to DoS, "Upcoming Elections," telegram, August 16, 1943, and DoS to US Consul (Beirut), "US Policy Towards Lebanese Government," telegram, August 22, 1943, in Browne, *Political History of Lebanon*, 2:404–8.

197. Munir Taqi al-Din, *Wiladat al-Istiqlal . . .* (Dar al-'Ilm li-l-Malayin, 1953), 42–43.

198. "Qanun Dusturi," *al-Jarida al-Rasmiyya* (November 10, 1943): 11501.

199. "Qarar 464/FC (10/11/1943)," facsimile, Sadaka Collection.

200. "Qarar 65/FC (10/11/1943)," facsimile, Sadaka Collection.

201. "Al-Khitab al-Ladhi Alqah Fakhamat al-Safir al-Misyu Jean Hellou al-Mandub al-'Am al-Mutlaq al-Salahiyya li-Faransa fi al-Sharq min Mahattat Radiyu al-Sharq Sabah al-Khamis fi 11 Tishrin al-Thani 1943," pamphlet, Sadaka Collection, 1. French aircrafts dropped the pamphlets on Beirut on November 13 and 18. See Wadsworth to DoS, 313 (Section 1), November 13, 1943, 890E.00/203, 5, in Browne, *Political History of Lebanon*, 3:31–36.

202. "Al-Khitab al-Ladhi Alqah Fakhamat al-Safir," 1. The hand-written inscription on this copy claims the pamphlet was dropped from a French aircraft over the Ras Beirut area at approximately eleven o'clock in the morning on Saturday, November 13, 1943.

203. "Tasrih Fakhamat al-Ustadh Émile Eddé Ra'is al-Dawla, Ra'is al-Hukuma al-Lubnaniyya," flyer, Sadaka Collection.

204. "Ijtima' al-Nuwwab Bayn Hirab al-Jund," *al-Nahar*, November 22, 1945.

205. Duplicate of the memo, titled "Mudhakarra," available in Sadaka Collection.

206. "Mahdar Jalsat al-Nuwwab al-Mun'aqida fi 11 Tishrin al-Thani Sanat 1943 al-Sa'a al-Rabi'a ba'd al-Zuhr," November 11, 1943, Sadaka Collection.

207. "Marsum," November 11, 1943, Sadaka Collection.

208. Meeting minutes of session held at Sa'ib Salam's home, November 12, 1943, Sadaka Collection.

209. The French attempted at least three different unsuccessful military incursions into the Bashamun stronghold: November 13, 15, and 17, 1943. See, respectively, "Sijil Hawadith Tishrin al-Thani 1943," *al-Nahar*, November 22, 1945; Republic of Lebanon, Ministry of National Defense, "Balagh 1," November 17, 1943, Sadaka Collection; Wadsworth to DoS, 317 (Section 1), November 17, 1943, 890E.00/218, in Browne, *Political History of Lebanon*, 3:58–62.

210. "Marsum 2 (13/11/1943)," in Taqi al-Din, *Wiladat al-Istiqlal*. The council consisted of a total of eleven persons: five of various ministries, the five governors, and a representative of the General Inspectorate for Administrative Departments. Also see Taqi al-Din, *Wiladat al-Istiqlal*, 81–82; "Al-Ayyam al-'Ashra al-Majida min Tarikh Lubnan," *Sawt al-Sha'b*, November 25, 1943; "Sijil Hawadith."

211. "Balagh Ila 'Umum Ma'muray wa-Muwwazzafay al-Jumhuriyya al-Lubnaniyya," flyer, n.d., Sadaka Collection.

212. These directives to the Ministry of Finance and BSL were issued on November 13, 1943 and are republished in Taqi al-Din, *Wiladat al-Istiqlal*.

213. Ashraf al-Ahdab (Public Works), Yusuf Sham'un (Education), Rashid Tabbara (National Economy), and Andre Tueini (Supply) issued the following joint statement: "Radio Orient broadcasted an announcement, the gist of which was our participation in the governing council. Because doing so would contradict the

administrative interests we have been tasked with safeguarding, we declare that we are unable to participate in this government." Statement attributed to Ashraf al-Ahdab, Yusuf Sham'un, Rashida Tabbara, and Andre Tueini, Sadaka Collection; "Sijil Hawadith"; Taqi al-Din, *Wiladat al-Istiqlal*.

214. Republic of Lebanon, Ministry of Interior, "Marsum 7/H," c. November 14, 1943, Iliya Harik Collection, Archives and Special Collections, Nami Jafet Library, American University of Beirut, Lebanon (henceforth Harik Collection).

215. For earlier scholarly accounts of some aspects of these popular mobilizations, see Thompson, *Colonial Citizens*, 253–54.

216. On these commitments, their attendant policies, and frustrations, see Wadsworth to DoS, 306 (Section 1), November 9, 1943; Wadsworth to DoS, 306 (Section 2), November 9, 1943; Wadsworth to DoS, 307, November 10, 1943; Wadsworth to DoS, 313 (Section 2), November 13, 1943, 890E.00/203; Wadsworth to DoS, 315 (Section 1), November 15, 1943, 890E.00/210; Wadsworth to DoS, 324 (Section 2), November 20, 1943; all in Browne, *Political History of Lebanon*, 3:1–12, 37–46, 70–71.

217. For example, see two flyers by 'Usbat al-Shabab al-Watani al-Lubnani, titled "Akhbar Hamma: Ila Muwatinina al-Lubnaniyyin," dated November 11 and 13, 1943, respectively, Sadaka Collection.

218. "Fi Khidmat Lubnan," no. 2, November 14, 1943, Harik Collection; "Fi Khidmat Lubnan," no. 3, November 19, 1943, Sadaka Collection.

219. Farjallah Hellou, "al-Haraka al-Wataniyya al-Lubnaniyya Tussajil Awwal Intisaratuha," *Sawt al-Sha'b*, November 27, 1943; "al-Mu'tamar al-Watani Yazur al-Fayha'," *Sawt al-Sha'b*, November 27, 1943.

220. Al-Shabab al-Watani al-Lubnani, flyer, November 11, 1943, Sadaka Collection; al-Shabab-al-Watani al-Lubnani,"Ya Abna' Bayrut al-Abat," flyer, n.d., Sadaka Collection; al-Shabab al-Watani al-Lubnani, flyer distributed on November 19, 1943, Sadaka Collection.

221. For example, see authorless flyer distributed in Saida on November 18, 1943, Sadaka Collection.

222. Al-Mu'tamar al-Watani, "Balagh," flyer distributed on November 18, 1943, Sadaka Collection.

223. Wadsworth to DoS, 313 (Section 1), November 13, 1943.

224. The exact membership of the National Congress is difficult to ascertain, in part because of the dearth of newspaper coverage at the time but also because the organization's membership and politics changed significantly after independence. Available communiqués issued by the congress in November 1943 feature the signatures of copresidents Ahmad Da'uq and Michel Far'un along with secretary Amin al-Halabi. Newspaper sources published shortly after the uprising indicate that the

executive committee included, in addition to Da'uq, Far'un, and al-Halabi: Elias Ba'aqlini, Hasan Buhsali, George Hanna, Amin al-Hanna, Farjallah Hellou, George Karam, Mohamad Khalid, Artin Madoyan, Alfred Nasr, Muhyi al-Din al-Nsuli, and Rene Sursuq. Memoirs of some of these members list others: 'Umar Bayhum, Elie Khayyat, and Taqi al-Din al-Sulh. See al-Mu'tamar al-Watani, "Balagh"; "al-Ayyam al-'Ashra"; "al-Mu'tamar al-Watani Yazur al-Fayha'," *Sawt al-Sha'b*, November 27, 1943; Artin Madoyan, *Hayat 'Ala al-Mitras: Dhikrayat wa-Mushahadat*, trans. Aradish Qaimujian (Dar al-Farabi, 2011 [1986]), 373–74.

225. Taqi al-Din, *Wiladat al-Istiqlal*, 150–52.

226. "Sijil Hawadith."

227. Taqi al-Din, *Wiladat al-Istiqlal*, 76–78.

228. A text distributed on November 12, 1943, asserted that "only your solidarity can serve the rights of your people; champion your government and abstain from your studies." See handwritten copy of typewritten flyer found on November 12, 1943, Sadaka Collection.

229. Petition addressed to AUB President Bayard Dodge, signed by the Students of the American University of Beirut, November 12, 1943, Sadaka Collection. For number of signatures, see Wadsworth to DoS, 313 (Section 2), November 13, 1943.

230. "First AUB Student Council Joined Struggle for Lebanese Independence," *Outlook*, November 24, 1970, 1.

231. Wadsworth to DoS, 313 (Section 1), November 13, 1943.

232. "First AUB Student Council."

233. On Friday November 13, 1943, Dodge canceled classes for "at least" Monday and Tuesday (November 16–17). Classes in fact did not resume until the end of the eleven-day uprising. See typewritten announcement in the name of AUB president addressed to the campus community, November 13, 1943, Sadaka Collection.

234. "First AUB Student Council"; Wadsworth to DoS, 313 (Section 1), November 13, 1943.

235. "First AUB Student Council."

236. "First AUB Student Council." The term of the first elected student council apparently coincided with the 1943–44 academic year. This election returned nine of the originally appointed eleven student council members. The fate of this second council, like that of the first, is not well documented. Most of the documents about the student council in the AUB archives date the organization's founding to 1949. Exceptions to this 1949-based narrative include "First AUB Student Council"; Najib B. Azzam, "The Student Council—A Short History," *Outlook*, November 30, 1971, 8.

237. Wadsworth to DoS, 313 (Section 1), November 13, 1943; Salma Sa'b, "The Story of the Lebanese Crisis," report, c. 1954, Folder 3, Box 30, Ruth Frances Woodsmall

Papers, Sophia Smith Collection, Smith College, Northhampton, Massachusetts; Ibrahim, *al-Haraka al-Nisa'iyya*, 148–49; Thompson, *Colonial Citizens*, 256–58.

238. Wadsworth to DoS, 313 (Section 1), November 13, 1943.

239. Sa'b, "Story of the Lebanese Crisis," 3–4.

240. For example, see "Sawt al-Mar'a," bulletin, November 23, 1943, Harik Collection. Also see Enclosure no. 1 in Clayton Lane (Beirut) to DoS, "Women's Magazine Sawt al-Mar'a," no. 113, July 8, 1947, 890E.917/7-847, National Archives and Records Administration, College Park, Maryland.

241. For example, see Wadsworth to DoS, 317, November 17, 1943, 890E.00/2018, in Browne, *Political History of Lebanon*, 3:58–62.

242. For example, see Hizb al-Islah, "Hafizu 'ala al-Dam al-Lubnani al-Bari'," November 19, 1943, pamphlet, Sadaka Collection.

243. Wadsworth to DoS, 315 (Section 1), November 15, 1943.

244. See authorless flyer distributed in Saida on November 18, 1943, Sadaka Collection.

245. William S. Farrel (Damascus) to DoS, no. 51, "Damascus Reactions to Frank-Lebanese Crisis," November 15, 1943, in Browne, *Political History of Lebanon*, 3:47–54.

246. In Egypt, groups like the Association of Arab Unity and the Arab Union in Cairo, as well as prominent figures like Mohamed Hussein Haykal and Mostafa al-Nahhas regularly expressed their solidarity with the Lebanese struggle to the US, British, and French governments. See Alex Kirk (Cairo) to DoS, no. 1412, "The Lebanese Crisis," November 20, 1943, 890E.00/308, in Browne, *Political History of Lebanon*, 3:77–109.

247. Wadsworth to DoS, 313 (Section 1), November 13, 1943.

248. Wadsworth to DoS, 315 (Section 1), November 15, 1943.

249. Wadsworth to DoS, 306 (Section 2), November 9, 1943; Wadsworth to DoS, 307, November 10, 1943; Paul H. Alling (Washington, DC) to DoS, memo, November 12, 1943, in Browne, *Political History of Lebanon*, 3:18–19; Wadsworth to DoS, 313 (Section 1), November 13, 1943; Wadsworth to DoS, 315 (Section 1), November 15, 1943.

250. WO 201/982, TNA. I thank Graham Pitts for sharing this folder with me.

251. Ziadeh, *Syria and Lebanon*, 78–79. Richard Casey, minister-resident for the Middle East, relayed the ultimatum to Carteaux through a note.

252. John Gilbert Winant (London) to DoS, B 136, 20 November 1943, 890E.00/244, in Browne, *Political History of Lebanon*, 3:72–73.

253. Wadsworth to DoS, 324 (Section 2), November 20, 1943.

254. For example, see Telegram from Jorge Akel, President, Syrian-Lebanese Assembly (Ecuador) to President Roosevelt, November 18, 1943; Telegram from

Lebanese Colony (Bogota, Colombia) to President Roosevelt, November 18, 1943; Telegram from Philippe Daou, Jorge Aucar, Jorge Skeff, Salom Ossami, and Abdalla Kalil (Manaos, Brazil) to President Roosevelt, November 19, 1943; Telegram from Lebanese Colony (Cartagena, Colombia) to President Roosevelt, November 19, 1943, all in Browne, *Political History of Lebanon*, 3:63–68

255. Wadsworth to DoS, 327 (Section 2), November 22, 1943, in Browne, *Political History of Lebanon*, 3:125–28.

256. Wadsworth to DoS, 327 (Section 2), November 22, 1943. Also see al-Shabab al-Watani al-Lubnani, "Ya Abna' Bayrut al-Abat," c. November 20, 1943, Sadaka Collection; untitled and undated flyer addressed to "the Lebanese people," c. November 20, 1943, Sadaka Collection; al-Mu'tamar al-Watani, al-Kata'ib wa-l-Najjada, al-Shabab al-Watani al-Lubnani, "Bayan Ila al-Umma," c. November 22, 1943, Sadaka Collection.

257. The caveat was that the French did not recognize the constitutional amendments. However, on November 25, 1943, Catroux communicated his acceptance of the amendments to al-Khuri and al-Sulh. See "al-Lajna al-Faransiyya wa-Ta'dil al-Dustur," *Sawt al-Sha'b*, November 26, 1943.

258. Wadsworth to DoS, 327 (Section 2), November 22, 1943; "Sha'b Lubnan Yahruz Intisaran Wataniyyan Ra'i'an bi-Wa'yahu wa-Ittihadahu wa-Nidalahu," *Sawt al-Sha'b*, November 26, 1943; "al-Ayyam al-'Ashra"; "Sijjil Hawadith."

259. "Fi Khidmat Lubnan," no. 4, November 23, 1943, Harik Collection; al-Mu'tamar al-Watani, "Balagh," November 23, 1943, Harik Collection; "al-Ayyam al-'Ashra."

260. "*Hikayat al-Istiqlal*," by Mansour Rahbani, *Hikayat*, Cairo Beirut Audio, n.d..

Chapter 2

1. Expelled officials included the Beirut public prosecutor, the head of the Census and Civil Status Department, the director of the Ministry of Interior, the *qa'immaqam* of Kisirwan, and the governors of Beirut and Mount Lebanon. See, for example, "Ihalat Ba'd Kibar al-Muwazzafin," *Sawt al-Sha'b*, November 27, 1943.

2. "Qadiyyat al-Ustaz Émile Eddé," *al-Nahar*, April 1, 1944; "Fasl al-Ustaz Edde," *al-Nahar*, April 4, 1944; Wadsworth to DoS, no. 346, "Lebanese Chamber Expels Emile Eddé," April 19, 1944, 890E.00/372, in Browne, *Political History of Lebanon*, 3:179–90.

3. Furlonge to Minister, British Legation (Beirut), no. 29/5/21, "Lebanese Cour de Justice," June 7, 1944, FO 371/40118, National Archives of UK (TNA), Richmond, United Kingdom; "Qanun Ilgha' al-Mahakim al-Mukhtalata (31/12/1946)," *al-Jarida al-Rasmiyya* (January 8, 1947): 17; Bertel E. Kuniholm (Beirut) to DoS, no. 1510, "Law of December 31, 1946, Concerning Abolition of Mixed Courts in Lebanon," March 3,

1947, 890E.05/3-347, National Archives and Records Administration (NARA), College Park, Maryland, United States.

4. Mobilizations for reform of the judicial system largely focused on the recruitment and promotion of judges, the authority to transfer judges and cases, and the division of jurisdiction between different types of courts. For example, see G. W. Furlonge to Minister, British Legation (Beirut), no. 29/5/5, December 31, 1943, FO 371/40118, TNA; Furlonge to Minister, British Legation (Beirut), no. 29/5, June 28, 1944, FO 371/40118, TNA; Kuniholm to DoS, no. 1448, "Composition of New Lebanese Tribunals to Succeed Former Mixed Courts," January 14, 1947, 890E.041/1-1447, NARA; As'ad Adib Rahhal, "The Conseil d'Etat, the Major Lebanese Administrative Court" (MA thesis, American University of Beirut [henceforth AUB], 1956), 34–85.

5. For example, see "Qanun al-Tanzim al-Qada'i (10/5/1950)," *al-Jarida al-Rasmiyya* (May 10, 1950): 248–315; "Marsum Ishtira'i 15 (9/1/1953)," *al-Jarida al-Rasmiyya* (January 14, 1953): 79–81; "Marsum Ishtira'i 7 (15/12/1954)," *al-Jarida al-Rasmiyya* (December 29, 1954): 980–87.

6. For example, see the multiple debates and draft laws that culminated in the 1946 abolition of mixed courts in FO 226/167, FO 371/40118, FO 371/45356, FO 371/52501 FO 371/61706, FO 93/147/1, and FO 141/1261, TNA.

7. For example, see Gabriel Menassa, *al-Tasmim al-Insha'i li-l-Iqtisad al-Lubnani wa-Islah al-Dawla* (Manshurat Jam'iyyat al-Iqtisad al-Siyasi al-Lubnaniyya, 1948); Andre Tueni, "Conceptions budgétaires et réalités nationales," *Les Conférences du Cénacle* 7, no. 1–2 (January 31, 1953): 1–26; Sa'ib Salam, "Hawl Bina' al-Dawla," *Muhadarat al-Nadwa* 8, no. 3 (February 15, 1954): 145–71.

8. For example, see al-Mu'tamar al-Thaqafi al-'Arabi al-Awwal, *Lubnan fi 'Ahd al-Istiqlal* (Dar al-Ahad, 1947); Republic of Lebanon, Ministry of Information, *Lubnan: Fi 'Ahduh al-Jadid* (Wizarat al-Anba', 1955); AUB, Department of Public Administration, *Dirasat 'an Hukumat Lubnan: Majmu'at Muhadarat Alqaha Mudirun 'Amun fi al-Hukuma al-Lubnaniyya Talbiya li-Da'wat Da'irat 'Ilm al-Idara al-'Ama fi al-Jami'a al-Amrikiyya fi Bayrut, 1954–1955* (Matba'at Dar al-Funun, 1956) (hereafter *Dirasat 'an Hukumat Lubnan*).

9. Raja S. Himadeh, *The Fiscal System of Lebanon* (Khayyat, 1961), 11–13; Raymond Philip Nahhas, "Structure and Behavior of Lebanese Bureaucracy" (MA thesis, AUB, 1963), 79–80. The ordinary budget estimate for 1944 was 34.02 million Syrian-Lebanese liras, whereas that of 1955 was 137.5 million Lebanese liras. Ordinary expenditures for 1944 totaled 27.67 million Syrian-Lebanese liras, whereas the 1955 total was 132.38 million Lebanese liras.

10. See Sa'id B. Himadeh, "Fiscal System," in *Economic Organization of Syria*, ed. Sa'id B. Himadeh (American Press, 1936), 13; Himadeh, *Fiscal System of Lebanon*, 11.

Between 1944 and 1949, total receipts for the Lebanese state nearly tripled. Between 1951 and 1955, receipts nearly doubled.

11. See Nahhas, "Lebanese Bureaucracy," 59, 62; Edward Bitar, "Personnel Administration in a Developing Country: A Study of the Lebanese Bureaucracy" (PhD dissertation, Louisiana State University, 1968), 143.

12. The precise figure of public sector employees is difficult to ascertain, in part because most contemporary estimates do not indicate whether they are only counting members of the permanent civil service. Other types of public sector jobs included salaried temporary employees and daily wage workers. In addition, while most estimates explicitly exclude members of the armed forces, others do not. For different figures, see George Grassmuck and Kamal Salibi, *A Manual of Lebanese Administration* (Public Administration Department of the AUB, 1955), ix; Nahhas, "Lebanese Bureaucracy," 62; Tawfiq Awwad, "al-Wazifa fi Lubnan," *Muhadarat al-Nadwa* 3, no. 5–6 (1949), 127.

13. Pierre Rondot, *Les institutions politiques du Liban. Des communautés traditionnelles à l'État moderne* (Institut d'Études de l'Orient contemporain, 1947), 89; Halim Faris Fayyad, "The Effects of Sectarianism on the Lebanese Administration" (MA thesis, AUB, 1956), 68, 71. A precise comparison across years is difficult because of inconsistencies in the method of calculating totals.

14. Bitar, "Personnel Administration," 140.

15. Himadeh, *Fiscal System of Lebanon*, 79.

16. Himadeh, *Fiscal System of Lebanon*, 96–98.

17. Himadeh, *Fiscal System of Lebanon*, 21. These budgets reflected growing receipts and expenditures, with only the telephone and Beirut water systems incurring periodic deficits.

18. Himadeh, *Fiscal System of Lebanon*, 77. These new laws and practices included additional regulations on the drafting, approval, execution, and oversight of the annual state budget and other appropriations. For example, see "Marsum Ishtira'i 9 (23/12/1954)," *al-Jarida al-Rasmiyya* (December 29, 1954): 1003–24; "Marsum Ishtira'i 10 (29/12/1954)," *al-Jarida al-Rasmiyya* (December 29, 1954): 1025–75.

19. I am drawing on Aradhana Sharma and Akhil Gupta's argument about the state as cultural artifact. See Aradhana Sharma and Akhil Gupta, "Introduction: Rethinking Theories of the State in an Age of Globalization," in *The Anthropology of the State*, ed. Aradhana Sharma and Akhil Gupta (Wiley-Blackwell, 2006), 1–42.

20. I am drawing on Timothy Mitchell's concept of "the state effect." See Timothy Mitchell, "Society, Economy, and the State Effect," in *State/Culture: State-Formation After the Cultural Turn*, ed. George Steinmetz (Cornell University Press, 1999), 76–97.

21. For example, see John Gerard Ruggie, "International Regimes, Transactions, and Change: Embedded Liberalism in the Postwar Economic Order," *International Organization* 36, no. 2 (1982): 379–415; Amy L. S. Staples, *The Birth of Development: How the World Bank, Food and Agriculture Organization, and Word Health Organization Changed the World, 1945–1965* (Kent State University Press, 2006).

22. This was indeed the case among advocates for greater state commitments to women's equal rights, public education, irrigation and electricity development, and central banking. The first two are discussed in subsequent chapters. On the latter two, see Owain Lawson, "Power Failures: Engineers and the Litani River, 1918–1978" (PhD diss., Columbia University, 2021), 118–290; Hicham Safieddine, *Banking on the State: The Financial Foundations of Lebanon* (Stanford University Press, 2019), 52–63.

23. See Irene L. Gendzier, *Notes from the Minefield: United States Intervention in Lebanon and the Middle East, 1945–1958* (Columbia University Press, 1997), 1–228; Rashid Khalidi, *Sowing Crisis: The Cold War and American Dominance in the Middle East* (Beacon, 2009), 1–90.

24. This strategy had its parallels in other parts of the Middle East and the Global South. See James L. Gelvin, "American Global Economic Policy and the Civic Order in the Middle East," in *Is There a Middle East? The Evolution of a Geopolitical Concept*, ed. Michael E. Bonine, Abbas Amanat, and Michael Ezekiel Gasper (Stanford University Press, 2011), 191–206; Nathan J. Citino, *Envisioning the Arab Future: Modernization in U.S.-Arab Relations, 1945–1967* (Cambridge University Press, 2017).

25. US Agency for International Development, *Tomorrow Becomes Today: A Program Report of the 10-Year Point Four Program in Lebanon, 1952–1962* (n.p., 1962), 45. The US Point Four program was officially called the Technical Cooperation Administration (TCA). The first US-Lebanon Point Four agreement was executed in late 1951. The Beirut office served as the headquarters for both Lebanese and all other Middle East operations.

26. For example, in 1951 the US TCA and the AUB entered into an agreement to expand existing programs at the AUB so as to offer two years of in-service training in agriculture, economics, engineering, and public health. This agreement also inaugurated a Public Administration Department at the AUB in the 1951–52 academic year. The TCA and AUB renewed their agreement for another two years in 1953, though financial support for in-service training in economics was ended (due to the Economics Department receiving a major Ford Foundation grant). In its place, the TCA supported teacher training through the AUB's Education Department. See Paul Beckett and Fredrick Bent, "Letters from Beirut," *Public Administration Review* 13, no. 1 (1953): 1–11; Paul Beckett, "Public Administration Training as Technical

Assistance: Some Further Observations Based on Experience in Beirut," *The Western Political Quarterly* 9, no. 1 (1956): 151–72.

27. The role of the United States in supporting what came to be known as the Litani River Project through the US Point Four Program in Lebanon is perhaps the most well-known example. Other projects include highway, public road, and water resource construction projects. See US Technical Cooperation Service for Lebanon, *Point 4 in Lebanon* (US Technical Cooperation Service for Lebanon, 1953); US Agency for International Development, *Tomorrow Becomes Today*. On the US role in the Litani River Project during the period under consideration, see Lawson, "Power Failures," 189–268.

28. See Central Intelligence Agency, "Report on the Arab States for the President," September 27, 1949, in *CIA Research Reports: Middle East, 1946–1976*, ed. Paul Kesaris (University Publications of America, 1983), microfilm, reel 1; National Security Council, Executive Secretary, "Report on United States Objectives and Policies with Respect to the Arab States and Israel," April 7, 1952; Afif I. Tannous, "Land Reform: Key to the Development and Stability of the Arab World," *Middle East Journal* 5 (1951): 1–20; Republic of Lebanon, Ministry of National Economy and United States Technical Cooperation Service, *Village Survey: Kasmie Rural Improvement Project: Lebanon* (Beirut: n.p., 1953).

29. This was most notable in the realm of labor mobilizations and Communist activism. On the US diplomatic mission's role in containing labor mobilizations and Communist activism, see Gendzier, *Notes from the Minefield*, 120–23. This is to say nothing of the role of the CIA, whose declassified reports betray a significant level of monitoring, infiltration, and disruption of both movements.

30. The electoral law governing each of these elections was a particularly contentious matter for the president, incumbent politicians, and would-be politicians. It determined the number of total seats, the number and size of electoral districts, and the apportionment of seats (including sectarian quotas); the eligibility of candidates and procedures for running and voting in elections, including any payments and deposits required for candidacy; the minimum age for candidacy and voting; and whether women had the right to participate in elections. Parliamentary elections engaged a growing share of the adult population, reflecting an increase in voter turnout both in absolute and relative terms. Relatedly, all of the five governorates featured reasonably high degrees of electoral competition. Of course the 1947 parliamentary elections, notorious for their corruption, were an exception. Furthermore, the voting increase rates in North Lebanon, South Lebanon, and Biqa' exceeded those of Beirut and Mount Lebanon. See Michael C. Hudson, *The Precarious Republic: Political Modernization in Lebanon* (Random House, 1968), 211–61.

31. Gordon Mattison (Beirut) to DoS, 44, January 23, 1946, 890E.00/1-2346, NARA; Wadsworth to DoS, "Reform Movement of Abdul Hamid Karami, and Its Implications," no. 1149, March 20, 1946, 890E.00/3-2046, NARA; "Mudhakarrat 'al-Islah' li-Ra'is al-Jumhuriyya," *al-Nahar*, May 8, 1946. Abdul Hamid Karami, Henri Far'un, Alfred Naccache, and Kamal Jumblatt established the Reform Bloc. Others associated include (in order of appearance in cited "Reform Memo") Habib Trad, 'Umar al-Da'uq, Muhammad Khalid, Luis Ziadeh, Muhammad al-'Abbud, Nuhad Arslan, Muhammad 'Umar Bayhum, Yusif Karam, Alfred Skaff, and Phillip Tamer.

32. Lowell C. Pinkerton (Beirut) to DoS, A-467, November 4, 1947, 890E.00/11-447, NARA; "Kutlat al-Taharur Tuqarrir Idha'at Bayan," *al-Nahar*, January 28, 1949; "Minhaj Kutlat al-Taharrur al-Watani," *al-Nahar*, January 29, 1949. Karami, Jawad Bulus, and Jumblatt were among the founders of the National Reform Bloc, established in the wake of the 1947 parliamentary elections. Others associated included Umar Bayhum, Alfred Naccache, and Philip Trad.

33. Al-Jabha al-Ishtirakiyya al-Wataniyya, "al-Nizam al-Dakhili – al-Barnamij al-Islahi," May 1951; Harold B. Minor (Beirut) to DoS, "National Bloc Secedes from National Socialist Front," Despatch 258, November 6, 1952, 783A.00/11-652, NARA; Minor to DoS, "Kamal Jumblatt Launches Open Attack on Chamoun," Despatch 611, April 20, 1953, 783A.00/4-2053, NARA. The PSF was established after the 1951 parliamentary elections by eight parliamentarians from Mount Lebanon (in order of appearance in cited booklet) Kamal Jumblatt, Anwar al-Khatib, Pierre Eddé, 'Abdallah al-Hajj, Kamil Sham'un, Emil Bustani, Ghassan Twayni, and Dhikran Tosbat. The PSF began to fragment shortly after Sham'un's election to the presidency in September 1952, and held its last official meeting in May 1953.

34. "Ta'assasat Ams al-Jabha al-Ishtirakiyya al-Sha'biyya," *al-Anba*, September 4, 1953; "Barnamij al-Jabha al-Ishtirakiyya al-Wataniyya," September 9, 1953, pamphlet, Archive Section, Al-Furat Bookshop, Beirut. Kamal Jumblatt, 'Abdallah al-Hajj, Nasib al-Matni, and Ali Bazzi established the front in September 1953 after the parliamentary elections of that year.

35. It is important to note that at issue is not so much the efficacy of such platforms or the degree of coalition members' commitment to them. Rather, it is the ubiquity and near common-sense understanding of such claims and the ways in which they bolstered the legitimacy of those espousing them.

36. More than half of the associations registered in 1958 with the Federation of Civic Organizations were established in the 1943–55 period. See *Dalil al-Jam'iyyat al-Ahliyya fi Lubnan* (Manshurat Ittihad al-Munazzamat al-Ahliyya, 1958).

37. The following description of al-Nadi al-Riyadi is drawn from the club's official website, www.riyadi.com.

38. The club played its first international basketball opponent in 1947, hosting Turkey's Galatasaray club (est. 1905).

39. "Marsum 2437 (7/12/1944)," *al-Jarida al-Rasmiyya* (December 13, 1944): 3–4; "Marsum 3447 (20/11/1950)," al-*Jarida al-Rasmiyya* (November 22, 1950): 770–71.

40. In December 1944, the Higher Committee for Sports and Physical Education (al-Lajna al-'Ulya li-l-Riyada wa-l-Tarbiyya al-Badaniyya, est. 1942) hosted a conference, whose recommendations led to the above-mentioned regulations and federations. In December 1946, the government established the Lebanese Olympic Committee and secured Lebanon's place on the International Olympic Committee. By 1955, the government agency overseeing sports was restructured as the Physical Sports and Scouts Service (Maslahat al-Riyada al-Badaniyya wa-l-Kashfiyya). For an example of the lobbying efforts, see "Bi-Munasabat al-Fashal al-Ladhi Asabana bi-l-Iskandraiyya: Ila al-Lajna al-Ulumbiyya," *Kul Shay'*, October 29, 1951.

41. On the series of petitions, meetings, and other forms of mobilization leading up to the 1944 law, see coverage in *al-Nahar* and *Sawt al-Sha'b* from January 4 through February 28, 1944.

42. "Qanun (29/4/1944)," in *al-Majmu'a al-Haditha.*

43. The law explicitly banned landlords from requiring more than three months' advanced rent and from imposing a rent hike for those who do not pay an advance of more than three months. However, the law did allow landlords to impose a 10 percent rent increase on rent paid monthly and a 5 percent rent increase if it was paid every two months.

44. "Qanun (5/5/1945)," "Qanun (19/2/1946)," and "Qanun (18/4/1947)" in *al-Majmu'a al-Haditha.*

45. In the lead-up to the 1944 law's passage, a group identified as the Tenants' Association (Jam'iyyat al-Musta'jirin) claimed the mantle of organized leadership. Beginning at least as early as 1949, statements were issued in the name of the Committee for the Defense of Tenants (Lajnat al-Difa' 'an al-Musta'jirin), while newspapers covering relevant mobilizations published statements by the organization.

46. "Qanun al-Ujur (30/3/1948)," "Qanun al-Ujur (29/4/1949)," "Qanun al-Ujur (24/3/1951)," "Qanun al-Ujur (4/3/1952)," "Qanun (9/10/1953)," "Qanun al-Ijarat (7/5/1954)," all in *al-Majmu'a al-Haditha.*

47. The government added the following grounds for eviction: the landlord's current domicile is no longer fit for habitation (1948), the tenant was absent from the property for one year (1954), and the tenant used the property for a purpose other than what it was leased for (1954).

48. Adil al-Sulh, *Hizb al-Istiqlal al-Jumhuri: Min al-Muqawama al-Wataniyya Ayyam al-Intidab al-Faransi* (Dar al-Tali'a, 1970), 123–26; al-Nadi al-Thaqafi al-Arabi,

Masirat al-Khamsin 'Aman: al-Nadi al-Thaqafi all'Arabi, 1944–1994 (Beirut: n.p., 1994), 15–16.

49. Salwa Mansur Jurdak, "The Evolution of Lebanese Party Politics: 1919–1947" (MA thesis, AUB, 1949), 112–21; Hizb al-Nida' al-Qawmi, "al-Qanun al-Asasi wa-Surat al-Ijaza al-Rasmiyya al-Qanuniyya min Hukumat al-Jumhuriyya al-Lubnaniyya bi-Insha' al-Hizb," pamphlet, 1944, Sadaka Collection; Hizb al-Nida' al-Qawmi, "Bayan ila al-Jumhur al-Karim," flyer, January 10, 1945; Kadhim al-Sulh, "Hizb al-Nida' al-Qawmi," *al-Liwa'*, January 25, 1945; Hizb al-Nida al-Qawmi, "Bayan Mujaz 'an Waqa'i' al-Ijtima' al-'Am," pamphlet, 1946, Sadaka Collection.

50. Donald R. Heath (Beirut) to DoS, "National Organization Becomes Political Party," Despatch 60, July 29, 1955, 783A.00/7-2855, NARA. The party did not secure official recognition from the Lebanese government until 1955.

51. On the Vanguard Organization, see Dylan Baun, *Winning Lebanon: Youth Politics, Populism, and the Production of Sectarian Violence, 1920–1958* (Cambridge University Press, 2021), 48–54. On the Ghasassina, see "al-Ghasassina Yaqimun Haflatahum al-Ula," *al-Nahar*, January 30, 1945; "Khitab al-Doktor Albeyr Saliba," *al-Nahar*, January 31, 1945; al-Ghasassina, "Ila Shabab Lubnan," February 25, 1945, Sadaka Collection.

52. In one notable example, the Kata'ib Party and the National Organization formed a joint committee in December 1951 to lead a seven-month campaign against the Beirut Electricity Company (Sharikat Kahruba' Bayrut). See "Muqata'at Sharikat al-Kahruba'" *al-Amal*, December 30, 1951. In a lesser-known 1955 instance, the Kata'ib Party and the Progressive Socialist Party announced a joint program that was explored through a series of meetings. See "Bayan Taqaddumi Ishtiraki-Kata'ibi," *al-Anba'*, October 7, 1955. Also see Jean Charaf, *Tarikh Hizb al-Kata'ib al-Lubnaniyya*, vol. 4, *1953–1967* (Dar al-'Amal li-l-Nashr, 2009), 335, cited in Dylan Baun, "Winning Lebanon: Popular Organizations, Street Politics and the Emergence of Sectarian Violence in the Mid-Twentieth Century" (PhD diss., University of Arizona, 2015), 55.

53. Perhaps the most well known of such instances of competition is the street brawl between members of the Kata'ib and SNP on June 9, 1949. See Dylan Baun, "The Gemmayzeh Incident of 1949: Conflict over Physical and Symbolic Space in Beirut," *Arab Studies Journal* 25, no. 1 (2007): 66–91. Other rivalries included that between Baydun's Vanguard Organization and Ahmad al-As'ad's Renaissance Party (Hizb al-Nahda). For example, see "Bayn Hizbay al-Nahda wa-l-Tala'i'," *al-Nahar*, September 3, 1946; "Bayn al-Tala'i' wa-l-Nahda," *al-Nahar*, September 12, 1946. Disagreements over policy recommendations were a more frequent form of party competition, especially when the parties in question did not share the same social base. For example, see CIA, "Differences between the Najjadah and the Talayi' on the

Palestine Question," January 31, 1949, CIA-RDP82-00457R002300220005-1, CREST Collection, Reading Room, Central Intelligence Agency, United States.

54. Tsolin Nalbantian, *Armenians Beyond Diaspora: Making Lebanon their Own* (Edinburgh University Press, 2020), 84–125.

55. Nalbantian, *Armenians Beyond Diaspora*, 84.

56. Nalbantian, *Armenians Beyond Diaspora*, 131.

57. "Tafasil Jalsat al-Mu'tamar al-Watani li-l-Hizb al-Shuyu'i fi Suriyya wa-Lubnan," *Sawt al-Sha'b*, January 5, 1944; "Qararat al-Mu'tamar al-Watani li-l-Hizb al-Shuyu'i fi Suriyya wa-Lubnan," "al-Mithaq al-Watani li-l-Hizb al-Shuyu'i al-Lubnani," "Ghayat al-Tanzim fi al-Hizb," all in *Sawt al-Sha'b*, Janaury 7, 1944.

58. See CIA's "Organizational Structure of the Lebanese Communist Party," January 11, 1949, CIA-RDP82-00457R002200470004-6; "Reorganization of the Lebanese Communist Party," April 7, 1949, CIA-RDP82-0047R002600170005-4; "Communist Agitation Among Palestinian Refugees," June 5, 1950, CIA-RDP82-00457R005000120009-7; "Communist Activity in Labor Unions—Leaflet and Letter," June 2, 1955, CIA-RDP83-00418R000300110006-6; all in Crest Collection; Raymond A. Hare (Beirut) to DoS, "New Emphases in the Communist Approach to Lebanon," Despatch 31, July 15, 1954, 783a.001/7-1554, NARA.

59. "Ahzab," *al-Nahar*, July 17, 1949; "al-Nizam al-Assasi li-l-Kata'ib al-Lubnaniyya," 1952; al-Kata'ib al-Lubnaniyya, "al-Kata'ib al-Lubnaniyya," undated two-page fact sheet, Sadaka Collection; "al-Tahawwul min Munnazama ila Hizb," *al-Amal*, November 4, 1952. For a critique of this transformation from a former party member and supporter, see George Naccache, "Pour les 17 ans de Phalanges," *L'Orient*, November 29, 1953.

60. Tawfiq al-Maqdisi and Lusian Jurj, *al-Ahzab al-Siyasiyya fi Lubnan 'am 1959* (Manshurat al-Jarida wa-l-Uruyan, 1959), 22.

61. Labib Zuwiyya Yamak, *The Syrian Social Nationalist Party: An Ideological Analysis* (Harvard University Press, 1969), 61–62.

62. Yamak, *Syrian Social Nationalist Party*, 62–71.

63. Rosemary Sayigh, The Palestinians: From Peasants to Revolutionaries (Zed Books, 2007), 98–147; Rosemary Sayigh, Too Many Enemies: The Palestinian Experience in Lebanon (Al Mashriq, 2015), 13–78.

64. Pinkerton to DoS, no. 65, April 11, 1949, 890E.00/4-1149, NARA; "al-Ittihad al-Filastini Yutali' Dawratay Thompson 'ala Halat al-Laji'in wa-Yashrah Laha Qadiyyatahum," *al-Nahar*, May 23, 1952.

65. CIA, "Visit of Akram Zu'aytir to Syria and Lebanon," Information Report dated January 31, 1949, CIA-RDP82-00457R00230011003-5, Crest Collection.

66. Al-Kutla al-Wataniyya, *Minhaj al-Hizb*, pamphlet, 1951, Sadaka Collection.

67. Safieddine, *Banking on the State*, 71–85.

68. Hizb al-Ittihad al-Dusturi, "al-Bayan al-Ta'sissi," in *al-Nizam al-Asassi li-Hizb al-Ittihad a-Dusturi*; Hizb al-Ittihad al-Dustirui, "al-Nizam al-Dakhili," pamphlet, n.d., Sadaka Collection; "Hizb am Kutla?" *al-Nahar*, December 5, 1954; "al-Dusturiyun Ya'udun ila al-Mu'tarak bi-Ismahum al-Jadid," *al-Nahar*, January 25, 1955; Armin H. Meyer (Beirut) to DoS, "Formation of Constitutional Union Party," Despatch 388, January 10, 1955, 783A.00/1-1055, NARA; Meyer to DoS, "Program of Constitutional Union Party," Despatch 458, February 9, 1955, 783A.00/2-955, NARA.

69. Al-Hizb al-Ishtiraki al-Masihi al-Lubnani, flyer, 1946, Sadaka Collection; CIA, "Christian Socialist Party," Intelligence Report dated January 21, 1947, CIA-RDP82-00457R000300010003-8, Crest Collection.

70. Minor to DoS, "Establishment of Lebanese Peoples Party," Despatch 327, 3 January 1952, 783A.00/1-352, NARA; Minor to DoS, "Preliminary Planning of Leaders of People's Party," Despatch 375, January 22, 1952, 783A.00/1-2252, NARA.

71. Pinkerton to DoS, A-40, 20 January 1948, 890E.00/1-2048, NARA; *Barnamij Hizb al-Ittihad al-Jumhuri*, pamphlet, 1947, Sadaka Collection; Hizb al-Ittihad al-Jumhuri, *Khitab al-Ustaz Ni'me Tabet fi al-Ijtima' al-Ta'sisi bi-Ism al-Lajna al-Tahdiriyya*, pamphlet, 1948, Sadaka Collection; "Hizb al-Ittihad al-Jumhuri Yandam li-l-Kutla al-Wataniyya," *al-Nahar*, December 3, 1950.

72. "Saba' Ahzab Mu'arida Tajtami'," *al-Nahar*, September 9, 1949.

73. "Al-Nass al-Kamil li-Rad al-Ahzab al-Mu'talifa," *al-Nahar*, November 19, 1949; "Jumblatt Yu'lin Inhilal Lajnat al-Ahzab," *al-Nahar*, January 5, 1951.

74. See "Insha' al-Jabha al-Sha'biyya," *al-Amal*, July 30, 1952; Minor to DoS, "The Popular Front—A New Type of Opposition in Lebanon," Despatch 93, August 14, 1952, 783A.00/8-1452, NARA; "Nurahib bi-Kult Ta'awun Yahduf li-l-Khayr," *al-Amal*, August 27, 1952; "Jabhat al-Mu'arada wa-l-Jabha al-Sha'biyya Ta'qudan al-Khanasir," *al-Nahar*, August 29, 1952. It would appear that this formal coordination between the two fronts gave way to differences in the lead-up to the September 15–16 general strike that forced al-Khuri's resignation, as mention of the coordination does not appear after the first week of September 1952.

75. Contemporary and historical accounts of the general strike take for granted this aspect of the downfall of al-Khuri as if it were a tactic readily available to elite politicians opposed to al-Khuri. For example, see Ziadeh, *Syria and Lebanon*, 117–25; Hudson, *Precarious Republic*, 105–107; Fawwaz Traboulsi, *A History of Modern Lebanon* (Pluto, 2007), 124–26. A more productive framework of these developments would be to view the 1952 general strike as the function of an alliance between Lebanon's increasingly mobilized popular sectors and the expanding coalition of elite opposition politicians.

76. "Al-Jabha al-Sha'biyya Tad'u ila Waqf al-Idrab," *al-Nahar*, September 17, 1952; "I'lan Fak al-Idrab," *al-Amal*, September 17, 1952; "Ittihad Naqabat Ashab al-Hiraf Yad'u ila Inha' al-Idrab," *al-Amal*, September 18, 1952; "Intiha' al-Idrab: Bayan min al-Jabha al-Sha'biyya," *al-Amal*, September 19, 1952; Minor to DoS, "Demise of President Beshara el-Khouri," Despatch 197, October 14, 1952, 783A.11/10-1452, NARA.

77. "Mu'tamar al-Ahzab al-Siyasiyya," *al-Nahar*, October 14, 1953; "Asbaha Ta'til al-Ijtima'at bi-Ilqa' al-Mutafajirat min Mayizat al-'Ahd," *al-Nahar*, October 15, 1953.

78. "Bayan al-Mu'tamar al-Watani al-'Am," *al-Anba'*, May 27, 1955; John K. Emerson (Beirut) to DoS, "Meeting of National Congress of Parties," Despatch 264, December 22, 1955, 783A.00/12-2255, NARA.

79. "Itifaq (22/12/1943)," *al-Jarida al-Rasmiyya* 9 (1944): 5.

80. For example, see al-Lajna al-Tanfiziyya li-l-Mu'tamar al-Watani al-Lubnani, "Bayan," October 23, 1944, Sadaka Collection.

81. "Mudhakkirat al-Mu'atamar al-Watani," *al-Nahar*, September 18, 1945.

82. For example, see "Brotokol (3/1/1944)," *al-Jarida al-Rasmiyya* 9 (1944): 5; "Brotokol (3/1/1944)," *al-Jarida al-Rasmiyya* 9 (1944): 5–6; "Brotokol (5/1/1944)," *al-Jarida al-Rasmiyya* 9 (1944): 6; "Marsum 'Adad 766/K (29/4/1944)" in *Majmu'at al-Qawanin*.

83. "Marsum Ishtira'i 1/K (16/3/1944)," in *Majmu'at al-Qawanin*. For contemporary debates about the politics and efficacy of the agreement, see Youssef Chaitani, *Post-Colonial Syria and Lebanon: The Decline of Arab Nationalism and the Triumph of the State* (I. B. Tauris, 2007), 18–24.

84. Formal negotiations on the monetary accord began on October 1, 1947, and concluded with the signing of the accord on February 6, 1948. The text of the accord is published as Annex no. 21 in *Tasmim al-Insha'i*. 625–46.

85. See Zuhayr Mikdashi, "The Monetary System of Lebanon" (MA thesis, AUB, 1956), 24–37; Salim Ahmad Hoss, "The Roles of Central Banking in Lebanon" (PhD diss., Indiana University, 1962), 51, 57–68; Raymond A. Mallat, *70 Years of Money Muddling in Lebanon, 1900–1970: A Guide to Monetary Management for Economic Development in Lebanon* (Aleph, 1973), 106–6. Between 1949 and 1955, the Lebanese government increased the degree to which Lebanese currency was backed by gold from 2 percent to 95 percent of face value.

86. See Elias Saba, "The Syro-Lebanese Customs Union: Causes of Failure and Attempts at Reorganization," *Middle East Economic Papers* (1960): 91–108; Carolyn L. Gates, "Laissez-Faire, Outward-Orientation, and Regional Economic Disintegration: A Case Study of the Dissolution of the Syro-Lebanese Customs Union," in *State and Society in Syria and* Lebanon, ed. Youssef M. Choueiri (St. Martin's, 1993), 62–73; Chaitani, *Post-Colonial Syria and Lebanon*, 54–58; Safieddine, *Banking on the State*, 34–42.

87. "Marsum 'Adad K/766 (29/4/1943)," in *Majmu'at al-Qawanin.*

88. "Marsum Ishtira'i 2 (23/3/1950)" and "Marsum 1560 (3/4/1950)," both in *al-Majmu'a al-Haditha*; Grassmuck and Salibi, *Manual*, 51–52.

89. The division of assets and liabilities were premised on the pre-1950 46–54 percent profit-sharing formula between Lebanon and Syria. See Vahe Karyergatian, "Monopoly in the Lebanese Tobacco Industry" (MA thesis, AUB, 1965), 86–87.

90. Prior to the breakup of the customs union and the parent Régie, the profit-sharing formula had five brackets applied progressively to each portion of profit, starting with an 85:15 ratio division of the first amount of profits and gradually rising to a 95:5 ratio division for the final portion of the profit.

91. Karyergatian, "Monopoly in the Lebanese Tobacco Industry," 55, 57, 81. Between 1949 and 1955, the total of acreage annually authorized for tobacco cultivation increased by 45 percent. The number of permits issued also rose from 7,122 (1951) to 9,969 (1955).

92. Republic of Lebanon, Ministry of National Economy, *Taqrir al-Sir Aliksandir Gib wa-Shurakah, 'an al-Tatawwur al-Iqtisadi fi Lubnan* (Beirut: n.p., 1948) [henceforth cited as Gibb & Partners, *Economic Development in Lebanon*], 136–38. The Beirut-Damascus line was constructed in 1895, while the others were constructed during 1902–11.

93. The Lebanese and Syrian governments signed the subsidization agreement with the DHP in 1925. Between 1930 and 1936, the DHP budget featured an annual total deficit that ranged from half a million to two million liras. Edwin B. Owen, "Ports, Roads and Railroads in Lebanon and Syria" (MA thesis, AUB, 1951), 104, fn. 1.

94. Gibb & Partners, *Economic Development in Lebanon*, 138–41. Also see Pinkerton to DoS, Airgram 3495, July 14, 1947, 890E.77/7-1447, NARA; Pinkerton to DoS, Airgram 1622, August 5, 1947, 890E.77/8-547, NARA.

95. Gibb & Partners, *Economic Development in Lebanon*, 139.

96. Usamah L. Farah, "The Lebanese Railway System: An Economic and Administrative Analysis" (MA thesis, AUB, 1973), 42–43.

97. Gibb & Partners, *Economic Development in Lebanon*, 138.

98. Unless otherwise noted, the following discussion on the Naqura-Beirut-Tripoli railway draws on CO 732/89/7, TNA; FO 371/52478, TNA; FO 957/20, TNA; FO 371/45359, TNA.

99. Pinkerton to DoS, A-261, May 29, 1947, 8900E.77/5-2947, NARA.

100. Carolyn L. Gates, *The Merchant Republic of Lebanon: Rise of an Open Economy* (I. B. Tauris, 1998), 80–135.

101. Samir A. K. Makdisi, "Post-War Lebanese Foreign Trade and Economic Development" (MA thesis, AUB, 1955), 172–89; Hoss, "Roles of Central Banking," 6–10; Gates, *Merchant Republic*, 111–15.

102. Arab League, Institute for Arab Research and Studies, *Muhadarat fi al-Iqtisad al-Lubnani Alqaha al-Doktor Albert Badre* (Matba'at Dar al-Hana, 1955); Government of the United Kingdom, Board of Trade, *Report of the United Kingdom Trade Mission to Iraq, Kuwait, the Lebanon, Syria, and Saudi Arabia* (H. M. Stationary Office, 1954), 57–64; "Basic Data on the Economy of Lebanon (June 1955)," *World Trade Information Service: Economy Reports* 1, no. 55–73 (1955); International Bank for Reconstruction and Development, "The Current Economic Position and Prospects of Lebanon," August 15, 1955; Yusif A. Sayigh, "Lebanon: Special Economic Problems Arising from a Special Structure," *Middle East Economic Papers* (1957): 60–88; Gates, *Merchant Republic*, 85–102.

103. Makdisi, "Post-War Lebanese Foreign Trade," 6–18.

104. See Ziad Munif Abu-Rish, "Conflict and Institution Building in Lebanon, 1946–1955" (PhD diss., University of California Los Angeles, 2014), 62–66; Ziad M. Abu-Rish, "Lebanon Beyond Exceptionalism," in *A Critical Political Economy of the Middle East and North Africa*, ed. Joel Beinin, Bassam Haddad, and Sherene Seikaly (Stanford University Press, 2021), 179–95.

105. The two most cited of these champions are Michel Chiha and Gabriel Menassa. For Chiha's writings, see his *Le Liban d'aujourdu'hui* (Éditions du Trident, 1942); *Essais*, vol. 1 (Éditions du Trident, 1950); and *Propos d'économie libanaise* (Éditions du Trident, 1965). For Menassa's writings, see his *al-Tasmim al-Insha'i*.

106. Toufic K. Gaspard, *A Political Economy of Lebanon, 1948–2002: The Limits of Laissez-faire* (Brill, 2004).

107. Menassa, *al-Tasmim al-Insha'i*; Albert Nassib Yusuf Badre, "The Economic Development of Lebanon with Special Emphasis on Finance" (PhD diss., State University of Iowa, 1950).

108. Safieddine, *Banking on the State*, 63–70. Also compare Menassa, *al-Tasmim al-Insha'i*, 147–293; Badre, "Economic Development of Lebanon,"160–252.

109. Safieddine, *Banking on the State*, 63–70.

110. Safieddine, *Banking on the State*, 75–81.

111. For examples, see Association of Lebanese Industrialists, *Dalil al-Sina'at al-Lubnaniyya 1949–1950* (Dar al-Ahad, 1950), 12–16; "al-Sina'iyyun Ya'lanun Lubnan Baladan Sina'iyyan," *al-Nahar*, May 29, 1949; "al-Sina'iyyun Yunaqishuna Radd al-Wizarat," *al-Nahar*, October 17, 1950; "Jam'iyyat al-Sina'iyyin Ta'rud," *al-Hayat*, September 13, 1953; "al-Sina'iyyun Yuqabilun Ra'is al-Majlis," *al-Nahar*, November 4, 1953.

112. I am drawing on a similar argument by Robert Vitalis, who critiques the "projection back into the past [i.e., the 1922–52 period] of post-1952 anti-capitalist discourses" to construct a narrative of failed attempts at autonomous (read nationalist) industrialization when in fact major manufacturing ventures were part of strategies for economic diversification. See Robert Vitalis, *When Capitalists Collide: Business Conflict and the End of Empire in Egypt* (University of California Press, 1995), 41–49.

113. See chapter 4.

114. For example, see Pinkerton to DoS, Despatch A-169, May 23, 1949, 890E.60/5-2349, NARA.

115. For example, see Pinkterton to DoS, Airgram A-425, October 29, 1948, 890E.6552/10-2948, NARA; Airgram A-320, October 12, 1949, 890E.61/10-1249, NARA; "Ittihad al-Muzari'in Yuwaddih Mawqifuh," *al-Nahar*, February 28, 1952.

116. See chapter 6.

117. Elizabeth Thompson, *Colonial Citizens: Republican Rights, Paternal Privilege, and Gender in French Syria and Lebanon* (Columbia University Press, 2000), 230–38; Chaitani, *Post-Colonial Syria and Lebanon*, 74–89.

118. For examples see, respectively, untitled petition (signed by Arab Women's Federation in Lebanon, the Union of Lebanese Women, the Women's Awakening Society, the Ghasassina Organization, Kata'ib Party, and the Najjada Organization) addressed to President Bishara al-Khuri, dated December 23, 1946, File 3, Box 1, Evelyne Bustrous Collection, Archives and Special Collections, Nami Jafet Library, American University of Beirut, Lebanon; this chapter's discussion of the Committee for the Defense of Tenants; "Nida' al-Ahzab wa-l-Hay'at ila -Muwatinin," *al-Nahar*, June 24, 1953.

119. "The Port of Beirut: The Resurgence of an Ancient Maritime Tradition," *The Dock and Harbour Authority* (October 1955): 171–74.

120. Compagnie du Port, des Quais et des Entrepôts de Beyrouth (CPQEB), *Marfa' Bayrut: Muftah Asiya: Ma'lumat 'Amma wa-Ta'rifat* (Beirut: n.p., 1955), 4. Compagnie du Port's Ottoman- and Mandate-era concessions covered the customs warehouses, the general warehouses, the free zone, the harbor station, workshops, and maintenance facilities. The government or other (private) Lebanese entities directly supervised the Office of the Port Captain, piloting, quarantining, beacons, the port police, and the customs administration.

121. Compagnie du Port, des Quais et des Entrepôts de Beyrouth (CPQEB), *Marfa' Bayrut*, 6–10.

122. Jad Mansour Karam, "The Free Zone of the Port of Beirut and the Its Effects on the Lebanese Economy" (MA thesis, AUB, 1963), 32–81; "The Port of Beirut," 732–74.

123. Ghurfat al-Tijara wa-l-Sina'a fi Bayrut, *Lubnan 1953* (Ghurfat al-Tijara wa-l-Sina'a fi Bayrut, 1953), 29–31. Trucks constituted the primary mode of regional transit trade across Lebanon and between the port and the many markets of the above-mentioned countries.

124. Makdisi, "Post-War Lebanese Foreign Trade," 47–58.

125. The repurchase clause in the Beirut port concession agreement was equally significant. The clause, which went into effect in 1955, featured a formula for determining a sale price that would still permit the Lebanese state to receive significantly greater income. See FO 371/121630, TNA.

126. For example, see BT 11/5070, TNA; James C. Lobenstine (Beirut) to DoS, "Possibility of Grant Economic Aid for Port of Tripoli," Despatch 339, December 30, 1953, 783A.5-MSP/12-3053, NARA.

127. "Tripoli: Relations with Lebanese Government," FO 1018/86, TNA.

128. For example, between 1950 and 1955 the Tripoli port experienced a 10 percent increase in the number of vessels docking and a 50 percent increase in the tonnage of goods imported through the Tripoli port. See Gulick, *Tripoli*, 92.

129. For example, see FO 371/40119, TNA; FO 371/110975, TNA. Some Lebanese politicians appear to have been particularly inspired by the Panamanian and Liberian governments' practices related to offering "flags of convenience." On this point specifically, see Chancery (Beirut) to Foreign Office, 13913/1/54, November 15, 1953, FO 371/110975, TNA.

130. Nicolas Salha, "Trade Agreements of Lebanon" (MA thesis, AUB, 1957), 21–119. These agreements variously covered conditions affecting trade in goods and services (i.e., quotas, licenses, customs, and other procedures) and methods of financing current trade between the signatories.

131. Salha, "Trade Agreements of Lebanon," 18–21. The agreement outlined the signatories' preferential trade relations and specific procedures concerning imports, exports, and transit trade, as well as trade-related payments and capital transfers.

132. Salha, "Trade Agreements of Lebanon," 9.

133. FO 371/110964, TNA.

134. UN Department of Economic and Social Affairs, *Economic Developments in the Middle East, 1945 to 1954: Supplement to World Economic Report, 1953–54* (United Nations Publications, 1955), 177.

135. Heath to DoS, "Proposed Purchase of Beirut Port Company by Lebanese Government," Despatch 494, May 14, 1956, 883A.053/5-1456, NARA.

136. Makdisi, "Post-War Lebanese Foreign Trade," 89–109; Ghurfat al-Tijara wa-l-Sina'a fi Bayrut, *Lubnan 1953*, 15–23. This comparison excludes Palestine. Beyond Syria, which remained the largest single regional trading partner, Saudi Arabia,

Egypt, Jordan, and Iraq (in that order) were the leading export destinations while Iraq, Saudi Arabia, Jordan, and Egypt (in that order) were the leading sources of imports.

137. Proposals for state-sponsored development of the tourism sector emerged from various parts of Lebanese society soon after independence. Compare, for example, Gabriel Menassa's 1948 proposals to those of Kamal Jumblatt when he was minister of national economy in 1947. See Menassa, *al-Tasmim al-Insha'i*, 396–417; Pinkerton to DoS, Airgram 189, April 23, 1947, 890E.15/4-2347, NARA; Pinkerton to DoS, Airgram A-208, May 2, 1947, 890E.15/5-247, NARA; Pinkerton to DoS, A-216, May 5, 1947, 890E.15/5/547, NARA.

138. Robert L. Clifford (Beirut) to DoS, "Basic and Annual Highway Report," Despatch 33, July 26, 1950, 883A.2612/7-2650, NARA, 1–2; "Annual Highway Report," no. 694, June 26, 1951, 883a.2612/6/2651, NARA; "Annual Highway Report," no. 642, May 28, 1952, 883a.2612/5-2852, NARA; UN, *Economic Developments*, 176–77. The Ministry of Public Works expanded upon Mandate-era roads, developing them into a three-tiered system of national highways, provincial roads, and local roads. It widened rural roads, doubled the length of paved roads, and doubled the total length of roadways open to automobile traffic.

139. For example, see UNESCO, *Lebanon: Suggestions for the Plan of Tripoli and for the Surroundings of the Baalbek Acropolis* (UNESCO, 1954); "Treasures of Lebanon and Syria," *UNESCO Courier*, no. 7 (1954): 11–14.

140. For example of government subsidization of Arab visitors, see "Marsum 1930 (25/5/1950)" in *Majmu'at al-Qawanin*. On the Société de Crédit Agricole et Industriel du Liban, see Hoss, "Roles of Central Banking," 46–47. In 1945 the government extended its 1942 agreement with the Société for ten additional years while increasing its investment amount from ten to fifteen million Syrian-Lebanese liras. In 1950, the government increased the amount by a further five million Lebanese liras.

141. UN Department of Economic and Social Affairs, *Economic Developments in the Middle East*, 166.

142. UN Department of Economic and Social Affairs, *Economic Developments in the Middle East*, 177.

143. Zeina Maasri, *Cosmopolitan Radicalism: The Visual Politics of Beirut's Global Sixties* (Cambridge University Press, 2022), 35.

144. "Qanun (7/5/1948)," in *Majmu'at al-Qawanin*.

145. Hasan al-Hasan, *al-Siyaha fi Lubnan: Madiyyan wa-Hadiran wa-Mustaqbalan* (Beirut: n.p., 1973), 32. The service was initially based in the Ministry of Trade, and subsequently a part of the Ministry of Economy, which was created via the 1944–45 merger of the Ministries of Trade and Supply.

146. Pinkerton to DoS, Airgram 322, July 15, 1947, 890E.502/7-1547, NARA.

147. For example, see "al-Istiyaf wa-l-Siyaha fi Lubnan," *al-Nahar*, August 6, 1947.

148. "Qanun Sadir (7/5/1948)," in *al-Majmu'a al-Haditha*. The law creating the GCTE initially specified a staff of thirty-four persons. The following discussion of the GCTE draws on Maasri, *Cosmopolitan Radicalism*, 31–35; Josette Kfoury, "Liban, pays de tourisme," *Revue de géographie de Lyon* 34, no. 3 (1959): 278–80.

149. Al-Hasan, *al-Siyaha*, 33–37.

150. "Marsum 9449 (7/6/1955)," *al-Jarida al-Rasmiyya* (June 15, 1955): 997; Kfoury, "Liban, pays de tourisme," 279; al-Hassan, *al-Siyaha*, 82.

151. Nadya Sbaiti, "Governing Summer in Mount Lebanon: *Istiyaf*, Tourism, and Mobility in the Interwar Arab East," *Journal of Tourism History* (2024): 1–19.

152. George Rayess, "Tourism, estivate et hivernage au Liban," *Les Conférences du Cénacle* 4, no. 3–4 (April 25, 1950): 44–67. Also see "Wad' Minhaj li-l-Siyaha wa-l-Istiyaf," *al-Nahar*, August 6, 1948; al-Hasan, *al-Siyaha*, 36.

153. The International Union of Official Tourism Organizations was created in 1946–47 and has its origins in the International Union of Official Tourist Propaganda Organizations (est. 1925). It was subsequently transformed into the UN World Tourism Organization in 1974.

154. See, respectively, "Marsum 14981 (14/5/1949)" and "Qarar 'Adad 7089 (15/10/1949)," both in *al-Majmu'a al-Haditha*; "Marsum 6012 (17/8/1954)" and "Marsum 8610 (10/3/1955)," both in *al-Majmu'a al-Haditha*; "Marsum 2115 (13/6/1950)," in *Majmu'at al-Qawanin*; "Marsum 9449 (7/6/1955)," in *al-Majmu'a al-Haditha*; and "Marsum 2174 (22/6/1950)," *al-Jarida al-Rasmiyya* (June 28, 1950): 428–39; "Qanun (2/1/1952)," *al-Jarida al-Rasmiyya* (January 9, 1952): 19; "Qanun al-Qimar (4/8/1954)," *al-Jarida al-Rasmiyya* (August 4, 1954): 583–85. The 1954 regulation of designated summer resorts established specific criteria for municipalities in Mount Lebanon to be recognized and listed as such resorts by the government, tourist agencies, and guide books. While the government legalized gambling in 1950 and empowered the commission to oversee the establishment, monitoring, and regulation of gambling establishments, the government revoked the legalization in 1952. The commission subsequently secured a law allowing for the establishment of a single casino, for which it would supervise the design, construction, and bids for management contracts. It was this law that resulted in the establishment of Casino du Liban (Kazino Lubnan) in 1959.

155. For example, see "Qanun (14/12/1950)," in *Majmu'at al-Qawanin*.

156. Maasri, *Cosmopolitan Radicalism*, 37.

157. See "Fi Mustahal Sanat al-Siyaha 1955," *Sawt al-Mara'* (February 1955), 10–11; al-Hasan, *al-Siyaha*, 82; "Iftitah Sayf al-Mughtaribin fi Lubnan," *Sawt al-Mar'a* (August 1955), 4; *Lubnan Balad al-Siyaha wa-l-Istiyaf* (Matba'at Dayr al-Mkallis, 1955).

158. Maasri, *Cosmopolitan Radicalism*, 36–38. In this sense, the commission further articulated, expanded, and deepened the ways in which "images, ideas, and practices of *istiyaf* . . . were crucial components in the tenuous and shifting interwar formation of nation and state" in Lebanon. See Sbaiti, "Governing Summer," 153.

159. "Marsum Ishtira'i 32 (17/2/1953)," *al-Jarida al-Rasmiyya* (February 25, 1953): 347–50. For some sense of the lead-up to and aftermath of the board's creation, see Minor to DoS, "Progress Toward Setting Up Economic Development Board for Lebanon," Despatch 128, August 27, 1952, 883A.00/8-2752, NARA; Bruins to DoS, Telegram 1550, February 18, 1953, 883A.00/2-1853, NARA; Hare to DoS, "Activities of Economic Planning and Development Board," Despatch 308, December 10, 1953, 883A.00/12-1053, NARA; Hare to DoS, "Problems Surrounding Economic Planning Board," Despatch 630, April 6, 1954, 883A.00/4-654, NARA.

160. The decree establishing and regulating the EPDB directed the board to study the need for and propose projects related to public works, agriculture, manufacturing, trade, banking, tourism, and social development (i.e., public health, education, housing, and social security). The board's president was to be the minister of national economy, who was joined by his ministry's director general for the supervision of companies; the directors general of the ministries of national economy, agriculture, and finance; and six economic experts.

161. Chancery (Beirut) to Middle East Secretariate, Foreign Office, 1107/2/53, April 3, 1953, FO 371/104500, TNA. Also see EPDB's report to parliament covering the first twenty months of its work, published as the annex to *al-Jarida al-Rasmiyya* (April 13, 1955).

162. Sami George Hajjar, "The Role of the Ministry of General Planning in the Economic Planning and Development of Lebanon" (MA thesis, AUB, 1962), 41–48.

163. Safieddine, *Banking on the State*, 43–70.

164. "Ta'sis Sharika li-l-Taslif," *al-Jarida al-Rasmiyya* (July 21, 1954): 540–47; Marsum 6807 (23/10/1954)," *al-Jarida al-Rasmiyya* (October 27, 1954): 751–67; Safieddine, *Banking on the State*, 79–81.

165. See E. A. Chapman-Andrews (Beirut) to the Marquess of Salisbury (London), 1106/9/53, September 2, 1953, FO 371/104502, TNA; Chapman-Andrews to the Marquess of Salisbury (London), 1106/11/53, September 9, 1953, FO 371/104502, TNA; "al-Hukuma Tuhil Qanun Insha' Masraf al-Taslif," *al-Nahar*, March 9, 1953; "Ijtima' Majlis al-Inma' al-Iqtisadi," *al-'Amal*, October 9, 1953; "Bank al-Taslif al-Zira'i wa-l-Sina'i," *al-'Amal*, October 10, 1953. For BCAIF loans in its first two years of operation, see Nadim George Khalaf, "Long Term Credit in Lebanon" (MA thesis, AUB, 1957), 88–103.

166. "Al-Sharika al-Wataniyya li-l-Ma' wa-l-Kahruba'," *al-Nahar*, October 30, 1953; "Mashru' Sharikat al-Ma' wa-l-Kahruba'," *al-Nahar*, February 16, 1954; "Mashru' al-Sharika al-Wataniyya li-l-Miyah wa-l-Kahruba'," *al-Nahar*, March 5, 1954.

167. Qanun (14/8/1954)," *al-Jarida al-Rasmiyya* (August 18, 1954): 619–22.

168. I am drawing on the argument of Owain Lawson. See his "Power Failures," especially 200–12.

169. International Bank for Reconstruction and Development, "Appraisal of Litani Power and Irrigation Project, Lebanon," August 15, 1955.

170. International Bank for Reconstruction and Development, "Report and Recommendations of the President to the Executive Directors on a Proposed Loan to the Litani Authority in Lebanon," August 16, 1955.

171. I am grateful to Owain Lawson for bringing this point to my attention. See Lawson, "Power Failures," 254–73.

172. See "Qanun (20/12/1951)," "Qanun (7/1954)," "Marsum 7695 (27/2/1952)," "Qanun (21/12/1951)," "Marsum 7694 (27/4/1952)," and "Qanun (4/12/1944): al-Mu'addal bi-Qawanin Muwazanat 1945 wa-1946 wa-1948 wa-1949 wa-1950 wa-1951 wa-1952," all in *al-Qawanin al-Haditha*.

173. Safieddine, *Banking on the State*, 84–85. Raymond Eddé apparently admitted that the 1956 Banking Secrecy Law was proposed in part to shield bank accounts from tax inspection.

174. Himadeh, *Fiscal System of Lebanon*, 22–30.

175. Himadeh, *Fiscal System of Lebanon*, 67–76.

176. Himadeh, *Fiscal System of Lebanon*, 35–47.

177. Jamil Shihab, "Wizarat al-Maliyya," in *Dirasat 'an Hukumat Lubnan*, 225–46.

178. This was in fact a regular complaint among senior bureaucrats in other ministries. See, for example, Najib Sadaka, "Wizarat al-Tarbiyya al-Wataniyya," in *Dirasat 'an Hukumat Lubnan*, 3. See also an attempt by the minister of finance to address this issue in "Ta'mim 41" in *Majumu'at al-Qawanin*.

179. It is worth noting that the growth in public sector employment appears to be commensurate, in relative terms, with that contemporaneously occurring in Syria. See Ralph Earl Crow, "The Civil Service of Independence Syria: 1945–1958" (PhD diss., University of Michigan, 1964), 122–23.

180. Underpinning these laws were two Mandate-era decrees in 1925, one that outlined procedures for appointment, promotion, discipline, and discharge, and one that outlined procedures for salaries, transfers, and leaves. See "Qarar 3021 (9/3/1925)" and "Qarar 3195 (1/7/1925)," both in *Majmu'at al-Qawanin*.

181. Bruins to DoS, Despatch 584, "Lebanese Government Salary Scales," May 12, 1952, 883A.061/5-1252, NARA.

182. Menassa, *al-Tasmim al-Insha'i*, 408–17; Awwad, "al-Wazifa fi Lubnan"; Department of Public Administration (AUB-DPA), *Arab Public Administration Conference, 1954* (Kashef, 1955); William Robson, "Civil Service Reform in Lebanon," unpublished report, Beirut, June 1949; Robert Culberston, "Report and Recommendations to the Government of Lebanon for a Program on Public Administration Improvement," unpublished report, Beirut, 1954.

183. "Marsum Ishtira'i 12 (5/1/1955)," "Marsum Ishtira'i 14 (7/1/1955)," and "Marsum Ishtira'i 30 (18/1/1955)," all in in *al-Majmu'a al-Haditha*.

184. Depending on the particular state institution, temporary workers could constitute a significant proportion of those employed. For example, the 1954 ordinary budget listed 677 permanent officials and 12 temporary employees for the Ministry of Justice at the same time that it listed 167 permanent and 104 temporary employees for the Ministry of National Economy. See Grassmuck and Salibi, *Manual*, 27, 79.

185. Technical positions included engineers (Ministry of Public Works), public school teachers (Ministry of Education), members of the gendarmerie and police (Ministry of Interior), and those of the consular services (Ministry of Foreign Affairs).

186. Applicants sat for both a written and oral examination. Passing the former was a condition for taking the latter. Individual ministries established ad hoc committees to design, administer, and evaluate examinations.

187. The government calculated monthly pension payments on the basis of 1/55 of the average monthly salary of the last two years of service multiplied by the total number of years of service. Alternatively, it calculated dismissal indemnities on the basis of one month's salary for every year of service for the first ten years, and two months' salary for every year of service thereafter—also calculating on the basis of the average monthly salary of the last two years of service.

188. Delay of promotion was one of several disciplinary measures to which civil servants were subject. Others were salary deduction, suspension, demotion, and dismissal.

189. For contemporary accounts of these dynamics during the 1943–55 period, see "Expose des Motifs" and "Note: Sur le project de loi reglementant l'administration public de l'Etat" in FO 1018/65, TNA; Robson, "Civil Service Reform in Lebanon," W. Houstoun Boswall (Beirut) to Ernest Bevin (London), no. 22, January 31, 1950, FO 371/82268, TNA; Bruins to DoS, "Lebanese Government Salary Scales"; Culberston, "Report and Recommendations to the Government of Lebanon"; Salam, "Hawl Bina' al-Dawla al-Lubnaniyya"; AUB-DPA, *Arab Public Administration*. For contemporary accounts of these dynamics during the 1956–75 period, see Umar Samih Lababidi, "Public Personnel Administration" (MA thesis, AUB, 1959), 31–33 and 40–45;

Lebanese Association of Political Sciences, *Abhath fi al-Tanzim al-'Idari* (Beirut: n.p., 1959); Nahhas, "Lebanese Bureaucracy," 218–34; Abdo Iskandar Ba'aklini, "The Civil Service Board in Lebanon" (MA thesis, AUB, 1963), 81–109; Aref Abdul Khalik, "Governmental Reforms in Lebanon 1965–1967" (MA thesis, AUB, 1968), 45–148.

190. Salam, "Hawl Bina' al-Dawla al-Lubnaniyya," 160.

191. See Lababidi, "Public Personnel Administration," 83–84.

192. Fayyad, "The Effects of Sectarianism."

193. The eruption centered on the publication of *Moslem Lebanon Today* (1953), a tract that claimed to provide a "frank discussion of the struggle on the part of Lebanon's non-Christian majority to secure a proportionate voice in the government." The ad hoc committee of Muslim politicians and organizations publishing the tract was provisionally chaired by Mohammed Jamil Bayhum and included al-Najjada, the National Organization, the Amiliyya Society, and the Young Men's Muslim Association. The tract's authors identified six arenas of discrimination requiring reform: the bureaucracy, rural development, urban rent control, education, government contracts, and the census. For critical responses, see "Sada al-Bayan al-Islami," *al-Amal*, March 5, 1953; "al-Bilad Ta'ish fi Jow Ta'ifi Mahmum Kajow 1942," *al-Nahar*, March 13, 1953; "Fi Bayan Khatir Adha'atih al-Hay'at al-Islamiyya," *al-Nahar*, March 14, 1953; "Muqarrarat Mu'tamar Bkriki," *al-Amal*, March 18, 1953; "Bayan Kata'ibi Khatir fi Kitab Maftuh," *al-Amal*, August 20, 1954; "Muqarrarat Ru'asa' al-Tawa'if al-Masihiyya fi al-Diman," *al-Hayat*, August 27, 1954.

194. "Bahth Huquq al-Tawa'if," *al-Nahar*, August 17, 1954; Lobenstine to DoS, "Danger of Confessional Strife Temporarily Averted," Despatch 144, September 1, 1954, 783A.00/9-154.

195. Heath to DoS, "Confessionalism Rears Once Again Its Ugly Head," Despatch 34, July 18, 1955, 783.A.00/7-1853, NARA.

196. The subsequent discussion of Naggear and Abd-El-Al's career trajectories draws on Owain Lawson, "A National Vocation: Engineering Nature and State in Lebanon's Merchant Republic," *Comparative Studies of South Asia and the Middle East* 41, no. 1 (2021): 71–87.

197. Harfush began his public sector career as a prosecutor in Mount Lebanon (1943–48), moving on to head the Social Affairs Service in the Ministry of National Economy (1948–51), and then becoming the director general of the Ministry of Social Affairs (1951–1960). Through the latter two positions, he played a critical role in the monitoring, controlling, and disrupting of the labor movement in Lebanon. Les Editions Publitec, *Who's Who in Lebanon, 5th ed., 1973–1974* (Imm. Gedeon, 1974), 485–86. Anis Saleh began his public sector career as a magistrate in Beirut (1947–51) before assuming the position of director general of the Ministry of Justice (1951–52)

and Ministry of Interior (1952), eventually leaving public service to work as a private sector lawyer. Al-Rumi joined the Lebanese Radio Station in 1950 as head of the Music Department, a position he continued to hold until his retirement in 1979. Shadir began his career in 1938 with the customs administration, moving to director of civil aviation in 1953, and holding the position of director general of transport until his retirement in 1966. Information on Harfush and Saleh has been collated from various US diplomatic sources cited throughout the subsequent chapters. On al-Rumi and Shadir, see, respectively, Halim al-Rumi, *Mudhakkarat Halim al-Rumi* (Riyad al-Rayyess, 1992); Fu'ad Shadir, *Nisf Qarn fi Khidmat al-Idara al-Lubnaniyya* (al-Matba'a al-Katholukiyya, n.d.).

198. Lababidi, "Public Personnel Administration," 86 & 112.

199. Iskandar E. Bashir, *Civil Service Reforms in Lebanon* (American University of Beirut, 1977), 21–47.

200. Minor to DoS, "Workers' Strikes in Lebanon," Despatch 649, May 31, 1952, 1–2, 883A.062/5-3152, NARA.

201. Lobenstine to DoS, "Annual Labor Report—Lebanon—1952," Despatch 484, February 18, 1953, 883A.06/2-1853, NARA; Hare to DoS, "Annual Labor Report—Lebanon—1953," Despatch 580, March 17, 1954, 7, 883A.06/3-1754, NARA; Heath to DoS, "Annual Labor Report—Lebanon—1955," Despatch 572, June 30, 1956, 3, 883A.06/6-3056, NARA.

Chapter 3

1. "Qanun (8/12/1953)," *al-Jarida al-Rasmiyya* (December 9, 1953): 1488–90.

2. Passive defense, which would later on be more commonly referred to as civil defense (*al-difa' al-madani*), was historically associated with the "home front" and developed in response to the ubiquity of air raids on European civilian population centers during World War II.

3. Coleman Noahson, "The Lebanese Army Code: A Translation and Comparison with Similar Regulations of the United States Army and a Brief Historical Background" (MA thesis, AUB, 1952), xxiv.

4. Noahson, "Lebanese Army Code," xxv.

5. Protocol signed between General Paul Beynet, Delegate General and Plenipotentiary of France, and Riad Bey Solh, President of the Lebanese Council of Ministers, Beirut, June 15, 1944, included as enclosure no. 8 in Wadsworth to DoS, "Lebanese Desiderata—Troupes Speciales and French Diplomatic Representation," no. 660, February 17, 1945, 890E.01/2-1745, NARA; "Risalat Fakhamat al-Shaykh Bishara al-Khuri Ra'is al-Jumhuriyya al-Lubnaniyya ila al-Sha'b al-Lubnani al-Karim," Beirut, September 21, 1944, Sadaka Collection.

6. "Tasallum al-Jaysh fi Tariq al-Tanfidh," *al-Nahar*, June 20, 1944; Noahson, "Lebanese Army Code," xxv.

7. For example, see al-Lajna al-Tanfiziyya li-l-Mu'tamar al-Watani al-Lubnani, "Bayan min al-Mu'tamar al-Watani al-Lubnani," October 23, 1944, Sadaka Collection.

8. "Al-Idrab fi Bayrut wa-Lubnan," *al-Nahar*, January 30, 1945; "Idrab al-Bilad fi Yawmih al-Thani," *al-Nahar*, January 31, 1945. Also see Wadsworth to DoS, no. 26, sections 1 & 2, January 30, 1945, 890E.01/1-3045, NARA.

9. "Nurid al-Jaysh!," flyer distributed in Beirut on January 27, 1945, calling for a student strike on January 29, 1945, Sadaka Collection; "al-Idrab fi Bayrut wa-Lubnan li-l-Mutalaba bi-l-Jaysh," *al-Nahar*, January 30, 1945.

10. "From the Student Council at AUB to Prime Minister Abdul Hamid Karami," hand-written duplicate of petition, January 29, 1945, Sadaka Collection.

11. "From the Student Council at AUB to Prime Minister Abdul Hamid Karami."

12. Letter on Behalf of Hay'at al-Talibat to British Minister, January 30, 1945, FO 226/272, TNA.

13. "Al-Madina Ta'ud ila Halatuha al-'Adiyya," *al-Nahar*, February 1, 1945.

14. "Bayan min Munazzamatay al-Kata'ib al-Lubnaniyya wa-l-Najjada ila al-Sha'b al-Lubnani al-Karim," flyer, January 30, 1945, Sadaka Collection.

15. "Al-Madina Ta'ud ila Halatuha al-'Adiyya," *al-Nahar*, February 1, 1945; Wadsworth to DoS, no. 26, sections 1 & 2, January 30, 1945, 890E.01/1-3045, NARA.

16. "Idrab al-Bilad fi Yawmih al-Thani," *al-Nahar*, January 31, 1945.

17. Pharaon to Beynet, no. 272, 29 January 1945 and Pharaon to Beynet, no. 273, January 29, 1945, included as enclosures no. 4 and no. 6 in Wadsworth to DoS, "Lebanese Desiderata"; "Mudhakarra Rasmiyya bi-Talab al-Jaysh," *al-Nahar*, February 2, 1945.

18. "Al-Majlis Yu'ayyid al-Hukuma," *al-Nahar*, February 6, 1945.

19. "Majlis al-Nuwwab Yatanaqash fi Qadiyyat al-Jaysh," *al-Nahar*, May 10, 1945.

20. Wadsworth to DoS, no.130, May 14, 1945, 890E.01/5-1445, NARA.

21. Nicola A. Ziadeh, *Syria and Lebanon* (Ernest Benn, 1957), 81.

22. Lajnat al-Tullab, "Tullab Lubnan Yastankirun Istiqdam al-Juyush al-Ajnabiyya," flyer, May 18, 1945, Sadaka Collection; "Ya Tullab Lubnan wa-Shababuha," flyer, May 20, 1945, Sadaka Collection; Wadsworth to DoS, no.142, May 20, 1945, 890E.01/5-2045, NARA; Wadsworth to DoS, no. 144, May 21, 1945, 890E.01/5-2145, NARA; Ziadeh, *Syria and Lebanon*, 82–3.

23. For example, see "Bayrut Tadrub Ta'yiddan li-Mawqif al-Majlis wa-l-Hukuma," *al-Nahar*, May 19, 1945; "Suriyya wa-Lubnan fi Ghalayan," *al-Nahar*, May 22, 1945.

24. "Suriyya wa-Lubnan fi Ghalayan."

25. "Suriyya wa-Lubnan fi Ghalayan."

26. For example, see "al-Tatawwu' li-l-Jaysh al-Watani," *al-Nahar*, May 27, 1945.

27. "Al-Hukuma Tatlub Waqf al-Idrab," *al-Nahar*, May 22, 1945.

28. "Bayrut Tada' Haddan li-Idrabuha," *al-Nahar*, May 23, 1945.

29. "Al-Tullab Yamshun fi Muzahara Rasina," *al-Nahar*, May 24, 1945.

30. "Idrab al-Madina, Idrab al-Muhamin wa-Muzaharat al-Talaba," *al-Nahar*, May 25, 1945.

31. "Idrab al-Madina, Idrab al-Muhamin wa-Muzaharat al-Talaba."

32. "Idrab al-Madina, Idrab al-Muhamin wa-Muzaharat al-Talaba."

33. "In'iqad al-Mu'tamar al-Watani fi Bayrut," *al-Nahar*, May 25, 1945.

34. "Bayrut Tasta'nif Nashatuha al-'Adi," *al-Nahar*, May 27, 1945.

35. "In'iqad al-Mu'tamar al-Watani fi Bayrut," *al-Nahar*, May 25, 1945.

36. "Bayrut Tasta'nif Nashatuha al-'Adi."

37. Wadsworth to DoS, "Transmitting Lebanese Notes of Protest Regarding French Action in Lebanon," no. 825, May 22, 1945, 890E.1/5-2245, NARA.

38. "Al-Mistir Idin Yu'akid Khabar Itlaq al-Madafi' al-Faransiyya," *al-Nahar*, June 1, 1945; "Mandub al-Nahar Yasuf Ba'd al-Mashahid fi Dimashq," *al-Nahar*, June 5, 1945.

39. "Al-Qa'id Yuballigh al-Hukuma," *al-Nahar*, June 2, 1945.

40. "Al-Hukuma al-Amirkiyya Tattahim Faransa," *al-Nahar*, June 2–3, 1945; "Ba'd Istilam al-Jaysh al-Britani al-Tasi' al-Amn," *Sawt al-Sha'b*, June 3, 1945.

41. "Al-Lajna al-'Askariyya Tada' Qanun al-Tatawwu'," *al-Nahar*, May 30, 1945; "al-Hukuma Taftah Bab al-Tatawwu'," *al-Nahar*, May 31, 1945.

42. "Bayrut Tabda' al-Idrab Sabah al-Khamis," *al-Nahar*, May 31, 1945.

43. "Idrab Lubnan al-Ra'i' fi Yawmih al-Awwal," *al-Nahar*, June 1, 1945.

44. "Idrab al-Bilad fi Yawmih al-Thani," *al-Nahar*, June 2, 1945.

45. "Idrab al-Bilad fi Yawmih al-Thani"; "Lubnan Yutabi' Idrabuh," *Sawt al-Sha'b*, June 3, 1945.

46. "Shakway Suriyya wa-Lubnan," *al-Nahar*, June 6, 1945; "Faransa Takhsha Qararat al-Jami'a al-'Arabiyya," *al-Nahar*, June 8, 1945; "Qararat al-Jami'a al-'Arabiyya," *al-Nahar*, June 9, 1945.

47. "Mu'tamar San Fransisko Yakhtim A'malah," *al-Nahar*, June 26, 1945.

48. For viewpoints of the US, British, Soviet, and French governments in the lead-up to the conferences, see Acting Secretary of State (Grew) to the Ambassador in France (Caffery), February 20, 1945, 500.CC/2–2045, *Foreign Relations of the United States 1945*, vol. 1, *General: The United Nations*, ed. Velma Hastings Cassidy, Ralph R. Goodwin, George H. Dengler (US Government Printing Office, 1967), https://history.state.gov/historicaldocuments/frus1945v01/d28; The Ambassador in

the United Kingdom (Winant) to DoS, March 17, 1945, 500.CC/3–1745, *Foreign Relations of the United States 1945*, vol. 1, https://history.state.gov/historicaldocuments/frus1945v01/d78

49. "Al-Wisaya la Tashmal al-Buldan al-Mustaqilla," *al-Nahar*, June 23–24, 1945.

50. "Mudhakkarat al-Mu'tamar al-Watani li-l-Hukuma," *al-Nahar*, June 8, 1945.

51. "Ta'yid al-Ahzab wa-l-Munazzamat wa-l-Jam'iyyat al-Mutalaba bi-Jala' al-Faransiyyin," *al-Nahar*, June 12, 1945.

52. Lebanon officially declared war on Germany and Japan on February 27, 1945. See "Lubnan Ya'lin al-Harb," *al-Nahar*, March 1, 1945.

53. For example, see "Mudhakkarat 'Usbat al-'Amal al-Qawmi ila al-Hukuma," *al-Nahar*, June 20, 1945.

54. "Ihtijaj al-Ittihad al-Nisa'i al-'Arabi al-'Am," *al-Nahar*, June 12, 1945.

55. "Ihtijaj al-Ittihad al-Nisa'i al-'Arabi al-'Am."

56. The subsequent three examples are drawn from "Al-Majlis al-Baladi wa-l-Mu'tamar al-Watani Yattakhidhan," *al-Nahar*, June 20, 1945.

57. See "Siyasat Amirka fi Suriyya wa-Lubnan," *al-Nahar*, June 26, 1945; "al-Hukuma al-Amirikiyya Tarfud Iqtirah Faransa," *al-Nahar*, June 27, 1945.

58. "Lubnan wa-Suriyya Yu'linan Irtiyahum li-Tasallum al-Jaysh," *al-Nahar*, July 11, 1945; Anglo French Joint Staff, decision no. 15, July 24, 1945, FO 226/295, TNA.

59. "Ijtima' Lubnani Suri fi Sawfar," *al-Nahar*, July 25, 1945; "Ra'is al-Jumhuriyya Ya'rud al-Jaysh," *al-Nahar*, August 2, 1945; Ninth Army to Minister, Beirut, August 2, 1945, FO 226/295, TNA.

60. "al-Balagh al-Britani al-Faransi al-Mushtarak," *al-Nahar*, December 14, 1945; "Ibtida' al-Marhala al-Hasima fi Tarikh Lubnan al-Mu'asir," *al-Nahar*, January 22–23, 1946; Ziadeh, *Syria and Lebanon*, 88–89; Stephen Hemsley Longrigg, *Syria and Lebanon under French Mandate* (Oxford University Press, 1958), 354.

61. "Al-Majlis al-Niyabi Yabhath Qadiyyat al-Jala'," *al-Nahar*, December 25, 1945.

62. "Idrab Jami' al-Mudun al-Lubnaniyya," *al-Nahar*, January 3, 1946; "Idrab Shamil Ra'i'," *Sawt al-Sha'b*, January 4, 1946.

63. "Mudhakarat al-Ahzab wa-l-Munazzamat," *Sawt al-Sha'b*, January 4, 1946.

64. "Mudhakarat al-Ahzab wa-l-Munazzamat."

65. "Mudhakarat al-Ahzab wa-l-Munazzamat."

66. "Mudhakarat al-Ahzab wa-l-Munazzamat."

67. "Mudhakarat al-Ahzab wa-l-Munazzamat."

68. "Qarar al-Majlis al-Niyabi," *Sawt al-Sha'b*, January 11, 1946; "Zuhur Qadiyyat Lubnan wa-Suriyya fi al-Midan al-Duwali," *Sawt al-Sha'b*, January 25, 1946; "Balagh Rasmi min al-Hukuma al-Lubnaniyya," *Sawt al-Sha'b*, January 31, 1946; "'Ard Qadiyyat al-Jala,'" *Sawt al-Sha'b*, February 7, 1946.

69. Mattison to DoS, no. 89, February 14, 1946, 890E.002/2-1446, NARA.

70. "Majlis al-Amn Yarja' Qarara," *al-Nahar*, February 16, 1946; "Bahth Qadiyyat Lubnan wa-Suriyya," *Sawt al-Sha'b*, February 17, 1946; Ziadeh, *Syria and Lebanon*, 90–91.

71. "Tafasil al-Jalsa al-Akhira," *Sawt al-Sha'b*, February 17–18, 1946; "Majlis al-Amn Yarfud Dun An Yattakhidh Qararan," *al-Nahar*, February 19, 1946; Ziadeh, *Syria and Lebanon*, 91–92.

72. "Akhar Munaqashat Majlis al-Amn," *Sawt al-Sha'b*, February 17–18, 1946; "Vyshinsky Ahbat al-Munawara," *Sawt al-Sha'b*, February 20, 1946.

73. "Hal Bada'at Mufawadat al-Jala' fi Baris," *al-Nahar*, February 26, 1946; Wadsworth to DoS, no. 144, March 15, 1946, 890E.01/3-1546, NARA; "Nuss al-Kitabayn al-Mutabadalayn bayn Beydo wa-Franjiyya," *Sawt al-Sha'b*, March 26, 1946.

74. For example, "Bayan al-Mu'tamar al-Watani," *Sawt al-Sha'b*, February 24, 1946.

75. "Minhaj al-Ihtifal bi-'id al-Jala'," *al-Nahar*, December 31, 1946; "Lubnan fi 'Id Jala' al-Juyush al-Ajnabiyya 'an Ardah," *Sawt al-Sha'b*, January 1, 1947.

76. "Mahrajan al-Jala' fi Lubnan," *al-Nahar*, January 3, 1947.

77. "Speech of the President of the Republic," enclosure no. 1 in Kuniholm to DoS, "Ceremonies Incident to Final Evacuation of Foreign Troops from Lebanon," no. 1436, January 3, 1947, 890E.407.1-341, NARA; "Khitab Ra'is al-Jumhuriyya bi-Yawm al-Jala'," *al-Nahar*, January 3, 1947.

78. "Mahrajan al-Jala' fi Lubnan Yanqalib 'idan Qawmiyyan Ra'i'an."

79. "Haflat al-Najjada fi 'id al-Jala'," *al-Nahar*, January 3, 1947; "'Adad Khas bi-Munsabat Mahrajan al-Munazzama bi-'id al-Jala'," *al-Iman*, January 6, 1947; "Mahrajan al-Hizb al-Shuyu'i Ihtifa' bi-l-Jala'," *Sawt al-Sha'b*, January 5–6, 1947; "Mahrajanan Kabiran li-l-Hizb al-Shuyu'i," *Sawt al-Sha'b*, January 10, 1947.

80. "Marsum 3860 (4/8/1945)," *al-Jarida al-Rasmiyya* 37 (1945): 670–72.

81. Munir Taqi al-Din, "Wizarat al-Difa' al-Watani," in AUB, Department of Public Administration, *Dirasat 'an Hukumat Lubnan: Majmu'at Muhadarat Alqaha Mudirun 'Amun fi al-Hukuma al-Lubnaniyya Talbiya li-Da'wat Da'irat 'Ilm al-Idara al-'Ama fi al-Jami'a al-Amrikiyya fi Bayrut, 1954–1955* (Matba'at Dar al-Funun, 1956) (hereafter *Dirasat 'an Hukumat Lubnan*), 23.

82. Taqi al-Din, "Wizarat al-Difa'," 24–25.

83. Taqi al-Din, "Wizarat al-Difa'," 30.

84. Taqi al-Din, "Wizarat al-Difa'," 30.

85. "The Military Attaché's Annual Report of the Lebanese Armed Forces for 1953," FO 371/110973, TNA.

86. "Annual Appreciation of the Lebanese Armed Forces for 1949," FO 371/82289, TNA.

87. "Military Attaché's Annual Report of the Lebanese Armed Forces for 1953"; "The Military Attaché's Annual Appreciation of the Lebanese Armed Forces for 1954," FO 371/115736, TNA.

88. "Military Attaché's Annual Appreciation of the Lebanese Armed Forces for 1954"; Taqi al-Din, "Wizarat al-Difa'," 27–28.

89. Asad Rustum, "al-Jaysh al-Lubnani: 1945–1950," hand-written manuscript, c. 1951, 10, File 4, Box 36, Series III, Asad Jibiril Rustum Collection, Archives and Special Collections Department, Jafet Memorial Library, American University of Beirut, Beirut, Lebanon.

90. Noahson, "Lebanese Army Code," xxxiii; "Marsum 4298 (13/11/1945)," *al-Jarida al-Rasmiyya* (November 21, 1945): 909–12; Rustum, "al-Jaysh al-Lubnani," hand-written manuscript, 12.

91. Taqi al-Din, "Wizarat al-Difa'," 31.

92. "Al-Hukuma Ta'tamid 5 Malayin Lira li-l-Jaysh," *al-Nahar*, February 3, 1945; Ninth Army to HM Minister Beirut, CO 4169, August 2, 1945, FO 226/295, TNA.

93. "Annual Appreciation of the Lebanese Armed Forces for 1949."

94. Anglo French Joint Staff, decision no. 15, July 24, 1945, FO 226/295, TNA; Ninth Army to HM Minister Beirut, CO 4169, August 2, 1945, FO 226/295, TNA.

95. Noahson, "Lebanese Army Code," xxxiii. For example, see "Isti'naf li-l-Tatawwu' fi al-Jaysh," *al-Nahar*, February 23, 1946; "al-Tatawwu' bi-l-Jaysh al-Lubnani," *Sawt al-Sha'b*, February 25, 1946. For post-1947 examples, see "Li-l-Tatawwu' fi al-Jaysh al-Lubnani," *al-Nahar*, September 16, 1953.

96. "Annual Appreciation of the Lebanese Armed Forces for 1951," FO 371/98542, TNA.

97. "The Military Attaché's Annual Appreciation of the Lebanese Armed Forces for 1954," February 22, 1955, FO 371/115736, TNA.

98. Taqi al-Din, "Wizarat al-Difa'," 23; "Military Attaché's Annual Report of the Lebanese Armed Forces for 1953."

99. For example, see "Isti'naf li-l-Tatawwu' fi al-Jaysh," *al-Nahar*, February 23, 1946.

100. US Army Attaché in Lebanon, "Results of Recruiting for Lebanese Army," September 27, 1951, Box 39, Center for Lebanese Studies, Oxford University.

101. The following discussion draws from Oren Barak, "Towards a Representative Military? The Transformation of the Lebanese Officer Corps Since 1945," *Middle East Journal* 60, no. 1 (2006): 83–84.

102. Noahson, "Lebanese Army Code," 74.

103. For example, see "al-Lajna al-'Adliyya Tadrus al-Tajnid al-Jabri," *al-Nahar*, November 5, 1948; "al-Lajna al-Idariyya wa-l-'Adliyya Tas'al 'an al-Abwab allati

Tusaddid Minha Muwazanat al-Tajnid," *al-Nahar,* November 6, 1948; "Ba'd an 'Ulhim Rijal Lubnan: Hay'atahu al-Nisa'iyya Tutalib bi-l-Tajnid," *al-Nahar,* May 16, 1952. Also see the series "Your Opinion on Conscription" in three consecutive issues of *Sawt al-Mara*: "Ra'yik fi al-Tajnid al-Ibari??," *Sawt al-Mar'a* (January 1949), 16–17; "Ra'yik fi al-Tajnid al-Ibari??," *Sawt al-Mar'a* (February 1949), 20–21 and 41; "Ra'yik fi al-Tajnid al-Ibari??," *Sawt al-Mar'a* (March 1949), 16–17.

104. For example, see Pinkerton to DoS, Telegram 373, July 21, 1949, 890E.20/7–2149, NARA; "SA Strike, Demanding Military Training," *Outlook,* December 22, 1951.

105. Taqi al-Din, "Wizarat al-Difa'," 33.

106. "Al-Tadrib al-'Askari li-l-Tullab al-Thanawiyyin," *al-Nahar,* November 4, 1955; "Military Training Toughens Young University Men," *Outlook,* December 21, 1954.

107. "Al-Tadrib al-'Askari li-l-Tullab al-Thanawiyyin"; "AUB Students Taking Military Training Will Appear in Independence Day Parade," *Outlook,* November 21, 1955.

108. The available sources make exclusive use of the male referent for students (s. *talib,* pl. *tullab*). Furthermore, the Lebanese government failed to institute a civil defense plan into which it could incorporate female students. As late as January 1954, there appears to be a civil defense plan neither in place nor in active development. See FO 371/104512, TNA.

109. Asad Rustum, "al-Jaysh al-Lubnani: 1945–1950," typed manuscript, c. 1951, 30–33, File 4, Box 36, Series III, Rustum Collection; Taqi al-Din, "Wizarat al-Difa'," 24–25.

110. Rustum, "al-Jaysh al-Lubnani," 32–35; Taqi al-Din, "Wizarat al-Difa'," 26–27, 29–31.

111. Rustum, "al-Jaysh al-Lubnani," 20.

112. "Marsum Ishtira'i 33 (19/1/1955)" and "Marsum Ishtira'i 34 (19/1/1955)," both in *al-Majmu'a al-Haditha.*

113. Noahson, "Lebanese Army Code," 1–75.

114. Taqi al-Din, "Wizarat al-Difa'," 34–37.

115. "The Military Attaché's Annual Report of the Lebanese Armed Forces for 1953."

116. Taqi al-Din, "Wizarat al-Difa'," 30–31.

117. For example, the US and British governments established a Foreign Service Institute Arabic Language and Area School in Beirut and Middle East Center for Arabic Studies in Shemlan, respectively. See Robert McClintock (Beirut) to DoS, Despatch 556, "Report on the Middle East Center for Arabic Studies at Shemlan, Lebanon," April 2, 1958, 883A.432/4-258, NARA.

118. See "Annual Appreciation of the Lebanese Armed Forces for 1949," 3; "Annual Appreciation of the Lebanese Armed Forces for 1951," 7; "The Military Attaché's Annual Report of the Lebanese Armed Forces for 1953," 7; "The Military Attaché's Annual Appreciation of the Lebanese Armed Forces for 1954," 6.

119. Irene L. Gendzier, *Notes from the Minefield: United States Intervention in Lebanon and the Middle East, 1945–1958* (Columbia University Press, 1997), 218–24.

120. The following discussion of the LAF during the Nakba draws entirely from Matthew Hughes, "Collusion across the Litani? Lebanon and the 1948 War," in *The War for Palestine*, ed. Eugene L. Rogan and Avi Shlaim (Cambridge University Press, 2007), 204–27. Hughes utilizes contemporaneous Lebanese army war diaries, field reports produced by the Arab Salvation Army, and the memoir of Arab Salvation Army commander Fawzi al-Qawuqji. For the official Lebanese government narrative, see Taqi al-Din, "Wizarat al-Difa'," 31–33.

121. The Arab League sponsored the organization of the Arab Salvation Army as an irregular, multistate, volunteer-based military force under the supervision and direction of the league's Military Committee.

122. Taqi al-Din, "Wizarat al-Difa'," 33–34.

123. On education policies during the mandate period, see Nadya Jeanne Sbaiti, "Lessons in History: Education and the Formation of National Society in Beirut, Lebanon, 1920–1960s" (PhD diss., Georgetown University, 2008).

124. République Française, Ministère des affaires étrangères, *Rapport à la Société des nations sur la situation de la Syrie et du Liban*, 15 vols. (Imprimerie Nationale, 1925–1939) (henceforth cited as *Rapport à la Société*), 1938, 141–42. There were 148 boys' schools and 29 girls' schools, with enrollments of 13,018 and 5,288, respectively.

125. *Rapport à la Société* (1938), 141–42.

126. *Rapport à la Société* (1938), 145–46.

127. *Rapport à la Société* (1938), 147.

128. Raymond Philip Nahhas, "Structure and Behavior of Lebanese Bureaucracy" (MA thesis, AUB, 1963), 96.

129. Nahhas, "Lebanese Bureaucracy," 96.

130. Nahhas, "Lebanese Bureaucracy," 96. Private schools' loss of ground to public schools and some of the causes of this phenomenon were discernable as early as the late 1940s. See Roderic D. Matthews and Matta Akrawi, *Education in Arab Countries of the Near East* (American Council on Education, 1949), 422.

131. On subsidies and other privileges to French and French-allied private schools during the Mandate period, see Elizabeth Thompson, *Colonial Citizens: Republican Rights, Paternal Privilege, and Gender in French Syria and Lebanon* (Columbia University Press, 2000), 60, 63–64. The network of French private schools that had

previously been accorded special status during the mandate "included the schools of the Frères Franciscains; the Alliance Israélite Universelle; the Jesuits, including Université Saint-Joseph; the Lazarists; the Marists; the Maronites; the Carmelites; and Greek Catholic schools like Collège Saint Sauveur in addition to the Sœurs de Besançon, Sœurs de Ste. Famille; École Dames de Nazareth; Collège Sacré-Cœur, and the Mission Laïque Française (MLF) schools." Nadya Sbaiti, "'If the Devil Taught French': Strategies of Language and Learning in French Mandate Beirut," in *Trajectories of Education in the Arab World: Legacies and Challenges*, ed. Osama Abi-Mershed (Routledge, 2009), 64–65.

132. For examples of government financial support, see "Tawzi' al-I'anat 'ala al-Madaris al-Khassa," *al-Nahar*, September 13, 1943; "al-Musa'adat al-Maliyya li-l-Madaris al-Khassa," *al-Nahar*, February 5, 1949; "130 Alf Lira li-I'anat al-Madaris al-Khass," *al-Nahar*, March 10, 1951. For example of private schools demanding a greater share of government spending on education, see *al-Shira'* 3, no. 176 (February 4, 1951), 4.

133. Nahhas, "Lebanese Bureaucracy," 96.

134. Nahhas, "Lebanese Bureaucracy," 96. The precise figures are 110 private secondary schools (both foreign and local) enrolling 20,911 students.

135. For example, see "Marsum 7152/K (15/10/1946)," "Marsum 13962/K (21/12/1948)," and "Marsum 1509 (29/3/1950)," all in *Majmu'at al-Qawanin*.

136. "Marsum 9583 (29/6/1955)," in *al-Jarida al-Rasmiyya* (June 29, 1955): 1035–38.

137. For 1945–46 enrollments, see Matthews and Akrawi, *Education*, 456. For 1953–54 enrollments, see Republic of Lebanon, Ministry of Education and Fine Arts (MoEFA), "The 1953–1954 Annual Report of the Schools, Teachers and Students in Lebanon," unofficial report and preissue copy, January 31, 1955, 18. 1953–54 enrollments in these public vocational schools were distributed as follows: 366 students in Beirut, 79 in Tripoli, 77 in Sidon, and 79 in Zahleh.

138. MoEFA, "1953–1954 Annual Report," 18. That year, there were only 3 private vocational schools outside of Beirut: 2 in Mount Lebanon (enrolling 41 students) and 1 in the Biqa' (enrolling 7 students).

139. Al-Mu'tamar al-Thaqafi al-Awwal, *Lubnan fi 'ahd al-Istiqlal* (Beirut: n.p., 1947), 16; Republic of Lebanon, Ministry of Information, *Lubnan fi 'Ahduh al-Jadid* (Beirut: n.p., 1955), 62; Najib Sadaka, "Wizarat al-Tarbiyya al-Wataniyya wa-l-Funun al-Jamila," in *Dirasat 'an Hukumat Lubnan*, 3, 9–10.

140. Riyad al-Sulh, "al-Bayan al-Wizari," September 25, 1943, in *al-Bayanat al-Wizariyya al Lubnaniyya wa-Munaqashatuha fi Majlis al-Nuwwab, 1927–1984*, vol. 1, *1926–1966*, ed. Yusif Qazma Khuri (Mu'assasat al-Dirasat al-Lubnaniyya, 1986).

141. al-Sulh, "al-Bayan al-Wizari."

142. Thompson, *Colonial Citizens*, 105–10, 143–45, 166–69.

143. "Marja'yun Tutalib bi-Haqqiha fi al-Ta'lim," *Sawt al-Sha'b*, October 3, 1943; "al-Nisa' Uqqaddimun Matalibahum," *al-Nahar*, April 5, 1949; "Matalib Lajnat Huquq al-Mar'a fi Lubnan," *al-Nahar*, March 10, 1953; "Trablus Tutalib bi-Madaris," *al-'Amal*, October 8, 1953; Sadaka, "Wizarat al-Tarbiyya," 7.

144. For example, see "Mashakil al-Ta'lim fi Lubnan," *al-'Amal*, October 14, 1953.

145. These guidelines manifested in three decrees outlining curricula for elementary (Decree #6998), high elementary (#6999), and secondary (#7001) schools; the eligibility for and substance of the Certificat (#7002), Brevet (#7003), and Baccalaureate Part 1 and Part 2 (#7004) examinations; and new regulations governing the opening and operation of private schools (#7000). The government amended the latter regulations in 1950 (#1436).

146. "Marsum 7002 (10/1946)," in *al-Majmu'a al-Haditha*. The mechanics program offered students a specialization in auto mechanics, turning, blacksmithing, welding, foundry, wood carving, or electricity, which encompassed telegraph, telephone, and radio.

147. "Marsum 7003 (10/1946)," in *al-Majmu'a al-Haditha*.

148. "Marsum 7004 (10/1946)," in *al-Majmu'a al-Haditha*.

149. Matthews and Akrawi, *Education*, 441.

150. Matthews and Akrawi, *Education*, 442, 453.

151. Matthews and Akrawi, *Education*, 430–31.

152. Matthews and Akrawi, *Education*, 432.

153. Matthews and Akrawi, *Education*, 435.

154. "Marsum 7000 (1/10/1946)" and "Marsum 1436 (23/3/1950)," both in *Majmu'at al-Qawanin*. Also see Creswell to DoS, no. 1355, "Transmitting Proposed Law Governing Private Schools, Together with Comments," October 17, 1946, 890E.42/10-1746, NARA; Dean G. Acheson (Washington, DC) to American Legation (Beirut), airgram, no. 149, December 30, 1946, 890E.42/10-1746, NARA; Kuniholm to DoS, no. 1500, "The Lebanese Educational Decree no. 7000," February 25, 1947, 890E.42/2-2547, NARA.

155. Articles 14–15 in "Marsum 7000."

156. "Marsum 16316 (20/9/1949)," *al-Jarida al-Rasmiyya* (September 28, 1949): 517–18. Munir Bashshour, *Bunyat al-Nizam al-Tarbawi fi Lubnan* (*Dirasa Naw'iyya*) (Wizarat al-Tarbiyya wa-l-Ta'lim, 1978), 187.

157. "Marsum 7002 (1/10/1946)," "Marsum 7003 (1/10/1946)," and "Marsum 7004 (1/10/1946)," all in *Majmu'at al-Qawanin*.

158. With the exception of janitors, drivers, and office boys (i.e., the lowest category of the civil service hierarchy), the government required those in higher categories to hold specific academic or vocational credentials. Secretaries and clerks had

to hold a Baccalaureate I diploma or its equivalent. More senior administrators had to hold at least a university degree.

159. On the Department of Public Instruction's role in the broader project of French colonial rule in Lebanon, see Sbaiti, "Lessons in History," 45–51.

160. On French language education's centrality to the colonial project in Lebanon, see Sbaiti, "'If the Devil Taught French,'" 59–83.

161. Philippe Takla, Minister of National Education and Fine Arts, to Prime Minister, memo, no. 4199, September 30, 1946, in MoEFA, *Manhaj al-Ta'lim* (n.p., n.d.).

162. Creswell to DoS, "Transmitting Proposed Law Governing Private Schools"; Ruth F. Woodsmall, *Study of the Role of Women: Their Activities and Organizations in Lebanon, Egypt, Iraq, Jordan and Syria (October 1954–August 1955)* (International Federation of Business and Professional Women, 1956), 9.

163. Matthews and Akkari, *Education*, 325–406.

164. "Cultural Treaty of the Arab League, November 20, 1946," republished from *Arab News Bulletin* 2, no. 2 (February 1, 1947) in *Middle East Journal* 1, no. 2 (1947): 207–09.

165. "Hal Tatawahhad Manahij al-Ta'lim fi al-Aqtar al- 'Arabiyya," *al-Nahar*, August 8 and 9, 1946; "al-Tarbiyya al-Wataniyya wa-l-Ikhlaqiyya fi al-Aqtar al-'Arabiyya," *al-Nahar*, August 10, 1946.

166. For example, in 1955 the Lebanese Ministry of Education hosted representatives of member states for a seminar series on education. See "Ghadan Tuftatah Halaqat al-Dirasasat fi al-Unesko," *al-Nahar*, November 2, 1955.

167. See Rajai Abou-Khadra, "UNESCO and the Arab Community" (PhD diss., Indiana University, 1957).

168. "Al-Isti'dadat al-Mu'tamar al-Unesko," *al-Nahar*, November 5, 1948; "Akhbar al- Unesko," *al-Nahar*, November 10, 1948; "Iftitah al-Ma'rad al-Fanni fi Qasr al-Yunesko," *al-Nahar*, December 1, 1948.

169. Herbert J. Abraham, "The General Conference of UNESCO," *World Affairs* 112, no. 1 (1949): 9–10.

170. Reference to the formation and work of the commission is made in "Wizarat al- Ma'arif Tanshur Manahij al-Ta'lim al-Jadida," *al-Nahar*, October 4, 1946; Secondary Schools Principals' Association (SSPA), Executive Committee, "A Preliminary Survey of Secondary Education in Lebanon with Relation to University Training," January 1957, 12–13. Also see Jennifer M. Dueck, *The Claims of Culture at Empire's End: Syria and Lebanon Under French Rule* (Oxford University Press: 2010), 103–11.

171. For example, see "Tawhid Manahij al-Ta'lim," *al-Nahar*, August 4, 1944.

172. "Ijtima' Lijan Tawhid Manahij al-Ta'lim," *al-Nahar*, August 31, 1944.

173. See "Siyasat al-Ta'lim," *al-Nahar*, October 4, 1944.

174. For example, see "Manahij al- Ta'lim wa-Mashyat al-Sulhafat," *al-Nahar*, September 20, 1945; "Islah Manahij al-Ta'lim," *al-Nahar*, August 28, 1946.

175. For example, see Abdallah al-Mashnuq, "Hikayat Manahij al-Ta'lim," lecture delivered in Bayt al-Najjada, December 6, 1944, published as a pamphlet by the Najjada Organization's Department of Education, Sadaka Collection; "Munir Nsuli Yafdah Mahzalat 'Hikayat Manahij al-Ta'lim' li-l-Ustaz Abdallah al-Mashnuq," pamphlet, n.d., Sadaka Collection.

176. For example, see "Wizarat al-Ma'arif Tanshur Manahij al- Ta'lim al-Jadida," *al-Nahar*, October 4, 1946.

177. See Abdullah al-Mashnuq, "The Story of the Curricula of Teaching," included as enclosure no. 2 to Creswell to DoS, "Transmitting Proposed Law Governing Private Schools."

178. "Al-Rabita al-Adabiyya li-l-Ta'lim al-Hurr," *al-Shira'* 3, no. 176 (February 4, 1951), 18; Matthews and Akkari, *Education*, 507; Dueck, *Claims of Culture*, 105–9. In 1951, the league listed Father Ignacius Maroun, principal of Sagesse College, as president; Iliyas Shibl Khuri, principal of the Universal College in 'Alay (al-Kulliyya al-Wataniyya fi 'Alay) as vice president; Badi' Hashim, principal of the National College in Shuwayfat (al-Kulliyya al-Wataniyya fi al-Shuwayfat) as treasurer; and Father Aftimus Skaf of the Catholic Schools (al-Madaris al-Kathalukiyya) as secretary.

179. SSPA, "Preliminary Survey," 5. In 1956, SSPA claimed it comprised thirty-three member schools, with al-Ahliyya School Principal Widad Makdissi Cortas playing a leading role. I thank Nadya Sbaiti for bringing the SSPA to my attention and providing me with a copy of its 1957 report. She discusses them in "Lessons in History," 325–32.

180. "Al-Nuss al-Kamil li-Muqarrarat Mu'tamar al-Ahbar al-Katholik fi Lubnan," *al-Shira'* 3, no. 176 (February 4, 1951): 12–13; "Fi Sabil Huriyyat al-Ta'lim Hifazan 'ala Huquq Muqaddassa," *al-Shira'* 3, no. 176 (February 4, 1951): 16; "al-Rabita al-Adabiyya li-l-Ta'lim al-Hurr," *al-Shira'* 3, no. 176 (February 4, 1951): 18.

181. For example, see "Huququna" *al-Shira'* 3, no. 176 (February 4, 1951): 4.

182. SSPA, "Preliminary Survey," 5. It should be noted that the Ministry of Education provided an exception to the Lebanese Baccalaureate as a condition for admission into the Beirut Women's College and the AUB's College of Arts and Sciences (only). Students entering the medical or engineering school at the AUB were still required to pass both parts of the Lebanese Baccalaureate.

183. SSPA, "Preliminary Survey," 19.

184. "Al-Rabita al-Adabiyya li-l-Ta'lim al-Hurr"; Elizabeth M. Holt, "'Bread or Freedom': The Congress for Cultural Freedom, the CIA, and the Arabic Literary Journal 'Hiwar' (1962–67)," *Journal of Arabic Literature* 44 (2013), 88.

185. SSPA, "Preliminary Survey."

186. Sbaiti, "Lesson in History"; Matthews and Akkari, *Education*, 325–406; Ralph Earl Crow, "The Civil Service of Independent Syria: 1945–58" (PhD diss., University of Michigan, 1964), 133–40.

187. SSPA, "Preliminary Survey," 14.

188. Nejib [Najib] Sadaka, interview by C. J. and R. W., notes, November 19, 1954, 1, Box 30, Woodsmall Papers.

189. MoEFA, "The 1953–1954 Annual Report," 89.

190. MoEFA, "The 1953–1954 Annual Report," 89.

191. "Al-Raghba fi Qubul al-Talamidh Mutawaffira Lada al-Wizara," *al-Nahar*, September 27, 1953; "Mashakil al-Tarbiyya wa-l-Ta'lim," *al-'Amal*, December 5, 1953; Leila Lababidy, Mr. Bustros, and Ms. Bustani, interview by R. W. and C. J., notes, Beirut, November 4, 1954, 1, Box 30, Woodsmall Papers; SSPA, "Preliminary Survey," 46.

192. MoEFA, "1953–1954 Annual Report," 21.

193. For example, see "al-Raghba fi Qubul al-Talamidh Mutawaffira Lada al-Wizara," *al-Nahar*, September 27, 1953.

194. MoEFA, "1953–1954 Annual Report," 23.

195. Sadaka, "Wizarat al-Tarbiyya," 5.

196. Sadaka, "Wizarat al-Tarbiyya," 11.

197. Sadaka, "Wizarat al-Tarbiyya," 8.

198. Sadaka, "Wizarat al-Tarbiyya," 8.

199. MoEFA, "1953–1954 Annual Report," 12.

200. MoEFA, "1953–1954 Annual Report," 91.

201. MoEFA, "1953–1954 Annual Report," 91.

202. Sbaiti, "Lessons in History," 291–305.

203. MoEFA, "1953–1954 Annual Report," 14.

204. MoEFA, "1953–1954 Annual Report," 14.

205. Nejib Sadaka, interview by C. J. and R. W., notes, November 19, 1954, 1.

206. Sbaiti, "Lessons in History," 299.

207. Sbaiti, "Lessons in History," 296, 315–16. Sbaiti points out that the French began to implement this policy in earnest in 1932.

208. MoEFA, "1953–1954 Annual Report," 95–97.

209. MoEFA, "1953–1954 Annual Report," 97.

210. SSPA, "Preliminary Survey," 41.

211. SSPA, "Preliminary Survey," 45.

212. For example, see "Ittihad al-Tullab Yuqati' al-Imtihanat," *al-Nahar*, April 20, 1952. In this respect, there was great continuity between the French colonial period,

the early postindependence period, and the 1960s. See Sbaiti, "Lessons of History," 313–31.

213. The only readily available outcome of this study is the already cited SSPA, "Preliminary Survey."

214. For example, see "Ittihad al-Tullab Yuqati' al-Imtihanat"; "al-Tahqiq fi Qadiyyat al-Bakaloriyya al-Muzzawwara," *al-Nahar*, October 23, 1952; "Qadiyyat al-Bakaloriya wa-Idrab al-Tullab," *al-Nahar*, February 11, 1954; "al-Siyasa allati La'ibat Dawraha fi Da'im al-Idrab wa-l-Tahrid 'Alayh," *al-Nahar*, February 11, 1954; "al-Tullab Yariddun," *al-Nahar*, February 12, 1954.

215. I am drawing on Sara Pursley's argument in her discussion of youth insurgency in Iraq between 1932 and 1958. See Sara Pursley, *Familiar Futures: Time, Selfhood, and Sovereignty in Iraq* (Stanford University Press, 2019), 110–15.

216. "Students Unite," *Outlook*, January 13, 1950; "Council Rejects Union Plan for New Student Cards," *Outlook*, November 25, 1950. The Student Union Committee appears to have existed as early as 1949, and was referred to by AUB student publication *Outlook* as the Lebanese Student Union. It possibly dates back to the 1943–46 student mobilizations that featured an active "Student Committee" (Lajnat al-Tullab). In 1950 the committee's membership included students from the Maqasid and Laïque schools, as well as USJ. The AUB does not appear to have ever been formally represented on the committee.

217. "SC Sends Racy, Sheikh to Talk Over Federation," *Outlook*, March 3, 1951; "New University Federation Now Forming Constitution," *Outlook*, March 17, 1951; "Fed. To Be 'National' not 'Lebanese,'" *Outlook*, April 21, 1951; "President Talhouk Forms Cabinet," Outlook, May 5, 1951; "Federation Elects Executive Committee, *Outlook*, May 12, 1951; "Ittihad al-Talaba al-Jami'iyin," *al-Nahar*, May 13, 1951; "SA Strike, Demand Military Training." Formal deliberations on the creation of the federation appear to have begun in January 1951, in parallel with university students at USJ and ALBA mobilizing in favor of government financial support and the creation of a public university. By March 17, 1951, initial consultations had produced two major decisions: to form the federation as a body independent of—rather than within—the Student Union Committee, and to establish a constitution-drafting committee. ALBA, AUB, and USJ students were represented in these consultations, with at least thirteen faculties from all three schools sending representatives. The constitution was finalized in April–May 1951, with the federation electing its inaugural executive committee on May 10, 1951.

218. See use of the new name to refer to the organization in "Boycott of Cinemas Comes to Abrupt End," *Outloook*, June 2, 1951; "Lajnat Ittihad al-Tullab Tufarriq

la-Tuwahhid," *al-Amal*, February 7, 1952; "Nida' Lajnat Ittihad al-Tullab al-Thanawiyyin," *al-Nahar*, May 6, 1952.

219. Hare to DoS, "Pro-Communist Re-Elected President of Students Union," Despatch 457, February 8, 1954, 783A.001/2-854, NARA.

220. On the AUB and SUC, see "Council Rejects Union Plan for New Student Cards."

221. "SA Strike, Demand Military Training"; Hare to DoS, "Pro-Communist Re-Elected President of Students Union." The vote took place in late December 1951, with supporters of the motion claiming the federation was a mouthpiece of university administrations. Yet by February 1954, the US embassy claimed the two-term president of the federation was pro-Communist and a thorn in the side of the both USJ administration and the Lebanese government.

222. For example, see "Da'wa min Maslahat al-Talaba," *al-Anba'*, October 9, 1954; "al-Nizam al-Asasi li-l-Shabiba al-Ishtirakiyya," *al-Anba'*, October 9, 1954.

223. Mustafa Zayn, "Nida' ila Jami' al-Tullab wa-l-Talibat fi Lubnan," flyer distributed on October 8, 1950, Sadaka Collection; Mustafa Zayn, "Nida' Har ila Jami' al-Tullab wa-l-Talibat fi Luban," flyer distributed on October 15, 1950, Sadaka Collection; Mustafa Zayn, "Nida' Rabitat al-Talaba fi Lubnan," flyer distributed on November 15, 1950, Sadaka Collection. Also see "Mulahaqat 'Rabitat al-Talaba," *al-Nahar*, October 15, 1950.

224. Mustafa Zayn, "Al-Mu'tamar al-Thani li-Ittihad al-Tullab al-'Alami," *al-Tariq* (October 1950): 73–80; J.C.C., "Students in World Politics: The Role of the I.U.S.," *The World Today* 7, no. 8 (1951): 346–56; Philip G. Altbach, "The International Student Movement," *Journal of Contemporary History* 5, no. 1 (1970): 156–74.

225. Hani al-Hindi, *al-Haraka al-Qawmiyya al-'Arabiyya fi al-Qarn al-'Ishrin (Dirasa Siyasiyya)* (Markaz Dirasat al-Wihda al-'Arabiyya, 2012), 89–95.

226. al-Hindi, *al-Haraka al-Qawmiyya al-'Arabiyya fi al-Qarn al-'Ishrin (Dirasa Siyasiyya)*, 91–92.

227. "Lubnan Yatazahar Ta'yiddan li-Masr," *al-Nahar*, October 24, 1951.

228. "Ishtibakan bayn Quwwat al-Amn wa-Mutathahirin min Talabt al-Jami'a," *al-Nahar*, January 27, 1952.

229. "Al-Jami'a Yussawidha Jow Mudtarib," *al-Nahar*, January 29, 1952; "Intiha' Idrab Talabat al-Jami'a al-Amirkiyya," *al-Nahar*, January 30, 1952.

230. "Tullab al-Ja'fariyya fi Sur Yatazaharun Ta'yidan li-Masr," *al-Nahar*, January 29, 1952.

231. "Al-Najjada wa-Hay'at Ukhra Tad'u Bayrut ila al-Idrab wa-Talabat al-Ma'ahid Yunazimun Tazahura Silmiyya Ihtijajiyya," *al-Nahar*, May 16, 1953; "Maynama Kan Tullab al-Ma'hid Yamshun fi Muzahara Silmiyya Ra'i'a," *al-Nahar*, May 17, 1953.

Representatives of eleven schools organized the Beirut student action, including those of the ʿAmaliyya School, Laïque School, and the Maqasid School.

232. These dynamics were part of the lead-up to the 1955 Baghdad Pact, which scholars commonly (erroneously) described as the target of the 1954 AUB student protest. On these dynamics and their relationship to the 1955 Baghdad Pact, see Ara Sanjian, "The Formulation of the Baghdad Pact," *Middle Eastern Studies* 33, no. 2 (1997): 226–66. For footage of the AUB student demonstration, see "Beirut Student Riots (1954)," video, British Pathé, https://www.britishpathe.com/asset/102884/.

233. Betty S. Anderson, *The American University of Beirut* (University of Texas Press, 2011), 142–45.

234. "Al-Tullab Yassirrun ʿala al-Tazahur," *al-Nahar*, March 27, 1954.

235. "Maʿraka Harbiyya maʿ al-Tullab," *al-Nahar*, March 28, 1954.

236. "Al-Hukuma Tasmah bi-Tashyiʿ al-Talib al-Maghdur," *al-Nahar*, March 30, 1954.

237. "Al-Tullab Yaʿlanun al-Idrab," *al-Nahar*, March 30, 1954; "Wazir al-Tarbiyya Yaqtarih ʿutlat al-Rabiʿ," *al-Nahar*, April 1, 1954.

238. "Idrab al-Tullab Yattasiʿ," *al-Nahar*, April 2, 1954; "Idrab al-Tullab Yattasiʿ Huna wa-Yataqallas Hunak," *al-Nahar*, April 3, 1954; "Bi-l-Ragham min Inthaʾ al-Idrab al-Hukuma Tuhaqqiq fi Qadaya al-Tullab," *al-Nahar*, April 6, 1954.

239. Carla Eddé, *L'USJ, Portrait d'une université* (Presses de l'Université Saint-Joseph, 2000).

240. Anderson, *American University of Beirut*.

241. Marie Aziz Sabri, *Pioneering Profiles: Beirut College for Women* (St. Paul's Printing Press, 1967), 18–38; Ellen Fleischmann, "'Under an American Roof': The Beginnings of the American Junior College for Women," *Arab Studies Journal* 17, no. 1 (2009): 62–84; Catherine Wadad Batruni, "Producing Pioneers: The American Junior College for Women and the Beirut College for Women, 1924–1973" (PhD diss., AUB, 2019).

242. "Al-Akadimiyya al-Lubnaniyya," *al-Nahar*, September 22, 1945; Wadad Makdisi Cortas, *A World I Loved: The Story of an Arab Woman* (Bold Type Books, 2009), 104–6.

243. "New President," *Outlook*, November 25, 1949; "Council Meeting," *Outlook*, December 22, 1949; "To Students," *Outlook*, December 22, 1949. In one instance, 156 students signed a petition demanding that the Student Council attend to the matter of tuition, book prices, and room and board fees.

244. "Open Letter," *Outlook*, December 16, 1950; "Restaurant Committee Submits Final Report—Fees Reduced 10 L.L. a Month," *Outlook*, January 13, 1950; "Council Meets; Students Shout: President Penrose Promises Further Reductions," *Outlook*,

January 20, 1950; "Saadi Walks Out," *Outlook*, January 27, 1950; "Bayan ila Tullab wa-Talibat al-Jami'a al-Amirkiyya fi Bayrut," flyer signed by Abdul Halim Saadi, c. 1950, Sadaka Collection.

245. "'Further Reductions' Denied," *Outlook*, January 27, 1950; "'Demonstrations Undermine Council'—President Penrose," *Outlook*, January 27, 1950; "Campus Battleground Purrs Quietly," *Outlook*, February 17, 1950.

246. "Idrab Tullab al-Yasu'iyya," *al-Hayat*, January 23, 1951.

247. "Idrab Tullab al-Madaris al-'Ulya Yattasi'," *al-Hayat*, January 24, 1951.

248. "Talhouk Stands Hot Questioning," *Outlook*, February 24, 1951; "Tullab al-Jami'a al-Amirkiyya Yuhaddidun Mawqifahum min Harakat Zumala'ihim," *al-Nahar*, February 9, 1951. Also see "Rise and Fall of Student Council," *Outlook*, May 16, 1966, 6.

249. "Al-Tullab al-Mudribun Yatazaharun," *al-Hayat*, January 31, 1951.

250. "Al-Talaba Yalqun 'ala al-Sulta Darsan fi al-Tadamun," *al-Nahar*, February 6, 1951.

251. "Al-Talaba Yalqun 'ala al-Sulta Darsan fi al-Tadamun."

252. "Al-Talaba Yalqun 'ala al-Sulta Darsan fi al-Tadamun."

253. "Al-Talaba Yalqun 'ala al-Sulta Darsan fi al-Tadamun."

254. "Majlis al-Wuzara' Yullabi Raghbat al-Talaba fa-Yaqqir Insha' al-Jami'a al-Wataniyya," *al-Nahar*, February 6, 1951.

255. "Majlis al-Wuzara' Yullabi Raghbat al-Talaba," *al-Nahar*, February 6, 1951.

256. "Khilaf fi Sufuf al-Talaba," *al-Nahar*, 8 February 1951; "al-Tullab Thalat Ara'," *al-Hayat*, February 10, 1951.

257. "Al-Tullab Yanhun Idrabahim wa-Ya'udun ila Durusihim," *al-Nahar*, February 13, 1951.

258. "Al-Majlis Yuwafiq 'Ala Insha' al-Jami'a al-Wataniyya," *al-Nahar*, February 14, 1951.

259. "Marsum 6267 (20/11/1951)," *al-Jarida al-Rasmiyya* (October 24, 1951): 600–605.

260. "Marsum Ishtira'i 25 (25/2/1953)," *al-Jarida al-Rasmiyya* (February 18, 1953): 232–85.

261. "Marsum Ishtira'i 212 (31/8/1942)," in Naqabat al-Mu'allimin, *Majmu'at al-Qawanin al-Muta'alliqa bi-Tanzim al-Hay'a al-Ta'limiyya fi al-Madaris al-Khassa fi Lubnan min Sanat 1942 ila Sanat 1968*, 1968, 9–16, Sadaka Collection.

262. Naqabat al-Mu'allimin, "Mashru' Qanun al-Mu'allimin fi al-Madaris al-Khassa," June 13, 1946, Sadaka Collection.

263. Majlis Naqabat al-Mu'allimin, "Bayan ila Mu'allimi al-Madaris al-Khassa fi al-Jumhuriyya al-Lubnaniyya," March 21, 1947, Sadaka Collection.

264. Naqabat al-Mu'allimin, *Nabdha fi Tarikh al-Naqaba*, c. 1957–58, 8, Sadaka Collection; "Teachers United," *Outlook*, December 22, 1949.

265. Majlis Naqabat al-Mu'allimin, "Matalib al- Mu'allimin wa-l-Mu'allimat fi al-Madaris al-Khassa fi al-Jumhuriyya al-Lubnaniyya," October 14, 1950, Sadaka Collection.

266. Majlis Naqabat al-Mu'allimin, "Matalib al-Mu'allimin wa-l-Mu'allimat"; "al-Naqaba Tada' al-Mushkila bayn Aydi al-Jam'iyya al-'Umumiyya," *al-Nahar*, October 19, 1950.

267. "Ta'yid Matalib al-Mu'allimin, *al-Nahar*, November 2, 1950; "Mudirat al-Kulliyya al-Ahliyya Tu'ayyid al-Mu'allimin," *al-Nahar*, November 8, 1950; "Mu'allimu al-Yasu'iyya Yu'ayyidun Naqabatahum," *al-Nahar*, November 9, 1950.

268. Majlis Naqabat al-Mu'allimin, "Bayan ila al-Mu'allimat wa-l-Mu'allimin fi al-Madaris al-Khassa fi al—Jumhuriyya al-Lubnaniyya," November 2, 1950, Sadaka Collection.

269. "Ashab al-Madaris Yatabanuna Qadiyyat al-Mu'allim," *al-Nahar*, November 16, 1950.

270. "Ashab al-Madaris Yatabanuna Qadiyyat al-Mu'allim." The fourteen schools were the Education College in Tripoli (Kulliyyat al-Tarbiyya wa-l-Ta'lim fi Trablus), al-Maqasid School in Sidon (Madrasat al-Maqasid fi Sayda), Universal College 'Alay (al-Jami'a al-Watania 'Alay), National College Shuwayfat (al-Kulliyya al-Watania al-Shuwayfat), Lebanese School Suq al-Gharb (al-Kulliyya al-Lubnaniyya Suq al-Gharb), Sisters of the Holy Heart School (Madrasat Rahibat al-Qalbin al-Aqdasin), Islamic Orphanage School (Dar al-Aytam al-Islamiyya), al-Maqasid School in Beirut (al-Maqasid fi Bayrut), al-Ahliyya School for Girls (Kulliyyat al-Banat al-Ahliyya), Sagesse Institute (Ma'had al-Hikma), Kfar Shima National School (Madrasat Kufr Shima al-Wataniyya), Basilian Oriental College in Zahleh (al-Kulliyya al-Sharqiyya Zahleh), College of the Apostle in Juniya (Madrasat al-Rusul Juniya), and College of the Three Doctors (Kulliyyat al-Thalathat al-Aqmar).

271. "Matalib al-Mu'allimin bayn al-Hukuma wa-Arbab al-Madaris," *al-Nahar*, December 1, 1950.

272. "Al-Mu'allimun Yandhirun al-Hukuma," *al-Nahar*, November 21, 1951; "Ba'd an Haddad al-Mu'allimun al-Idrab wa-Ayadahum al-Talaba," *al-Nahar*, December 3, 1950; "Bayan ila al-Mu'allimin wa-l-Mu'allimat," *al-Nahar*, December 15, 1950; "Naqabat al-Mu'allimin Tashkur al-Sultat," *al-Nahar*, December 22, 1950. The syndicate issued two strike threats that were ultimately averted, one scheduled for December 3 and another for December 18.

273. "Wa-Akhar Dawa' . . . al-Idrab 'an 'Amalak," *al-Nahar*, February 11, 1951.

274. "Mu'allimu al-Madaris al-Madaris Yatawaqafun 'an al-'Amal Yowman Wahidan," *al-Nahar*, February 17, 1951.

275. "Al-Mu'allimin Yu'ajilun Idrabahum li-l-'Arbi'a'," *al-Hayat*, February 25, 1951.

276. "Qararat al-Mu'allimin Turfa' li-l-Sulutat," *al-Nahar*, February 27, 1951.

277. "Al-Majlis Yaqur bi-l-Ijma' Mashru' Qanun al-Mu'allimin," *al-Nahar*, February 28, 1951.

278. For example, see "Bayan min Naqabat al-Mu'allimin al-Lubnaniyyin," *al-Nahar*, May 29, 1952. For the outcome of these meetings and the new system they put in place, see MoEFA, *Majmu'at Ta'limat wa-Tafsirat Sadira 'an Wizaratay al-'Adl wa-l-Tarbiyya wa-l-Ta'lim*, August 26, 1952, Sadaka Collection.

279. "Naqabat al-Mu'allimin Tutalib al-Sulatat bi-Wad' Qanun Jadid," *al-Nahar*, October 21, 1953.

280. See Naqabat al-Mu'allimin, *Qanun Tanzim al-Hay'a al-Ta'limiyya fi al-Ma'ahid al-Khassa* (Matba'at Sadir, 1956).

281. "Mu'allimu al-Madaris Ya'linun al-Idrab idha Lam Yanalu Matalibahum," *al-Nahar*, November 24, 1954; "Mu'allimu al-Madaris al-Khassa Yudhakkirun al-Hukuma," *al-Nahar*, June 25, 1955; "Matalib Naqabat al-Mu'allimin," *al-Nahar*, October 27, 1955; "Matalib Naqabat al-Mu'allimin bi-Lajnat al-Tarbiyya," *al-Nahar*, June 30, 1955.

282. Naqabat al-Mu'allimin, "Min Naqabat al-Mu'allimin ila Awliya' al-Talaba fi al-Madaris al-Khassa," flyer, October 30, 1955, Sadaka Collection; Naqabat al-Mu'allimin, "Bayan ila al-Mu'allimat wa-l-Mu'allimin fi al-Madaris al-Khassa," flyer, November 1, 1955, Sadaka Collection; "Wazir al-Tarbiyya Yufawid al-Mu'allimin 'ala Asas Ta'liq al-Idrab," *al-Nahar*, November 2, 1955; "al-Mu'allimun Madun fi Idrabihum al-Samit," *al-Nahar*, November 3, 1955; "al-Mu'allimun Yu'ajilun Idrabihum 4 Asabi'," *al-Nahar*, November 4, 1955.

Chapter 4

1. Heath to DoS, "Celebration of May 1 in Lebanon; Views of ICFTY Representative Boudali on Lebanese Labor Movement," Despatch 652, May 13, 1955, 783A.00-MAY DAY/5-1355, NARA.

2. Heath to DoS, "Celebration of May 1 in Lebanon."

3. Heath to DoS, "Celebration of May 1 in Lebanon."

4. "Ihtifalat al-Hizb al-Taqaddumi al-Ishtiraki bi-'Id Awwal Ayar," *al-Anba'*, May 6, 1955; Heath to DoS, "Celebration of May 1 in Lebanon."

5. "Khitab Kamal Jumblat bi-Mahrajan 'Alay," *al-Anba'*, May 6, 1955.

6. "Majlis al-Amn Yasta'rid Halat al-Amn," *al-Nahar*, May 1, 1955.

7. "Majlis al-Amn Yasta'rid Halat al-Amn"; "Ba'dama Ahbat Rijal al-Amn Muhawalat al-Shuyu'iyyin Hafalat Awwal Ayyar," *al-Nahar*, May 3, 1955.

8. "Ta'til Yawm al-Ithnayn Lam Yakun fi al-Hisabat," *al-Nahar,* May 3, 1955.

9. Couland, *al-Haraka al-Naqabiyya,* 95–335; al-Buwari, *Tarikh al-Haraka,* 98–209; Elizabeth Thompson, *Colonial Citizens: Republican Rights, Paternal Privilege, and Gender in French Syria and Lebanon* (Columbia University Press, 2000), 100–103, 156–63, 229–30, 235–243; Malek Abisaab, *Militant Women of a Fragile Nation* (Syracuse University Press, 2010), 12–63.

10. See République Française, Ministère des affaires étrangères, *Rapport à la Société des nations sur la situation de la Syrie et du Liban,* 15 vols. (Imprimerie Nationale, 1925–1939) (henceforth cited as *Rapport à la Société*); Fuad Abu-Izziddin and George Hakim, "A Contribution to the Study of Labour Conditions in the Lebanon," *International Labour Review* 28 (1933): 673–82; "Working Conditions in Handicrafts and Modern Industry in Syria," *International Labour Review* 29 (1934): 407–11; "Conditions of Work in Syria and the Lebanon under French Mandate," *International Labour Review* 39 (1939): 513–26.

11. *Rapport à la Société* (1925), 44–54; "Conditions of Work in Syria and the Lebanon," 517.

12. A 1926 amendment to the Ottoman Law of Associations empowered the cabinet to dissolve any formal group that violated the stipulations of the law. See "Ta'dil Qanun al-Jam'iyyat, 26 Ayar 1926," in *Majmu'at Qawanin wa-Marasim Hukumat al-Jumhuriyya al-Lubnaniyya, May 1926–January 1929,* vol. 1 (Adab, 1931), 270. A 1934 law built on Ottoman-legislated controls on workers, replacing the post-1912 Ottoman guild-like organizational form (*naqabat al-asnaf*) with what many contemporaries and later researchers have translated as "professional associations" (*naqabat al-hiraf wa-l-mihan*). See "Qarar 294 LR (20/1/1934)" in *Majmu'at al-Qawanin.*

13. According to the International Labor Organization (ILO), the High Commission first conducted a significant study of "conditions of work" in 1937, the results of which it included *Rapport à la Société* (1938). "Conditions of Work in Syria and the Lebanon," 514.

14. Thompson, *Colonial Citizens,* 156–60.

15. Thompson, *Colonial Citizens,* 159; al-Buwari, *Tarikh al-Haraka,* 230.

16. Carolyn L. Gates, *The Merchant Republic of Lebanon: Rise of an Open Economy* (I. B. Tauris, 1998), 35–42, 46–50, 57–58.

17. Thompson, *Colonial Citizens,* 236–38.

18. "Qarar bi-Insha' al-Makhazin al-Ta'awuniyya," *Bayrut,* March 24, 1943.

19. *Rapport à la Société* (1939), 27; "Marsum 203," *al-Jarida al-Rasmiyya* (January 30, 1943): 10856–57.

20. Kuniholm to DoS, "The Anti-Communist Labor Movement in Lebanon," no. 115, March 3, 1947, 890E.504/3-347, NARA, 7.

21. Kuniholm to DoS, "The Anti-Communist Labor Movement in Lebanon."

22. "Marsum Ishtira'i 29/ET (12/5/1943)," in *Majmu'at al-Qawanin.*

23. Thompson argues the cornerstone of the transformation to a colonial welfare state in Lebanon was the establishment of "basic social rights to health, education, and job security in the form of both legal protections and fiscal commitments from the state." See Thompson, *Colonial Citizens*, 167.

24. Ilham Khuri-Makdisi, *The Eastern Mediterranean and the Making of Global Radicalism, 1860–1914* (University of California Press, 2010), 107; Fu'ad al-Shimali, *Naqabat al-'Ummal* (Beirut: n.p., 1929), republished as part of Fu'ad al-Shimali, *Kitabat Majhula* (Dar al-Mada, 2001), 118–21.

25. Mustafa al-Aris, *Mustafa al-Aris Yatadhakkar* (Dar al-Farabi, 1982), 43.

26. "Al-Ihtifal bi-Awwal Ayyar," *Sawt al-Sha'b*, May 6, 1942.

27. "Ihtifal Bayrut bi-Yawm Awwal Ayyar," *Sawt al-Sha'b*, May 5, 1943.

28. "Al-'Ummal fi Bayan al-Wizari," *Sawt al-Sha'b*, October 24, 1943.

29. This was particularly so with the workers in the tobacco and electricity sectors. For example, see Abisaab, *Militant Women*, 22–29, 42–46.

30. The role of workers in the 1936 Bint Jubayl revolt is one example. See Malek Abisaab, "Shiite Peasants and a New Nation in Colonial Lebanon: The Intifada of Bint Jubayl, 1936," *Comparative Studies of South Asia, Africa, and the Middle East* 29, no. 3 (2009): 483–501.

31. "Nida' min Mumaththili Naqabat wa-Jam'iyyat al-'Ummal," *Sawt al-Sha'b*, August 26, 1943; al-Buwari, *Tarikh al-Haraka*, 205–6.

32. "Naqabat al-Sawwaqin wa-l-Intikhabat al-Niyabiyya," *Sawt al-Sha'b*, July 10, 1943.

33. "Kayf Sawwat al-Lubnaniyyun Ams," *Sawt al-Sha'b*, September 1, 1943.

34. "Sha'b Lubnan Yahruz Intisaran Wataniyya Ra'i'an," *Sawt al-Sha'b*, November 26, 1943; "al-Ayyam al-'Ashra al-Majida fi Tarikh Lubnan," *Sawt al-Sha'b*, Novemnber 26, 1943; "al-Haraka al-Wataniyya al-Lubnaniyya Tussajil Awwal Intisarataha," *Sawt al-Sha'b*, November 27, 1943; "al-Haraka al-Wataniyya Tu'allaf Bayna Jami' al-Lubnaniyyin," *Sawt al-Sha'b*, November 28, 1943.

35. Thompson, *Colonial Citizens*, 158–61, 237–38.

36. "Ummal al-Masani' fi Dawahi Bayrut," *Sawt al-Sha'b*, January 2, 1944.

37. Couland, *al-Haraka al-Naqabiyya*, 265–68.

38. Couland, *al-Haraka al-Naqabiyya*, 331.

39. "Wafd Naqabat al-'Ummal wa-l-Mustakhdamin Yuqabil Ma'ali Ra'is al-Wizara" *Sawt al-Sha'b*, October 31, 1943.

40. "Wafd Naqabat al-'Ummal wa-l-Mustakhdamin Yuqabil Ma'ali Ra'is al-Wizara."

41. "Naqabat al-'Ummal Tarfa' Matalib li-l-Hukuma," *Sawt al-Sha'b*, January 30, 1944.

42. *Sawt al-Sha'b*, April 28, 1944.

43. "Mustafa al-'Aris Yabrik," *Sawt al-Sha'b*, January 7, 1946.

44. "Mustafa al-Aris: Muqabala ma' Radiyu Uryan," *Sawt al-Sha'b*, April 4, 1944; "Awwal Ayar: Yawm Ittihad," *Sawt al-Sha'b*, May 4, 1944.

45. *Sawt al-Sha'b*, July 10, 1943; *Sawt al-Sha'b*, July 30, 1943.

46. "Qanun (30/9/1944)," *Majmu'at al-Qawanin*.

47. See relevant issues of *al-Nahar* and *Sawt al-Sha'b*.

48. See relevant issues of *al-Nahar* and *Sawt al-Sha'b*.

49. The following account draws from "I'tida' Jadid min Rijal al-Darak," *Sawt al-Sha'b*, July 25, 1945; "Ba'd I'tida' al-Darak," *Sawt al-Sha'b*, July 27, 1945; "Qadiyyat 'Ummal Ma'mal al-Jawf fi al-Hazmiyya," *Sawt al-Sha'b*, August 1, 1945; "'Ummal Ma'mal al-Jawkh La Yazalun bi-l-Sijn," *Sawt al-Sha'b*, August 5, 1945; "Qadiyyat 'Ummal wa-'Amilat Ma'mal al-Jawkh," *Sawt al-Sha'b*, August 10, 1945; "al-Hukuma wa-Matalib 'Ummal al-Jawkh," *Sawt al-Sha'b*, August 15, 1945; "Qadiyyat 'Ummal Ma'mal al-Hazmiyya," *Sawt al-Sha'b*, August 16, 1945; "'Ummal Ma'mal al-Ajwakh wa-'Amilatuh," *Sawt al-Sha'b*, September 26, 1945; "'Ummal al-Hazmiyya Mazalu Mudribin," *Sawt al-Sha'b*, September 27, 1945; "Qadiyyat 'Ummal al-Hazmiyya la tazal 'Arda li-l-Mumatala wa-l-Tassaruf," *Sawt al-Sha'b*, October 24, 1945.

50. "Wa-Akhiran Hullit Qadiyyat 'Ummal al-Hazmiyya," *Sawt al-Sha'b*, November 16, 1945.

51. For example, see its role in the 1945 National Wool Company strike in above referenced sources.

52. "Wafd Naqabat al-'Ummal wa-l-Mustakhdamin Yuqabil Ma'ali Ra'is al-Wizara," *Sawt al-Sha'b*, October 31, 1943.

53. M. T. Audsley, "Brief Notes Regarding My Visit to Beirut and Damascus From 11th to 17th May, and the Subsequent Developments as Reported by the Commercial Secretary, His Majesty's Legation, Beirut, June 20, 1946, LAB 13/590, TNA. It was a legal expert in the Ministry of Justice, Anis Saleh, that apparently spearheaded the drafting of the law and the selective incorporation of feedback given to him.

54. "Qanun al-'Amal al-Ladhi 'Uhil li-l-Majlis," *Sawt al-Sha'b*, July 24, 1945; "Tashri' al-Naqabat al-Jadid," November 14, 1945.

55. "Lajnat al-Naqabat Tadrus Tashri' al-'Amal," *Sawt al-Sha'b*, November 21, 1945; "Karras Naqabi Jadid," *Sawt al-Sha'b*, January 20, 1946; al-Buwari, *Tarikh al-Haraka*, 262–63.

56. For example, see "Shu'un al-'Ummal," *Sawt al-Sha'b*, February 11, 1946; "Matalib 'Ummal Lubnan," *Sawt al-Sha'b*, March 14, 1946.

57. Foreign Office, Research Department, "Trade Unions in the Middle East," July 1945, 14–16, FO 1018/46, TNA.

58. Couland, *al-Haraka al-Naqabiyya*, 404–7.

59. That was primarily due to the involvement of the syndicates of bank employees, commercial employees, and drivers.

60. Far'un was closely connected to President al-Khuri through a number of connections, most notably as the banking partner of his brother-in-law.

61. For example, the government provided the Syndicate of Commercial Employees a copy of the draft labor law long before it did so to the FWES.

62. For example, see "Jabhat al-'Amal Tas'a li-Insaf al-'Ummal," *al-Nahar*, June 4, 1946.

63. For example, see "Matalb Jabhat al-'Amal," *al-Nahar*, March 2, 1946; "Min Jabhat al-'Amal ila al-Majli al-Niyabi," *al-Nahar*, June 7, 1936. The front's primary intervention into the draft labor law was through written commentary submitted to the government in May 1946.

64. See "Hadith Mustafa al-Aris," *Sawt al-Sha'b*, May 6, 1946; "al-'Ummal al-Lubnaniyyun," *Sawt al-Sha'b*, May 6, 1946; "Wihdat al-Haraka al-Naqabiyya," July 11, 1946.

65. "Shu'un al 'Ummal," *Sawt al-Sha'b*, February 10, 1946.

66. "Ijtima' Ham li-l-Mutalaba bi-Qanun al-'Amal," *Sawt al-Sha'b*, February 17–18, 1946.

67. Wadsworth to DoS, "Minimum Wage Legislation in Recent Strikes; A Study of Legal and Political Imponderables in Newly-Independent Lebanon," 1297, August 13, 1946, 890E.5045/8-1346, NARA, 1–5.

68. "Qanun (30/9/1944)," in *Majmu'at Qawanin*.

69. For example, see "Shu'un al-'Ummal," *Sawt al-Sha'b*, February 17, 1946.

70. For example, see "Matalib 'Ummal wa-Muwazzafi al-Sharika Dhawat al-Imtiyaz," *Sawt al-Sha'b*, February 25, 1946; "'Ummal al-Sharikat Dhuwat al-Imtiyaz," *Sawt al-Sha'b*, February 26, 1946.

71. "'Ummal al-Sharikat al-Ajnabiyya," *Sawt al-Sha'b*, February 17, 1946.

72. "'Ummal al-Sharika Dhuwat al-Imtiyaz," *Sawt al-Sha'b*, April 10, 1946.

73. "Qarar Gharib Jadid li-Wizarat al-Dakhiliyya," *Sawt al-Sha'b*, April 12, 1946; Wadsworth to DoS, A-69, April 12, 1946, 890E.5045/4-1246, NARA.

74. "Yajib Hal Mushkilat al-'Ummal bi-Tahqiq Matalibahim al-Mashru'a," *Sawt al-Sha'b*, April 11, 1946; Wadsworth to DoS, A-69, April 12, 1946.

75. "Idrab 'Ummal al-Kahruba' fi Yawmih al-Awwal," *Sawt al-Sha'b*, April 14–15, 1946; "Intisar 'Ummal al-Tramway wa-l-Kahruba'," *Sawt al-Sha'b*, May 5–6, 1946.

76. "Al-Sha'b Yu'ayyid 'Ummal al-Kahruba," *Sawt al-Sha'b*, April 21, 1946.

77. "Wazir al-Dakhiliyya Yata'arrad li-Hujum al-Nuwwab al-'Anif," *Sawt al-Sha'b*, April 14, 1946; "al-Nuwwab Yashjubun Waqif Wazir al-Dakhiliyya min al-'Ummal," *Sawt al-Sha'b*," April 17, 1946.

78. "Wazir al-Dakhiliyya Yughalit bi-Bayanah,'" *Sawt al-Sha'b*, April 19, 1946.

79. "Qanun (27/5/1946)," in *Majum'at al-Qawanin*.

80. "Idrab 'Ummal al-Tramway wa-Matalibuhum," *Sawt al-Sha'b*, May 1, 1946; Wadsworth to DoS, "Minimum Wage Legislation," 7–8.

81. "Intisar 'Ummal al-Tramway wa-l-Kahruba'," *Sawt al-Sha'b*, May 5–6, 1946; Wadsworth to DoS, "Minimum Wage Legislation,", 8–9.

82. "al-'Ummal wa-Tashri' al-'Amal," *Sawt al-Sha'b*, May 5–6, 1946.

83. "Kayfa Inqada Awwal Ayyar fi Lubnan," *Sawt al-Sha'b*, May 4, 1946; "Naqabat al-'Ummal wa-l-Mustakhdamin Tuqarrir I'lan al-Idrab al-'Am al-Ithnayn 20 Ayyar," *Sawt al-Sha'b*, May 18, 1946.

84. "Idrab Juz'i Yadum 'Iddat Sa'at," *al-Nahar*, May 21, 1946.

85. "Al-Munaqasha Ams fi Qanun al-'Amal," *al-Nahar*, May 18, 1946; "Ijtima' al-Lajna al 'Adliyya al-Niyabiyya ma' Mumathili Naqabat al-'Ummal," *Sawt al-Sha'b*, May 19, 1946.

86. Al-Aris, *Mustafa al-Aris*, 179–80.

87. "Al-Munaqasha Ams fi Qanun al-'Amal."

88. "Idrab Juz'i Yadum 'Iddat Sa'at," *al-Nahar*, May 21, 1946; "Idrab Mu'ajjal wa-Idrab Mu'ajjal," *al-Nahar*, May 22, 1946; Sadir Yunis, "Mouvement syndical au Liban," *Le Jour*, August 12, 1965.

89. "Safar al-Ra'is fi Majlis al-Nuwwab," *al-Nahar*, May 29, 1946; "Qanun al-'Amal fi Majlis al-Nuwwab," *al-Nahar*, May 30, 1946; "Munaqashat Qanun al-'Amal," *Sawt al-Sha'b*, May 30, 1946; "Mashru' Qanun al-'Amal fi Lubnan," *al-Nahar*, June 7, 1946; "Mutaba'at Dars Mashru' Qanun al-'Amal," *Sawt al-Sha'b*, June 7, 1946.

90. "Mushkilat Ujur 'Ummal al-Tramway," *al-Nahar*, June 1–2, 1946; Wadsworth to DoS, "Minimum Wage Legislation in Recent Strikes," 11–12.

91. "Ujur 'Ummal al-Tramway," *al-Nahar*, May 31, 1946.

92. "Bayn al-'Ummal wa-l-Hukuma," June 14, 1946.

93. "Idrab Mustakhdimi wa-'Ummal al-Rejji," *al-Nahar*, June 12, 1946.

94. Abisaab, *Militant Women*, 29.

95. "Al-Idrabat fi Bayrut," *al-Nahar*, June 18, 1946; "Idrabat al-'Ummal," *Sawt al-Sha'b*, June 26, 1946; Wadsworth to DoS, "Minimum Wage Legislation in Recent Strikes," 7.

96. "Idrab Muwwazafi al-Rayji wa-l-Kahruba'," *al-Nahar*, June 15, 1946; Wadsworth to DoS, "Minimum Wage Legislation in Recent Strikes," 13.

97. "Intiha' Idrab 'Ummal al-Kahruba'," *al-Nahar*, June 21, 1946.

98. "Wa-Akhiran 'Ada al-Nur ila Bayrut," *al-Nahar,* June 20, 1946.

99. Wadsworth to DoS, "Minimum Wage Legislation in Recent Strikes," 13.

100. Wadsworth to DoS, "Minimum Wage Legislation in Recent Strikes," 13.

101. "Wa-Akhiran 'Ada al-Nur"; Wadsworth to DoS, "Minimum Wage Legislation in Recent Strikes," 13.

102. "Fashal al-Masa'i wa-l-Mufawadat li-Hal al-Idrabat," *al-Nahar,* July 10, 1946; "Ma'arik Jadida min Ajl al-Sikara," *al-Nahar,* July 11, 1946; Wadsworth to DoS, "Minimum Wage Legislation in Recent Strikes," 14.

103. "Mustakhdimu al-Sikka Yuwasilun al-Idrab," *al-Nahar,* July 11, 1946; Wadsworth to DoS, "Minimum Wage Legislation in Recent Strikes," 14.

104. "Wazir al-Dakhiliyya Yusadir al-'Ummal idha lam Ya'udun ila al-'Amal," *al-Nahar,* July 11, 1946.

105. "Mustakhdimu al-Sikka Yuwasilun al-Idrab"; "al-Idrabat la Tazal Mustamirra," *al-Nahar,* July 12, 1946; Wadsworth to DoS, "Minimum Wage Legislation in Recent Strikes," 14.

106. For an account that incorporates oral history interviews, see Abisaab, *Militant Women*, 75–77

107. "Ba'd Itlaq al-Darak Risasahim 'ala al- 'Ummal wa-l-'Amilat al-'Azl min al-Silah," *Sawt al-Sha'b,* June 30, 1946; Wadsworth to DoS, "Minimum Wage Legislation in Recent Strikes," 14.

108. Abisaab, *Militant Women*, 77; Malek Abisaab, "Nisa' Halmna Butun: Warda Butrus Ibrahim, Ayqunat al-Jumhuriyya al-Lubnaniyya al-Ula," *al-Adab*, February 17, 2017.

109. "Idrab 'Ummal al-Kahruba' bi-Homs wa-Hama," *al-Nahar,* July 11, 1946; "al-Idrabat wa-l-Musadarat bi Halab," *al-Nahar,* July 12, 1946.

110. "Mahkamat al-'Amal Tanqid al-Hukm li-Maslahat al-Sharika," *al-Nahar,* July 12, 1946.

111. "Al-Idrabat La Tazal Mustamirra," *al-Nahar,* July 12, 1946; "'Ummal al-Rayji Ya'udun li-l-'Amal?," *al-Nahar,* July 13, 1946.

112. "Intaha al-Idrab al-Hamd li-Allah,"*al-Nahar,* July 16, 1946.

113. "Asbab Idrab Muwazafi Bank al-Isdar," *al-Nahar,* August 7, 1946; "Thalathat Idrabat fi al-Madina," *al-Nahar,* August 22, 1946.

114. Nsuli primarily provided this support through editorials in his *Beirut.* For examples, see issues of April 30, May 18, and July 6, 1946.

115. Malek Abisaab argues that in the absence of the security forces' murder of Wadra Butrus, the labor code would not have passed for many years. While I am sympathetic to this argument, I believe it overlooks the extent of labor militancy at this time and the growing pressure it constituted on the Lebanese parliament,

cabinets, and president as well as their allies in the US and UK diplomatic missions. For Abisaab's argument, see his "Nisa' Halmna Butun: Warda Butrus Ibrahim, Ayqunat al-Jumhuriyya al-Lubnaniyya al-Ula," *al-Adab*, February 17, 2017.

116. "Mulahazat Ashab al-Hiraf," *al-Nahar*, March 20, 1946.

117. Terrance Shone (Beirut), Minute 105/29/46, June 1, 1946, FO 371/52492, TNA.

118. See W. Harpham (Beirut Legation Commercial Secretary) to M. T. Audsley (Cairo), CS.109/2-46, June 10, 1946; Audsley, "Brief Notes Regarding My Visit to Beirut and Damascus"; M. T. Audsley (Labor Advisor, Cairo) to HAN Brown (Ministry of Labour and National Service London), July 26, 1946.

119. Wadsworth to DoS, A-88, May 16, 1946, 890E.5045/5-I646, NARA. Murr offered to meet with the Socony-Vacuum representative, which he very well might have.

120. It is worth noting that Joseph Donato, formerly of the Social Section of the French High Commission and now in the Social Affairs Service of the Ministry of National Economy, "played a major role in drafting those provisions of the Labor Code . . . which pertain to union activities." See Kuniholm, "Anti-Communist Labor Movement in Lebanon," 8.

121. "al-Majlis al-Niyabi Yussaddiq Qanun al-'Amal," *al-Nahar*, August 23, 1946; Republic of Lebanon, Ministry of National Economy, Social Affairs Service, *Qanun al-'Amal al-Sadir bi-Tarikh 23 Aylul 1946* (Matba'at Dar al-Funun, 1946).

122. Several authors and institutions drew attention to these problems in the subsequent decade and a half. See Robert J. Lampman, "The Lebanese Labor Code of 1946," *Labor Law Journal* 5, no. 7 (1954): 491–95; International Labor Organization, Report of the Committee on Freedom of Employers' and Workers' Organizations, Appendix 2, Supplement (Geneva: International Labor Organization, 1956), 279–91; Arthur E. Mills, *Private Enterprise in Lebanon* (American University of Beirut, 1959), 130–33.

123. Lane to DoS, "Lebanese Law Against Incitement to Strike," July 23, 1946, 890E.5045/7-2346, NARA.

124. "Hijrat Abna' al-Qura ila al-Mudun," *al-Nahar*, May 8, 1951.

125. Gates, *Merchant Republic*, 50–53, 83–84; Saqr Abu Fakhr, "al-Filastiniyyun fi Lubnan: Dawr Thaqafi Mumayyaz wa-Isham Mashhud fi al-'Umran," in *Awraq Filastiniyya wa-'Arabiyya: Takrim li-Rif'at Sidqi al-Nimer fi al-Dhikra al-'Ula li-Rahilih*, ed. Anis Sayigh (al-Dar al-'Arabiyya li-l-'Ulum, 2008), 149–56.

126. Gates, *Merchant Republic*, 109–35.

127. Republic of Lebanon, Ministry of National Economy (MoNE), *Industrial Census—1955* (Beirut: n.p., 1957). The report defines an establishment as "the individual plant . . . in which goods are produced . . . an organization in a single location,

under a single management . . . in which materials or components are transformed into products for the use of others." It distinguishes between a production establishment and an "enterprize," which it defines as the "commercial or legal unity or entity that owns or controls one or more establishments." The industrial census identified 4,860 active establishments in Lebanon during 1955, of which 2,174 employed 5 persons or more. Of those, 1,861 participated in the census.

128. MoNE, *Industrial Census*, 74.

129. MoNE, *Industrial Census*, 81.

130. MoNE, *Industrial Census*, 7.

131. MoNE, *Industrial Census*, 7.

132. MoNE, *Industrial Census*, 7.

133. MoNE, *Industrial Census*, 9. The survey geographically classifies establishments on the basis of the administrative unit of the governorate (*muhafaza*). Therefore the "governorate of Beirut" refers to the administrative unit, as distinct from metropolitan Beirut, which includes significant areas and populations of the Ba'abda and Matn districts of the Mount Lebanon governorate (3).

134. MoNE, *Industrial Census*, 9.

135. MoNE, *Industrial Census*, 9.

136. MoNE, *Industrial Census*, 9.

137. MoNE, *Industrial Census*, 9.

138. MoNE, *Industrial Census*, 9. It also worth noting that these two districts also contained 53 of the enterprises of Mount Lebanon employing fifty workers or more, which also accounted for more of such enterprises than the 29 in Beirut. In 1951, 1,144 establishments totaled 147.2 million liras in invested capital. Of these establishment, 8.7 percent (99) accounted for at least 34.4 percent of the total invested amount. Another 55 percent (630) establishments accounted for at most 8.1 percent of the invested capital. On these 1951 figures, see Kurt Grunwald, "The Industrialization of Lebanon and Syria," *Weltwirtschaftliches Archiv* 76 (1956), 161.

139. MoNE, *Industrial Census*, 9. By the early 1960s, this urban agglomeration would be reimagined as Greater Beirut (Bayrut al-Kubra). On this, see Samir Kassir, *Beirut*, trans. M. B. Deveoise (University of California, 2010), 419–26.

140. MoNE, *Industrial Census*, 8.

141. Beirut to DoS, "Annual Labor Report—Lebanon—1950," Despatch 250, December 15, 1950, 883A.06/12-1550, NARA, 3; Beirut to DoS, "Annual Labor Report—Lebanon—1951," Despatch 462, March 7, 1952, 883A.06/3-752, NARA, 3.

142. Maroun S, Jalkh, "Money Supply and Cost of Credit in Lebanon," included as enclosure in Health to DoS, "Banking Practices and Interest Rates in Lebanon," Despatch 363, February 29, 1956, 10, 883A.10/2-2956, NARA.

143. Kassir, *Beirut*, 413. The significance of the construction sector to labor politics is evidenced by the inclusion of a section on building permits (including surface areas and number of floors) issued for Beirut in the annual labor reports of the US Embassy in Beirut beginning in 1951.

144. "Annual Labor Report—Lebanon—1950," 10, 20.

145. Beirut to DoS, "Annual Labor Report—Lebanon—1949," Despatch 134, March 30, 1950, 883A.06/3-3050, NARA, 3; Beirut to DoS, "Annual Labor Report—Lebanon—1952," Despatch 484, February 18, 1953, 883A.06/2-1853, NARA, 14.

146. A 1952 newspaper article reporting on a general conference of drivers claimed the total number of drivers in Lebanon of all types (*min jami' al-fi'at*) was 45,000, including those that are unemployed. See "Abhath Mu'tamar al-Sawwaqin fi Lubnan," *al-Nahar*, May 22, 1952. Also see Republic of Lebanon, Ministry of National Economy, *Taqrir al-Sir Aliksandir Gib wa-Shurakah, 'an al-Tatawwur al-Iqtisadi fi Lubnan* (Beirut: n.p., 1948), 115–35; Meyer to DoS, "Motor Vehicle Registration—Lebanon," Despatch 494, February 28, 1955, 983A.71-2-2855, NARA; John K. Emmerson to DoS, Despatch 357, February 24, 1956, 983A.71/2-2456, NARA.

147. MoEFA, "1953–1954 Annual Report," 4. Of these, at least 80 percent were full-time and 14 percent were part-time (46). Another 1,000 persons worked as directors, supervisors, or administrators in private schools (44).

148. See relevant discussion in chapter 2 and chapter 3.

149. Malek Abisaab is one the few historians who has attempted to address the resultant scholarly gap. His work specifically explores the histories and experiences of women tobacco factory workers in Lebanon from the late Ottoman period through the 1980s. See Abisaab, *Militant Women*.

150. MoNE, *Industrial Census*, 7; "Annual Labor Report—Lebanon—1949," 5; "Annual Labor Report—Lebanon—1951," 5; "Annual Labor Report—Lebanon—1952," 16.

151. MoNE, *Industrial Census*, 7.

152. Abisaab, *Militant Women*, 29, 47; "Annual Labor Report—Lebanon—1951," 4; "Annual Labor Report—Lebanon—1952," 14. See next footnote for information on textile manufacturing.

153. "Annual Labor Report—Lebanon—1951," 5; Edma Bayouth, "Women in Industry and Handicrafts: Women in Factories," File 7, Box 34, Woodsmall Papers.

154. MoEFA, "1953–1954 Annual Report," 37. During the 1953–54 school year, women accounted for 47 percent of all (public and private) school teachers.

155. Young Women's Christian Association, Lebanon (YWCAL), *Status of Women in Lebanon* (YWCAL, 1951), 19; Marie Neshaka, "The Role of Women in Business and General Employment in Lebanon," June 1955, Woodsmall Papers.

156. The exclusion of domestic workers from the labor law (referred to as *khadam* at the time) appears to be part of the original draft and was not something introduced in parliamentary debate or challenged therein. On domestic workers in Lebanon at this time, see Ray Jureidani, "In the Shadows of Family Life: Toward a History of Domestic Service in Lebanon," *Journal of Middle East Women's Studies* 5, no. 3 (2009): 74–101.

157. "Annual Labor Report—Lebanon—1949," 2.

158. "Annual Labor Report—Lebanon—1949," 2.

159. Samir Khalaf, *Prostitution in a Changing Society: A Sociological Survey of Legal Prostitution in Beirut* (Khayats, 1965). Of the 130 Beirut women sex workers surveyed in 1963, 48 percent began sex work during the 1943–55 period, and another 31 percent began such work prior to then—meaning that 87 percent of those surveyed were sex workers during the 1943–55 period (29).

160. MoNE, *Industrial Census*, 40.

161. "Annual Labor Report—Lebanon—1949," 9–10.

162. For example, see "Mustawa al-Ma'isha wa-'Ajz al-Tabaqatayn al-Mutawassita wa-l-Faqira," *al-'Amal*, February 17, 1952; Terence Shone to Ernest Bevin, no. 34, February 21, 1946, FO FO371/52492, TNA; Foreign Office, Research Department, "Trade Unions in the Middle East"; Chancery to Foreign Office, July 21, 1948, FO1018/46, TNA.

163. "Al-'Ummal Yatlibun Mukafahat al-Batala wa-Tanzim al-Iqtisad," *al-Hayat*, September 15, 1953.

164. Gates, *Merchant Republic*, 109.

165. Gates, *Merchant Republic*, 109.

166. "Hijrat Abna' al-Qura ila al-Mudun."

167. For example, see "Qadiyyat al-'Ummal Qabl al-Mashru' al-Insha'i," *al-Nahar*, March 30, 1946; "Rabitat al-'Atilin 'an al-'Amal," *al-'Amal*, February 6, 1952; "al-'Ummal Yatlibun Mukafahat al-Batala wa-Tanzim al-Iqtisad."

168. Palestine was the principal single export market for Lebanese-Syrian goods beginning in the mid-1930s and through 1947, notwithstanding World War II–related disruptions. See Samir A. K. Makdisi, "Post-War Lebanese Foreign Trade and Economic Development" (MA thesis, AUB, 1955), 89–97.

169. "Annual Labor Report—Lebanon—1950," 12.

170. For example, see Robert L. Clifford to DoS, "Effect of Korean War on Money and Commodity Markets in Lebanon," Despatch 66, August 29, 1950, 883A.13/8-29-50, NARA. Also see previously cited 1950, 1951, and 1952 annual labor report of the US diplomatic mission in Beirut, as well as Heath to DoS, "Annual Labor Report—Lebanon—1954," Despatch 727, June 17, 1955, 883A.06/6-1755, NARA.

171. For details on demands, draft laws, and debates between 1946 and 1950, see FO 1018/56, FO 1018/57, and FO 371/82303, TNA. On the 1952 draft law, see Nadim Harfush, "Wizarat al-Shu'un al-Ijtima'iyya wa-Mayadin Nashatuha," in AUB, Department of Public Administration, *Dirasat 'an Hukumat Lubnan: Majmu'at Muhadarat Alqaha Mudirun 'Amun fi al-Hukuma al-Lubnaniyya Talbiya li-Da'wat Da'irat 'Ilm al-Idara al-'Ama fi al-Jami'a al-Amrikiyya fi Bayrut, 1954–1955* (Matba'at Dar al-Funun, 1956), 49–50.

172. For example, see Minor to DoS, "Election of an Executive Committee Composed of Twenty Members Representing Communist Labor Unions and Women's Organizations to Study 'Social Security Programs,'" Despatch 606, April 17, 1953, 883A.062/4-1753, NARA; M. T. Audsley, "Notes Recording Events during the Past Three of Four Months Connected with Syndicates (Trade Unions) in the Lebanon," 3–4, FO371/115744, TNA.

173. See Doxoadis Associates, "First Outline of the Lebanon Housing Program," September 27, 1957, 1–9, included as Enclosure #1 in Heath to DOS, "Transmittal of Doxiadis Associates' Reports on Lebanon's Housing Program," Despatch 249, May 18, 1957, 883A.02/11-1857, NARA.

174. The Lebanese government developed a number of housing proposals during 1952–55 in collaboration with Point Four, the UN Technical Assistance Program, and the Economic Research Institute at the American University of Beirut. See Harfush, "Wizarat al-Shu'un al-Ijtima'iyya," 52–54.

175. "Kitab Maftuh wa-Mashruh ila Ma'ali Wazir al-Iqtisad al-Watani min Mustafa al-Aris," in Mustafa al-Aris, *Mumayyizat al-Wad' al-Naqabi fi Lubnan* (Beirut: n.p. 1948), 5–20.

176. "Al-Ijtima'at al-Naqabiyya al-Mushtaraka," in *Mumayyizat al-Wad' al-Naqabi*, 21–31.

177. Chancery to Foreign Office, July 21, 1948.

178. "Ijtima' al-Lajna al-Tahdiriyya," in al-Aris, *Mumayyizat al-Wad' al-Naqabi*, 31–33.

179. "Annual Labor Report—Lebanon—1952," 5.

180. Beirut to DoS, "Annual Labor Report—Lebanon—1953," Despatch 580, March 17, 1954, 883A.06/3-1754, NARA, 4.

181. Beirut to DoS, "Annual Labor Report—Lebanon—1954," Despatch 727, June 17, 1955, 883A.06/6-1755, NARA, 5; Beirut to DoS, "Annual Labor Report—Lebanon—1955," Despatch 572, June 30, 1956, 883A.06/6-3056, NARA, 8–9.

182. Kuniholm to DoS, "The Anti-Communist Labor Movement in Lebanon," 1511, March 3, 1947, 890E.504/3-347, NARA, 1, 10; Foreign Office, Research Department, "Trade Unions in the Middle East," 14–16.

183. Kuniholm to DoS, "The Anti-Communist Labor Movement," 2–4.

184. "Annual Labor Report—Lebanon—1949," 19.

185. "Annual Labor Report—Lebanon—1954," 3–4; "Annual Labor Report—Lebanon—1955," 5–6.

186. "Annual Labor Report—Lebanon—1952," 4.

187. Beirut to DoS, A-291, September 8, 1949, 890E.5043/9-849, NARA.

188. "Annual Labor Report—Lebanon—1954," 4; "Annual Labor Report—Lebanon—1955," 5–6.

189. "Annual Labor Report—Lebanon—1953," 2–3.

190. Hare to DoS, "Former Members of ICFTU Affiliate Jami'at Granted License to Form New Federation," Despatch 793, June 22, 1954, 883A.06/6-2254, NARA.

191. "Annual Labor Report—Lebanon—1954," 4–5; "Annual Labor Report—Lebanon—1955," 5–6.

192. "Annual Labor Report—Lebanon—1954," 5–6; "Annual Labor Report—Lebanon—1955," 5–6.

193. "Annual Labor Report—Lebanon—1955," 4–6.

194. For example, see "Annual Labor Report—Lebanon—1950," 22–23.

195. "Lajnat al-Tahqiq fi Mu'tamar al-'Ummali Tasdur Qarar bi-l-Muwafaqa 'ala al-Saffa," *Sawt al-Sha'b*, October 3 , 1945.

196. "Intisar Kabir li-l-'Arab 'ala al-Sahyuniyya wa-Ansaruha fi Mu'tamar al 'Ummal," *Sawt al-Sha'b*, October 10, 1945; "Annual Labor Report Lebanon 1953," 5.

197. "Annual Labor Report—Lebanon—1955," 6.

198. International Labour Organisation, Seventh Report of the International Labour Organisation to the United Nations (1953), 197–99.

199. "Annual Labor Report—Lebanon—1951," 13.

200. "Women's Work in the Lebanon," *International Labour Review* 58 (1948): 395; Joseph Donato, "Lebanon and Its Labour Legislation," *International Labour Review* 64 (1952): 64–92; J. A. Hallsworth, "Freedom of Association and Industrial Relations in the Countries of the Near and Middle East," Parts 1 & 2, *International Labour Review* (1954): 364–84, 526–41.

201. International Labour Office, *Official Bulletin* 37, no. 1 (1954): 120–27.

202. "The Anti-Communist Labor Movement," 1.

203. Irene L. Gendzier, *Notes from the Minefield: United States Intervention in Lebanon and the Middle East, 1945–1958* (Columbia University Press, 1997), 115–23.

204. Minor to DoS, "Our Approach to Lebanese Labor," Despatch 314, December 21, 1951, 883A.06/12-2151, NARA.

205. FO 371/82305, TNA; FO 371/104522, TNA; FO 371/110985, TNA; FO 371/115744, TNA.

206. Lampman, "Lebanese Labor Code," 499; Benjamin T. Hourani, "Unionism in the Lebanese Labor Law of 1946: A Case Study Approach," (MA thesis, AUB, 1959), 159. According to a different 1952 source, there had been a cumulative total of 6,000 cases at the Beirut arbitration council and 300 at all the other councils combined since the system was first introduced. See Edward W. Samuel Jr., "A Contribution to the Study of Lebanese Labor Syndicates" (MA thesis, AUB, 1952), 5.

207. Lampman, "Lebanese Labor Code," 499; Hourani, "Unionism," 159.

208. The parliament set the amount at 500 Lebanese liras in February 1949. It subsequently increased the amount to 1,000 liras nearly three months later.

209. It is worth recalling that such demands date back to January 1944, when the Workers and Employees' Syndicates Committee included it as part of the mobilizations leading to the passage of the labor law.

210. Harfush, "Wizarat al-Shu'un al-Ijtima'iyya, 43–44. The internal reorganization of February 1948 created three specialized departments: labor, social services, and social security. The minister of national economy decreed the establishment of the labor inspectors in May 1949: two of the inspectors were assigned to Beirut and each of the other four were assigned to one of the remaining four governorates. See Pinkerton Beirut to DoS, A-234, May 14, 1947, 890E.504/5-1447, NARA; Pinkerton to DoS, A-158, May 16, 1949, 890E.5043/5-1649, NARA. Also see E. Paul Tenney to DoS, no. 14, "Lebanese Directorate of Social Affairs," August 23, 1949, 890E.40/8-2349, NARA, which identifies Nadim Harfush as the director of Social Affairs Service, Nicola Khayr as chief of labor, Joseph Donato as chief of social services, and Habib Nahhas as chief of social insurance.

211. Beirut to DoS, no. 185, "Labor Developments—October," November 6, 1950, 2, 883A.06/11-650, NARA.

212. Marsum 4868 (9/5/1951) *al-Jarida al-Rasmiyya* (May 16, 1951): 333–34.

213. Beirut to DoS, no. 85, "Labor Developments—February," March 2, 1950, 2, 883A.06/3-250, NARA.

214. "Marsum 5633 (10/8/1951)," *al-Jarida al-Rasmiyya* (August 15, 1951): 491–95. The government reorganized the ministry in 1953 as part of a broader set of administrative reorganizations. See "Marsum Ishtira'i 23 (4/2/1953)," *al-Jarida al-Rasmiyya* (February 11, 1953): 190–99.

215. "Marsum 4868 (9/5/1951)," *al-Jarida al-Rasmiyya* (May 16, 1951): 333–34.

216. Kuniholm to DoS, "The Anti-Communist Labor Movement in Lebanon." 7–9.

217. Hourani, "Unionism," 157.

Chapter 5

1. "Mahrajan al-Mar'a al-Lubnaniyya," *Sawt al-Mar'a* (April 1953): 7, 43.

2. For example, the Welfare Workshop of Furn al-Shubbak (Mashghal al-'Inaya Furn al-Shubbak, est. 1942) and the Association for Elderly Shelter in 'Alay (Jam'iyyat Ma'wa al-'Ajaza – 'Alay, est. 1947).

3. For example, the Mar Iliyas School and Orphanage Association (Jam'iyyat Madarasat wa-Maytam Mar Iliyas, est. 1947) and the Lebanese Association for the Blind (al-Jam'iyya al-Lubnaniyya li-Ighathat al-Darir, est. 1953).

4. For example, the Association for the Protection of Lebanese Girls (Jam'iyyat Himayat al-Fatat al-Lubnaniyya, est. 1923), the Association for Crime Prevention and Prison Improvement (Jam'iyyat Mukafahat al-Jarima wa-Tahsin al-Sujun, est. 1928), and the Batrun Women's Righteousness and Charity Association (Jam'iyyat al-Birr wa-l-Ihsan li-l-Nisa' fi al-Batrun, est. 1954).

5. For example, the Women's Awakening Society (Jam'iyyat al-Nahda al-Nisa'iyya, est. 1923).

6. Elizabeth Thompson, *Colonial Citizens: Republican Rights, Paternal Privilege, and Gender in French Syria and Lebanon* (Columbia University Press, 2000), 94–100; Ellen Fleischmann, "The Other 'Awakening:' The Emergence of Women's Movements in the Modern Middle East, 1900–1940," in *Globalizing Feminism, 1789–1945*, ed. Karen Offen (Routledge, 2010), 97–98.

7. Miss Ibtihaj Kaddoura, interview by R. W. and C. J., Beirut, October 26, 1954, Box 30, Woodsmall Papers. The neighborhoods included 'Ayn al-Muraysa and Mina' al-Husn, Ashrafiyya, Basta, Hurj and Tariq al-Jadida, Musaytba and Burj Abi Haydar, Ras al-Naba', Zaydaniyya and Sana'i', and Zuqaq al-Blat. Most of the associations of which were established in 1945–46.

8. "List of Member Agencies: Union of Child Welfare," Box 30, Woodsmall Papers. The women's organizations constituted a subset of thirty-one organizations. These women's organizations were the Young Women's Christian Association Committee on Child Labor, the Center for Maternal and Infant Hygiene (Centre Hygiene Maternal Infantile), the Greek Orthodox Orphanage (Offre de Diner Gratuite), the Sisters of the Good Shepherd's Shelter for Delinquent Girls, the Juveniles Protection Union (Ittihad Himayyit al-Ahdath), the Child Welfare Association, Solarium's Hospital for Children, the Union of Lebanese Women's Kindergarten, the Women's Renaissance's Rural School for Girls, the Beirut College for Women's Neighborhood House, the Zahleh Kindergarten (Hadanat El Tufl Zahleh), the Zahleh Day Care Nursery, the Muslim Girl Scouts in Tripoli, the Tripoli Day Care Nursery, the Orphanage for Muslim Girls in Tripoli, the Orphanage for Girls in Akkar, and the Home for Babies in Tripoli. Listed in order of document.

9. These included the Arab Women's Federation in Lebanon, the Union of Lebanese Women, and the Women's Awakening Society, among others. Political parties included the Ghassasina Organization, Kata'ib Party, and the Najjada Organization. See untitled petition addressed to President Bishara al-Khuri, dated December 23, 1946, File 3, Box 1, Evelyne Bustrous Collection, Archives and Special Collections, Nami Jafet Library, American University of Beirut, Lebanon.

10. "Conference for Non-Government Organizations in Lebanon," Box 30, Woodsmall Papers. Twenty-five organizations formed the conference in 1949. By 1950, its membership had grown to encompass sixty organizations. By 1954 the conference comprised sixty-four organizations.

11. In addition to organizations represented on the executive committee, the Conference on NGOs in Lebanon also included the Federation of Lebanese Women's Organizations, the Union of Lebanese Women, and the Union of Child Welfare Societies. See "Conference for Non-Government Organizations in Lebanon."

12. For example, see "Wafd al-Jam'iyyat al-Nisa'iyya bi-Wizarat al-Tamwin," *al-Nahar*, April 13, 1944.

13. "Ittifaq al-Ahzab wa-l-Hay'at al-Lubnaniyya 'ala Nasrat Marakish," *al-Anba'*, August 28, 1953; "Bayan al-Mu'tamar al-Watani al-'Am," *al-Anba'*, May 27, 1955; John K. Emerson, Charge d'Affairs (Beirut) to DoS), "Meeting of National Congress of Parties," Despatch 264, December 22, 1955, 783A.00/12-2255, NARA.

14. Barakat Al-Farr, "Juvenile Delinquency in Lebanon" (MA thesis, American University of Beirut, 1957).

15. Al-Farr, "Juvenile Delinquency in Lebanon," 4.

16. Al-Farr, "Juvenile Delinquency in Lebanon," 35. Of the 826 cases identified, 135 ended in dismissal or no punishment. Other possible outcomes included a period of supervision by the association, remaining with one's family under specific conditions, or institutionalization in either a government-run reformatory (for males only) or in one of the privately operated reformatories that the government financially supported.

17. Al-Farr, "Juvenile Delinquency in Lebanon," 24–26.

18. Thompson, *Colonial Citizens*, 96.

19. A 1951 YWCA survey on the status of women in Lebanon identified ninety-three "women's clubs, whose membership ranges from 30 women as a minimum to 1,200 as a maximum." A 1956 survey of "the role of women, their activities, and organizations in Lebanon, Egypt, Iraq, Jordan, and Syria" sponsored by the International Federation of Business and Professional Women identified at least 103 such organizations. See, respectively, Young Women's Christian Association, Lebanon (YWCAL), *Status of Women in Lebanon* (1951), 7; Ruth F. Woodsmall, *Study of the Role*

of Women: Their Activities and Organizations in Lebanon, Egypt, Iraq, Jordan and Syria (October 1954–August 1955) (International Federation of Business and Professional Women, 1956), 19.

20. YWCAL, *Status of Women*, 7; Woodsmall, *Study of the Role of Women*, 19.

21. Ruth F. Woodsmall, "Study of the Role of Women, Their Activities, and Organizations in Lebanon, Egypt, Iraq, Jordan, and Syria," unpublished draft manuscript, 209–12, Woodsmall Papers.

22. "Talab bi-Ta'lif Jam'iyya Nisa'iyya Jadida," *Sawt al-Sha'b*, January 10, 1944.

23. "Jami'at Nisa' Lubnan," *Sawt al-Mar'a* (December 1948), 5.

24. The magazine title byline read "A Monthly Women's Magazine."

25. Enclosure no. 1 in Clayton Lane to Department of State, "Women's Magazine Sawt al-Mar'a," no. 113, July 8, 1947, 890E.917/7-847, National Archives and Records Administration (NARA), College Park, Maryland.

26. Enclosure no. 1 in Clayton Lane to Department of State, "Women's Magazine Sawt al-Mar'a."

27. Thompson, *Colonial Citizens*, 215–17.

28. The "Lebanese Child-Welfare Society" featured a similar trajectory. The Arab Women's Federation in Lebanon first established a child welfare committee, headed by Zahiyya Hasan, in 1938. In 1948, Hasan, in collaboration with others, reestablished the committee as an independent organization. See "The Story of the Lebanese Child-Welfare Society," *Sawt al-Mar'a* (April 1949), 7.

29. Mrs. Ni'mat Muhiddin Koronfol, interview by R. W. and C. J., notes, October 25, 1954, Box 30, Woodsmall Papers.

30. Mrs. Ni'mat Muhiddin Koronfol, interview by R. W. and C. J. The 1953 annual budget of the Child Welfare Association was 31,000 Lebanese liras. In 1954, it received 2,000 liras from the Lebanese government and 15,000 liras from the Municipality of Beirut.

31. Mrs. Ni'mat Muhiddin Koronfol, interview by R. W. and C. J.

32. "al-Jam'iyyat al-Nisa'iyya," *Sawt al-Mar'a* (December 1948), 15; Mrs. Yakon, interview by R. W. and C. J., Beirut, notes, October 21, 1954, Box 30, Woodsmall Papers.

33. On the history, contemporary activities, and plans of the Lebanese YWCA as of 1954, see "Plan for Developing YWCA Community Centers in Lebanon," 26 January 1954, Box 30, Woodsmall Papers.

34. Jam'iyyat al-Shabbat al-Muslimat, *al-Bayan al-Sanawi* (1948), 1–2, Sadaka Collection.

35. Mrs. Evelyn Bustrus [Eveline Bustros], interview by C. J., notes, Beirut, October 13, 1954, Box 30, Woodsmall Papers; Mrs. Albert Rihani, interview by R. W. and C. J., notes, Beirut, October 22, 1954, Box 30, Woodsmall Papers.

36. R. W. and C. J., "Mimis Village Welfare Girl's School," November 3, 1954, Box 30, Woodsmall Papers.

37. Mrs. Rihani and Mrs. George Dabbas, interview by R. W., notes, Munsif, October 27, 1954, Box 30, Woodsmall Papers.

38. R. W. and C. J., "Visit to Bechfeen," October 16, 1954, Box 30, Woodsmall Papers.

39. Najla Salim Sa'b, *al-Salib al-Ahmar wa-Ittifaqiyyat Jinef* (Matba'at Iliyas Habib Khuri, 1966), 138.

40. For a sense of how the Lebanese Red Cross Society developed in terms of activity areas and capacities between 1945 and 1955, see "al-Taqrir al-Sanawi li-l-Salib al-Ahmar," *al-Nahar,* July 18, 1946; De Marquise de Freige and Mrs. Alfred Kittaneh, interview by C. J. and R. W., notes, Beirut, November 11, 1954, Box 30, Woodsmall Papers.

41. For example, see "Ra'is Ittihad al-Salib al-Ahmar Yatahddath 'an al-Mu'assassa al-Lubnaniyya wa-Yashruh al-Dawr al-Muwakkal ilayha fi Ighathat al-Laji'in," *al-Nahar,* February 8, 1949.

42. Sources differ on the precise date of the federation's establishment. It was most likely the product of several meetings held between 1921 and 1925, but there is disagreement about which meeting constituted the founding event.

43. Nazik Sarkis, "al-Ittihad al-Nisa'i al-Lubnani al-'Arabi," *Sawt al-Mar'a* (December 1948), 14.

44. *Bayan al-Ittihad al-Nisa'i al-'Arabi al-Rabi', 1936–1941* (Sader, 1941).

45. "A'mal Jam'iyyat al-Ittihad al-Nisa'i," *al-Mar'ad* (February–April 1931), 21.

46. "Nahdat al-Mar'a al-Lubnaniyya al-Suriyya," *al-Ma'rad* (August–October 1931), 21.

47. "al-Ittihad al-Nisa'i al-Lubnani al-'Arabi," *Sawt al-Mar'a* (December 1948); "The Arab Women's Federation of Lebanon," *Sawt al-Mar'a* (April 1949), 2–3.

48. See "The Arab Women's Federation of Lebanon"; YWCAL, *Status of Women in Lebanon,* 7.

49. For example, see "al-Ittihad al-Nisa'i fi Trablus," *al-Nahar,* May 17, 1946; "al-Ittihad al-Nisa'i fi Ziyarat Zahleh," *al-Nahar,* June 13, 1946.

50. YWCAL, *Status of Women in Lebanon,* 7. In 1951, Women's Solidarity included twenty-six women's organizations.

51. Woodsmall, *Study of the Role of Women,* 19. The International Alliance of Women was the name adopted by the International Women's Suffrage Alliance in 1946. The precise date on which the women's federation in Lebanon joined the International Council of Women remains unknown.

52. These conferences were organized under various rubrics like "Eastern Women's," "Arab Women's," and "international." There were such conferences in Beirut

(1928) and Jerusalem (1929), the Eastern women's conferences in Beirut/Damascus (1930), Tehran (1932), and Cairo (1938), and the International Women's Suffrage Alliance conference in Istanbul (1934). For an overview of these events, see Charlotte Weber, "Making Common Cause?: Western and Middle Eastern Feminists in the International Women's Movement, 1911–1948," (PhD diss., Ohio State University, 2003), 121–68. On the Arab and Eastern women's conferences, see Marie Sandell, "Regional Versus International: Women's Activism and Organisational Spaces in the Inter-War Period," *International History Review* 33, no. 4 (2011): 607–25; Charlotte Weber, "Between Nationalism and Feminism: The Eastern Women's Congresses of 1930 and 1932," *Journal of Middle East Women's Studies* 4, no 1 (2008): 83–106. On the International Women's Suffrage Alliance conference, see Kathryn Libal, "Staging Turkish Women's Emancipation: Istanbul, 1935," *Journal of Middle East Women's Studies* 4, no. 1 (2008): 31–52; Nicole A. N. M. Van Os, "Ottoman Muslim and Turkish Women in an International Context," *European Review* 13, no. 3 (2005): 467–71.

53. *Al-Mu'tamar al-Nisa'i al-'Arabi* (Dar al-Ma'arif, 1944).

54. *Al-Mu'tamar al-Nisa'i al-'Arabi*, 27–28.

55. *Al-Mu'tamar al-Nisa'i al-'Arabi*, 56–61.

56. *Al-Mu'tamar al-Nisa'i al-'Arabi*, 42 and 61. The delegation from Lebanon included Iqbal Dhuq, Jamal Karam Harfush, Najla Kfury, Najla Sa'b, Shafiqa Salam, Zahiyya Salman, Rose Shahfa, Hunayna Tarsha, Habiba Yakun, and others. See Zahiyya Qaddura, *Tarikh al-'Arab al-Hadith* (Dar al-Nahda al-' Arabiyya, 1973), 580; Salma Sa'igh, *Suwar wa-Dhikrayat* (Dar al-Hadara, 1964), 63.

57. *Muqarrarat al-Mu'tamar al-Nisa'i al-'Arabi al-Rabi'* (Manshurat al-Ittihad al-Nisa'i al-'Arabi, 1958), 17–18.

58. *Al-Mu'tamar al-Thalith li-l-Ittihad al-Nisa'i al-'Arabi al-'Am: al-Muhadarat wa-l-Dirasat wa-l-Qarrarat* (Matba'at al-Bayan, 1954)

59. See UN Office of Public Information, *The United Nations and the Status of Women* (United Nations, 1961), 3–6; UN Commission on the Status of Women, "Report of the Commission on the Status of Women to the Economic and Social Council," February 25, 1946. For a focused study on women's lobbying during the interwar years in general, and at the League of Nations in particular, see Carol Miller, "Geneva—the Key to Equality: Inter-war Feminists and the League of Nations," *Women's History Review* 3, no. 2 (1994): 219–45.

60. UN, *United Nations and the Status of Women*, 6; United Nations, *A Short History of the Commission on the Status of Women* (UN Women, 2019), 4.

61. UN Economic and Social Council, Official Records, Fifth Year, Eleventh Session, Supplement no. 6: "Commission on the Status of Women, Report of the Fourth Session (May 8–19, 1950)," 1; UN Economic and Social Council, Official Records, Sixth

Year, Thirteenth Session, Supplement no. 10: "Commission on the Status of Women, Report of the Fifth Session (April 30–May 14, 1951)," 1.

62. Nova Robinson, "'Sisters of Men': Syria and Lebanese Women's Transnational Campaign for Arab Independence and Women's Rights, 1910–1940" (PhD diss., Rutgers University, 2015), 401–2. The other Arab woman referred to was Alice Kandalft Cosma (1895–c. 1965), who served as the Syrian delegate to the commission from 1947 to 1951 and was elected as an officer in 1947.

63. "Taqrir," *al-Tariq* (March–April 1949), 65–70; Lajnat Huquq al-Mar'a, *Lajnat Huquq al-Mar'a al-Lubnaniyya 1947–1987* (Beirut: n.p., n.d.), 8–17.

64. Thurayya Khatib 'Adra, "Ahdaf Lajnat Huquq al-Mar'ah," *al-Tariq* (July 1949), 95.

65. In addition to what is discussed in this chapter, the CWR credits itself with pressuring the Ministry of Education through a combination of meetings and demonstrations to open public schools in specific neighborhoods within Ashrafiyya (1949), Tripoli (1951), Tariq al-Jadida (1952), and Ghobayri (1953). See Lajnat Huquq al-Mar'a, *Lajnat Huquq al-Mar'a*, 19–20.

66. I am drawing on some of the key characteristics Masha Kirasirova identified as a pillar of the Lebanese leftist milieu in Lebanon in her discussion of the Partisans of Peace. See Masha Kirasirova, "The Partisans of Peace in Lebanon and Syria: How Anti-Nuclear Activism in the 1950s Revitalized the Arab Left," *International Journal of Middle East Studies* 55 (2023): 650–74.

67. CIA, "Women's International Democratic Federation (WIDF)," report, c. 1956, 23–24, CIA-RDP78-00915R000600140010-9, CREST Collection. Members of the Lebanese women's movement appear to have participated in the second (Budapest, December 1948) and third (Copenhagen, June 1953) congresses as well as the Conference in Defense of Children (Vienna 1952) and the World Congress of Mothers (Lausanne, 1955). A group of Communist and Communist-sympathizing women's organizations and delegations established the Women's International Democratic Federation in November 1945 in Paris. The coalition went on to become one of the primary international women's organizations during the Cold War era. It held consultative status at the UN Economic and Social Council by the late 1940s. See Francis de Haan, "The Women's International Democratic Federation (WIDF): History, Main Agenda and Contributions (1945–1991)," in *Women and Social Movements (WASI) Online Archive*, ed. Thomas Dublin and Kathryn Kish Sklar (2012), 2.

68. CIA, "Women's International Democratic Federation (WIDF)," 37.

69. "Lajnat Huquq al-Mar'a Tahtafil bi-Yawm al-Mar'a al-'Alamiyya," *al-Tariq* (March–April 1949), 65–70.

70. On frustrating General Security, see a 1951 General Security memo on the CWR that claims "Despite proof of the communism of their goals . . . the press

continues to publish articles about them. . . . Their propaganda is increasing and so is people's willingness to support them. I therefore have the honor to request that you take steps to limit such propaganda in the local press." Head of General Security Farid Chehab to Ministry of Interior, memo (labeled secret), October 4, 1951, File 9C/10, Box 10, Emir Farid Chehab Collection, Middle East Centre Archive, St. Antony's College, Oxford, England. On General Security's surveillance of the CWR, see Head of General Security Farid Chehab to Ministry of Interior, memo (labeled secret), September 28, 1950, File 8C/10, Box 10, Chehab Collection. The memo requests "the Ministry of Post and Telegraph to supply us with a copy of each telegram issued [by the CWR, Partisans of Peace, and others] so as to identify their signatories."

71. "Al-Hukuma Tamna' Mahrajana Yawm al-Mar'a," *al-Nahar*, March 6, 1949; "Akhbar al-Mujtama'," *Sawt al-Mar'a* (April 1949), 24.

72. "Lajnat Huquq al-Mar'a Tahtafil bi-Yawm al-Mar'a."

73. "Mahrajan Yawm al-Mar'a Yukhtam bi-Muzahara," *al-Nahar*, March 8, 1949.

74. The Lebanese parliament received at least two telegrams protesting the detentions, one from 'Adra and Thabit of the CWR, and another from the attorney Iliyas Shahin. See Republic of Lebanon, Parliament, Sixth Legislative Assembly, Second Extraordinary Session, Fifteenth Meeting (March 15, 1950), minutes.

75. "Ihtifal Ra'i' bi-Dimashq li-Munasabat Yawm al-Mar'a al-'Alami," *al-Akhbar*, March 13, 1955.

76. "Al-Mar'a al-Lubnaniyya Tahtafil bi-Yawm 8 Adhar," *al-Akhbar*, March 20, 1955; "Ihtifalat Trablus wa-l-Shamal Biyawm al-Mar'a al-"alami," *al-Akhbar*, March 13, 1953; "Ijtima' Nisa'i li-Munasabat 8 Adhar fi 'Ayn Harsha (al-Biqa'), *al-Akhbar*, March 20, 1955.

77. Al-Munazzama al-Kata'ibiyya al-Nisa'iyya, *al-Qanun al-Asasi*, March 1, 1941.

78. "Ila al-Lubnaniyyat: Nida' al-Ra'is al-A'la bi-Munasabat Insha' "al-Munazzama al-Nisa'iyya al-Kata'ibiyya," *al-Amal*, March 28, 1948; "Ijtima'at 'Adida fi al -Muqata'at. . .al-Khutwa al-Jadida li-l-Munazzama al-Nisa'iyya," *al-Amal*, April 4, 1948; "Min Ahadith al-Munazzama al-Nisa'iyya," *al-Amal*, April 25, 1948.

79. "Ittisa' al-Haraka al-Nisa'iyya," *al-Amal*, February 6, 1950.

80. Al-Munazzama al-Kata'ibiyya al-Nisa'iyya, *al-Qanun al-Asasi*, 2.

81. "Al-Ijtima' al-Nisa'i al-Kabir fi Bayt al-Kata'ib: Huquq al-Mar'a 'ala Basit al-Bahth wa-l-Tamhid li-l-Mu'tamar al-'Am al-Muqbil," *al-Amal*, February 14, 1950.

82. The following discussion of Matar's initial involvement with the CWR is based on Linda Matar, *Mahattat min Sirat Hayati* (Dar al-Farabi, 2013), 39–42.

83. Thompson, *Colonial Citizens*, 118.

84. The transcripts' of these deliberations evidently first appeared in Akram Zu'aytir, "al-Mu'atamar al-Suri A'ta al-Mar'a Haqq al-Intikhab ma' Waqf al-Tanfiz,"

Majallat al-Hawadith (July 27, 1975), 69–72. They were subsequently reproduced as an appendix in Hanifa Khatib, *Tarikh Tatawwur al-Haraka al-Nisa'iyya fi Lubnan wa-Irtibatuha bi-l-'Alam al-'Arabi, 1800–1975* (Dar al-Hadatha, 1984), 193–205. Also see Thompson, *Colonial Citizens*, 117–20.

85. "Al-Mar'a al-Lubnaniyya: Fi Nazrat Nuwwab al-Balad," *al-Mar'a al-Jadida* 4 (1924), 229–32. Also see Thompson, *Colonial Citizens*, 122–23.

86. "Al-Mar'a al-Lubnaniyya."

87. Helen Miller Davis, *Constitutions, Electoral Laws, Treaties of States in the Near and Middle East* (Duke University Press, 1953), 294.

88. Davis, *Constitutions*, 172–3. In January 1947, the Lebanese parliament amended this clause rendering it as "the electoral laws in force." See Davis, *Constitutions*, 294.

89. Turkey is the only Middle Eastern state to grant women suffrage prior to the post–World War II period. France did not grant women voting rights until in 1945, rights that were subject to fulfilling a literacy requirement, a provision that would endure until 1965.

90. Thompson, *Colonial Citizens*, 171–74.

91. Thompson, *Colonial Citizens*, 141–48.

92. Thompson, *Colonial Citizens*, 142.

93. Emily Faris Ibrahim, "Sawt al-Mar'a: Huquq Jadida," *al-Tariq* (December 29, 1943), 15–17.

94. Anderson, *American University of Beirut*, 138.

95. "Al-Ittihad al-Nisa'i al-'Arabi Yutalib bi-Haqq al-Mar'a fi al-Intikhab," *Sawt al-Sha'b*, June 30, 1943; Thomspson, *Colonial Citizens*, 248–50, 260–61.

96. Emily Faris Ibrahim, "al-Mar'a fi al-Barlaman," *al-Tariq* (September 19, 1944), 6–7; Emily Faris Ibrahim, "al-Mar'a wa-l-Shar'," *al-Tariq* (December 31, 1944), 10–11; Salwa Mahmasani Mumneh, "Nurid li-l-Bilad Nahda Shamila," *Sawt al-Mar'a* (May 1947), 23.

97. Nahiyya Ghalmiyya, "al-Mar'a fi al-Barlaman," *Sawt al-Mar'a* (May 1948), 26.

98. For example, see Rose Gharib, "Limaza Yussawwit al-Ummi wa-la Tussawwit al-Mar'a al-Muthaqqafa," *al-Mar'a al-Jadida* (March 1949), 6–7.

99. The UN General Assembly adopted the Universal Declaration of Human Rights on December 10, 1948. See "The Universal Declaration of Human Rights," *The American Journal of International Law* 43, no. 3, Supplement, Official Documents (July 1949): 127–32.

100. For example, see Nahiyya Ghulmiyya, "al-Mar'a al-Insan fi Shar'at Huquq al-Insan," *Sawt al-Mar'a* (June 1949), 20–21.

101. UN Economic and Social Council, Commission on the Status of Women, "Report of the Commission on the Status of Women to the Economic and Social

Council," February 25, 1947, 12; "Report of the Second Session of the Commission on the Status of Women (5–19 January 1948)," published as UN Economic and Social Council, Official Records, Third Year, Sixth Session, Supplement no. 5, 4–5; "Report of the Third Session of the Commission on the Status of Women (March 21–April 4, 1949)," published as UN Economic and Social Council, Official Records, Fourth Year, Ninth Session, Supplement no. 5, 5–6.

102. Caroline Green, "Campaigning Against Women's Rights? Britian's Global Colonial Legacy in the Early UN Women's Rights Agenda 1950–1962," *The International History Review* 46, no. 6 (2024), 947–61. The UN General Assembly passed the convention in December 1952, which went into effect in July 1954. See United Nations, Treaty Collection, Status of Treaties, Chapter 16: Status of Women, 1, Convention on the Political Rights of Women, at https://treaties.un.org/.

103. "Madha Taf'al Munazzamat al-Ummam min Ajl al-Mar'a," *Sawt al-Mar'a* (April 1949), 2–5.

104. "Gharb wa-Sharq fi Lajnat Shu'un al-Mar'a," *al-Nahar*, March 27, 1949; "Sharq wa-Gharb fi Mu'tamar Shu'un al-Mar'a," *al-Nahar*, March 29, 1949; "Mwa'ith Siniyya fi Lajnat Shu'un al-Mar'a," March 30, 1949; "al-Jadal al-'Qim fi Lajnat Shu'un al-Mar'a," *al-Nahar*, March 31, 1949; al-Tabdhir wa-l-Iqtisad fi Qasr al-Unesko," *al-Nahar*, April 1, 1949; "Mandubat Suriyya Tuthir Qadiyyat al-Laji'in," *al-Nahar*, April 3, 1949.

105. See correspondence to and from the Arab Women's Federation in Lebanon ("Arab Lebanese Women's Union"), the Union of Lebanese Women, Sawt al-Mar'a ("Sout al-Maraat"), and the Young Women's Christian Association in Lebanon, in UN 175/02 Part B, Commission on the Status of Women, Third Session, Interoffice Memorandum from Section for Non-Governmental Organizations to Edward Lawson, March 4, 1949, cited in Robinson, "'Sisters of Men,'" 413, fn. 849.

106. For a general overview of consultative status at the UN, see UN Office of Public Information, *The United Nations and the Status of Women*, 8–12. On the accreditation process at the Beirut session of the CSW, see UN 175/02 Part B, Commission on the Status of Women, Third Session, Accreditations Policy, cited in Robinson, "'Sisters of Men,'" 413, fn. 851. On the actual list of organizations with that status in attendance at the session, see UN 175/02 Part B, Commission on the Status of Women, Third Session, NGOs participating in Third Session of the Commission on the Status of Women, August 11, 1949, cited in Robinson, "'Sisters of Men,'" 413, fn. 853.

107. For example, Laure Tabet ("Mrs. George Tabet") officially participated as a representative of the International Council of Women, Emily Faris Ibrahim ("Emilie Fares Ibrahim") participated as a representative of the Women's International Democratic Federation, and Edma Bayouth participated as a representative of the global

Young Women's Christian Association. See "Report of the Third Session of the Commission on the Status of Women (March 21–April 4, 1949)," 2.

108. "Akhbar al-Mu'tamarat al-Nisa'iyya," *Sawt al-Mar'a* (April 1949), 1; "Lajnat Shu'un al-Mar'a al-Lubnaniyya Tarfa' Muqarrartiha ila al-Hukuma fi Ijtima' Ams," *al-Amal*, April 5, 1949.

109. Robinson, "'Sisters of Men,'" 421, fn. 872.

110. "Al-Nisa' Uqaddimina Matalibahunna ila al-Hukuma: Musawat al-Mar'a bi-l-Rajul fi Midan al-Hayat Kafa," *al-Nahar*, April 5, 1949, 2 and 4.

111. This was a particularly important point given the ongoing division between the AWFL and the Women's Solidarity coalitions.

112. "Qarar Raqam 17: Qanun al-Initikhabat fi Suriyya, 10 Aylul 1949," *al-Jarida al-Rasmiyya* 46 (September 12, 1949).

113. For example, see "Kayfa Tahsul al-Mar'a al-Lubnaniyya 'Ala Huquqiha al-Siyasiyya," *al-Amal*, February 19, 1950.

114. "Hal Tuwafiqin 'Ala I'ta' al-Mar'a Haqq al-Intikhab??," *Sawt al-Mar'a* (May 1949), 16–17; "Na'am! Yajib An Tanal al-Mar'a Haqq al-Intikhab," *Sawt al-Mar'a* (June 1949), 16.

115. For example, see "Akhbar al-Mujtama'," *Sawt al-Mar'a* (June 1949), 28.

116. Habiba Sha'ban Yakun, "Imnahu al-Mar'a Huququha al-Siyasiyya," *al-'Urwa al-Wuthqa* 14, no. 2 (February 1949): 6–9, cited and discussed in Anderson, *The American University of Beirut*, 139.

117. "Talibat al-Junyur Kolege Yatabanayn al-Hamla," *al-Nahar*, January 21, 1950.

118. Jamal Karam Harfush, "Shahada fi al-Mar'a," *Muhadarat al-Nadwa* 3, no. 7–8 (1949): 182–200.

119. George Hanna, *al-Mar'a: Jasad wa-Ruh* (Dar al-Thaqafa, 1950).

120. The first of these meetings took place on March 26, 1950. The executive committee was formed at the meeting of April 27, 1950. For the minutes of one of these meetings, see "Mahdar Ijtima' al-Lajna al-Mukallafa min Qibal al-Hay'a al-Nisa'iyya," April 12, 1950, reproduced in Antun Masra and Toni Atallah, *Laure Mughayzil: Nisf Qarn Difa'an 'an Huquq al-Mar'a al-Lubnaniyya*, vol. 1 (Mu'assassat Joseph wa-Laure Mughayzil, 1999), 427. For a contemporary account of the creation of the Executive Committee, see "The Lebanese Woman and Elections," *Sawt al-Mar'a*, (May 1951), 41.

121. A scan of the petition text is reproduced in Masra and Atallah, *Laure Mughayzil*, 160–63.

122. Masra and Atallah, *Laure Mughayzil*, 160.

123. For a detailed account of this public meeting, see "al-Mar'a al-Lubnaniyya Qalat Ams 'Aliyya fi Mu'tamariha al-'Am," *al-'Amal*, June 16, 1950.

124. For example, see "Tazahur Nisa'iyya Kubra," *al-Amal*, February 6, 1951. In this public meeting held at the Officer's Club (Nadi al-Dubbat), the committee hosted approximately two hundred women representing nearly seventy women's organizations.

125. The meeting was held on June 4, 1951. For details, see "al-Hay'at al-Naqabiyya Tu'ayyid Huquq al-Mar'a," *al-Nahar*, June 5, 1951.

126. The meeting was held on February 14, 1952. For details, see "Muqarrarat al-Lajna al-Tanifidhiyya al-Nisa'iyya bi-Hudur Mumathilli al-Ahzab wa-l-Hay'at al-Lubnaniyya," *al-Amal*, February 16, 1952. Also see "Qadiyyat al-Mar'a Qadiyya Wataniyya: al-Hay'at al-Siyasiyya Tua'yyid Huquq al-Mar'a," *al-Nahar*, February 22, 1952.

127. For example, see "al-Lubnaniyya 'Indama Taghtarib: Ma'ali Wazir al-Kharijiyya Yatahaddath ila Sawt al-Mar'a," *Sawt al-Mar'a* (August 1950), 7; "Sawt al-Mar'a Tastaqi Rijal al-Qada' fi Huquq al-Mar'a," *Sawt al-Mar'a* (August 1950), 12; Ka'di Ka'di, "Haqq al-Mar'a fi al-Intikhab," *Sawt al-Mar'a* (August 1950), 6.

128. Emily Faris Ibrahim, *al-Haraka al-Nisa'iyya al-Lubnaniyya* (Dar al-Thaqafa, 1966), 156.

129. "Usbu' al-Mar'a fi Lubnan Huwwa Usbu' al-Nidal al-Silmi," *al-Nahar*, January 4, 1951.

130. Ibrahim, *al-Haraka al-Nisa'iyya al-Lubnaniyya*, 168–70; Emily Faris Ibrahim, "al-Mar'a wa-l-Siyasa," 5, study by author c. 1983 published in Laure Moghaizel, *Nisf Qarn Difa'an Huquq al-Mar'a fi Lubnan: Watha'iq min al-Tarikh 1947–1997: Arshif Laure Mughayzil*, vol. 1 (Mu'assasat Joseph wa-Laure Moghaizel, 1999), 278–84.

131. As one US diplomat put it, "Informed observers agree that the government is trying to quiet the women and that there is little strong support for the ballot for them in the Chamber." Lowell C. Pinkerton to Department of State, "Women Demonstrate for Ballot," Dispatch no. 474, March 26, 1951, 783A.07/3-2651, NARA.

132. For example, see Salma Sa'igh, "Ba'da al-Ma'raka," *Sawt al-Mar'a* (April 1951), 1.

133. John H. Bruins to Department of State, "Lebanese Women Seek Right to Vote," Dispatch 345, February 8, 1951, 783A.07/2-851, NARA; Lowell C. Pinkerton to Department, "Further Activities of Lebanese Feminists," Dispatch 397, February 28, 1951, 783A.07/2-2851, NARA.

134. Pinkerton, "Women Demonstrate for Ballot."

135. Ibrahim, *al-Haraka al-Nisa'iyya al-Lubnaniyya*, 165–66.

136. "Sadara al-Marsum al-Ishtira'i bi-Ta'dil Qanun al-Intikhabat al-'Amma," *al-Nahar*, November 7, 1952.

137. For example, see 'Abdul Rahman Labban, "Hawl Manh al-Mar'a al-Lubnaniyya al-Muta'allima Haqqaha al-Siyasi," *Sawt al-Mar'a* (December 1952), 10–11 and

47; Rose Gharib, "al-Mar'a wa-l-Huquq al-Sihasiyya," *Sawt al-Mar'a* (February 1953), 5–6; Maliha Zaydan, "'Adl al-'Ahd al-Jadid fi Intisar Qadiyyat al-Mara," *Sawt al-Mar'a* (February 1953), 34; Tammam Dawud, "'Ala Hamish Huquq al-Mar'a," *Sawt al-Mar'a* (February 1953), 36–37.

138. "Al-Hay'at al-Nisa'iyya wa-Qanun al-Intikhabat," *al-Nahar*, November 8, 1952. Also see "Haqq al-Mar'a la Yumkin an Yatajaza'," *al-Amal*, November 10, 1952; "al-Hay'at al-Nisa'iyya Tahtajj 'ala Qanun al-Intikhabat," *al-Nahar*, November 15, 1952.

139. Ibrahim, *al-Haraka al-Nisa'iyya al-Lubnaniyya*, 182–83. Also see "Bayan Maslahat al-Qadaya al-Nisa'iyya fi al-Kata'ib: al-Mar'a la Tarmi al-Silah," *al-Amal*, November 8, 1952.

140. "Al-Lajna al-Tanfidhiyya li-l-Hay'at al-Nisa'iyya Tahtajj 'ala Hurman al-Ummiyyat Huquqihin," *al-Nahar*, November 26, 1952.

141. "Manih Jami' al-Nisa' Huquqihin wa-Jawab al-Ra'is 'an Mudhakarat al-Hay'at al-Nisa'iyya," *al-Amal*, January 23, 1953.

142. "Munihat al-Mar'a Kul Huquqaha," *al-Amal*, February 19, 1952.

143. Quoted in Ibrahim, *al-Haraka al-Nisa'iyya al-Lubnaniyya*, 196.

144. "Awwal Lubnaniyya Takhud al-Ma'raka al-Intikhabiyya," *Sawt al-Mar'a* (July 1953), 8.

145. "Awwal Lubnaniyya Takhud al-Ma'raka al-Intikhabiyya."

146. "Kalimat al-Mar'a," *Sawt al-Mar'a* (June 1953), editorial page.

147. "Tarshih al-Nisa' li-l-Intikhabat," *al-Telighraf.*

148. Laure Tabet, "Limadha 'Addalt 'An Khawd al-Ma'raka al-Initkhabiyya," *Sawt al-Mar'a* (July 1953), 9.

149. "Awwal Lubnaniyya Takhud al-Ma'raka al-Intikhabiyya."

150. For example, see the campaign paraphernalia of Michel Asmar (Ashrafiyya-Rumayl-al-Sayfi Beirut District), Jamil al-Birji (al-Kura Disctrict), Hannan Haddad and Rashid 'Azaar (Jizzin Maghdusha District), Rashid and Salim al-Khuri (Jizzin Maghdusha District), and 'Abdallah Sa'ada (al-Kura District), in 1953 Elections Folder, Sadaka Collection.

151. For example, see the campaign flyer of Zuhayr 'Usayran (Musaytba-Zuqaq al-Blat-Ras Bayrut Beirut District) in 1953 Elections Folder, Sadaka Collection.

152. For example, see the campaign brochure of Ra'if Abi al-Lama' (Unspecified Beirut District) in 1953 Elections Folder, Sadaka Collection.

153. "Kayfa Intakhabna," *Sawt al-Mar'a* (August 1953); Asma Tubi, "Hal Najahat al-Mar'a al-Lubnaniyya fi Khawd al-Ma'raka al-Intikhabiyya am Fashalat?," *Sawt al-Mar'a* (August 1953), 8–9.

154. Tubi, "Hal Najahat al-Mar'a," 9.

155. One exception is Mirna al-Bustani al-Khazin (b. 1937), who was appointed in 1963 to serve the remainder of the term of her father (Emile al-Bustani), who died in office.

156. *al-Nahar*, June 17, 1954.

Chapter 6

1. Jean Ducruet, *Les capitaux européens au Proche-Orient* (P.U.F., 1964); Şevket Pamuk, *The Ottoman Empire and European Capitalism, 1820–1913* (Cambridge University Press, 1987); V. Necla Geyikdaği, *Foreign Investment in the Ottoman Empire: International Trade and Relations, 1854–1914* (I. B. Tauris, 2011), 53–134.

2. Geyikdaği, *Foreign Investment*, 74–134; Donald Quataert, "Transportation," in *An Economic and Social History of the Ottoman Empire, 1300–1914*, ed. Halil İnalcık and Donald Quataert (Cambridge University Press, 1994), 798–823.

3. "Société Anonyme Ottomane des Tramways et de l'Électricité de Beyrouth," *Recueil Financier* (1910). The company listed the following officers in 1910: Najib Pasha Malhama (president); Victor Limauge (vice president); and seven managers (Philippe Effendi, Habibi Effendi Malhama, Adolphe Laloux, Ch. Thoney, Edouard Denis, Issac Fernandez, and Nouri Bey). Also see Jens Hanssen, *Fin de Siècle Beirut: The Making of an Ottoman Provincial Capital* (Oxford University Press, 2005), 99.

4. See "Qarar 2642 (31/5/1924)," French High Commission in Syria and Lebanon, *al-Nashra al-Rasmiyya li-l-A'mal al-Idariyya fi al-Mafwadhiyya al-'Ulya* (1924), 145–48; Omar Ajam, *L'equipement électrique du Liban* (Les presses de l'imprimerie Catholique, 1952), 169.

5. "Société Anonyme Ottomane des Tramways et de l'Électricité de Beyrouth."

6. Hanssen, *Fin de Siècle Beirut*, 98, fns 60, 61. Ibrahim Sabbagh originally made his fortunes in Beirut's silk and textile trade during the last decades of nineteenth century.

7. Hanssen, *Fin de Siècle Beirut*, 100.

8. For the history of the establishment and development of the OBGC, including its purchase of OBTEC, see Jacques Thobie's "Mouvement d'affaires et mounvement ouvrier: La compagnie ottoman du Gaz de Beyrouth, 1887–1914" in his *La France et l'est méditerranéen depuis 1850: Économie, finance, diplomatie* (Editions Isis, 1993). Also see "Qarar 2642 (31/5/1924)."

9. For the history of the establishment and development of the Beirut Water Company, see Hanssen, *Fin de Siècle Beirut*, 98; Geyikdaği, *Foreign Investment*, 113.

10. Hanssen, *Fin de Siècle Beirut*, 98–99.

11. Simon M. W. Jackson, "Mandatory Development: The Political Economy of the French Mandate in Syria and Lebanon, 1915–1939" (PhD diss., New York University, 2009), 216.

12. Hanssen, *Fin de Siècle Beirut*, 101.

13. Ajam, *L'équipement électrique*, 169.

14. "Qarar 2511 (20/3/1924)," *Majmu'at al-Muqarrarat 1934–1935*, 482–83; Jackson, "Mandatory Development," 254, fn 8.

15. Jackson, "Mandatory Development," 200–323.

16. Jackson, "Mandatory Development," 253–54.

17. Jackson, "Mandatory Development," 253–54.

18. Jackson, "Mandatory Development," 254.

19. Jackson, "Mandatory Development," 254–55.

20. International Court of Justice (ICJ), *"Électricité de Beyrouth" Company Case* (*France vs. Lebanon*) (International Court of Justice, 1957), 18; Ajam, *L'equipement électrique*,169–70.

21. "Decision no. 2642 (31/5/1924)"; ICJ, *"Électricité de Beyrouth,"* 19–20.

22. "Qanun (2/7/1954)," *al-Jarida al-Rasmiyya*, no. 29 (July 14, 1954): 523–28.

23. This agreement technically constituted a renewal of the tramline component of the 1906 concession, which the Ottoman government granted to OBTEC. See "Order no. S-143 (10/6/1925)," *al-Nashra al-Rasmiyya li-l-A'mal al-Idariyya fi al-Mafwadhiyya al-'Ulya* (1925), 127.

24. This agreement technically constituted a readaptation of the electricity components of the 1885 and 1906 concessions, which the Ottoman government granted to the OBGC and OBTEC. See "Order no. S-143 (10/6/1925)."

25. See references in "Qanun (2/7/1954)"; "Marsum 8904 (10/7/1952)," *al-Jarida al-Rasmiyya*, no. 29 (July 10, 1952), 729–31.

26. "Qanun," *Majmu'at Qawanin*, 3: 958.

27. "Order 2511 (20/3/1924)."

28. ICJ, *"Électricité de Beyrouth,"* 19–20.

29. Carla Eddé, "La mobilisation 'populaire' à Beyrouth à l'époque du Mandat, le cas des boycotts des trams et de l'électricité," in *France Syrie et Liban 1918–1946: Les ambiguitiés et les dynamiques de la relation mandataire*, ed. Nadine Meouchy (IFEAD, 2002).

30. Jackson, "Mandatory Development," 200–50, 286–318.

31. For example, "Indhar Sharkiat al-Tram Tantahi Muddatah," *al-Nahar*, November 29, 1945.

32. Samir Kassir, *Beirut*, trans. M. B. Deveoise (University of California, 2010), 302.

33. Kassir, *Beirut*, 267.

34. Ajam, *L'equipement électrique*, 30.

35. Elizabeth Thompson, *Colonial Citizens: Republican Rights, Paternal Privilege, and Gender in French Syria and Lebanon* (Columbia University Press, 2000), 181.

36. Ajam, *L'equipement électrique*, 23.

37. Carolyn L. Gates, *The Merchant Republic of Lebanon: Rise of an Open Economy* (I. B. Tauris, 1998), 77.

38. Jackson, "Mandatory Development," 255, fn 10.

39. Bassim A. Faris, *Electric Power in Syria and Palestine* (American Press, 1936), 125–33.

40. Republic of Lebanon, Ministry of National Economy, *Taqrir al-Sir Aliksandir Gib wa-Shurakah, 'an al-Tatawwur al-Iqtisadi fi Lubnan* (Beirut: n.p., 1948) (henceforth cited as Gibb & Partners, *Economic Development in Lebanon*), 179–80.

41. For example, "al-Kahurba' fi al-Shuf," *al-Nahar*, September 1, 1950.

42. Gibb & Partners, *Economic Development in Lebanon*, 186–88; "Kahruba' Ba'albak," *al-Nahar*, September 1, 1945.

43. For example, "'Addadat Sharikat al-Ta'tim wa-l-Tajmid," *al-Amal*, January 22, 1950.

44. "Brotokol (5/1/1944)," *al-Jarida al-Rasmiyya*, no. 9 (March 1, 1944): 6.

45. "Marsum 766 (29/2/1944)," *al-Jarida al-Rasmiyya*, no. 10 (March 8, 1944): 1–2.

46. "Marsum 14385 (17/2/1949)," *al-Jarida al-Rasmiyya*, no. 8 (February 23, 1949), 131–33.

47. For example, see "Zahleh Tatazahar Didd Sharikat al-Nur," *al-Nahar*, December 21, 1949; "Ma Hiya Asbab Inqita' al-Kahruba'," *al-Nahar*, December 22, 1949; "Hal wa-Hal Thum Hal?," *al-Amal*, January 5, 1950; "Dayr al-Qamar wa-l-Damur wa-Bayt al-Din Tahtaj 'ala Ta'rifat al-Kahruba' wa-Tutalib bi-Rafdiha," *al-Amal*, January 20, 1950; "Di'f al-Tayyar al-Kahruba'i wa-As'ar al-Sharika," *al-Nahar*, November 21, 1950; "Ma'amil al-Balat Tashku min Sharikat al-Kahruba' li-l-Hukuma," May 10, 1951, *al-Nahar*.

48. ". . . Wa-Hadhihi Wahida bi-Alf," *al-Amal*, January 8, 1950; "Sharikat al-Ta'tim wa-Qafz al-'Addadat," *al-Amal*, January 10, 1950; "Sharikat 'al-Ta'tim' Tatala'ab bi-l-Ta'rifa," *al-Amal*, January 11, 1950.

49. I am drawing on the work of Owain Lawson. See his "Power Failures: Engineers and the Litani River, 1918–1978" (PhD diss., Columbia University, 2021).

50. Lawson, "Power Failures," 175–89.

51. US Department of Interior, Bureau of Reclamation, *Development Plan for the Litani River Basin, Republic of Lebanon*, 3 vols. (Bureau of Reclamation, 1954).

52. "As'ar al-Kahruba' fi al-Damur," *al-Amal*, January 17, 1950; "Directive 3837 (30/12/1950)," *al-Jarida al-Rasmiyya*, no. 1 (1951): 10–12; "Directive 3962 (9/1/1951)," *al-Jarida al-Rasmiyya*, no. 3 (1951): 27–28; Ajam, *L'equipement électrique*, 146.

53. "Qanun (11/1/1951)," *al-Jarida al-Rasmiyya*, no. 4 (1951), 35–41.

54. "Lettre n° 912, du 1er juin 1950, addressée par le Président-Directeur General de la Société au Président de la République libanaise," ICJ, *"Électricité de Beyrouth,"* 183–84.

55. "Lettre n° 1601, du 26 Septembre 1950, addressée par le Président-Directeur General de la Société au Président de la République libanaise," ICJ, *"Électricité de Beyrouth,"* 185.

56. Ajam, *L'équipement électrique*, 101–3; ICJ, *"Électricité de Beyrouth,"* 24–25.

57. Ajam, *L'équipement électrique*, 57–60.

58. Wahib Maaluf, *Na'ib al-Sha'b al-Kadih: Sirat 'Abdallah al-Haj (1899–1975)* (Dar al-Nahar, 2007), 97–98.

59. "Hamla Shamila 'ala Sharikat Kahruba' Bayrut," *al-Amal*, December 19, 1951; ICJ, *"Électricité de Beyrouth,"* 24–25, 35.

60. "Sharikat Kahruba' al-Matn bi-l-Mazad," *al-Nahar*, July 24, 1951.

61. "Muqata'at Sharikat al-Kahruba': Ijtima' bayn al-Hay'a al-Wataniyya wa-l-Kata'ib al-Lubnaniyya," *al-Amal*, December 30, 1951.

62. "Al-Hukuma Tu'alij Qadiyyat al-Kahruba'," *al-Amal*, January 2, 1952; "Lajnat al-Kahurba' Qaddamat Taqriruha," *al-Amal*, February 2, 1952.

63. "Bayan Sharikat Kahruba' Lubnan," *al-Amal*, January 2, 1952.

64. "Bayan ila al-Sha'b al-Lubnani min Hizb al-Kata'ib al-Lubnaniyya wa-l-Hay'a al-Wataniyya," *al-Amal*, January 4, 1952.

65. For example, see "Ghadan fi Bayt al-Katai'ib: Ijtima' 'Am li-l-Hay'at wa-l-Naqabat al-Wataniyya," *al-Amal*, February 3, 1953.

66. "Fi al-Mu'tamar al-Sha'bi al-Kabir," *al-Amal*, February 5, 1952.

67. "Brochure intitulée 'La Question de l'Électricite à Beyrouth' diffusée fin décembre 1951 par la Société pour informer l'opinion," ICJ, *"Électricité de Beyrouth,"* Annex 41.

68. "Arrêté n° 1843, due 22 décembre 1951 nommant une Commission chargée d'enquêter sur le prix de reient du kWh et de recommander un abaissement des tarifs," ICJ, *"Électricité de Beyrouth,"* 42–43; "Dossier remis le 19 janvier 1952 à la Commission d'Information créée par Arrêté n° 1842 du 22 décembre 1951," ICJ, *"Électricité de Beyrouth,"* Annex 43.

69. "Al-Mufawadat li-Takhfid As'ar al-Kahruba'," February 3, 1952.

70. "Lettre n° 176, du 29 janvier 1952, du Directeur de l'Exploitation au Directeur Général du Contrôle," ICJ, *"Électricité de Beyrouth,"* 209–10.

71. "Rapports du 15 mai 1952 des Experts hollandaise, MM. Ringers et Bakker," ICJ, *"Électricité de Beyrouth,"* 107–10.

72. "Lettre n° 176, du 29 janvier 1952."

73. "Lettre n° 176, du 29 janvier 1952."

74. "Lettre n° 176, du 29 janvier 1952."

75. "Lettre n° 176, du 29 janvier 1952."

76. "Lettre n° 176, du 29 janvier 1952."

77. "Lettre n° 176, du 29 janvier 1952."

78. "Mantiqat Bahmadun Tuqati' al-Kahruba'," *al-Nahar*, February 2, 1952.

79. "Muqarrat Naqabat Mustakhdimi al-Fanadiq wa-l-Mata'im wa-l-Maqahi," *al-Amal*, March 16, 1952.

80. "Lettre n° 215, du 4 février 1952, du Président de la Société et du Directeur de l'Exploitation au Directeur Général du Control," ICJ, *"Électricité de Beyrouth,"* 210–11.

81. "Qadiyyat al-Kahruba' Tantaqil ila Baris," *al-Nahar*, February 8, 1952; "Mudira Sharikat al-Kahurba' Yusafiran," al-'Amal, February 9, 1952.

82. "Lettre n° 449, du 16 janvier 1952, du Directeur Général du Contrôle à la Société," ICJ, *"Électricité de Beyrouth,"* 128; "Lettre n° 179, du 30 janvier 1952, de Directeur d'Exploitation au Directeur Général du Contrôle," ICJ, *"Électricité de Beyrouth,"* 129.

83. "Rapport de la Commission d'Information nommée par arrété n° 1843 du 22 décembre 1951, remis fin février 1952," ICJ, *"Électricité de Beyrouth,"* 204–9.

84. "Ijtima' f al-Saraha bi-Hudur Mudir al-Sharika," *al-Amal*, February 28, 1952; "Procès-verbal de la Réunion tenue le 11 mars 1952 dans le bureau du Directeur Général de la Justice a Beyrouth" ICJ, *"Électricité de Beyrouth,"* 188–93.

85. "Sharika al-Kahruba' Taqbal Faj'a bi-Takhfid al-As'ar," *al-Nahar*, March 11, 1952.

86. "Ta'lif Lajnat Tahqiq 'Ulya li-l-Imtiyazat," *al-Nahar*, March 12, 1952.

87. "Ordinance no. 7830 (14/3/1952)," *al-Jarida al-Rasmiyya*, no. 12 (1952), 221–22.

88. "Lettre n° 627, du 29 mars 1952, de la Directeur d'Exploitation au Directeur Général des Travaux Publics et du Contrôle à Beyrouth" and "Lettre n° 662 du 7 avril 1952, de la Directeur d'Exploitation au Directeur Général des Travaux Publics et du Contrôle à Beyrouth," ICJ, *"Électricité de Beyrouth,"* 132–34.

89. "Le règlement du litige avec la Société d'Électricité: Communiqué du Ministère des Travaux Publics du 27 mars 1952," *Commerce du Levant*, April 2, 1952.

90. "Procès-verbal de la Réunion tenue le 11 mars 1952 dans le bureau du Directeur Général de la Justice a Beyrouth."

91. "Lettre n° 656 du 3 avril 1952, du Directeur d'Exploitation au Directeur Général du Travaux Publics et du Contrôle à Beyrouth," ICJ, *"Électricité de Beyrouth,"* 507–8.

92. "Indhar al-Hukuma bi-wujub Inha' al-Qadiyya fi 'Ashrat Ayyam," *al-Nahar*, April 24, 1952.

93. Ringers and Bakker, "Rapport," 107.

94. "Lettre n° 88/L, du 25 avril 1952, du Président de la Commission Supérieure d'Enquête au Directeur d'Exploitation. Note juridique, annexée, du Gouvernement Libanais, en date du 1er avril," ICJ, *"Électricité de Beyrouth,"* 134–36.

95. "Lettre n° 830, du 30 avril 1952, du Directeur d'Exploitation au Président de la Commission Supérieure," ICJ, *"Électricité de Beyrouth,"* 136–37.

96. Ringers and Bakker, "Rapport."

97. Ringers and Bakker, "Rapport," 108.

98. Ringers and Bakker, "Rapport," 108.

99. Salma Sa'igh, "Madha fi al-Bayt al-Lubnani," *Sawt al-Mar'a*, 3.

100. Republic of Lebanon, *Mahadir Majlis al-Nuwwab*, May 8, 1952.

101. *al-Anba'*, May 30, 1952.

102. These were *al-Bayraq*, *Bayrut*, *al-Nahar*, *al-Nida'*, *Sada Lubnan*, and *al-Teleghraf*.

103. "Brochure intitulée 'La Question de l'Électricite à Beyrouth'": "Dossier remis le 19 janvier 1952."

104. "Lettre du 26 juin 1952 de President-Directeur General de la Société et du Directeur de l'Exploitation au Directeur General du Contrôle," ICJ, *"Électricité de Beyrouth,"* 216.

105. "Mashru' Hal Mushkilat al-Kahruba'," *al-Amal*, July 7, 1952.

106. "Mashru' Hal Mushkilat al-Kahruba'."

107. "Fawz Ra'in' li-l-Sha'b," *al-Amal*, July 11, 1952; "Marsum 8904 (10/7/1952)," *al-Jarida al-Rasmiyya*, no. 29 (1952), 729–31.

108. "al-Hay'at Tu'lin Intiha' Muqata'at al-Kahruba' . . . Fawz Ra'i' li-l-Sha'b," *al-Amal*, July 11, 1952.

109. "Lettre n° 1548, du 15 julliet 1952, du Ministre des Travaux Publics à la Société," ICJ, *"Électricité de Beyrouth,"* 218–20.

110. For example, see "Ila Mustahliki al-Kahruba' bi-Bayrut," *al-Amal*, August 1, 1952; "Sharkiat al-Kahruba' la Tazal Tab'ath bi-l-Qawanin wa-l-Anzima," *al-Amal*, August 3, 1952.

111. "Marsum 9228 (19/8/1952)," *al-Jarida al-Rasmiyya*, no. 35 (1952), 791–96.

112. "Marsum (5/9/1952)," *al-Jarida al-Rasmiyya*, no. 37 (1952), 824–29

113. "Ordinance no. 9380 (5/9/1952)," *al-Jarida al-Rasmiyya*, no. 37 (1952), 485–89.

114. Caroline Attié, *Struggle in the Levant: Lebanon in the 1950s* (I. B. Tauris, 2004), 46–47.

115. Attié, *Struggle in the Levant*, 48–51; Irene L. Gendzier, *Notes from the Minefield: United States Intervention in Lebanon and the Middle East, 1945–1958* (Columbia University Press, 1997), 160–66.

116. "Lettres du président-général de la Société au ministre des Travaux Publics"; "Le ministre des Travaux Publics de la République libanaise au président directeur général de la Société Électricité de Beyrouth," ICJ, *"Électricité de Beyrouth,"* 123–24.

117. "Lettres du président-général de la Société au ministre des Travaux Publics"; "Rapport de la Commission d'Information nommée par arrêté n° 1843."

118. "Le ministre des Travaux Publics au président directeur général."

119. "Le ministre des Travaux Publics au président directeur general,"126.

120. "Lettre n° 332, du 23 février 1953, du président-directeur général de la Société au ministre des Travaux Publics," ICJ, *"Électricité de Beyrouth,"* 274–75.

121. "Lettre n° 332, du 23 février 1953, du président-directeur général de la Société au ministre des Travaux Publics," 274.

122. *al-Nahar,* March 2, 1953.

123. *al-Anba',* October 10, 1952.

124. *al-Anba',* March 13, 1953.

125. "Lettre n° 559, du 2 mars 1953, du ministre des Travaux Publics au président-directeur général de la Société," ICJ, *"Électricité de Beyrouth,"* 275–76.

126. "Lettre n° 398, du 2 mars 1953, du président-directeur général de la Société au ministre des Travaux Publics" ICJ, *"Électricité de Beyrouth,"* 276–79.

127. "Lettre n° 615, du 4 mars 1953, du ministre des Travaux Publics à la Société," ICJ, *"Électricité de Beyrouth,"* 280.

128. "Lettre n° 431, du 6 mars 1953, de la Société au directeur général du Contrôle," ICJ, *"Électricité de Beyrouth,"* 281.

129. "Order no. 757 (19/3/1953)," *al-Jarida al-Rasmiyya,* no. 11 (1953). For the letter from the government notifying the EDB of provisional control, see "Lettre n° 760, du 20 mars 1953, du directeur général du Contrôle signifiant l'arrêté n° 757 à la Société," ICJ, *"Électricité de Beyrouth,"* 284–85. For the response from the EDB protesting provisional control, see "Lettre n° 1, du 24 mars 1953, du représentant de la Société au ministre des Travaux Publics," ICJ, *"Électricité de Beyrouth,"* 287–88.

130. "Télégramme n° 106, du 25 mars 1953, du ministre des Travaux Publics au président-directeur général de la Société," ICJ, *"Électricité de Beyrouth,"* 298

131. "Lettre n° 217, du 31 mars 1953, du président-directeur général de la Société au ministre des Travaux Publics," ICJ, *"Électricité de Beyrouth,"* 298–99.

132. "Application Instituting Proceedings," ICJ, *"Électricité de Beyrouth,"*13.

133. *"Électricité de Beyrouth,"* 300–26.

134. Two examples of such communications are the initial letter protesting the extension of provisional control and the EDB public response to the pamphlet the government distributed to justify extending provisional control. See, respectively,

"Lettre n° 28, du 13 avril 1953, du représentant de la Société au ministre des Travaux Publics," ICJ, *"Électricité de Beyrouth,"* 297–98; "Commentaire et réponse au Livre Blanc," ICJ, *"Électricité de Beyrouth,"* 325–45.

135. "Application Instituting Proceedings," ICJ, *"Électricité de Beyrouth,"* 8–15; "International Court of Justice," *International Organization* 7 (November 1953): 556–57.

136. ICJ, *"Électricité de Beyrouth,"* 521–39.

137. "Qanun (2/7/1954)," *al-Jarida al-Rasmiyya* (July 14, 1954), 523–28.

138. "Qanun (2/7/1954)."

Conclusion

1. For example, see Walid Khalidi, *Conflict and Violence in Lebanon: Confrontation in the Middle East* (Harvard Center for International Affairs, 1980).

2. Despite their different theoretical frameworks, several scholars concur on this: Kamal Salibi, *Crossroads to Civil War: Lebanon, 1958–1976* (Caravan Books, 1976); Iliya Harik, *Lebanon: Anatomy of Conflict* (American Universities Field Staff, 1981); Farid al-Khazen, *Breakdown of the State in Lebanon, 1967–1976* (Harvard University Press, 2000); Samir Khalaf, *Civil and Uncivil Violence in Lebanon: A History of the Internationalization of Communal Conflict* (Columbia University Press, 2002).

3. For example, see Caroline Attié, *Struggle in the Levant: Lebanon in the 1950s* (I. B. Tauris, 2004); Dylan Baun, *Winning Lebanon: Youth Politics, Populism, and the Production of Sectarian Violence, 1920–1958* (Cambridge University Press, 2021).

4. For example, see Michael C. Hudson, *The Precarious Republic: Political Modernization in Lebanon* (Random House, 1968); Michael Johnson, *Class & Client in Beirut: The Sunni Muslim Community and the Lebanese State 1840–1985* (Ithaca Press, 1988).

5. Jillian Schwedler has made a similar argument about Jordan in *Protesting Jordan*. Also see Jillian Schwedler, "State Capacity and Contention: A View from Jordan," in *Making Sense of the Arab State*, ed. Steven Heydemann and Marc Lynch (University of Michigan Press, 2024), 231–46.

6. I am drawing on the work of Steven Heydemann, who argues that "states exhibit asymmetrical institutional capacities, varying from higher in some domains . . . and lower in others." Steven Heydemann, "Seeing the State or Why Arab States Look the Way They Do," in *Making Sense of the Arab State*, ed. Steven Heydemann and Marc Lynch (University of Michigan Press, 2024), 28–29.

7. Youssef Chaitiani, *Post-Colonial Syria and Lebanon: The Decline of Arab Nationalism and the Triumph of the State* (I. B. Tauris, 2007).

8. Hicham Safieddine, *Banking on the State: The Financial Foundations of Lebanon* (Stanford University Press, 2019).

9. I am drawing on the work of Steven Heydemann wherein he analyzes the changes in the organization of social conflict during different phases of Syrian state formation. See Steven Heydemann, *Authoritarianism in Syria: Institutions and Conflict 1946–1970* (Cornell University Press, 1999). All quotes from page 10 of said work.

10. Peter Mansfield, "Nasser and Nasserism," *International Journal* 28, no. 4 (1973): 670–88; Elie Podeh, "The Drift Towards Neutrality: Egyptian Foreign Policy during the Early Nasserist Era, 1953–55," *Middle Eastern Studies* 32, no. 1 (1996): 159–79; Reem Aboud-El-Fadl, "Neutralism Made Positive: Egyptian Anti-Colonialism on the Road to Bandung," *British Journal of Middle Eastern Studies* 42, no. 2 (2015): 219–40.

11. Reem Abou El Fadl, "Nasserism," in *The Oxford Handbook of Contemporary Middle-Eastern and North African History*, ed. Amal Ghazal and Jens Hanssen (Oxford University Press, 2016).

12. Irene L. Gendzier, *Notes from the Minefield: United States Intervention in Lebanon and the Middle East, 1945–1958* (Columbia University Press, 1997).

13. Michael W. Suleiman, *Political Parties in Lebanon: The Challenge of a Fragmented Political Culture* (Cornell University Press, 1967), 250–60; Hudson, *Precarious Republic*, 153–61.

14. Suleiman, *Political Parties*, 232–49; Hudson, *Precarious Republic*, 142–46. It is worth noting the Michael Hudson included the Kata'ib in his section on "The Establishment and Its Politics" and not "The Radical Outsiders."

15. Chancery (Beirut) to Levant Department, "Formation of New Political Party by President Chamoun," September 11, 1958, FO 371/134135/VL10162, TNA; Suleiman, *Political Parties*, 260–62.

16. Suleiman, *Political Parties*, 121–55; Hudson, *Precarious Republic*, 197–200.

17. Suleiman, *Political Parties*, 155–72; Hudson, *Precarious Republic*, 192–97.

18. Safieddine, *Banking on the State*, 175. For example, see Michael C. Hudson, "The Problem with Authoritative Power in Lebanese Politics: Why Consociationalism Failed," in *Lebanon: A History of Conflict and Consensus*, ed. Nadim Shehadi and Dana Haffar Mills (I. B. Tauris, 1988), 224–40; Robert Fisk, *Pity the Nation: Lebanon at War* (Andre Deutch, 1990).

19. For example, see Leonard Binder, ed., *Politics in Lebanon* (John Wiley & Sons, 1966); Elie Adib Salem, *Modernization Without Revolution: Lebanon's Experience* (Indiana University Press, 1973).

20. For example, see Theodor Hanf, *Coexistence in Wartime Lebanon: Decline of a State and Rise of a Nation* (I. B. Tauris, 1993).

21. Nisreen Salti, "No Country for Poor Men: How Lebanon's Debt Has Exacerbated Inequality," Malcolm H. Kerr Carnegie Middle East Center, September 2019, https://carnegieendowment.org/research/2019/10/no-country-for-poor-men-how-lebanons-debt-has-exacerbated-inequality.

22. Salti, "No Country for Poor Men."

23. Lydia Assouad, "Rethinking the Lebanese Economic Miracle: The Extreme Concentration of Income and Wealth in Lebanon, 2005–2014," *Journal of Development Economics* 161 (2023).

24. Reinoud Leenders, *Spoils of Truce: Corruption and State Building in Postwar Lebanon* (Cornell University Press, 2012); Hannes Baumann, *Citizen Hariri: Lebanon's Neoliberal Reconstruction* (Oxford University Press, 2016).

25. Safieddine, *Banking on the State*, 175–80.

26. Jad Chaaban, "I've Got the Power: Mapping Connections Between Lebanon's Banking Sector and the Ruling Class," Working Paper no. 1059, Economic Research Forum, October 2016; Salti, "No Country for Poor Men."

27. The World Bank, "Lebanon: Normalization of Crisis Is No Road to Stabilization," May 16, 2023, https://www.worldbank.org/en/news/press-release/2023/05/16/lebanon-normalization-of-crisis-is-no-road-to-stabilization.

28. Timur Azhari, "'Not Legal' but Necessary: Lebanon's Banks Tighten Restrictions," *Al Jazeera*, February 3, 2020, https://www.aljazeera.com/economy/2020/2/3/not-legal-but-necessary-lebanons-banks-tighten-restrictions.

29. Georgia Dagher and Sami Zoughaib, "A Collapsing Society: The Urgency of a Social Protection Floor," The Policy Initiative, June 16, 2022, https://www.thepolicyinitiative.org/article/details/166/a-collapsing-society-the-urgency-of-a-social-protection-floor; The World Bank, "Lebanon Poverty and Equity Assessment 2024: Weathering a Protracted Crisis," 2024.

30. Eric Verdeil, "Infrastructure Crises in Beirut and the Struggle to (Not) Reform the Lebanese State," *Arab Studies Journal* 26, no. 1 (2018): 84–113.

31. I am drawing on Heydemann, "Seeing the State," 25–28, and Bassel F. Salloukh, "What We Talk about When We Talk about the State in Postwar Lebanon," in *Making Sense of the Arab State*, ed. Steven Heydemann and Marc Lynch (University of Michigan Press, 2024), 147–54.

32. This conceptual and methodological problem parallels the critique by critical scholarship on authoritarianism in the Middle East and North Africa that challenges the tendency to focus on the "absence of democracy" as the primary analytic puzzle rather than the "presence of authoritarianism" to understand the working of political incumbency, economic development, and social mobilization.

33. On the garbage protests, see Carole Kerbage, "Politics by Coincidence: The Harak Faces Its 'Peoples,'" AUB Policy Institute, December 2016; Joanne Randa Nucho, "Garbage Infrastructure, Sanitation, and New Meanings of Citizenship in Lebanon," *Postmodern Culture* 30, no. 1 (2019). On the municipal elections, see Mona Harb, "Cities and Political Change: How Young Activists in Beirut Bred an Urban Social Movement," Working Paper no. 20, Power2Youth, September 2016.

34. See Habib Battah, "A City Without a Shore: Rem Koolhaas, Dalieh, and the Paving of Beirut's Coast," *The Guardian*, March 17, 2015, https://www.theguardian.com/cities/2015/mar/17/rem-koolhaas-dalieh-beirut-shore-coast; Abir Saksouk-Sasso, "Making Spaces for Communal Sovereignty: The Story of Beirut's Dalieh," *Arab Studies Journal* 23, no. 1 (2015): 296–318; Fatima Fouad el-Samman, "Hold on to Dalieh," *The Public Source*, September 9, 2024, https://thepublicsource.org/raouche-dalieh-beirut; Neila Hyndman-Rizk, "A Question of Personal Status: The Lebanese Women's Movement and Civil Marriage," *Journal of Middle East Women's Studies* 15, no. 2 (2019); Maya Mikdashi, *Sextarianism: Sovereignty, Secularism, and the State in Lebanon* (Stanford University Press, 2022), 128–42.

35. See Marwan G. Rowayheb and Makram Ouaiss, "The Committee of the Parents of the Missing and Disappeared: 30 Years of Struggle and Protest," *Middle Eastern Studies* 51, no. 6 (2015): 1010–26; Samee Suleiman, "An Ethnography of Disability Rights and Displacement in Lebanon in the Aftermath of War" (PhD diss., Brown University, 2023).

36. See Lea Bou Khater, *The Labour Movement in Lebanon: Power on Hold* (Manchester University Press, 2022).

Index

Note: Names beginning with "al-" are alphabetized on the major portion of the name

Stanford Studies in Middle Eastern and Islamic Societies and Cultures

Lara Deeb and Sherene Seikaly, editors

Plots and Deeds: Agrarian Annihilation and the Fight for Land Justice in Palestine 2026
PAUL KOHLBRY

Race and the Question of Palestine 2025
LANA TATOUR AND RONIT LENTIN, EDITORS

Dust That Never Settles: Literary Afterlives of the Iran-Iraq War 2025
AMIR MOOSAVI

The Revolution Within: Islamic Media and the Struggle for a New Egypt 2025
YASMIN MOLL

Unruly Labor: A History of Oil in the Arabian Sea 2024
ANDREA WRIGHT

The Incarcerated Modern: Prisons and Public Life in Iran 2024
GOLNAR NIKPOUR

Elastic Empire: Refashioning War Through Aid in Palestine 2023
LISA BHUNGALIA

Colonizing Palestine: The Zionist Left and the Making of the Palestinian Nakba 2023
AREEJ SABBAGH-KHOURY

On Salafism: Concepts and Contexts 2023
AZMI BISHARA

Revolutions Aesthetic: A Cultural History of Ba'thist Syria 2022
MAX WEISS

Street-Level Governing: Negotiating the State in Urban Turkey 2022
ELISE MASSICARD

Protesting Jordan: Geographies of Power and Dissent 2022
JILLIAN SCHWEDLER

Media of the Masses: Cassette Culture in Modern Egypt 2022
ANDREW SIMON

States of Subsistence: The Politics of Bread in Contemporary Jordan 2022
JOSÉ CIRO MARTÍNEZ

Between Dreams and Ghosts: Indian Migration and Middle Eastern Oil 2021
ANDREA WRIGHT

Bread and Freedom: Egypt's Revolutionary Situation 2021
MONA EL-GHOBASHY

Paradoxes of Care: Children and Global Medical Aid in Egypt 2021
RANIA KASSAB SWEIS

The Politics of Art: Dissent and Cultural Diplomacy in Lebanon, Palestine, and Jordan 2021
HANAN TOUKAN

The Paranoid Style in American Diplomacy: Oil and Arab Nationalism in Iraq 2021
BRANDON WOLFE-HUNNICUTT

Screen Shots: State Violence on Camera in Israel and Palestine 2021
REBECCA L. STEIN

Dear Palestine: A Social History of the 1948 War 2021
SHAY HAZKANI

A Critical Political Economy of the Middle East and North Africa 2020
JOEL BEININ, BASSAM HADDAD, AND SHERENE SEIKALY, EDITORS

Showpiece City: How Architecture Made Dubai 2020
TODD REISZ

Archive Wars: The Politics of History in Saudi Arabia 2020
ROSIE BSHEER

Between Muslims: Religious Difference in Iraqi Kurdistan 2020
J. ANDREW BUSH

The Optimist: A Social Biography of Tawfiq Zayyad 2020
TAMIR SOREK

For a complete listing of titles in this series, visit the Stanford University Press website, www.sup.org.